THE EFFECTIVENESS OF THE INTER-AMERICAN COURT OF HUMAN RIGHTS

The Inter-American Court of Human Rights has the most developed jurisprudence on indigenous rights, yet this case law is understudied. This book addresses this gap by exploring the Court and its cases from both the perspective of international law and the legal protection of indigenous territories.

Setting out the network of actors and institutions involved in such litigation, it examines the motivations and constraints in domestic politics affecting international orders (and by extension the impact of the Court). It provides both an important statement on the effectiveness of international tribunals and a fascinating insight into the evolution of indigenous rights.

Volume 96 in the series Studies in International Law

Studies in International Law

Recent titles in this series

International Law and the War with Islamic State: Challenges for Jus ad Bellum and Jus in Bello
Saeed Bagheri

Private Actors as Participants in International Law: A Critical Analysis of Membership under the Law of the Sea
Armando Rocha

Truth and Transitional Justice: Localising the International Legal Framework in Muslim Majority Legal Systems
Alice Panepinto

State Responsibility for Non-State Actors: Past, Present and Prospects for the Future
Richard Mackenzie-Gray Scott

International Agreements between Non-State Actors as a Source of International Law
Melissa Loja

Judicial Decisions in International Law Argumentation: Between Entrapment and Creativity
Letizia Lo Giacco

South-South Migrations and the Law from Below: Case Studies on China and Nigeria
Oreva Olakpe

Territorial Status in International Law
Jure Vidmar

Marine Bioprospecting, Biodiversity and Novel Uses of Ocean Resources: New Approaches in International Law
Edited by Niels Krabbe and David Langlet

The Standard of Review Before the International Court of Justice: Between Principle and Pragmatism
Felix Fouchard

Global Lawmaking and Social Change: The Varieties of Customary International Law
Gregor Novak

The Effectiveness of the Inter-American Court of Human Rights: The Case of Indigenous Territorial Rights
Gabriela CB Navarro

For a complete list of titles in this series see www.bloomsbury.com/uk/series/studies-in-international-law/

The Effectiveness of the Inter-American Court of Human Rights

The Case of Indigenous Territorial Rights

Gabriela CB Navarro

•HART•
OXFORD • LONDON • NEW YORK • NEW DELHI • SYDNEY

HART PUBLISHING

Bloomsbury Publishing Plc

Kemp House, Chawley Park, Cumnor Hill, Oxford, OX2 9PH, UK

1385 Broadway, New York, NY 10018, USA

29 Earlsfort Terrace, Dublin 2, Ireland

HART PUBLISHING, the Hart/Stag logo, BLOOMSBURY and the Diana logo are trademarks of Bloomsbury Publishing Plc

First published in Great Britain 2024

A catalogue record for this book is available from the British Library.

A catalogue record for this book is available from the Library of Congress.

ISBN: HB: 978-1-50997-906-6
ePDF: 978-1-50997-908-0
ePub: 978-1-50997-907-3

Typeset by Compuscript Ltd, Shannon

Preface

THE LAST THREE decades saw quite a remarkable increase in international legal developments in the field of rights of indigenous peoples, not the least inspired and driven by the growing acceptance of the 2007 UN Declaration on the Rights of Indigenous Peoples (UNDRIP). One of the major – if not the major – issue of such rights concerns the precise definition of the contents of land-related rights, or territorial rights, and their effective implementation. For obvious reasons, very much depends in this context on the legal (and political) developments on the national level; recent studies such as those conducted in the framework of the International Law Association (ILA) Committee on the Implementation of the Rights of Indigenous Peoples[1] have shown considerable progress in some jurisdictions but also severe setbacks in others. This somewhat mixed assessment applies in particular to the Americas with their quite numerous and politically increasingly active indigenous peoples.

The Americas are also the place of the Inter-American System of Human Rights (IASHR) with the 1969 American Convention on Human Rights (ACHR) as its cornerstone. The monitoring of the effective implementation of its substantive provisions is the task of two organs, the Inter-American Commission of Human Rights (IACHR) and the Inter-American Court of Human Rights (IACtHR). Notwithstanding a somewhat slow start (the first judgment in a contentious case, *Velásquez Rodriguez v Honduras*, in 1988) and persisting problems relating, inter alia, to the still limited number of states-parties having recognized the jurisdiction of the IACtHR, its progressive jurisprudence as concerns e.g. the interpretation of states' obligations flowing from their membership in the ACHR, has attracted widespread scholarly attention.

Since its first decision concerning indigenous (territorial) rights, the landmark-case of *Awas Tingni v Nicaragua* of 31 August 2001, the IACtHR has handed down a considerable number of judgments related to such rights, the most recent one being *Lhaka Honhat v Argentina* of 6 February 2020. It seems therefore almost natural to explore, from a scholarly perspective, this emerging jurisprudence, and not only as to its contents as this has been done to varying extents in a number of publications but to address a much more complex issue, namely the effectiveness of this jurisprudence, or even more generally, the

[1] See ILA, Kyoto Conference (2020) Implementation Of The Rights Of Indigenous Peoples, Kyoto, 2020.

effectiveness of the whole IASHR. And this is exactly what the present book is about, thereby opening up new avenues of scholarly research and offering new insights – a truly innovative approach which is all the more welcome as there continues to be some hesitation as to the recognition of the effectiveness of the indigenous rights jurisprudence of the IACtHR, its actual relevance for the persons concerned.

In doing so, the book adopts Laurence Helfer's four dimensions of effectiveness which include norm-developing effectiveness, case-specific effectiveness, embeddedness, and *erga omnes* effectiveness. Based thereupon, the author formulates her research question which she divides into four specific problems: 1. To what extent is the IACtHR effective in developing international law on the matter of territorial protection, considering both the recognition of rights and the design of reparation measures? 2. To what extent is the IACtHR effective in compelling compliance with its judgments in territorial cases? 3. To what extent is the IACtHR effective in promoting the embeddedness of its territorial rights parameters within domestic legal systems? 4. How do norm development, compliance, and embeddedness relate one to another in territorial cases issued by the IACtHR?

The book is structured into five chapters. The first chapter addresses the aspect of norm-development effectiveness with regard to territorial rights protected by the IACtHR. Interestingly enough, this is not only done by virtue of Article 21 ACHR protecting the right to (collective) property, but also on the basis of other substantive rights such as the rights to life and physical integrity. While the book rightly hails the case-law studied as a true breakthrough model for the enhanced protection of indigenous rights, in particular the Court's approach to recognize collective social rights including collective property, the author convincingly points to some weaknesses of this jurisprudence: first, the persisting restrictions to collective property rights, namely 'excessive' consideration of the protection of the right to property owned by individuals, and insufficient safeguards for the exploration of natural resources by indigenous peoples; second, and this is quite a well-known problem around the globe, the insufficient protection of human rights defenders. In order to overcome these shortcomings, the chapter proposes to focus not only on the right to cultural identity but to explore to a much stronger extent than has been done so far (only in two cases involving Surinam), the potential of the right to self-determination. The chapter concludes with another line of criticism as regards the Court's jurisprudence, the lack of sufficient argumentation.

The second chapter is, again, concerned with the aspect of norm-development effectiveness by addressing the – from an international comparative law perspective – probably most innovative contribution of the IACtHR to the universal system of human rights protection, namely its truly innovative development and use of 'reparations'. Not surprisingly, the focus is on the two obviously most relevant elements, namely restitution and compensation, but also other elements, such as satisfaction or non-repetition, are dealt with.

It is indeed fascinating to read how the Court developed its approach as regards restitution measures as an aspect of the protection of the traditional territory of indigenous communities or how it 'invented' a right to the provision of public services as a kind of restitution measure. The same assessment applies to the distinction between collective damage resulting into collective compensation on the one hand and the traditional approach of individual damages. But, just as before, the book does not limit itself with this analysis of what is rightly to be considered quite an achievement, but again puts forward some – in my opinion very well-founded – criticism which refers to what the author considers the 'insufficient and paternalistic monetary compensation' on the one hand and the quite obviously still insufficient protection of the collective property, on the other hand.

The third chapter is devoted to the second criterion of effectiveness, i.e. its case-specific dimension. In the present context, this concerns the effectiveness of the reparation measures in the view of the IACtHR. The whole enterprise is based on an original dataset on domestic compliance with the territory-related decisions of the IACtHR. The book shows – again convincingly – the rather disparate range of such domestic compliance: Full compliance in the *Awas Tingni* case; slow and 'hampered' compliance in the Suriname cases; a rather discouraging rate of actual compliance, i.e. no restitution of the traditional territories, in the Paraguayan cases; prompt, but only partial compliance in the cases against Panama and Ecuador; and finally, only very first steps towards compliance as regards Colombia, Brazil and Honduras. In more substantive terms, this means that partial compliance prevails insofar as no State has challenged as such the Court's decisions nor refused to pay compensation; the fact that no State opposed publishing of the decisions should not be a surprise. It is also very true and needs to be emphasized that the IACtHR plays a most pro-active role in the supervision of the implementation of its judgements, a role that is unique in international law – but is it really successful and/or effective? One might wonder indeed reading the book's well-founded critique concerning the – sometimes almost excessive – temporal delays in the domestic implementation of the decisions and the most considerable shortcomings when it comes to rehabilitation, accountability and restitution measures.

The final three chapters are not only the largest one but possibly also the most important one as they are is devoted to the third, and arguably the most crucial, criterion of effectiveness, namely the embeddedness of international litigation in the domestic legal orders – obviously, that is the real litmus test. The book's treatment of this element, i.e. basically three case-studies on the situation in Nicaragua, Paraguay and Brazil is a truly fascinating read – albeit rather sobering if not disappointing or even discouraging.

The chapter on Nicaragua shows how a State initially opted for quite a full compliance but slowly and fundamentally changed its position into what the book rightly describes as 'open defiance'. This tragic and truly deplorable development reflects the general development in this country with President Ortega's rule having turned into an outright dictatorship characterized by grave and continuous violations of the most basic human rights. So, one might indeed argue that Nicaragua's defiance of the IACtHR in the indigenous territory rights cases is not so much based on resistance against the Court's stance in these very specific cases but reflects the general resistance against any international human rights monitoring – an approach shared by all right- or left-wing dictators in Latin America (and elsewhere, for that matter). Nonetheless, this is, of course, as stated above, a most discouraging development.

The chapter on Paraguay clearly reveals the dilemma so frequently observed throughout Latin America: With the advent of agribusiness as a most promising means to generate income for quite a number of non-indigenous persons and, one should also admit that, also for indigenous persons who choose – or are forced to choose – to renounce their traditional way of livelihood, (claims for) territorial rights are increasingly seen, by the majority population, as an outdated obstacle on the road to economic growth – an obstacle which has to be removed. In contrast to the situation in Nicaragua where, in my mind, non-compliance with international human rights monitoring is simply part of the general (current) structure of that State, the situation in Paraguay and so many other States throughout the world has much less or nothing to do with a general rejection of international human rights monitoring but with what is considered as an intrusion into a nation's sovereign decision to determine the ways and means to overcome poverty and generate economic growth. Again, one might argue that this approach is not only based on a renaissance of ideas of national sovereignty but is intrinsically linked with the just mentioned world-wide trend, the backlash against human rights.

The chapter on Brazil seems to confirm this rather pessimistic assessment. Again, the strong interests of a very powerful agribusiness with apparently excellent connections with the political leadership have generated serious setbacks for the protection of indigenous territorial rights, a development that was further aggravated by the impact of the COVID 19-pandemic on indigenous populations. On the other hand, the book quite convincingly stresses the 'heterogeneity' of the Brazilian society and political landscape in which powerful political groups rely on and use international human rights monitoring in general and the IACtHR jurisprudence in particular as a means to support their fight for indigenous (territorial) rights. Thus, it remains indeed to be seen which way Brazil will follow in the future.

This brings us to the final section entitled 'Conclusion'. It is here where the book answers the research questions with well-formulated summaries of the research; the general answer might be called a 'mixed one': While there are clear signs of effectiveness in all three dimensions (norm-development, case-studies and domestic embeddedness), there remain serious shortcomings regarding all three categories which call for additional measures or reform as developed by the book.

There are, however, also developments which nurture some kind of optimism – the adoption of the legal parameters, developed by the IACtHR, by an increasing number of national Constitutional Courts such as those of Colombia, Peru, and Bolivia. And indeed, it might be this increasingly close inter-relationship between the IACtHR and the national Constitutional Courts, if fully extended to the area of indigenous territorial rights, that might turn out to be the key for a future development more favorable to the effective implementation of such rights on the national level.

This present book is an excellent piece of scholarly research. It is based on a truly impressive study of relevant case-law and the pertaining literature which constitute the basis for a well-balanced analysis presenting both the achievements and the persisting shortcomings of the Court's innovative jurisprudence. This in turn serves as the basis for interesting and innovative proposals how to overcome these shortcomings.

Professor Dr. Dr. Rainer Hofmann
Chair of Public Law, International Public Law and European Law,
Faculty of Law, Goethe-University Frankfurt (Germany)
Frankfurt, July 2024

Acknowledgements

THIS BOOK IS a rewritten version of the PHD Dissertation defended by me at Johann Wolfgang Goethe University in Frankfurt am Main. The research was supervised by Professor Rainer Hofmann, to whom I am enormously grateful for his guidance and kindness.

During my doctoral research, I was able to build an incredible network of female researchers that was decisive for the conclusion of the present work. From different countries and fields and at different levels and moments, they contributed to a clear comprehension of the object of study, refining the conclusions and my understanding of my position as a young female researcher. In particular, I want to express my gratitude to Dr Carina Calábria, Julia Lieberman and Catarina Woyames Dreher as they were central interlocutors of the outcomes of the research. We established and have maintained a very insightful dialogue and I am extremely proud to have built my results from our fruitful conversations. I am also very grateful for the relevant contributions from Dr Ximena Soley, Professor Courtney Hillebrecht, Dr Salome Addo Ravn, Professor Hélène Trigoudja, Professor Sabrina Ragone, Professor Clara Sandoval-Villalba, Julia Wetterslev, Dr Caroline Silva and Dr Jane Mende.

I am also very thankful for the period I was able to spend as a visiting scholar at the Max Planck Institute for Comparative Public Law and International Law in Heidelberg. The research stay was crucial for advancing my research, which was aided by the vast and impressive library of the institute in Heidelberg. There I also found the space to share my ideas and engage in dialogue with the greatest set of researchers, who care deeply for the academic study of transformative constitutionalism in Latin America and the Caribbean. I want to express particular thanks to Professor Armin von Bogdandy, Dr Mariela Morales and Dr Pedro Vilarreal, for their insightful contributions during the Coloquio Iberoamericano.

Furthermore, I also very much appreciated the opportunity to visit the Danish National Research Foundation's Centre of Excellence for International Courts and Governance (iCourts) twice during the book's development. First, in 2019 during the iCourts and Pluricourts Summer School, and second in 2022 as a visiting scholar. I am particularly thankful to Professor Mikael Madsen, Professor Laurence Helfer and Professor Shai Dothan for their meaningful insights.

This doctoral thesis would not have been possible without the emotional and warm support from my dear friends in Frankfurt, my partner and my family. Above all, I want to emphasize my deepest gratitude for all the love, support and understanding they shared throughout the time that I pursued my doctoral thesis.

I am sincerely honoured and grateful to the Federal University of Lavras for the opportunity to develop my research and for providing the necessary funding. I owe sincere gratitude to the students who I have worked with closely, and from whom I am constantly learning.

The PHD dissertation was honoured with the WISAG-Preis 2022, as the best PHD dissertation in the social sciences or humanities that deals with processes and conditions of social integration.

Table of Contents

List of Illustrations

Tables

Figures

Introduction

OVER THE LAST two decades, the Inter-American Court of Human Rights has developed the most advanced binding case law in the field of territorial rights, expanding the entitlement of rights, amplifying the reach of established guarantees, recognising implicit rights and ordering a wide range of remedies. The case law represented a breakthrough model for the protection of traditional peoples' rights, becoming an inspiration for human rights bodies and treaties all around the world. It is fair to say that Inter-American jurisprudence is 'at the forefront of the progressive development of international indigenous rights' (Pasqualucci 2006). The Court's rulings are a consolidated model for the protection of Indigenous peoples, redressing centuries of marginalisation and injustice, and thus giving Indigenous and ethnic peoples an opportunity to become actors of their own trajectory. The Court has even showed sensitivity towards cultural peculiarities, adjusting conventional rights to the peculiar conditions of traditional peoples.

Indigenous peoples have experienced centuries of marginalisation and dispossession as a legacy of colonisation. In recent times, due to increased pressure over natural resources, their traditional territory has become severely endangered due to extensive environmental damage and escalating violence. Despite historical discrimination, it has only been in recent decades that international law and international courts have presented efforts to redress past violations. Currently, the central international treaties for Indigenous rights include the International Labour Organization (ILO) Indigenous and Tribal Peoples Convention (Convention 169, adopted in 1989) and the UN Declaration on the Rights of Indigenous Peoples, adopted in 2007 (UNDRIP). The treaties recognise, among other things, the property rights to ancestral territory, the right to free, prior and informed consultation, political rights, non-discrimination and the right to cultural identity. The rights to traditional territories and the natural resources throughout those territories are the most pressing of issues, as land is considered to be essential grounds for physical and cultural survival.

In Latin America and the Caribbean, there are more than 800 Indigenous peoples living in various situations, but all of them share indications of dispossession, land encroachment, and lack of access to health, education, drinkable water, sanitation and political participation. Structural discrimination and exclusion are two other common patterns among Indigenous peoples (Del Popolo 2017). Such similar contexts have been analysed as violations of human rights by the regional system, the Inter-American System of Human Rights (IAS).

The IAS is part of the Organization of American States (OAS) and is regulated by three main documents: the 1948 OAS Charter; the 1948 American Declaration of the Rights and Duties of Man; and the 1969 American Convention on Human Rights ('the Convention' or ACHR). It is composed of two organs: the Inter-American Commission on Human Rights[1] ('the Commission', or IACHR) and the Inter-American Court on Human Rights[2] ('the Court', or IACtHR). The IACHR receives, analyses and investigates individual petitions related to the violation of human rights and monitors the human rights situation in Member States. The Court is a judicial institution with the purpose of applying and interpreting the Convention. Only state parties and the IACHR have standing before the Court. There are different levels of state participation in the IASHR: all 35 independent countries of the American continent are signatories of the OAS Charter and of the Declaration, while only 25 countries have ratified the Convention and 20 have accepted the Court's jurisdiction.[3]

The Court has jurisdiction to review violations of the Convention and of other treaties which explicitly accept the Court's jurisdiction. It initiated its activities in 1979, but the first decision on the merits in a contentious case was issued only in 1988 (*Velásquez Rodriguez v Honduras*). Until 2022, it presided over 357 contentious cases. Three different moments can be observed in the Court's rulings (Grossman 2009): the first focused on mass and gross violations caused by internal conflicts or dictatorships; the second dealt with self-amnesty laws and rights to truth and accountability; and the third focused on vulnerable groups and structural discrimination. The three moments do not completely overlap with one another, as the Court still currently deals simultaneously with the three categories of cases (Abramovich 2009). A fourth wave could be appointed, ie the contested recognition of direct justiciability of social, cultural and economic rights through the application of Article 26 of the Convention (Mac-Gregor et al 2018).

It is very important to bear in mind that the Inter-American Court has adopted a far more forward-looking attitude towards the realisation of human rights among states compared to its European counterpart, the European Court of Human Rights (ECtHR) (Burgorgue-Larsen 2017). Principles such

[1] For an overall analysis of the IASHR, see Abramovich (2009); Dulitzky (2011); Dejusticia (2015); Cavallaro et al (2019).

[2] For an overall analysis of the Inter-American Court, see: Corte Interamericana de Derechos Humanos (2005); Burgorgue-Larsen and Úbeda de Torres (2009) Pasqualucci (2014) Haeck et al (2015).

[3] The countries that have accepted the Court's jurisdiction are Argentina, Barbados, Bolivia, Brazil, Chile, Colombia, Costa Rica, Dominican Republic, Ecuador, El Salvador, Guatemala, Haiti, Honduras, México, Nicaragua, Panamá, Paraguay, Perú, Suriname, Trinidad and Tobago, Uruguay and Venezuela, although Trinidad and Tobago and Venezuela have denounced the Convention. Dominica, Jamaica and Grenada have signed the Convention, but have not accepted the Court's jurisdiction. The countries that have signed the OAS Charter but not the Convention are Antigua y Barbuda, the Bahamas, Belize, Canada, Cuba, Guyana, Saint Kitts and Nevis, Saint Lucia, Saint Vincent and the Grenadines, and the United States.

as subsidiarity and contingency are barely mentioned by the Inter-American Court.[4] In fact, it has extensively interpreted Article 2 of the Convention, ordering states to adapt the domestic legal system to conventional parameters as well to adopt very specific public policies. It has promoted the conventionality control theory under which all state powers are obliged to adopt the Court's interpretation on human rights (Hitters 2009; Torelly 2017; Mac-Gregor 2017). The Court has even reviewed very delicate and controversial political questions, such as in vitro fertilisation, same-sex marriage, freedom of speech and judicial structure. As a consequence, over the years, the Court has had a considerable impact in Latin American countries. Despite concerning shortcomings,[5] the Court has, in a short period of time, promoted constitutional alterations, the revocation of amnesty laws, the prosecution of high-ranking state authorities for mass violations, the adoption of normative frameworks and the implementation of procedural guarantees (Alessandri 2015).

There has been a growing concern in international law research regarding understanding the after-effects of international litigation within domestic politics (Hillebrecht 2014; Alter 2014; Shany 2016; Alter et al 2018), overcoming a focus strictly on compliance (Helfer and Slaughter 1997; Posner and Yoo 2005). Particularly in the case of the Inter-American System, studies have indicated the transformative role of the Court (Bogdandy et al 2017a) and its impact within both the state and society (Engstrom 2019b).

In this framework, the central question the present book answers is: to what extent is the Inter-American Court of Human Rights effective with regards to the territorial rights of Indigenous and ethnic peoples in Latin America? The research adopts a four-dimensional concept of effectiveness, which include norm-developing effectiveness, case-specific effectiveness, embeddedness and *erga omnes* effectiveness (Helfer 2014). The research analyses the first three dimensions in relation to the Court's case law on territorial rights. Therefore, the research question is divided into four specific problems:

1. To what extent is the IACtHR effective in developing international law on the matter of territorial protection, considering both the recognition of rights and the design of reparation measures?
2. To what extent is the IACtHR effective in compelling compliance with its judgments in territorial cases?
3. To what extent is the IACtHR effective in promoting the embeddedness of its territorial rights' parameters within domestic legal systems?
4. How do norm development, compliance and embeddedness relate one to another in territorial cases issued by the IACtHR?

[4] The only exceptions that have been made have been in cases involving transitional justice, when the country counts on an adequate reparation system for multiple victims. See Sandoval (2018).

[5] Some of the shortcomings appointed include: the Court is not a permanent organ; it has inadequate funding and reduced staff; the political organ has failed to exert pressure over non-compliant states; and there is a lack of quality control of elected judges (Pasqualucci 2006).

When answering these questions, the book not only analyses the level of effectiveness in each of the categories, but also suggests paths for enhancement of the effectiveness, analysing which elements have promoted or hindered the impact of the judgments. In addition, the book considers the relationship among the three dimensions of effectiveness, analysing how increased effectiveness in one dimension might influence the extent of effectiveness in the other dimensions. It demonstrates that full understanding of effectiveness is achieved only by comprehensively analysing each of its dimensions and the interrelation played among them.

Understanding the Court's effectiveness in the field provides elements for more adequate and improved strategies for litigators, social movements and civil society actors who defend territorial rights and, more broadly, socio-economic rights. It also allows international tribunals and bodies to revaluate their strategies in implementing social, cultural and economic rights. From another perspective, the research contributes to the understanding of limits and possibilities regarding the expansion of regional tribunals' mandates through interpretation methods. Territorial case law is the furthest the American Court has gone in terms of the indirect recognition of socio-economic rights, internationally recognised as forward looking and creative. The Court has widely expanded its mandate on the protection of civil and political rights, interpreting an individualistic framework in order to recognise social, economic and cultural rights from a collective point of view. The understanding of the Court's effectiveness in these utmost forward-looking decisions is relevant when forming an understanding of the Inter-American System, as well as a detailed study of possible venues and consequences of the self-expansion of regional courts' mandates through interpretation methods. Furthermore, as the book provides a unique empirical analysis of different theories on effectiveness, it provides an original methodology that could be further applied to other courts or other fields of rights.

OVERVIEW OF INDIGENOUS AND ETHNIC CASES

From the time of its creation until December 2022, the Inter-American Court ruled on 29 contentious cases involving Indigenous and ethnic peoples. In most of the cases (12), the central issue was territorial protection and land demarcation.[6] The second most common issue included massacres or

[6] *Mayagna (Sumo) Awas Tingni v Nicaragua* (2001), *Yakye Axa v Paraguay* (2005), *Sawhoyamaxa v Paraguay* (2006), *Saramaka v Suriname* (2007), *Xámok Kásek v Paraguay* (2010), *Kichwa de Sarayaku v Ecuador* (2012), *Kuna de Madungandí y Emberá de Bayano v Panama* (2014), *Garífuna de Punta Piedra v Honduras* (2015), *Garífuna Triunfo de la Cruz v Honduras* (2015), *Kaliña y Lokono v Suriname* (2015), *Xucuru v Brazil* (2018) and *Lhaka Honhat v Argentina* (2020).

internal conflict (six cases).[7] In two of these cases,[8] land demarcation was also a central issue, as it was a way to ensure the return of the peoples to their land. Other issues analysed by the Court include forced disappearances (two cases),[9] violence against women (two cases),[10] political rights (one case),[11] criminalisation of Indigenous leaderships (two cases),[12] extrajudicial executions (two cases),[13] labour rights (one case)[14] and freedom of expression (one case).[15] Considering that land is the most pressing issue for Indigenous peoples and the central aspect of communal property for the cultural and physical survival of traditional peoples, the present research focuses on the 14 cases issued by the Court in which the violation to the right to communal property has been recognised.

Territorial cases are understood as those in which the Inter-American Court recognised the right to communal property over ancestral territory, imposing the state the duty to delimit, demarcate and title traditional peoples' lands. In such cases, the Court recognised an ensemble of rights, including judicial remedies, right to life and political guarantees. However, all the rights recognised and the reparation measures issued are deeply related to the protection of traditional territories.

The Court does not offer any exhaustive concept of Indigenous peoples. Instead, it presents several common characteristics and considers, primarily, self-identification. Additionally, it does not distinguish Indigenous from ethnic (or tribal) peoples for the purpose of recognition of territorial rights, following the equivalence contained in the Convention 169 from the ILO (ILO 169). The common characteristics considered by the Court include: strong bond with land and natural resources; regulation, at least partially, by customary rules and codes; and social, cultural and economic elements that distinguish the groups from the national community.[16] In addition to such objective characteristics, the Court has reiterated the importance of self-identification as one of the main criteria for classification as Indigenous or tribal people.[17] Self-identification

[7] *Plan de Sánchez v Guatemala* (2004), *Moiwana v Suriname* (2005), *Río Negro Massacres v Guatemala* (2012), *Operation Genesis v Colombia* (2013), *Miembros de la Aldeia Chicupac y comunidades vecinas del Municipio del Rabinal v Guatemala* (2016) and *Coc Max et al v* Guatemala (2018).

[8] *Moiwana v Suriname* (2005) and *Operation Genesis v Colombia* (2013).

[9] *Tiu Tojín v Guatemala* (2008) and *Chitay Nech et al v Guatemala* (2010).

[10] *Fernandez Ortega y otros v Mexico* (2010) and *Rosendo Cantu y otra v Mexico* (2010).

[11] *Yatama v Nicaragua* (2005).

[12] *López Alvarez v Honduras* (2006) and *Norín Catrimán y otros v Chile* (2014).

[13] *Aloeboetoe v Suriname* (2001) *and Escué Zapata v Colombia* (2001).

[14] *Buzos Miskutos v Honduras* (2021).

[15] *Pueblos Indígenas Maya Kaqchikel de Sumpango y otros v Guatemala* (2021).

[16] *Saramaka People v Suriname*, Preliminary Objections, Merits, Reparations, and Costs, IACtHR Series C No 172 (28 November 2007) §79.

[17] *Kaliña and Lokono Peoples v Suriname*, Merits, Reparations and Costs, IACtHR Series C No 309 (25 November 2015) §48.

ought to be sustained even if the state does not recognise the community as an original people,[18] or in cases where some community members adhered to other forms of culture[19] or to other communities.[20] Errors or contradictions in the state registry of the community do not interfere in the identification.[21]

In cases involving territorial rights before the Court, non-Indigenous traditional peoples were parties in five cases (*Moiwana v. Suriname, Saramaka v Suriname, Operation Genesis v Colombia, Garífuna de Punta Piedra v Honduras and Garífuna Triunfo de la Cruz v Honduras*). The traditional peoples were African American groups with distinguishable history and culture: the *Maroons*, in Suriname, the *Garífunas*, in Honduras, and the black rural communities, in Colombia.

Regarding the factual background of the cases, only five of the communities had property titles for their traditional territories before the cases were brought forth. In the other 10 cases, the communities' lands were neither titled nor demarcated, not even in cases where the communities occupied their traditional lands. The factual situation of the territory contrasts with legal and constitutional recognition of land rights in the domestic system, demonstrating that the issue involves a lack of effectiveness of rights and not a lack of legal affirmation of such rights: nine of the 10 countries involved constitutionally recognised Indigenous territorial rights before the litigation. An extremely precarious situation experienced in the three cases against Paraguay, in which the communities were living along the highway or on minimal lands, with no access to traditional sources of food, water or shelter. Traditional communities were living outside their traditional territory in two cases involving forced displacement: one provoked by a massacre (*Moiwana v Suriname*) and one caused by internal conflict (*Operation Genesis v Colombia*).

Other than the titling and demarcation of traditional territory, a central issue for almost all cases was the use and exploration of natural resources. The contested harmful activities included logging (four cases), mining/oil concessions (three cases) and creation of a nature reserve (three cases). The factual background illustrates that there is currently pressure regarding natural resources in the region. It also reveals the intimate connection between Indigenous rights and environmental protection. Finally, an increasing concern related to Indigenous rights is the protection of human rights defenders (HRD), as violence and murder against land and environmental activists increase considerably. From the cases analysed, six of them involve murder or threats to Indigenous leadership, generating a scenario of insecurity.

[18] *Garífuna Triunfo de la Cruz v Honduras*, Preliminary Objections, Merits, Reparations and Costs, IACtHR Series C No 305 (8 October 2015) §57.

[19] *Saramaka v Suriname* §164.

[20] *Sawhoyamaxa v Paraguay*, Merits, Reparations and Costs, IACtHR Series C No 146 (29 March 2006) §206.

[21] *Xákmok Kásek v Paraguay*, Merits, Reparations and Costs, IACtHR Series C No 214 (24 August 2010) §§37 and 49.

EFFECTIVENESS OF INTERNATIONAL COURTS

The aim of this book is to analyse the effectiveness of the IACtHR. However, the concept of effectiveness of international courts has varied greatly over the years and among different scholars. This section aims to briefly describe the different theories on effectiveness of international courts, demonstrating how scholars have conceptualised the relationship between international litigation and changes in the domestic sphere.

At first, the effectiveness of courts was understood as a synonym of compliance with its decisions (Helfer and Slaughter 1997), even though it was sometimes counterbalanced with usage rates and the success of treaty regimes (Posner and Yoo 2005). More recently, a list of functions and goals has been indicated, expanding the parameters for measuring the effectiveness of courts beyond dispute settlement (Bogdandy and Venzke 2014; Alvarez 2014), while some studies have turned to analysing the authority and legitimacy of international courts (Bogdandy and Venzke 2010; Alter et al 2018). Specifically with respect to the Inter-American System, research has analysed the structural impact of litigation, which is related to non-repetition measures (Corzo Sosa et al 2013) or, more broadly, influences on civil society and government offices (Engstrom 2017). Finally, a prominent group of scholars has indicated the transformative role of the IAS and its dialogue with domestic actors with the purpose of alleviating poverty and reducing discrimination (Bogdandy et al 2017b; Bogdandy et al 2017a).

One of the first studies regarding the effectiveness of international courts was presented by Slaughter and Helfer in 1997 in which they identified effectiveness as a tribunal's 'ability to compel compliance with its judgments by convincing domestic government institutions, directly and through pressure from private litigants, to use their power on its behalf' (Helfer and Slaughter 1997: 278). In an attempt to understand why the ECJ and the ECHR were effective courts, the authors established a checklist of factors that influenced effectiveness. Later in 2005, the authors clarified that their concept of effectiveness was more relative than absolute (Helfer and Slaughter 2005). Similar to Helfer and Slaughter, Posner and Yoo also considered compliance to be a measure for effectiveness, although it should be complemented by the level of usage and success of the respective treaty regime (Posner and Yoo 2005). They presented a sceptical analysis, describing international courts as mere problem-solving devices, incapable of transforming a state's interests.

From a similar perspective, Helfer and Alter proposed a differentiation between compliance and effectiveness, stating that, while there is conformity between state behaviour and specified legal rule in both, only effectiveness involves desired changes in behaviour that are attributable to that rule (Alter and Helfer 2017; Raustiala 2000). Despite this differentiation, in cases of compulsory jurisdiction, effectiveness could be measured by state compliance.[22] The authors

[22] See also Hawkins and Jacoby (2010); Huneeus (2011); Gonzalez-Salzberg (2017).

proposed recognising effects beyond compliance and, while analysing the Andean Tribunal of Justice, the following effects were indicated: inculcation of the rule of law; opposition to corruption; and effects on states that were not parties (Alter and Helfer 2017).

The characteristics of international courts have considerably altered over the years, and so has their role on domestic politics. Facing such alterations, Alter suggests that design features of new-style courts (compulsory jurisdiction and access by non-state litigators) promoted a wider influence of international decisions within domestic politics. Alter attributes four functions to international courts: dispute settlement; administrative review; constitutional review; and law enforcement. She also analyses why some courts are more effective than others, arguing that effective courts are those that are able to rely on a coalition of compliance constituencies who support the rule of law (Alter 2014).

From another perspective, Yuval Shany proposes a goal-based approach in which effectiveness is assessed against predefined goals contained in their stated mission and/or affirmed by their constituencies. For an analysis of the decisions' outcomes, one should consider compliance (effect on involved parties), the impact of case law (effect on the wider public), docket size, acceptance of jurisdiction, available budget and legitimacy. These elements can, depending on the circumstances, suggest lower or higher rates of effectiveness. Lastly, the author proposes two complementary assessment of the analysis: efficiency (overall impact assessment) and cost-effectiveness (relationship between structural attributes and effectiveness) (Shany online). The assessment of a tribunal's goals is based upon the normative assumption that international courts should be constrained by the expectations of one set of constituencies, focusing on the mandate providers. The author recognises that the goals could have ambiguities and could vary in time. Four general goals are indicated (norm support, resolving disputes, regime support and legitimising public authority), b it is not clear as to how to assess the idiosyncratic goals of international courts (Shany 2016).

Using a similar perspective, it is possible to analyse the international tribunal's effectiveness by assessing how they fulfil their functions. Bogdandy and Venzke affirm that international adjudication can exercise four functions: dispute settlement; lawmaking; reinforcing rights expectations; and controlling and reaffirming domestic institutions (Bogdandy and Venzke 2014, 2010). Similarly, Alvarez proposes dispute settlement, fact finding, lawmaking and governance as being the functions of international courts (Alvarez 2014).

Focusing on how domestic audiences react to an international court's litigation, Alter, Helfer and Madsen proposed a theory on de facto authority of international tribunals. The theory offers a 'yardstick to evaluate how a range of contextual factors shapes de facto authority of ICs via an analysis of audiences' practices towards ICs (Alter et al 2018). The study of the authority analyses the interaction among legal, social and political structures, as well as the behaviour of actors situated within these structures, encompassing a wider audience than just the parties in the litigation. The theory prescribes five types of de facto authority: no authority; narrow authority; intermediate authority; extensive authority; and popular authority. While narrow authority examines the practice of the litigants involved in the dispute, intermediate authority extends to the behaviour and decisions of similarly situated actors, including potential future litigants and compliance partners. Extensive authority is reached when the court's authority reaches a broader range of legal actors, shaping both law and politics. Lastly, popular authority occurs when the recognition of the IC's decisions reaches the public in general. The five levels of authority are not necessarily sequenced according to time, and authority can contract and expand over time, as well as vary in different matters (Alter et al 2018).

Specifically regarding the Inter-American System, one very prominent group of scholars has researched about the *Ius Commune Constitutionale en America Latina* (ICCAL). ICCAL analyses the legal phenomenon of dialogue between national and international courts aiming at transforming reality of gross social inequality in the context of transition from dictatorship. The concept promotes 'the transformative potential of human rights, democracy and rule of law in Latin America', transforming a context characterised by structural deficiency and social inequality. ICCAL proposes to identify, frame and develop a web of comparative constitutional law and regional human rights law, including its institutions, stakeholders and actors. The studies of the scholar hub include themes such as the conventionality control, the constitutional block, mechanisms of domestic opening (*interamericanización*), the impact of the reparations system and institutional empowerment (Morales Antoniazzi 2016; Bogdandy et al 2017b; Bogdandy et al 2014; Bogdandy et al 2017a).

Using a similar approach, the Inter-American Human Rights Network has analysed the impact of the IAS in the implementation of human rights in Latin America. Even though avoiding a close definition on impact, the scholars 'have developed a grounded and contextual understanding of how the IAS influences the politics and struggles between actors and institutions seeking to advance the realisation of human rights and those who resist such social and political change', proposing elements that could increase the positive effects of the system (Engstrom 2016). In relation to the reduction of the analysis of the Court's effects on domestic legal orders merely as compliance, Engstrom proposed three criticisms: the role of the System in the interpretation and enhancement of human rights standards; the insertion of the System within domestic political debates; and the creation of opportunities for domestic actors to pressure for change (Engstrom 2017). He defines effectiveness as 'the degree to which international human rights institutions work to improve human rights conditions and decrease the likelihood of the repetition of abuses, while providing satisfactory recourse to the victims' (Engstrom 2019a: 4), a concept that, even though includes compliance, is not restricted to it.

Other terms have been used in reference to the effectiveness of international courts, such as engagement (the use of international human rights parameters by domestic courts) (Torelly 2019), institutional empowerment (the use of IAS by state officials helping to overcome institutional resistance and to promote the defence of human rights, reconfiguring conflicts among social groups) (Parra-Vera 2019), transconstitutionalism (the relationship between different legal orders in regard to a common constitutional problem, which can be bilateral or multidimensional) (Neves 2013) and efficacy chain (separating efficacy into five layers, ie observance, application, strengthening, implementation and adequacy) (Calabria 2018).

The literature on the effectiveness of international courts has gradually evolved to the understanding that even though compliance is an important proxy, analyses of effectiveness should not be restricted to it. The distinction between the two concepts becomes blurry when a tribunal issues society-wide reparations, such as non-repetition measures. In these cases, impact and compliance might overlap one another. This is the case of the Inter-American Court, whose non-repetition reparation measures have a reach beyond the parties, ie human rights courses for public officials, implementation or adaptation of legal measures, creation of public policies, among others. In another perspective, a compliance assessment does not sufficiently explain problematic situations of delayed compliance, partial compliance and the selection of effects (Dothan 2017). Lastly, new courts have exerted multiple and innovative activities, promoting dialogue with state actors, civil society and victims. A focus exclusively on compliance disregards this complex network and its after-effects in domestic political conjuncture.

Regarding the researches that present specific functions or goals for international courts, they provide an interesting and up-to-date approach that extends the comprehension of courts as mere dispute settlement devices. However, the enumeration of a closed list of goals might overlook the specificities of some courts that expand their own mandate or assume innovative functions, considering the particular context of their constituencies. Specifically in the case of the Inter-American Court, the assessment of these goals are quite a challenging task, considering the existence of multiple levels of acceptance in the system's parameters (the simultaneous presence of signatories of the OAS Charter, signatories of the OAS Charter and the ACHR and signatories of the OAS Charter and the ACHR, which accepted the Court's jurisdiction) (Calabria 2018). Even if we exclusively consider the last group of countries, considering the political instability characteristic of LAC and the enormous distinctions among the countries, it would be very challenging to assess a common stipulated goal for the Inter-American Court.

Despite the variation in terms and definitions presented by the literature, the most recent studies have in common the concern with the after-effects of international litigation within domestic politics. The concern is even more present among researches conducted on the IAS, considering the peculiarities of the Inter-American Court (a new-style court) and the transformative constitutionalism within the region. It is possible to summarise some of the elements analysed by the theories as being relevant for the increased effectiveness of international litigation: partnerships with local constituencies and the formation of a network; institutional empowerment through non-repetition measures; the influence of international organisations, including financial institutions and human rights mechanisms; and the level of compliance.

In an attempt to consolidate the different conceptions of effectiveness, Helfer divides the scholarship into four groups: case-specific effectiveness (or compliance), embeddedness effectiveness (influence in domestic legal orders), norm-development effectiveness and *erga omnes* effectiveness (systemic precedential effects for state parties not involved in the litigation). The present book adopts such classification, analysing the three first dimensions of effectiveness (Helfer 2014).

In addition to adopting Helfer's systematisation of the different dimensions on effectiveness, the book closely dialogues with the researches on domestic impacts beyond compliance. The study analyses, specifically in the case of territorial rights: the reliance on compliance partners (Alter 2014) and the strengthening of a network of key actors (Engstrom and Low 2019); the unblocking effect on public policies, the reshaping of domestic political disputes (Rocha Reis 2019) and the institutional empowerment (Pegram and Rodriguez 2019; Engstrom 2016); the dialogue between domestic and international courts and the application of the conventionality control (Góngora Mera 2014; Ferrer Mac-Gregor 2017); and the transformative potential of the Court's decisions in a context characterised by marginalisation and poverty (Morales Antoniazzi et al 2020).

OUTLINE OF THE BOOK

The book is presented in six chapters and a conclusion. In chapters one and two, the norm-development effectiveness of the decisions is analysed. Effectiveness is assessed considering three criteria: coherence (among cases and among rights); consistent level of reasoning; and the potential of the developed norms to promote the self-determination of Indigenous peoples. While the first two criteria are analysed through a careful review of the decisions, the third compares the reasoning with the international *corpus iuris* of Indigenous rights and the requests of Indigenous peoples and their representatives.

Chapter one details the parameters established by the Court and the interpretation methods applied in order to recognise the territorial rights of Indigenous and ethnic peoples. It also describes how the Court was able to recognise collective social rights through an extensive interpretation of individual civil and political rights guaranteed in the Convention. In order to protect the ancestral territory, central concern of the cases, the Court affirmed an ensemble of rights, including right to life, access to judicial remedy and cultural identity. Even though the case law is considered to be a breakthrough model for the enhanced protection of Indigenous rights, contradictions and omissions are presented as an attempt to improve decisions in future cases. The chapter concludes by reinforcing the interdependence among human rights and the protection of traditional Indigenous territories, and proposes an integral approach centred in the right to self-determination.

Chapter two focuses on the Court's reparation system, characterised by victim-centred and transformative approaches. The chapter details how the Court has applied the principles of *pro personae* and integral reparation to build culturally adequate remedies aimed at redressing centuries of marginalisation, presenting an original quantitative dataset and analysing each category of measure: compensation; satisfaction; restitution; rehabilitation; accountability; and non-repetition. The Court has adopted a varied catalogue of reparation measures, from monetary compensation to the adoption of legislation and the provision of basic public services. Despite the recognition of the importance of the applied remedies, concerns are presented, such as the insufficient and paternalistic monetary compensation and an inadequate protection of the collective property. The interconnected model presented in the previous chapter is analysed as possible solution for improvement of the reparations.

Chapter three focus on case-specific effectiveness, presenting an original dataset on compliance with territorial decisions. It provides a quantitative analysis of compliance rates and qualitatively describes the domestic implementation of the decisions. The analysis of the case-specific effectiveness reveals a concerningly low rate of compliance, as well as delayed and conflicting implementation processes within the countries. Partial compliance prevails, as no state has challenged the Court's decision, paying compensation and also publishing the decisions, while, on the other hand, rehabilitation, accountability and restitution measures have low rates of compliance. The chapter also analyses elements appointed by scholars related to compliance, and it proposes venues for the improved implementation of case law.

Even though compliance levels are low, the implementation process has fomented domestic embeddedness of the normative parameters. Chapters four, five and six present the embeddedness effectiveness by analysing the influence of international litigation in the domestic legal orders of selected states (Nicaragua, Paraguay and Brazil). Differently from chapters one to three, in which all cases were analysed, the embeddedness assessment is pursued through inference-oriented research and case study. Considering the complexity of embeddedness, three countries were selected. For selection of the countries, three criteria were adopted: the representativeness of the countries among other Latin American and the Caribbean (LAC) countries; the lapse of time between the decision and the study; and compliance levels. Regarding the first, the three countries are representative of the LAC situation in terms of the protection of territorial rights, as all of them have a consolidated legislative framework recognising

Indigenous and ethnic territorial rights, but lack the implementation of such rights. They also have similar levels of 'opening' towards the Inter-American System, as regional treaties on human rights have a special hierarchical position in the three countries. Regarding the lapse of time, while the territorial cases against Nicaragua and Paraguay were the first ones issued by the Court, Brazil was condemned in the second most recent case analysed by this research. The varying lapse of time could indicate the relation between time and effectiveness. Lastly, the chosen cases present contrasting rates of compliance (full compliance in *Awas Tingni v Nicaragua*, intermediate compliance level in the three cases against Paraguay and initial steps in *Xucuru v Brasil*) and could indicate different patterns of embeddedness.

Chapter four analyses the deep transformation that occurred in Nicaragua, a country that went from full compliance with the *Awas Tingni* case to the recent denouncement of the Inter-American System. The chapter details how the adoption of an advanced legislation on territorial rights was not enough to counter violations, addressing the implementation gap in the country. Chapter five analyses the territorial protection in Paraguay after the Court's decisions. The country struggles to comply with the vague reparations ordered by the Court while the communities endure the same wretched conditions from before the litigation. As the agribusiness sector takes a considerable role in the country, both in politics and in the economy, the rights violations increase. The gradual adoption of a protective indigenist legal framework was not enough to counter the violations, presenting a merely symbolic feature. In Chapter six, the setbacks in the Brazilian indigenist framework after the *Xucuru* case are detailed. It demonstrates how the rising of a populist far-right Government promoted deep setbacks in what used to be one of the most protective domestic legislation. On the other hand, it also details how national human rights institutions and domestic NGOs have adopted the Inter-American parameters in order to strength the mobilisation against the setbacks.

The book concludes with a description of the different levels of effectiveness identified in each of the three dimensions analysed and asserting the relationships between them. Instead of finishing with a dual analysis of effectiveness (effective or non-effective), the book concludes that the effectiveness of the IACtHR has varied according to time and to domestic context. Furthermore, the book demonstrates the indissolubility among each dimension of effectiveness, as they are interconnected, influencing one another.

The IACtHR has demonstrated great effectiveness in the following aspects: the development of international parameters for the protection of territorial rights; the development of a reparation system for territorial rights; the strengthening of domestic institutions and NGOs; and the promotion of the domestic adoption of international territorial rights. However, the Court has demonstrated a low level of ability to compel states to comply with its decisions. The effectiveness has varied considerably over time and according to each domestic context. Lastly, however, the improvement on the legal parameters on territorial rights did not guarantee full enjoyment of the rights since the implementation gap is a consequence of deep social and historical elements. Indigenous peoples' struggle for self-determination continues decades after the strategic litigation and even after full compliance, demonstrating the persistence of discrimination and the inability to overcome the impacts of colonisation exclusively through strategic litigation.

1

The Inter-American Law-Making on Territorial Cases: The Recognition of Rights

THE CONSTRUCTION OF collective social and cultural rights is the most innovative aspect of the Inter-American Court's rulings on territorial rights, adjusting the American Convention to cultural peculiarities of Indigenous and ethnic peoples through creative interpretation methods. This chapter focuses on the lawmaking of Indigenous territorial rights, analysing the norm-development effectiveness of the Court's decisions. This book analyses the territorial cases, since land is the most vital threshold for traditional peoples' survival. In all 14 analysed cases, the right to property over traditional lands is the central issue. In addition, considering the interdependence between land and the enjoyment of other conventional rights, the Court has declared the violation of an ensemble of rights, all related to the protection of the traditional territory. Effectiveness is assessed considering three criteria: coherence (among cases and among rights); consistent level of reasoning; and the potential of the developed norms to promote the self-determination of Indigenous peoples.

The chapter begins with a quantitative analysis of the recognised rights, demonstrating the Court's focus on territorial rights and procedural guarantees. Before a detailed analysis of the construction of each right and freedom, the interpretation methods applied by the Court are presented, as well as the prominent dialogue that is taking place between international and domestic courts. Thereafter, the chapter analyses each right that the Court declared as having been violated, thus chronologically presenting the praetorian innovations. Such innovations are seen as being at the forefront of international Indigenous law and are considered the most forward-looking binding precedent on the matter. Despite recognised advances in the recognition of rights, there is room for improvement in the rulings of the Court; this will be presented and analysed in the conclusion of the chapter.

1.1. OVERVIEW OF THE VIOLATED RIGHTS

In all 14 analysed cases, the Court recognised international responsibility only for violation of the American Convention of Human Rights (San Jose,

22 November 1969) (ACHR). In all cases, the Court declared violated the right to property (Article 21) and the right to judicial protection (Article 25), combined with the obligation to respect rights and to not discriminate (Article 1.1). The recognition of the right to a fair trial (Article 8.1) and the obligation to adopt measures in the domestic system (Article 2) are also prominent in the rulings. On a few occasions, the Court has recognised a violation of the right to juridical personality (Article 3), the right to life (Article 4.1), the right to personal integrity (Article 5.1), the freedom of expression (Article 13), the freedom of association (Article 16), rights of the child (Article 19), the freedom of movement (Article 22), the right to participate in the government (Article 23) and social rights (Article 26). A peculiarity of the Inter-American Court is the use of the principle of *iura novit curia*, according to which the Court is linked to facts reported by the parties, but not to the claim regarding specific articles of the Convention. According to this principle, the Court can declare a violation of an article even if the Commission or the representatives had not claimed so, as long as the violation is related to the facts presented (see Table 1.1).

In all decisions, the Court has at least partially accepted the claims of the Commission, declaring international responsibility for almost all rights claimed. In some situations, the Court did not accept a claim for a specific right at first, but changed its positioning in future cases. This happened with the right to personal integrity (denied in *Sawhoyamaxa v Paraguay* (2006),[1] but accepted in *Xákmok Kásek v Paraguay* (2010)[2]); the right to participate in government and freedom of expression (both denied in *Kichwa de Sarayaku v Ecuador*[3] (2012)), but accepted in *Kaliña and Lokono v Suriname*[4] (2015) and *Lhaka Honhat v Argentina*[5] (2021)) and the recognition of the direct justiciability of social rights (Article 26), claimed in *Kichwa de Sarayaku* and *Yakye Axa v Paraguay* (2005),[6] both by the representative CEJIL, and recognised in *Lhaka Honhat* (2020).

The data shows that the right not to be discriminated (Article 24) has received little attention in Indigenous and ethnic cases – it was claimed only twice and never accepted, even though the factual background in the Indigenous cases reflects elevated levels of discrimination. The prominence of the right

[1] *Sawhoyamaxa Indigenous Community v Paraguay*, Merits, Reparations and Costs, IACtHR Series C No 146 (29 March 2006).

[2] *Xákmok Kásek Indigenous Community v Paraguay*, Merits, Reparations and Costs, IACtHR Series C No 214 (24 August 2010).

[3] *Kichwa Indigenous People of Sarayaku v Ecuador*, Merits and Reparations, IACtHR Series C No 245 (27 June 2012).

[4] *Kaliña and Lokono Peoples v Suriname*. Merits, Reparations and Costs, IACtHR Series C No 309 (25 November 2015).

[5] *Indigenous Communities of the Lhaka Honhat (our land) Association v Argentina*, Merits, Reparations and Costs, IACtHR Series C No 400 (6 February 2020).

[6] *Yakye Axa Indigenous Community v Paraguay*, Merits, Reparations and Costs, IACtHR Series C No 125 (17 June 17 2005).

Table 1.1 Articles declared violated by the Court

Case/Article of the ACHR	1	2	3	4	5	7	8	11	13	16	17	19	21	22	23	24	25	26
Mayagna (sumo) Awas Tingni v. Nicaragua	C	C											C				C	
Moiwana v Suriname	C V				V		C V						V	V			C V	
Yakye Axa v Paraguay	C V	C V		C V			C V						C V				C V	V
Sawhoyamaxa v Paraguay	C V	C V		C V	C V		C V						C V				C V	
Saramaka v Suriname	C V	C V	V										C V				C V	
Xamok Kásek v Paraguay	C V	C V	C V	C V	V		C V					C V	C V				C V	
Kichwa de Sarayaku v Ecuador	C V	C V		C V	C V	C V	C V		C V				C V	C V	C V		C V	V
Operation genesis v Colombia	C V			C V	C V		C V	C V			C V	C V	C V	C V		C V	C V	
Kuna de Madugandí *y* Emberá de Bayano v Panama	CV	CV					CV						CV			C V	CV	
Garífuna Triunfo de la Cruz v Honduras	C V	C V		V			C V						C V				C V	
Garífuna de Punta Piedra v Honduras	C V	C V		V			V						C V		V		C V	
Kaliña *y* Lokono v Suriname	C V	C V	C V										C V				C V	
Xukuru v Brazil	C	C			C		C						C				C	
Lhaka Honhat v Argentina	C V	C V	V				C V		C V	V			C V	V	C V		C V	V

C. Claimed by the Commission V. Claimed by the victims' representatives. In grey, declared violated by the Court. Data obtained from the submission of the case by the Commission, brief of pledges and evidence proposed by the representatives and the Court's decisions on merits. Original compilation.

to property is reflected by the territorial emphasis on the selected cases. The Court has affirmed as the central instrument for the protection of traditional territories the recognition of a collective right to traditional property, which is complemented by procedural rights (access to justice – Articles 8 and 25) and by multiple substantive rights according to each specific situation. In all cases, cultural identity is a central element for an analysis of the Convention and the promotion of a particular worldview. Besides the rights explicitly foreseen in the Convention, the Court also recognised rights protected under the international *corpus iuris* and derived from a broader interpretation of the Convention. They are the right to free, prior and informed consultation (recognised under the right to property), the right to cultural identity and the right to self-determination.

The Convention enshrines only individual civil and political rights. The expansion of its reach to encompass collective social, cultural and economic rights was pursued with innovative interpretation methods. The interpretative and expansive management of the Convention guaranteed very progressive judicial lawmaking, expanding the reach of already enshrined rights and affirming implicit rights.

The central interpretation method used by the Court is the so-called 'evolutionary interpretation', or interpretation *pro personae*, according to which international treaties are considered living instruments that must be interpreted according to the evolution of times and to the current living conditions, ensuring the best protection available for human beings.[7] This evolutionary interpretation shall always be extensive, avoiding any interpretation that restricts human rights protection, according to Article 29.b of the Convention.[8] In other words, the conventional rights flow from the human person and cannot be limited by the state or by the Court.

The application of Article 29.b also favours a normative opening, as it allows the Court to resort to the *corpus iuris* of international law, interpreting the Convention in light of several international treaties related to the case, which include either binding or soft law. In this regard, the Vienna Convention on the Law of the Treaties (Vienna, 23 May 1969) is mentioned, and more particularly, Article 31.2.[9] The *corpus iuris* considered by the Court is vast and encompasses documents from the Inter-American System itself (American Declaration of the Rights and Duties of the Man, Protocol of San Salvador

[7] *Mayagna (Sumo) Awas Tingni Community v Nicaragua*, Merits, Reparations and Costs, IACtHR Series C No 79 (31 August 2001) §146.

[8] ACHR, Art 29: 'No provision of this Convention shall be interpreted as: … b. restricting the enjoyment or exercise of any right or freedom recognized by virtue of the laws of any State Party or by virtue of another convention to which one of the said states is a party'.

[9] Vienna Convention, Art 31.2: 'The context for the purpose of the interpretation of a treaty shall comprise, in addition to the text, including its preamble and annexes: (a) Any agreement relating to the treaty which was made between all the parties in connexion with the conclusion of the treaty; (b) Any instrument which was made by one or more parties in connexion with the conclusion of the treaty and accepted by the other parties as an instrument related to the treaty'.

and several Reports and Informs from the Commission), decisions from other regional systems and reports from UN human rights mechanisms.[10] Regarding treaties celebrated in the international sphere, the most commonly mentioned are the ILO Indigenous and Tribal Peoples Convention (27 June 1989) and the UN Declaration on the Rights of Indigenous Peoples (13 September 2017). Additionally, the *corpus iuris* includes domestic legislation and judicial precedents, not only from the state involved in the dispute, but also, comparatively, from other Latin American and Caribbean (LAC) states. The cross-referencing is a crucial tool to reaffirm the legitimacy of the Court, and it has become a reiterated practice in its jurisprudence, and not only on territorial rights (Sandholtz 2020).

The use of evolutionary interpretation has served to specify undetermined concepts of the Convention or even to identify the reach of certain rights, attaching a multicultural and collective meaning to Indigenous cases (for example, the right to collective property and the right to a dignified life) (Burgorgue-Larsen 2014: 121–4). The Court has also used transformative concepts, which expand the state's obligations regarding the Convention. Two transformative concepts that are of great importance to territorial cases include the right not to be discriminated against and the vulnerability.[11] Both of these concepts are committed to the changing of the factual circumstances of exclusion and marginalization (Burgorgue-Larsen 2014: 129). The awareness of the historical conditions of Indigenous and ethnic groups, marginalised and excluded since colonization, leads to the reinforcement of states obligations in order to achieve equality (Russo and Wences 2016: 303). Another transformative concept applied is the cultural integrity, as the alleged violations were analysed by the Court under the lens of Indigenous socio-cultural aspects. The cultural parameter was used to transform individualistic and liberal rights into collective socio-cultural rights and did so using an 'interculturalistic approach' (Russo and Wences 2016: 303). As the recognition encompasses sociological and anthropological elements, thus overcoming a legalist approach, reports and testimonials from expert witnesses played an essential role in the interpretation of the Convention.

1.2. RIGHT TO COLLECTIVE PROPERTY

The right to collective property is the most fundamental right assured by the Court to traditional peoples. It represents one of the most forward-looking

[10] Committee on Economic, Social, and Cultural Rights, Human Rights Committee, Committee on the Elimination of Racial Discrimination, Special Rapporteur on the rights of indigenous peoples, Office of the High Commissioner for Human Rights, Human Rights and Committee of the International Covenant on Civil and Political Rights.

[11] For further analysis on the use of vulnerability in the Inter-American system, see Estupiñan-Silva (2014).

developments of the tribunal, which has become a reference for international and domestic courts around the world. The centrality of property rights in Indigenous matters is related to a factual condition, the indissoluble bond between Indigenous communities and their territory, as an imperative condition for not only physical survival, but also socio-cultural continuity. In fact, traditional lands represent more than a place to live, but also an inseparable mechanism to guarantee traditional culture, social organisation, religion, medicine, food supply and the economy. It provides not only social identification, but also spiritual and cultural distinctiveness. The Court's interpretation of the right to property considers such an attachment of Indigenous peoples to their territory, recognising that territorial rights are a pressing issue for the survival of traditional peoples.

The Court's interpretation concerning collective property right changed over the years, assuming a progressively wider scope. At first, the Court recognised the right to collective property based upon an enlarged interpretation of the right to property. Then, it included ILO 169 in its legal framework. The next steps were the recognition of rights over natural resources and to prior consultation. At last, the Court approached the compatibility of Indigenous rights and environmental concern.

1.2.1. Right to Collective Property – First Cases

The first time the Court recognised the right to Indigenous territory was in *Mayagna (Sumo) Awas Tingni v Nicaragua* (2001). As the Convention has no explicit mention of Indigenous territorial rights, the Court used methods of interpretation to enlarge the Convention-established rights and to protect traditional communities' lands: the interpretation *pro personae*, or evolutionary; the historical analysis of the Convention; the use of Indigenous customary law and the reference to the Nicaraguan Constitution.[12] The Court interpreted Article 21 of the Convention (right to property)[13] in light of all the arguments listed above and affirmed that the right to property should be recognised in respect to a 'communitarian tradition regarding a communal form of collective property of the land, in the sense that ownership of the land is not centred on an individual but rather on the group and its community'. Additionally, the Court considered that, 'For indigenous communities, relations to the land are not merely a matter of possession and production but a material and spiritual element which they must fully enjoy, even to preserve their cultural legacy and transmit it to future generations'. Therefore, the Tribunal stated that the mere

[12] *Awas Tingni v Nicaragua* (n 7) §§146–53.

[13] ACHR, Art 21.1: 'Everyone has the right to the use and enjoyment of his property. The law may subordinate such use and enjoyment to the interest of society'.

possession of lands was considered sufficient for the obtainment of official recognition of the territory, respecting ancestral occupation of the lands. Based upon the Nicaraguan Constitution, the recognition of the Indigenous right to property imposed duties on the state to delimit, demarcate and title traditional territory, as well as to abstain from any act that could harm total use and enjoyment of the property.[14]

The arguments were reaffirmed in *Moiwana v Suriname* (2005), the first territorial case regarding a non-Indigenous traditional people. The case was related to a massacre that was followed by forced displacement. Just as in *Awas Tingni*, the Court equated possession of the territory to an official title and declared a violation of the right to property, affirming the state's obligation to demarcate the ancestral lands.[15] In the subsequent case, *Yakye Axa v Paraguay*, a new interpretation method is added to the one previously mentioned: a systematic interpretation, based upon the *corpus iuris* of the international law of human rights. The Court decided to interpret the Convention based upon the treaties from the whole system of which a case is a part, resorting, therefore, to ILO 169 for interpretation of the right to communal property.[16] As the Yakye Axa Indigenous territory had been sold on the stock market, the Court presented, for the first time, considerations regarding a confrontation between the right to private property and the right to collective territory, both of which are protected under Article 21. Instead of recognising the prevalence of one of the rights, the Court established that the state should solve the conflict based upon legality, necessity and proportionality. Cultural identity and the survival of Indigenous peoples were considered by the Court as compelling arguments in defence of restrictions to private property. Therefore, the Court recognised that, only in the eventual impossibility that the original lands are acquired and, also, in agreement with the community, alternative lands and/or payment of fair compensation could be offered.[17] With regards to a time framework, the right to communal property shall be recognised as long as the cultural bond with the land persists, otherwise it will lapse.[18]

Sawhoyamaxa was a similar case, in which the Court summarised its precedents in the following terms:

> 1) traditional possession of their lands by indigenous people has equivalent effects to those of a state-granted full property title; 2) traditional possession entitles indigenous people to demand official recognition and registration of property title; 3) the members of indigenous peoples who have unwillingly left their traditional lands, or lost possession thereof, maintain property rights thereto, even though they lack legal

[14] *Awas Tingni v Nicaragua* (n 7) §§149 and 153.

[15] *Moiwana Community v Suriname*, Preliminary Objections, Merits, Reparations and Costs, IACtHR Series C No 124 (15 June 2005) §§125–35.

[16] *Yakye Axa v Paraguay* (n 6) §§123–31.

[17] ibid §§142–52.

[18] *Sawhoyamaxa v Paraguay* (n 1) §§131–33.

title, unless the lands have been lawfully transferred to third parties in good faith; and 4) the members of indigenous peoples who have unwillingly lost possession of their lands, when those lands have been lawfully transferred to innocent third parties, are entitled to restitution thereof or to obtain other lands of equal extension and quality.[19]

The arguments created and strengthened in these four initial cases are the basis for recognition of the collective property right of traditional communities and are mentioned and reinforced in all future cases.

1.2.2. Right to Use Natural Resources

The Court affirmed that protection of traditional communal property must ensure the control and use of natural resources, which are fundamental for economic, social and cultural survival. Therefore, the right to property protects 'those natural resources traditionally used and necessary for the very survival, development and continuation of such people's way of life'.[20] The first time the Court ruled about the use of natural resources in traditional territory was in *Saramaka v Suriname* (2010), even though mining concessions in traditional territory were reported in *Awas Tingni*. Considering that the right to property is not absolute and that 'law may subordinate [the] use and enjoyment [of property] to the interest of society',[21] the Court established that states could restrict the right to collective property provided the restrictions are: a) previously established by law; b) necessary; c) proportional, and d) with the aim of achieving a legitimate objective in a democratic society. Even though the Convention does not prevent the state (itself or through third parties) to develop projects and public work on the territory, the impact of the activities should never endanger the survival of the members of Indigenous peoples.[22] Specifically regarding concessions for the exploration of natural resources in Indigenous and ethnic lands, the Court established three procedural safeguards: consultation; benefit sharing; and social and environmental studies. In addition to the procedural safeguards, the Court stated that exploration of natural resources should not endanger the cultural and physical survival of the community, as the safeguards 'are intended to preserve, protect and guarantee the special relationship that the members of the [Indigenous] community have with their territory'.[23]

[19] *Sawhoyamaxa v Paraguay* (n 1) §128.

[20] *Saramaka People v Suriname*, Preliminary Objections, Merits, Reparations, and Costs, IACtHR Series C No 172 (28 November 2007) §122.

[21] ACHR Art 21.1.

[22] *Lhaka Honhat v Argentina* (n 5) §175.

[23] *Saramaka v Suriname*, Interpretation of the Judgment on Preliminary Objections, Merits, Reparations and Costs, IACtHR Series C No 185 (12 August 2008) §36.

First, the community must receive reasonable benefits from such concessions because of the restrictions or deprivations of their right to property. It is important to note that the Court only mentioned participation with regards to the profit, with no consideration regarding compensation for possible damages. In addition, the details of the benefit-sharing (rates, form and moment of payment) are not clear, nor the procedures for their stipulation. Second, independent and technically capable entities must perform, with the states' supervision, a prior environmental and social impact assessment, in accordance with international parameters of excellence.[24] Technical studies should ensure that planned activities do not endanger the survival of the community, as well as offer a prospect of the damages and the potential risks.[25] The third safeguard, the right to prior consultation, is discussed more in depth below.

The use of natural resources and the application of the safeguards were considered by the Court in several future cases, always with the same argumentation and the same results.[26] In the majority of them, the Court ruled on terrestrial resources. The exception is the *Garífuna Triunfo de la Cruz*, in which the Court affirmed that states have a duty to guarantee the enjoyment of beaches and seashores, according to traditional uses and customs.[27] In one most recent case, *Kaliña and Lokono v Suriname*, the Court added as an argument the 'Guiding Principles on Business and Human Rights', considering that the exploration of resources to the detriment of the community was carried out by private actors, under concessions made by the state.[28] The innovation is of paramount importance, as private companies are essential partners for implementation of the decisions. Even though only states are subject to the Court's authority, the affirmation of the guiding principles might be essential for the reinforcement of state duties to regulate and control the private sector in violation of human rights (Londoño-Lázaro et al 2017).

Regarding the relationship between Indigenous peoples and their environment, since the very first case, the Court considered it to be a crucial element within the traditional worldview, complementing the cultural identity. However, the specific use of environmental protection to strengthen the reasoning of the right to collective property was performed for the first time in *Kaliña and Lokono v Suriname*. The environmentally protected area was considered not only in terms of its biological aspects, but also in terms of its socio-cultural dimension. As the Indigenous use of natural resources entails, in general,

[24] *Saramaka v Suriname* (n 20) §§129–40.

[25] *Kichwa de Sarayaku v Ecuador* (n 3) §205.

[26] *Xákmok Kásek v Paraguay* (n 2) §§155–62 (creation of a protected wooded area); *Kichwa de Sarayaku v Ecuador* (n 3) (oil exploration); *Garífuna Triunfo de la Cruz v Honduras* §§154–57 (touristic exploitation and the creation of a nature reserve); *Kaliña and Lokono v Suriname* (n 4) §§199–230 (mining and the creation of a nature reserve).

[27] *Garífuna Triunfo de la Cruz Community and its members v Honduras*, Preliminary Objections, Merits, Reparations and Costs, IACtHR Series C No 305 (8 October 2015) §§131–37.

[28] *Kaliña and Lokono v Suriname* (n 4) §224.

sustainable practices that are essential for conservation strategies, the respect for the rights of Indigenous peoples have a positive impact on environmental conservation. After an analysis of several international treaties regarding environmental protection,[29] the Court established three criteria in order to achieve the compatibility of such rights: 'a) effective participation, b) access and use of their traditional territories, and c) the possibility of receiving benefits from conservation'.[30]

1.2.3. Right to Consultation

The right to free, prior and informed consultation is a genuine praetorian construction, as there is no provision in the Convention regulating it, even though the recognition follows an international trend regarding Indigenous rights. The first time the right to consultation was recognised was in *Saramaka* (2007), when the Court decided that the right to consultation is a safeguard applied in case of restrictions to traditional territory. In the decision, consultation was considered to be a consequence of Article 21, the right to property, as a mechanism to ensure the use and enjoyment of the traditional territory and its natural resources. The Court mentioned the interpretation applied by the Human Rights Committee (HRC) regarding Article 27 of the International Covenant on Civil and Political Rights (ICCPR) and decided that the protection of traditional communities' cultural rights depends on their participation in the decision-making process. Other international treaties and reports on the matter, such as the UNDRIP, ILO 169 and reports from various UN bodies, are also mentioned as arguments. In addition, the Court stated that consultation should be carried on 'in good faith, through culturally appropriate procedures and with the objective of reaching an agreement'. The consultation must take place prior to the harmful activities and the community must be well informed about possible risks and impacts. Lastly, consent must be achieved in cases regarding the 'large-scale development or investment projects that would have a major impact on *Saramaka* territory'. The formal elements of the consultation, especially regarding who should be consulted, should be defined by the community, according to its practice.[31]

In *Xákmok Kásek* (2010) the right to consultation was analysed in relation to the creation of a nature reserve. The Court succinctly affirmed the state's

[29] Protocol of San Salvador, Art 11; Rio Declaration on Environment and Development, Principle 22; Addis Ababa Principles and Guidelines for the Sustainable Use of Biological Diversity (CBD Guidelines); Convention on Biological Diversity; Ramsar Convention on Wetlands; World Heritage Convention; Convention on Biological Diversity; and United Nations Framework Convention on Climate Change.

[30] *Kaliña and Lokono v Suriname* (n 4) §181.

[31] *Saramaka v Suriname* (n 20) §§16–18, 131, 134.

duty to ensure effective participation of the members of the community, based upon ILO 169.[32] In *Kichwa de Sarayaku* (2012), the recognition of the right to consultation was deepened and altered. In this case, the grounding for the recognition was indicated as the cultural identity of Indigenous peoples since it was considered to be an essential component of the close relationship among such communities, their traditional lands and their worldview. The Court mentioned the ILO 169 and the UNDRIP to reaffirm the obligation. In the decision, the Court refers to several domestic laws and judicial decisions from Member States of the Organization of American States[33] that adopt the right to prior consultation, concluding that 'the obligation to consult, in addition to being a treaty-based provision, is also a general principle of international law'.[34] Contrary to *Saramaka*, in *Kichwa de Sarayaku* the right to consent is not mentioned, even though the case involved a large scale project with severe impacts on the community (MacKay 2018: 41).

In *Kichwa de Sarayaku*, the scope of the obligation to consult is expanded, possibly considering its foundation on cultural identity instead of exclusively on property rights. In *Saramaka*, the obligation was recognised for activities on traditional territory (namely, the use of natural resources), but in *Kichwa de Sarayaku* it is expanded to 'any administrative or legislative measure that may affect their rights, as recognised under domestic and international law, as well as the obligation to guarantee the rights of Indigenous peoples to participate in decisions on matters that concern their interests'.[35] The criteria established in *Kichwa de Sarayaku* is reproduced in two future cases. In *Garífuna de Punta Piedra* and in *Garífuna Triunfo de la Cruz*, both against Honduras (2015), consultation is justified based upon ILO 169, domestic law and as a general principle of international law. There is no mention of the right to consent.[36]

In *Kaliña and Lokono v Suriname* (2015), the right to consultation is analysed not only as a derivation of Article 21, but also from Article 23 of the Convention (the right to participate in the Government). Just as in *Saramaka*, the ICCPR and the ICESCR are applied as interpretation guides for the right to property, with the application of the decisions issued by the HRC and the CESCR. However, contrary to *Saramaka*, the right to consent is not mentioned. The most recent recognition of the right to consultation is the case *Lhaka Honhat*, in which it is affirmed based upon Article 23 of the Convention, with the same content as in previous cases. One novelty of the case is the

[32] *Xákmok Kásek v Paraguay* (n 2) §§155–62.

[33] It is noteworthy that the Court mentions several domestic constitutions and laws by only citing the number of the Article in which the right to consult is assured. The text of the Articles is not included and there is no analysis of discrepancy among them, as Säuberli (2015) points out.

[34] *Kichwa of Sarayaku v Ecuador* (n 3) §§159–65.

[35] ibid §166.

[36] *Garífuna Punta Piedra Community and its members v Honduras*, Preliminary Objections, Merits, Reparations and Costs, IACtHR Series C No 304 (8 October 2015) §§215–24; *Garífuna Triunfo de la Cruz v Honduras* (n 27) §§154–61.

differentiation between new projects and the maintenance of already constituted public works, since 'activities merely to adequately maintain or improve public works do not always require the intervention of prior consultation procedures'.[37]

The right to consultation and to consent are usually applied in international law based upon the right to self-determination (Tomaselli 2016). In the rulings of the Court, however, consultation was interpreted as a derivation of self-determination only in the first case, *Saramaka*, through mention of the UN bodies' case law. In future cases, the right was based upon the right to property and the right to cultural identity.

1.2.4. The Duty to Perform *Saneamiento*

Following the recognition of the right to communal property under Article 21, the Court affirmed the state's obligation to delimit, demarcate and title ancestral territories. In more recent decisions, the Court included a fourth state's obligation regarding Indigenous and ethnic peoples' territory: the duty to perform title clearance, or *saneamiento*, removing any interference or invasion in the communal property and ensuring full use and enjoyment of the property right. *Saneamiento* is a Spanish term from civil law that means the vendor's obligation to guarantee peaceful possession over the sold property (Muñoz Machado 2016).

The Court does not define *saneamiento* but presents its content instead. The tribunal ruled on the *saneamiento* duty in three cases. In *Garífuna de Punta Piedra* (2015) the analysis of the duty was swift, stating 'the Court reminds the State's obligation to guarantee use and enjoyment of the right to Indigenous and ethnic property, for which many measures can be adopted, among them, the *saneamiento*'. The Court affirmed the state should relocate private occupants of the traditional territory and pay for improvements they had eventually made.[38] In *Xucuru v Brazil* (2018) the Court analysed the matter under the lens of the legal certainty, affirming that the *saneamiento* should include eviction of third-party occupants and the guarantee that the property title does not contain any encumbrance in the name of a third party. The Court distinguished the weighting of rights between private owners and Indigenous peoples for the purpose of land demarcation (analysed in *Yakye Axa*, *Sawhoyamaxa* and *Xákmok Kásek*) from the duty to perform *saneamiento*, since the latter emerges only once the property title has already been guaranteed to the Indigenous community. The balancing between rights is not

[37] *Lhaka Honhat v Argentina* (n 5) §179.
[38] *Garífuna Punta Piedra v Honduras* (n 36) §181.

applicable during the *saneamiento*, and it is the state's obligation to guarantee full use and enjoyment of the property.[39]

In the most recent case, however, the Court recognises the importance of securing the rights both from private occupants and Indigenous peoples. In *Lhaka Honhat v Argentina* (2020), the Indigenous land was occupied by *criollos*, vulnerable rural settlers whose connection to the land is also determinant for their way of life. The Court cited for the first time the UN Declaration on the Rights of Peasants and other People Working in Rural Areas (New York, 17 December 2018), recognising the state's obligation towards the *criollo* population. Even though affirming the conventional obligation to relocate the non-Indigenous population, the Court affirmed that the state should respect the rights of the criollo population, appreciating the dialogue process underway. For the Court, 'this type of procedure has the potential to allow the State to comply with its diverse obligations and realise the rights involved'.[40]

As analysed in chapters four and five, property title has not been enough to guarantee the effectiveness of territorial rights, since Indigenous peoples struggle against third-party occupation and land encroachment even after titling of ancestral territories. The recognition of the duty to perform *saneamiento*, even though late in the Court's case law, is a landmark recognition in international law and it reveals an effort to tackle one central form of violation of territorial rights.

1.2.5. Criticism of the Court's Position Regarding Property Rights

Even though the Court's rulings on the protection of traditional territory is internationally recognised as a model for the rights of Indigenous peoples, some criticism has been presented. The quality and importance of the Court's precedents regarding territorial rights is unquestionable, as it still represents the most forward-looking position on the matter of the demarcation of traditional lands. The literature is reasonably unanimous in recognising the advances brought forth by the case law. However, criticism might be presented with the purpose of promoting a better protection to Indigenous and ethnic peoples' traditional territories. The criticism of the Court's reasoning regarding territorial rights can be divided into two groups: first, criticism regarding an excessive focus on land protection under the right to private property; second, the lack of sufficient safeguards for the exploration of natural resources.

[39] *Xucuru Indigenous People and its members v Brazil*, Preliminary Objections, Merits, Reparations and Costs, IACtHR Series C No 346 (5 February 2017) §§121–29.

[40] *Lhaka Honhat v Argentina* (n 5) §139.

A. *Is the Protection under Property Rights Adequate?*

In a first group of criticism, the protection of Indigenous interests under the right to property is criticised. Overall scepticism of the protection of Indigenous territory under property rights has been raised by some authors, alleging that the multicultural turn that defined Indigenous rights under property title has been used as a neoliberal strategy to impose capitalistic values on Indigenous and ethnic peoples (Hale 2011; Correia 2018; Wetterslev 2020). For Offen, the territorial turn has satisfied very distinct intentions, from property stabilisation to conservationism and attraction of foreign investments, but it might improve social justice only if accompanied by the 'transfer of appropriate financial resources, genuine administrative power, and progressive laws instituting them' (2003: 66). Similarly, analysing the cartographic-legal strategy in Nicaragua and Belize, Wainwright and Bryan affirmed that 'the power of Indigenous mapping for legal cases must be weighed against the political struggles they derive from and are intended to advance', otherwise it might only reinforce state power and deepen capitalist relations (Wainwright and Bryan 2009: 169).

Recognising the relevance of the recognition of property rights but criticising its centrality, Antkowiak defends that the centrality of the right to property in the Court's case law should be replaced using the right to a dignified life (*vida digna*). For the author, the property approach is flawed, because it sustains an idealised cultural relationship, ignoring the fact that culture may evolve over time, adopting recent technologies and new means of survival. Additionally, even if such innovations are considered, the protection of the lands through the right to private property is not enough to provide shelter for minimum Indigenous rights, as it allows for multiple restrictions to the property. The use of the right to *vida digna* in conjunction with other rights foreseen in the Convention would increase claims related to the fulfilment of other rights, such as political rights and land rights (Antkowiak 2014).

Similarly, Dulitzky proposes a racial approach in addition to the cultural approach to property, focusing on structural discrimination and broader historic and systematic exclusion. The author criticises the preponderance of the cultural approach to territorial claims, ignoring the fluidity of culture and avoiding having to protect economic aspects of the territory. Additionally, the inclusion of collective territories under the protection of property rights creates some inconsistencies related to porous boundaries or collective use of land among several communities.[41] Lastly, Dulitzky criticises the lack of a clear prevalence of traditional territorial rights over private owners, considering that, in both the *Yakye Axa* and *Sawhoyamaxa* cases, 'the Court allows the states to sacrifice Indigenous and Afro-descendant territorial rights in favour of the economic interests of third parties having no particular link to the land'

[41] See Shelton (2013: 969–70).

(Dulitzky 2010: 49–52). The same lack of prevalence was observed later in both cases involving the *Garífuna* communities against Honduras and in the most recent case, *Xucuru v Brazil*, demonstrating a concerning trend in the case law.

A point of concern is the fact that the Court has repeatedly proposed the alternative to offer substitute lands or compensation instead of the traditional territory's demarcation. The alternative may solve economic concerns, but does not encompass cultural and spiritual dimensions of the claim (Shelton 2013: 970). The Court seems to ignore the distinction between land and traditional territory, ignoring, as a consequence, the impossibility to substitute spiritual and cultural relations with a unique portion of space and the natural resources within. It is interesting to note that limitations to the use of Article 21 (property rights) as a mechanism to protect Indigenous peoples' territory were recognised by Judge Ramírez in a separate opinion in one of the first cases, *Sawhoyamaxa v Paraguay*. He argued that when property rights were mentioned in reference to traditional peoples' territory it should not be understood as 'the absolute ownership that is characteristic of ordinary civil law', but instead as qualified, with unique characteristics, or it could 'prove extremely disadvantageous. He also recognises the intimate connection between historical conditions of exclusion of Indigenous peoples and the classical right to private property, urging for a replacement of such a connection by new types of ownership.[42]

Recognising the protection of collective Indigenous territory under Article 21 was a creative and bold innovation of the Court, assuring Indigenous peoples use and control over their lands, as well as an attempt to repair centuries of exclusion and invisibility. It might not be ideal, overlooking cultural and racial peculiarities in some cases (Dulitzky 2010; Antkowiak 2014; Shelton 2013), but it was the best instrument available for territorial protection within the Court's limited mandate. Even though the protection is framed under Article 21, it should not be considered equal to private property, considering the cultural peculiarities of Indigenous peoples.[43] The central aim of the Court has been the protection of the vital relationship between traditional peoples and their territories. For that purpose, land protection has been assessed in parallel with other essential rights already recognised by the Court, such as the right to a dignified life, the right to cultural identity and the right to self-determination. This interpretation of Article 21 based upon the interdependence among rights (mainly the right to cultural identity and self-determination) offers a strong and culturally adequate guarantee for the protection of traditional territories. Moreover, the Court has transformed a civil individual right into a socio-cultural right, imposing positive obligations to states. However, despite the recognition of the right to property, the Court has established safeguards

[42] *Sawhoyamaxa v Paraguay* (n 1) Separate Opinion of Judge García-Ramírez §§10–16.
[43] ibid.

for restrictions on and exploration of the property, which have been criticised for their leniency with regards to the violation of rights, as is presented in the next section.

B. *Are the Safeguards Sufficient for the Protection of Traditional Territories?*

In a second group of criticism, the protection of the territory under the property right is considered adequate, but the exceptions established by the Court for the exploration of natural resources are indicated as insufficient. The Court has permitted the exploration of natural resources as long as four safeguards are met: three procedural safeguards (consultation, benefit sharing and socio-environmental impact assessment); and one material guarantee (the absence of threats to the physical and cultural survival of the community). There are two central lines of argumentation for the inefficacy of the exceptions. First, the Court should not prioritise procedural guarantees over substantial one. Second, the procedural safeguards are insufficient and offer a low level of protection.

According to the first group of criticism, even though the Court mentions a substantive guarantee, it has never been analysed. On at least two occasions the existence of harmful activities endangering the survival of the community was extensively proved: *Kichwa de Sarayaku* (the burying of explosives throughout the territory); and *Kaliña and Lokono* (extensive deforestation and mining activities). In none of them was the substantive safeguard analysed. Accordingly, MacKay criticises the Court's preference to assign procedural measures instead of ruling on substantive guarantees. As the author stated, the Court's case law presents an 'undue emphasis on permissible restrictions to rights, rather than focusing on the content of those rights' (MacKay 2002: 40). The ultimate purpose of the Court – to ensure the cultural and physical survival of traditional communities – is replaced by a review of possible restrictions to this right through the application of lenient procedural elements (MacKay 2002).

The undue priority of procedural guarantees is worsened, as they do not offer sufficient guarantees for the protection of traditional territories. The central concern is the affirmation of the right to consultation instead of the right to free, prior and informed consent. In *Saramaka*, the Court designated the consent as obligatory, but only for large-scale projects. In three future cases related to procedural safeguards (*Kichwa de Sarayaku, Garífuna de Punta Piedra* and *Kaliña and Lokono*), the right to consent is not even mentioned, constituting a dangerous setback in the decisions. Even if one considers the higher level established by the Court in *Saramaka*, in which consent was demanded for large-scale projects, the protection is insufficient. The Court seems to ignore the fact that small-scale projects may just as well cause irreparable damages to traditional communities, harming, for example, sacred sites (Antkowiak 2014: 171).

The recognition of the right to consent is affirmed in international law because of the right to self-determination. Since 2007, the UNDRIP has protected the right to free, prior and informed consent (Article 32.2). The right is also adopted by several UN bodies, for example the Committee to Eradicate Racial Discrimination, the UN Permanent Forum on Indigenous Issues, the Committee on Economic, Social and Cultural Rights and the Human Rights Committee, among others (Tomaselli 2016: 223–5). In contrast, the position adopted by the Court recognising only the right to consultation offers a lower threshold of protection, ignoring what the Court itself called the *corpus iuris* of international law of human rights. Therefore, not only does the Court offer insufficient protection, but this protection is incoherent with the Court's reasoning, as it has repeatedly mentioned UN documents and decisions, omitting passages on the right to consent.[44] With the recent adoption of the ADRIP in 2016, the Court's parameters became lower than the Inter-American levels of protection. The American Declaration enshrines the right to consent in the same terms used by the UNDRIP (Article XXIII(2)).

The problem of adopting a lower level than international law has been criticised in a different context by the former president of the Court, Judge Trindade, as explained in a separate opinion in *Sawhoyamaxa*:

> An international human rights tribunal can never let itself lower the international protection standards, more so when the parties are in a flagrantly vulnerable position, if not abandoned, condemned – many of them since birth – by their fellowmen to social exclusion, and to chronic poverty, which, as I see it, constitutes, the deprivation of all human rights.[45]

Briefly, the right to consultation as ordered by the Court offers insufficient and incoherent protection by not recognising the right to free, prior and informed consent.

Another fragile aspect of the procedural safeguards is the absence of any concern regarding possible damages caused by the exploration of natural resources. The Court could have established the obligation to avoid and minimise possible damages or, if this was not possible, to restore, rehabilitate and compensate damages, just like multiple international treaties do.[46] It would be an essential guarantee to assure the minimum impact possible in the traditional peoples' way of living, and, therefore, guarantee their right to cultural and physical survival.

To conclude the analysis of the Court's recognition of the right to property, the Court has offered forward-looking protection and assured, by means

[44] See Pasqualucci (2009: 98); MacKay (2002: 44); Shelton (2013: 975); KAS and IDEHPUCP (2017).

[45] *Sawhoyamaxa v Paraguay* (n 1) Separate Opinion of Judge Cançado Trindade §71.

[46] ILO 169, Art 15.2; World Bank OP 4.10 Indigenous Peoples (July 2005, rev April 2013) §1; UNDRIP Article 32.3; ADRIP Art 24.5.

of interpretation methods, the expansion of the right to property to achieve the collective right over traditional territories in accordance with the traditional worldview. The expansion of Article 21 promoted the protection of the cultural and physical survival of Indigenous and Afro-descendent peoples. However, the Court stipulated and gave undue emphasis to precarious procedural safeguards, permitting unjustified restrictions to the territory that might, in some cases, endanger the cultural and physical survival of traditional peoples.

1.3. ACCESS TO A REMEDY FOR LAND DEMARCATION AND LAND PROTECTION

The violation of the right to judicial protection (Article 25) was recognised in all 14 analysed cases, while the violation of the right to a fair trial (Article 8) was affirmed 11 times. Considering the intimate relationship between the two rights, the Court has analysed their violation in combination. The Court considers the right to judicial remedies as one of utmost importance, as it is intended to protect citizens before judges or courts against acts that violate their fundamental rights. It is not enough that the remedies formally exist; they must also be effective, respect the due process of law and be executed in a reasonable amount of time. Additionally, the effectiveness of the judicial proceedings is intimately related to their further execution.

In cases of Indigenous territorial rights, states have the duty to offer an effective land titling proceeding, which should not only be foreseen in the legal system, but also effectively applied. The American Convention was interpreted in light of ILO 169, Article 14.3, which enshrines the duty to establish domestic legal proceedings to resolve land claims.[47] The domestic law should also provide effective instruments for the protection and control of traditional lands, mainly against unauthorised external interference.[48] Lastly, it is the obligation of the states to regulate the free, prior and informed consultation of traditional peoples in accordance with ILO 169.[49] Cultural identity is a central element that should be respected in such proceedings, as the socio-economic conditions of Indigenous peoples and their customary law, values and customs need to be respected. Internal mechanisms of decision of the communities shall be respected, as long as they are in accordance with human rights.[50]

In the majority of the countries involved in the territorial litigation, there was already a procedural mechanism for land titling in the domestic law, but

[47] *Yakye Axa v Paraguay* (n 6) §§95–96.
[48] *Garífuna Punta Piedra v Honduras* (n 36) §233.
[49] *Garífuna Triunfo de la Cruz v Honduras* (n 27) §§196–200.
[50] *Kaliña and Lokono v Suriname* (n 4) §251–55.

the state was condemned for its inadequacy[51] or ineffectiveness.[52] The only state that has no legal provision regarding the demarcation and titling of traditional lands is Suriname, which was condemned three times. In Nicaragua, the right to land demarcation was constitutionally foreseen, but there was no legal provision of mechanism for land titling.

The lack of investigation of gross human rights violations is considered itself a violation of Articles 8.1 and 25, as the inactivity of the state reveals disregard for the principle of due diligence.[53] Another fact analysed under Articles 8.1 and 25 was the criminalisation of Indigenous leaderships, mainly when criminal charges run without a defence counsel or for unreasonable amount of time.[54] An innovation inaugurated in *Kaliña and Lokono* is the interpretation of the right to a juridical remedy in combination with the right to access information (Article 13).

1.4. LAND DISPOSSESSION AS A VIOLATION OF THE RIGHTS TO LIFE AND PERSONAL INTEGRITY

The right to life is the most basic and crucial right, as it is ground for the realisation of any other right. The obligation of states to ensure it includes not only negative measures (not to be arbitrarily deprived of life), but also positive actions intended to offer access to minimum conditions for a decent life. In the Court's rulings, the recognition of the right to life has been associated with the right to personal integrity, protecting the individual against any harm to its physical, moral and mental integrity. Among the territorial cases, the violation of the right to life in a negative perspective was declared twice, while, from a positive perspective, it was declared as having been violated three times. The violation of the right to personal integrity was recognised four times.

1.4.1. Right to a Dignified Life

The right to life was interpreted by the Court as not only a right to survive, or not to be arbitrarily deprived of life, but also as imposing to the state several

[51] *Yakye Axa v Paraguay* (n 6) §§97–98; *Sawhoyamaxa v Paraguay* (n 1) §§102–12; *Xákmok Kásek v Paraguay* §§145–54.

[52] *Awas Tingni v Nicaragua* (n 7) §§137–38; *Kichwa of Sarayaku v Ecuador* (n 3) §§272–78; *Operation Genesis v Colombia* §§404–10; *Kuna Indigenous People of Madungandí and the Emberá Indigenous People of Bayano and their members v Panama*, Preliminary Objections, Merits, Reparations and Costs, IACtHR Serie C No 284 (14 October 2014) §§170–73; *Garífuna Punta Piedra v Honduras* (n 36) §§231–42; *Kaliña and Lokono v Suriname* (n 4) §§252–58; *Xucuru v Brazil* (n 39) §§150–62; *Lhaka Honhat v Argentina* (n 5) §§158–68.

[53] *Moiwana v Suriname* (n 15) §§139–67; *Kichwa of Sarayaku* v Ecuador (n 3) §§265–71; *Operation Genesis v Colombia* §§370–403.

[54] *Yakye Axa v Paraguay* (n 6) §§106–16; *Kuna of Madungandí v Panama* (n 52) §§183–87.

obligations related to creating minimum conditions for a dignified life, or *vida digna*. In relation to Indigenous cases, the concept was applied three times, in the trilogy of cases against Paraguay, in order to guarantee minimum conditions of life for the communities. The Court already counted on consolidated precedents regarding the right to *vida digna*, which were used as a parameter in the territorial cases.[55] In the three Paraguayan Indigenous cases, the communities had been displaced from their lands in the last century and were living on a minimal amount of land, in extremely impoverished conditions, with no access to basic public services, water supply, housing, sewage or nutritional security. They had been waiting for the public administration to respond to their claims for land restitution for several years, which contributed to the deterioration of the social conditions and caused the deaths of several community members, mainly children and the elderly.

The Court affirmed that 'the State has the duty to take positive, concrete measures geared toward fulfilment of the right to a decent life, especially in the case of persons who are vulnerable and at risk, whose care becomes a high priority'.[56] The right to *vida digna* implies an indirect justiciability of social rights, as the Court interprets it in parallel with Article 26 of the Convention along with several articles of the Additional Protocol to the American Convention, with regard to economic, social and cultural rights. Special consideration was given to the vulnerability of Indigenous populations and the essential relationship between the protection and demarcation of traditional land and access to basic conditions of human life, such as housing, nutrition, water, etc.

Two basic criteria are established for the recognition of the state's positive obligation: the knowledge about real and immediate risk to life and the lack of the state's measures to minimise the situation. Additionally, the fact that the state did not take sufficient measures to assure the return of the communities to their traditional territory overly prolonged the impoverished conditions and reinforced the state's responsibility, as the lack of lands directly contributed to their lack of access to sources of food and water.[57] In *Xákmok Kásek*, the Court specifically analysed several components of the right to *vida digna*: access to and quality of water, diet, health and education. Cultural elements and Indigenous peculiarities were considered for the analysis of such elements.

Although the cases are remarkably similar, there is a central difference in the first case, *Yakye Axa*. The Court recognised the violation of the right to life in general terms, given the state omission. Nevertheless, the Commission had also claimed the recognition of the state responsibility regarding the death of

[55] *Street Children v Guatemala, Merits*, IACtHR Series C No 63 (19 November 1999); *Juvenile Reeducation Institute v Paraguay*, Preliminary Objections, Merits, Reparations and Costs, IACtHR Series C No 112 (2 September 2004). See Pasqualucci (2008).

[56] *Yakye Axa v Paraguay* (n 6) §162.

[57] *Sawhoyamaxa v Paraguay* (n 1) §§155, 163–64.

16 members due to causes that could have been avoided with adequate basic services. The Court decided that it did not have enough evidence to establish the causes of said deaths. Such decision was not unanimous, since judges Burelli, Trindade and Robles dissented.[58] In the subsequent Indigenous case, *Sawhoyamaxa*, the Court recognised the violation of the right to life due to the lack of general dignity conditions available to the community and due to the death of 19 Indigenous members. The decision was unanimous, demonstrating an evolutionary interpretation of Article 4.1. The position of the Court was reaffirmed in *Xákmok Kásek*, in which the state is condemned due to a violation of the right to life for not providing minimum conditions for a decent existence and for the death of 18 persons.

The last time the Court recognised the right to a dignified life was in *Xákmok Kásek*, not only among territorial cases, but in all its rulings. The Court seems to transition from an indirect recognition of social rights to a direct one through Article 26 of the Convention. In *Operation Genesis v Colombia* (2013), both the representatives and the Commission alleged violation of the right to a dignified life considering the precarious conditions of the Afro-descendent communities living in provisional shelters after forced displacement.[59] However, the Court did not specifically analyse this claim, and did not even mention the right to a dignified life. The precarious conditions were only considered to be a violation of the right to personal integrity.[60]

1.4.2. Right not to be Arbitrarily Deprived of Life

The negative perspective of the right to life is the right not to be arbitrarily deprived of life, which includes guarantees against the state and the right to be protected by the state from private actors. In Indigenous territorial cases, the right constitutes a fundamental guarantee, as the struggle for traditional territory is most frequently followed by violence, murders and threats.[61] Indeed, seven out of all 14 territorial cases involve either threats against or murders of Indigenous leaderships.

In the territorial cases, the violation of the right not to be arbitrarily deprived of life was declared twice: in *Operation Genesis* and *Kichwa de Sarayaku*. In *Kichwa de Sarayaku*, violation of the right to be protected by the state was

[58] *Yakye Axa v Paraguay* (n 6) §§176–78.

[59] *Escrito de solicitudes, argumentos y pruebas, Operation Genesis v Colombia* (29 January 2012) §§516–23; Informe sobre Fondo, Interamerican Commission of Human Rights Info no 64/11 (31 March 2011) §§301–09.

[60] *Comunidades Afrodescendientes desplazadas de la Cuenca del Río Cacarica (Operación Génesis) v Colombia*, Preliminary Objections, Merits, Reparations, and Costs, IACtHR Series C No 270 (20 November 2013) §§320–24.

[61] UNHRC, 'Report of the Special Rapporteur on the rights of indigenous peoples' (10 August 2018) A/HRC/39/17.

declared regarding a permanent risk created by the permission given by the state to place explosives on the traditional territory. The Court issued a provisional measure when the case was still before the Commission, which was not complied with by the state. Over 1,400 kilograms of pentolite were buried in the soil and its activation or detonation was a real and potential possibility, creating a permanent situation of risk to the lives and personal integrity of the members of the community. The violation of the right to life was declared in relation to the right to personal integrity (Article 5). In *Operation Genesis*, the death of a community leader by paramilitary forces was attributed to the state having owed collaboration, which was thus provided by public agents, to those groups.[62]

The violation of the right to life was dismissed in both cases related to the Garífuna People against Honduras, in which representatives and the Commission claimed a declaration of the violation of the right to life, concerning the death of Indigenous leaderships. In *Garífuna Triunfo de la Cruz*, the Court stated that the state's obligation to protect arises only when it has knowledge of a situation of real and imminent risk to determinate persons, as well as a reasonable possibility to avoid the situation. The Court considered that it did not have sufficient evidence to determine knowledge by the state or that the risk was imminent.[63] Four members of the community had been killed. In *Garífuna de Punta Piedra*, the Court recognised that the community received several threats over the years, caused by conflict generated by the lack of regularisation of the traditional territory. The Court attested that at least 13 state organisations knew about threats to the community, but none of them had specific knowledge about specific threats to their leader. He was murdered, but the Court considered that there was no violation of the state's obligation to protect due to the lack of knowledge of his specific situation. However, the Court reiterated the duty to protect the community against threats and to investigate the murder.[64]

In both situations, the dismissal of the request to recognise the state's responsibility for the murders is critical, considering the importance of the for protection of HRD, in general, and Indigenous leaderships in contexts of worsening disputes over natural resources and territory. In both cases there were claims for provisional measures for the protection of the communities and their representatives. The Court dismissed the measures, alleging the lack of a relationship between the provisional measures claimed and the facts presented in the proceedings. The protection of leaderships against attacks during the proceedings and after the final decision is a matter that might claim a better approach from the Court, which should be aware of the social context of LAC and the escalation of murders and threats against HRD. In that sense, the Court

[62] *Operation Genesis v Colombia* (n 60) §§281–82.
[63] *Garífuna Triunfo de la Cruz v Honduras* (n 27) §§201–14.
[64] *Garífuna Punta Piedra v Honduras* (n 36) §§257–80.

should take the factual context into consideration for its review of requests regarding violations of the rights to life and personal integrity. The Court might also take into consideration the fact that the conflict remains after the delivery of the final decision and that it may even be intensified, considering the length of time to implementation.[65] In the case *Garífuna Triunfo de la Cruz*, conflicts only worsened after the decision and five Indigenous leaderships were abducted in 2020. The Court ordered provisional measures in their defence.

1.4.3. Right to Personal Integrity (Article 5.1)

The right to personal integrity (Article 5.1) was declared violated on four occasions, each of which was related to the lack of territorial protection, cultural identity and right to life. In *Moiwana* (2005) the psychological distress caused by the massacre was considered a violation of the right to human treatment. Three central elements were considered to have constituted the suffering. First, the impossibility to perform a proper ritual for deceased members and honour them, which constituted a gross moral violation for the community. Second, the forced separation from traditional lands, of vital spiritual, cultural and material importance. Finally, the obstruction of the attempts to obtain justice and the lack of investigation into the massacre. For the three of them, cultural identity was a central element for analysis and the Court considered expert witness opinions and testimonials as an important mechanism to attest to the suffering of the victims.[66]

In *Xákmok Kásek* (2010) the violation was declared by the Court taking into consideration the sorrow the community experienced due to wretched living conditions and the death of the community's members. In addition, the separation from the traditional land and the progressive loss of culture were considered.[67] The violation of Article 5 was recognised again in *Kichwa de Sarayaku* (2012) due to the state's permission to place explosives on the traditional territory, causing a permanent risk to the physical integrity of the community's members. The representatives alleged that they received threats and suffered attacks that could be deemed as a violation of personal integrity. The Court dismissed the allegation on the ground of lack of evidence.[68] In *Operation Genesis* (2013), the state was responsible for the violation of the right to personal integrity of communities in situation of forced displacement, considering its failure to ensure basic humanitarian assistance and the return to their territory, as well as for its collaboration with paramilitary forces, which

[65] See Correia et al. (2017), justifying the application of special measures to protect human rights defenders.

[66] *Moiwana v Suriname* (n 15) §§87–103.

[67] *Xákmok Kásek v Paraguay* (n 2) §§235–44.

[68] *Kichwa of Sarayaku v Ecuador* (n 3) §§244–54.

conducted violent activities against the community.[69] The representatives had alleged the lack of basic living conditions constituted a violation of the right to a dignified life instead, but the Court did not review the argument.

The Court dismissed the recognition of a violation of the right to personal integrity on two occasions. First, in *Sawhoyamaxa*, the recognition had been claimed by the Commission, but the Court asserted that the facts had already been analysed regarding right to life. In *Xucuru*, the omission of the state to protect the community against threats and violence was alleged to be a violation of Article 5, but the Court considered that the related facts were presented extemporaneously and could not be considered. Even so, the Court recognised a general situation of violence and conflict, considering that the leader of the community survived an attempted murder, while the two members of the community who accompanied him had died.[70]

One question that deserves attention is the relationship between the right to life and the right to personal integrity in cases in which the factual situations simultaneously create an imminent risk to both the lives and the personal integrity of the community's members. In the cases *Xákmok Kásek* and *Kichwa de Sarayaku*, violation of Articles 4.1 and 5.1 were declared in combination, whereas only the right to a dignified life was declared in *Yakye Axa* and *Sawhoyamaxa*, and only the right to personal integrity was declared in *Operation Genesis*, even though the factual conditions were similar. It might seem that extreme conditions that threaten the lives of persons simultaneously threaten their personal integrity, whether it be of a moral or physical character. Therefore, it would be possible to say that whenever the Court recognised the violation of Article 4.1 due to the state's omission to prevent risks to Indigenous communities, it should be combined with Article 5.1. Lastly, there is room for improvement in the recognition of a risk situation as a violation of a right. In the case of the right to personal integrity, the risk can be understood as sorrow and therefore as a violation of moral integrity. However, in the case of the right to life, the parameters for considering the risk to be a violation are not clear.

1.5. THE DIRECT JUSTICIABILITY OF SOCIAL RIGHTS

Lhaka Honhat v Argentina (2021) is one of the most paradigmatic cases among the territorial cases, since it is the first time the Court recognises the direct justiciability of the rights to a healthy environment, to adequate food, to water and to take part in cultural life.[71] The recognition was not unanimous among the

[69] *Operation Genesis v Colombia* (n 60) §§320–24.

[70] *Xucuru v Brazil* (n 39) §§171–81.

[71] The application of Art 26 follows a general trend in the jurisprudence that started in August 2017 (*Lagos del Campo v Peru*, Merits, Reparations and Costs, IACtHR Series C No. 366 (31 August 2017), regarding labour rights; *Trabajadores Cesados de Petroperú et al v Perú*, Preliminary exceptions, Merits, Reparations and Costs, IACtHR Series C No 344 (23 November 2017).

judges. In fact, there was a tie and the president of the Court gave the casting vote. The rights to food and water had already been indirectly recognised in the cases against Paraguay through the right to a dignified life and the right to cultural identity had been recognised as an implicit right (see below). On the other hand, it was the first time the Court recognised the right to a healthy environment among all contentious cases.

Before specifying each of the recognised rights, the Court affirms the justiciability of Article 26, mostly by reaffirming its former jurisprudence: 'the Court has asserted its competence to determine violations of Article 26 of the American Convention and has indicated that this protects those economic, social, cultural and environmental rights (ESCER) derived from the [OAS Charter]'.[72] The content and scope of Article 26, in turn, should be established in light of the international *corpus iuris*.

In order to affirm the recognition of each of the rights, the Court follows a similar path: assures the legal recognition of the right, details its contents and correlates the right with the facts of the case. For legal recognition of the rights, the Court includes a multitude of international documents from a variety of range (domestic, regional and international) and enforceability level (declarations, conventions, protocols and regulations). The Court also established the interdependence among the social rights and their impact to already recognised conventional rights. Lastly, the Court affirmed the particular impact of the violation for Indigenous peoples and other vulnerable groups, considering their traditional way of life.

Regarding the right to a healthy environment, the Court stressed the importance of prevention of any environmental damage, affirming that the obligation to fulfil the right encompasses the following measures in relation to potentially harmful activities: '(i) regulate; (ii) supervise and monitor; (iii) require and approve environmental impact assessments; (iv) establish contingency plans, and (v) mitigate, when environmental damage has occurred'.[73] Regarding the right to food, the Court adopted the interpretation by the UN Committee on Economic, Social and Cultural Rights (CESCR), affirming nutrition should be available, accessible and adequate, also ensuring long-term food security. Similarly, the right to water should encompass availability, quality, accessibility and sustainability. Lastly, the Court affirmed that the right to take part in a cultural life encompasses the right to cultural identity, protecting 'the distinctive features that characterise a social group without denying the historical, dynamic and evolutive nature of culture'.[74]

After establishing the content of the rights and their interdependence, the Court generally analysed the facts of the case and recognises the violation of the rights. The Court did not analyse how in the concrete case each of the rights

[72] *Lhaka Honhat v Argentina* (n 5) §195.
[73] ibid §208.
[74] ibid §240.

were violated and which state actions or omissions were considered. The omission is worrisome when the novelty of the rights is considered. There is no clear pattern of violation established for further cases.

As mentioned, the decision was not unanimous and the dissenting judges presented separate opinions to justify their votes. Judge Vio Grossi indicated that the Court 'lacks competence to examine the violation of such rights under the provisions of Article 26 of the Convention',[75] considering Article 26 should be interpreted not as recognising the Court direct justiciability for social rights. He expressed hard criticism against the majoritarian position of the Court:

> It would appear that, for the judgment, the literal meaning of what was agreed is totally irrelevant and, consequently, that it is considered a mere formalism, allowing the judgment to attribute a meaning and scope to this provision that is unrelated to what the States expressly agreed, as if they really meant to agree something else, which is evidently illogical.[76]

Judge Sierra Porto presented similar arguments, but focusing on legal certainty. He considered problematic the use of soft law instruments as convenience dictates and the disregard of the position of Protocol of San Salvador in the regional system. The recognition of the right to water was particularly criticised, since it is not recognised by the OAS Charter. In that sense,

> it could be argued that Article 26 of the Convention contains all the rights that the Court would like to make justiciable in a specific case and that it is not necessary for them to be alleged by the parties or that there is brief mention of them in the OAS Charter. It will be sufficient to include numerous citations of other declarations, treaties or soft law documents, in addition to referring to "a vast corpus iuris" to create an international obligation for the States.[77]

For Sierra Porto, the recognition of the direct justiciability has weakened one of the most significant innovations of the Court: the protection of Indigenous rights under Article 21 of the Convention. The rights to cultural identity, healthy environment, water and food could have been recognised under Article 21, strengthening the state's obligations towards Indigenous peoples.

Lastly, Judge Pérez Manrique recognised the Court's jurisdiction on ESCR under Article 26, but considered that in the specific case it was not appropriate or necessary to declare an autonomous violation of Article 26, since the ESCR could have been declared violated under the right to property (Article 21), considering the state's failure to protect the traditional territory against third-party occupation.

The innovation brought forth by the decision is considerable, establishing a new framework for the protection of Indigenous rights in the Inter-American System. However, there are some alarming features in the decision in terms of

[75] ibid, Partially Dissenting Opinion of Vio Grossi §4.
[76] ibid §24.
[77] *Lhaka Honhat v Argentina* (n 5), Partially Dissenting Opinion of Sierra Porto §10.

legal certainty: first, the lack of analysis of the facts in correlation with each right, undermining the perception of what state's behaviour is damning; second, the tie among the judges with very strong criticism among the separate opinions; and third, the difficulty to foresee all the rights that are protected under Article 26, since the Court's innovation occurs only on a case-by-case analysis.

1.6. OTHER CORRELATED TERRITORIAL RIGHTS RECOGNISED

The recognition of territorial rights in the Court's rulings has focused on the affirmation of the rights to property and a dignified life. However, the territorial protection has been complemented by the affirmation of other rights according to specific situations of a given case. The rights of the child (Article 19) were specifically mentioned in cases characterised by severe impoverished living conditions affecting children's development. The violation was declared three times, in *Sawhoyamaxa, Xákmok Kásek* and *Operation Genesis*.[78] The Court reiterated the cultural peculiarities of Indigenous children, affirming the state's obligation to promote and protect cultural diversity so that minors could enjoy their own culture, language and religion.

The violation of the right to juridical personality (Article 3) was declared four times: two of them related to individual personality and two of them related to the collective personality of the community. In *Sawhoyamaxa* and *Xákmok Kásek*, the communities had scarce access to public services, including the registration of births and deaths. The Court recognised that several communities' members were born and died with no official registration or documentation of their existence. When interpreting Article 3 of the Convention, the Court considered the recognition of personality to be an indispensable instrument for the possibility of being the holder of rights, especially when regarding persons in situations of vulnerability, exclusion and discrimination.[79]

The recognition of the right to collective personality was an important development in the case law, adapting the Convention to cultural peculiarities of Indigenous peoples. In *Saramaka* and *Kaliña and Lokono*,[80] the violation was recognised due to the lack of recognition of the juridical personality of the traditional communities, from a collective perspective. The Court considered that the state should offer a legal mechanism to ensure that members of the community could collectively enjoy the right to property, which was to be achieved by means of recognition of the community itself as a personality capable of exercising and enjoying the right to property. The Court affirmed the state's obligation to adopt legislative and other measures that 'recognize and

[78] *Sawhoyamaxa v Paraguay* (n 1) §177; *Xákmok Kásek v Paraguay* (n 2) §§256–64; *Operation Genesis v Colombia* (n 60) §§327–31.

[79] *Sawhoyamaxa v Paraguay* (n 1) §186–94; *Xákmok Kásek v Paraguay* (n 2) §§245–55.

[80] *Saramaka v Suriname* (n 20) §§159–74; *Kaliña and Lokono v Suriname* (n 4) §§101–14.

take into account the particular way in which the *Saramaka* people view themselves as a collectivity capable of exercising and enjoying the right to property'.[81]

The *Saramaka* case presents a contradiction, as the Court states the importance of recognition of collective juridical personality for Indigenous communities, but the Court itself did not recognise the *Saramaka* community as an injured party in the case; only its members. The Court demanded a position from the state that the tribunal itself had not yet adopted. In subsequent cases, the Court recognised Indigenous communities as holders of rights and the contradiction was solved. The decision was unanimous in *Saramaka*, but not in *Kaliña and Lokono*. In a partially dissenting opinion, Judge Pérez-Pérez[82] argued that the definition of 'person' exclusively encompasses human beings. The Judge mentioned the Court's precedents regarding the violation of the right to individual personality, including *Saramaka*, but considers the violation of Article 3 to be 'not only unjustified, but also unnecessary'.[83]

Freedom of movement and residence (Article 22) is a right commonly related to massacres and internal conflicts in the Inter-American case law. Responsibility for the violation of the right was recognised in two territorial cases, *Moiwana* and *Operation Genesis*. In *Moiwana*, the case relates to a massacre in traditional territory and the lack of investigation into the actions. Religious and cultural elements were considered central for a safe return, as the community believed that the return to their land would be possible only after 'making peace' with the spirits of the deceased through several specific rituals and bringing about justice for their murders.[84] *Operation Genesis* is related to internal displacement imposed on traditional communities by acts of violence carried out by paramilitary groups, as well as the lack of actions undertaken by the state to ensure the return of the community to their traditional land. The Court mentioned consolidated precedents regarding internal displacement that affirmed the state's obligation 'to adopt measures of a positive nature to reverse the effects of their said situation of weakness, vulnerability and defencelessness'.[85] In order to analyse general conditions in the country regarding internal displacement, domestic and international decisions were mentioned. The Court declared violation of Article 22.1, combined with Articles 5.1 and 1.1.[86] There is a substantial distinction between the two cases

[81] *Saramaka v Suriname* (n 20) §174.

[82] Judge Pérez-Pérez was a part of the Court between 2010 and 2015. He composed the Court during the judgment of three indigenous cases (*Kuna de Madugandí, Garífuna Triunfo de la Cruz and Garífuna de Punta Piedra*) in which the community was considered an injured party, but on no occasion did he present a dissenting opinion. See Advisory Opinion OC-22/16 Voto Parcialmente Disidente del Juez Alberto Pérez-Pérez.

[83] *Kaliña and Lokono v Suriname* (n 4), Partially Dissenting Opinion of Judge Alberto Pérez-Pérez. §3–10.

[84] *Moiwana v Suriname* (n 15) §§104–21.

[85] *Operation Genesis v Colombia* (n 60) §315.

[86] id §§315–24.

regarding the arguments applied. Meanwhile, in *Moiwana*, cultural identity and Indigenous peculiarities played a leading role in the identification of the violation of freedom of residence, in *Operation Genesis*, the Court used general arguments related to internal displacement. No reference to cultural identity was made, relating it to restrictions of movement and residence, even though they were presented by the representatives.

The most recent innovations in the Court include the affirmation of the rights to participate in the government (Article 23) and the right to obtain information (Article 13). Both rights have been recognised only twice, in *Kaliña and Lokono* and *Lhaka Honhat*. The recognition signals a change in the view of the Court, as the Commission had already requested the violation of Article 23 twice and, in both cases, the Court considered that the state's acts had already been contextualised under Articles 21 and 25 of the Convention.[87] In *Kaliña and Lokono*, the Court ruled that there was a violation of Article 23 in relation to Articles 1.1, 2, and 21 via the principle of *iura novit curia*. The Court recognised the state's failure to ensure effective participation, as it did not consult affected communities regarding the exploration of natural resources in traditional territory, declaring it a violation of Articles 21 and 23, without offering any additional justification. There are some considerable advantages in the configuration of the right to Indigenous participation under Article 23, instead of exclusively under Article 21. First, when participation is grounded in Article 21, it is subject to restrictions by the state in case of public interest. In contrast, Article 23 claims regulation without subordination. Additionally, when Indigenous participation is protected under Article 23, it offers a more generalised approach and it may be applied even if it is not related to property rights (MacKay 2018: 37).

In addition, the Court recognised in *Kaliña and Lokono* the violation of the right to information (Article 13) in relation to the violation of the right to judicial protection (Article 25) and Articles 1.1 and 2. The right to seek and receive information from states was conceived as a component of the right to freedom of thought and expression. According to the Court, a violation of the right occurs when the state denies requested information without any justification, in an arbitrary decision. In the case under analysis, Indigenous leaders had requested information regarding third parties' title to the land, but the state did not respond to them.[88]

1.7. IMPLICIT RIGHTS: SELF-DETERMINATION AND CULTURAL IDENTITY

The rights to self-determination and to cultural identity are genuinely praetorian constructions, as they are not enshrined in the ACHR. While the first one

[87] *Awas Tingni v Nicaragua* (n 7) §§ 157–60; *Kichwa of Sarayaku v Ecuador* (n 3) §126.
[88] *Kaliña and Lokono v Suriname* (n 4) §§259–67.

was recognised only twice in the case law, the second is widely mentioned and became a central parameter for the analysis of human rights violations in cases involving Indigenous rights.

Cultural identity represents, simultaneously, an autonomous right and an interpretation principle that encompasses individual and collective rights (Chiriboga 2006). In all Indigenous cases, including territorial ones, cultural elements were an essential threshold for the interpretation of the rights through the use of cultural identity as a transformative interpretation concept (Burgorgue-Larsen 2014). However, specifically regarding the affirmation of the right to cultural identity as a specific right, both the recognition and the reasoning have not been uniform. The first time cultural identity was recognised as a right was in *Yakye Axa*. The right was considered to be a consequence of the right to a dignified life, alongside rights to health, education and access to food and water.[89] *Kichwa de Sarayaku* was the first case in which the Court offered a thorough analysis of the right to cultural identity, built upon the principle of non-discrimination (Article 1.1). The Court affirmed that the 'recognition of the right to cultural identity is an ingredient and a crosscutting means of interpretation to understand, respect and guarantee the enjoyment and exercise of the human rights of Indigenous peoples and communities protected by the Convention'.[90] International treaties were mentioned in order to justify the right to cultural identity, as well as decisions issued by UN organs and regional systems. The Court recognised the obligation of states to respect the right to cultural identity, as it was a consequence of a multicultural, pluralistic and democratic society.[91]

A similar extensive approach of the right of cultural identity was expected in future cases regarding Indigenous territories. However, upcoming decisions have revealed constraint at any mention of the right. After the decision in *Kichwa de Sarayaku*, the right to cultural identity was declared violated on two separate occasions, both regarding the lack of consultation prior to restrictions upon the traditional territory, with a very quick reasoning. First, in *Garífuna de Punta Piedra*, the right was declared as have been violated in relation to Articles 21, 1.1 and 2 of the Convention.[92] There is no previous reasoning, just a reference of *Kichwa de Sarayaku* in a footnote. In *Kaliña and Lokono*, after affirming the relationship between safeguards to protect traditional territory and the rights to property, dignified life and cultural identity, the Court declared that the lack of consultation violated the rights to collective property, cultural identity and political rights.[93] Again, the reach and the basis of the right to cultural identity were not analysed. In *Xucuru*, there is very brief mention of the

[89] *Yakye Axa v Paraguay* (n 6) §§124, 135 and 147.
[90] *Kichwa of Sarayaku v Ecuador* (n 3) §213.
[91] ibid §159.
[92] *Garífuna Punta Piedra v Honduras* (n 36) §224.
[93] *Kaliña and Lokono v Suriname* (n 4) §§181 and 197–98.

right to cultural identity in relation to property rights, but without any further elaboration.[94] Despite the short reasoning for the recognition of cultural identity as a right, it has been widely mentioned as interpretation means, applied by the Court in order to clarify the content of the right to collective property, the state's duties in regard to traditional peoples and the adequacy of remedies for land demarcation.[95]

As seen above, in *Lhaka Honhat*, for the first time, the Court recognised the direct justiciability of the right to take part in a cultural life through Article 26. For the first time, the Court, based upon the CESCR interpretation, delimited the content of the right, establishing five fundamental elements: availability, accessibility, acceptability, adaptability and appropriateness. States have not only the obligation to fulfil the right through the adoption of appropriate legislative, administrative, judicial, budgetary, promotional and other measures necessary, but also to protect the right from third parties' interventions.

In summary, the right to cultural identity received widespread recognition and reasoning in *Kichwa de Sarayaku* and was twice declared as having been violated after this decision, with scarce analysis. On the other hand, it is safe to affirm that cultural identity is a fundamental element for the interpretation of Indigenous territorial rights, as it has been applied on several occasions, regarding the rights to property, dignified life, personal integrity, consultation as well as the rights of children. The principle has also been widely accepted in order to establish adequate reparations measures, adjusting them to an Indigenous worldview. As Säuberli stated, 'the right to cultural identity remains an important means to interpret other rights rather than representing an independent, substantive provision in itself' (Säuberli 2015: 591).

The right to self-determination has received little attention in the Inter-American Court. It was mentioned only twice as being *ratio decidendi*, in *Saramaka* and *Kaliña and Lokono*, both against Suriname. In the decisions, the Court mentioned the right to self-determination to interpret the right to property. The Court adopted the concept foreseen in the common Article 1 of the International Covenant on Civil and Political Rights (IICCPR) and the International Convent on Economic, Social and Cultural Rights (ICESCR),[96] as well as the interpretation of such treaties by their respective bodies (the HRC and the CESCR). The mention of self-determination exclusively in cases related to Suriname relates to the fact that the state is the only one with no internal legal protection for traditional peoples and the only one that has not ratified any of the ILO conventions regarding traditional peoples. In order to

[94] *Xucuru v Brazil* (n 39) §115.

[95] *Awas Tingni v Nicaragua* (n 7) §§149–51; *Moiwana v Suriname* (n 15) §131; *Sawhoyamaxa v Paraguay* (n 1), §159; *Saramaka v Suriname* (n 20) §§121–22; *Xákmok Kásek v Paraguay* (n 2) §§171–82; *Kuna of Madungandí v Panama* (n 52) §§112–13; *Garífuna Triunfo de la Cruz v Honduras* (n 27) §§158.

[96] *Saramaka v Suriname* (n 20) §93; *Kaliña and Lokono v Suriname* (n 4) §122.

expand the reach of the property right to collective lands, the Court presented specific argumentation in the cases against Suriname, based upon the ICCPR and the ICESCR. The Court also mentioned self-determination indirectly on two other occasions, in which the right was enshrined in national constitutions under analysis: in *Awas Tingni*, in reference to the Nicaraguan Constitution, and in *Kichwa de Sarayaku*, in reference to the Ecuadorian Constitution.

In *Lhaka Honhat*, despite not mentioning specifically the right to self-determination, the Court considers self-determination as a central element of the right to property: 'the adequate guarantee of communal property does not entail merely its nominal recognition, but includes observance and respect for the autonomy and self-determination of the Indigenous communities over their territory', encompassing the right to freely enjoy the natural resources within the traditional territory according to the guarantee in the ADRIP, Articles VI and IX.

The right of Indigenous peoples to self-determination is a very controversial one, generating profound discussions at both international and regional levels, mostly related to the recognition of internal sovereignty.[97] Both the UNDRIP and the ADRIP approval were delayed for several years (25 for the former, 30 for the latter) and the central point of controversy was the reach of the right to self-determination to include Indigenous peoples. This would probably explain the apprehension of the Court to mention such a right, avoiding backlash from the states. However, with the approval of the ADRIP in 2016, the right was recognised in the American system. Therefore, it would be expected that self-determination would play a more vital role in future cases, thus expanding the protection of Indigenous rights.

Contrary to international Indigenous law, which is constructed mainly upon the right to self-determination (Tomaselli 2016). the Inter-American Court adopts an approach that focuses on the right to property. It represents profound impacts to the protection offered by the Court. For example, regarding the use of natural resources, the Court stated that, based upon the right to cultural identity, traditional communities have the right to explore natural resources that are essential for their cultural and physical survival, with no mention to economic use. From a different perspective, if the approach was built upon the right to self-determination, it might guarantee 'free disposal of their resources and wealth' (ICCPR, Article 1.2), independently of their survival. From a similar perspective, the right to consultation is based upon the property right interpreted under the right to cultural identity, which is limited to consultation regarding matters that may affect the property. It could receive wider content when constituted as a political right derived under self-determination, imposing the obligation to free, prior and informed consent in all matters affecting traditional peoples. (Schettini 2012: 77–79).

[97] See: Anaya (2000); Thornberry (2005); Xanthaki (2007); Charters (2009).

1.8. THE NORM DEVELOPMENT EFFECTIVENESS OF THE CASES

Over two decades, the Inter-American Court managed to develop very advanced protections for Indigenous and ethnic peoples, overcoming an individualistic framework. In a region characterised for centuries by exclusion and marginalisation, the flourishing jurisprudence has given voice to the victims of gross human rights violations and offered them substantial support in obtaining reparations and justice. The evolution of case law is simultaneously noticeable in procedural and material aspects, reinforcing the position of the victim in the proceedings at the same time as more rights have been recognised. Undoubtedly, the Court has developed a forward-looking and progressive model of protection of Indigenous peoples' rights. The Court's approach has not only recognised the importance of the legal protection of the traditional territory, but has also guaranteed an ensemble of procedural and substantive rights aggregated by the protection of cultural identity; a crosscutting means of interpretation.

The present topic will analyse the effectiveness of the case law in developing international rights or, in other words, norm-development. In general, application of international law by an international court develops the applicable norms, since it should at least clarify ambiguities and fill *lacunae*. However, in the case of innovative and forward-looking courts, as the Inter-American Court, norm-development evolves to a concrete lawmaking, in which new rights are created, either by the expansion of recognised rights or as implicit guarantees. The first step to comprehend effectiveness of international courts is to assess their capacity to sustain such norm-development. The assessment enables a better comprehension of the development, as well as the indication of paths for improvement. Furthermore, norm-development can influence compliance and embeddedness with the cases, as the reasoning is crucial for convincing states to follow them.

As already detailed, the Court has been creative with regards to the protection of Indigenous rights, expanding the protection of already enshrined rights (rights to life and property) and recognising implicit rights (rights to self-determination and cultural identity). Even though internationally acknowledged as forward-looking and a reference for the entire world, there is still room for enhancement. There has been a lack of coherence in some cases and insufficient reasoning, in others. Incoherence has occurred both internally (incongruity between the content of recognised rights and their effectiveness to solve the violation) and externally (different approaches to similar situations, ruling out justified case law evolution). Lastly, there are some areas that could be more developed by the Court, in order to provide an up-to-date protection to Indigenous and ethnic people.

External incoherence is the most common issue. The recognition of the right to self-determination is an example, as it has been extensively analysed only in two cases, both against Suriname. In other cases, the Court has not justified the absence of any reference to the right. The right to personal integrity is another example, as it is not clear as to whether the creation of a permanent and grave life risk is considered a violation of mental integrity or not. The recognition of the right to cultural identity has been incoherent, as after its first point of recognition, it was applied in only a few cases in very brief mentions. This incoherence should be counterbalanced, however, with the fact that the Court is greatly innovating in an overly complex field, deciding over different contexts and experiencing different compositions. Full coherence is only a regulative ideal and differences on the decisions are not only justified by the complexity, but also expected.

The right to property is the one with the gravest internal incoherencies. The primary aim of the expansion in the reach of property right is the protection of the physical and cultural survival of the community. However, the Court has given disproportionate relevance to procedural safeguards rather than protecting the substantive content of the right. Worse still, procedural safeguards have not been sufficient for guaranteeing the right, as interpretation of the right to consultation has been inconsistent: the Court has not applied the right to consent since *Saramaka* and has applied a standard lower than that of the international *corpus iuris*, even when mentioning such documents. Furthermore, the right to collective property over traditional territories has been characterised by an undue relevance of cultural aspects, overlooking economic and racial elements that might be essential for some cases. This focus on culture relates to the concept of Indigenous and ethnic peoples, as the Court has stipulated a definition of Indigenous peoples centred in cultural characteristics and self-identification and has applied them to the interpretation of the property right in all cases. In some decisions, little attention has been given to peculiarities of the victims of the case, neglecting the immanent diversity among traditional peoples in Latin America and the Caribbean and offering an inadequate form of protection. For Afro-descendent groups, racial discrimination is a central issue and thus could have been explored.

The second point of concern is the lack of argumentation. As the Court innovates with regards to the recognition of rights, it is fundamental to elucidate thoroughly the reach and the meaning of the recognised right, thus promoting legal certainty. One of the most recent innovation of the Court, the recognition of the violation of Article 23 in respect to the lack of consultation, suffers from insufficient reasoning, since it is analysed in only one brief paragraph, despite the importance of the right. The recognition of the direct justiciability of ESCR is one of great concern, since the argumentation on the Court's jurisdiction on the matter is considerably short. Similarly, as appointed, the Court does not analyse how each of the recognised ESCR was violated in the specific case. The reasoning just recognises the interdependence among them and generally indicates the state's harmful activities and omissions.

The criticism presented is not directed to the content of the innovations, but instead to the Court's approach to them, characterised in some cases by the absence of reasoning and coherence. It is exactly because the innovations are considered an extraordinary improvement in traditional peoples' rights that they should be sufficiently justified and elaborated on, avoiding any possible resistance and assuring legal certainty. Besides improving the already recognised rights, there are some critical areas that have been avoided by the tribunal.

It is crucial to improve the protection of Indigenous leaderships, by recognising the intimate relationship between the protection of traditional territory, violence against human rights defenders (HRD) and cultural peculiarities. The protection of HRD is an urgent problem, considering the escalation of the violence against Indigenous and environmental defenders (Global Witness 2019). The Court has failed to offer such protection during the analysis of violations to the right to life and personal integrity, as well as when ruling on third-party occupation to the territory. Violence against Indigenous leadership emerges because of the state's omission regarding collective property rights, namely, the absence of the delimitation, demarcation, entitlement and final delivery of the property. Attacks against leaderships affect the whole community, considering the cultural peculiarities of traditional communities and their social organisation. The interpretation of the rights to personal integrity and life in these cases should occur in parallel with the recognition of the rights to property, cultural identity and self-determination, which expands the state's duties regarding the protection of HRD and attenuate the burden of proof, favouring an enhanced protection of land and environmental defenders. The *Garífuna* cases against Honduras exemplify how the Court failed to offer sufficient protection to HRD. The Court did not recognise the violation of the right to life in respect to the murders of the Indigenous leaders alleging lack of evidence and lack of knowledge by the state about the specific circumstances. An interpretation connecting the land insecurity, the importance of traditional leaders and the permanent situation of violence could facilitate the recognition of the violation to the right to life and personal integrity and, therefore, improve the protection of HRD in Honduras. Violence against Garífunas leaders only increased after the judgment, demonstrating the gravity of the scenario and the insufficient response given by the Court.

Further developments in the Court's case law could benefit from a perspective on the relationship between business and human rights. In most of the cases, multinational companies were involved in the violation of territorial rights either for the exploration of natural resources or for owning the traditional lands and refusing to negotiate the sale. In *Sawhoyamaxa*, the state had alleged the existence of a bilateral investment agreement (BIT) with Germany that prohibited expropriation of goods belonging to German investors, such as the owners of the ancestral lands. It could have been an opportunity for the Court to advance in the relationship between business and human rights protection, but instead the Court dismissed the allegation, briefly affirming that enforcement of BIT's should always respect the American Convention.[98] Only in *Kaliña and Lokono* has the Court directly approached the matter by citing the UN Guiding

[98] *Sawhoyamaxa v Paraguay* (n 1) §§139–41.

Principles for Business and Human Rights and overtly affirming the obligation of companies to respect human rights and the state's duty to protect against human rights abuse from private companies. The matter has been analysed in depth in a recent case regarding Indigenous workers. In the 2021 case *Lemoth Morris and others v Honduras*, the Court ruled on the obligations of private companies towards labour accidents in a business and human rights perspective, as well as state's obligation to protect human rights through regulation, supervision and application of penalties.

One recent innovation in international law that might contribute to the Court's jurisprudence is the recently adopted Regional Agreement on Access to Information, Public Participation and Justice in Environmental Matters in Latin America and the Caribbean (Escazú Agreement). The Agreement is the first international treaty imposing duties on the state regarding the protection of environmental defenders, in addition to stipulating multiple procedural rights on environmental protection and increasing public participation on the matter. The binding regional treaty was signed in 2018 in the framework of the United Nations Economic Commission for Latin America and the Caribbean (ECLAC) and entered into force in April 2021.[99]

A further improvement for the case law is an intersectional approach (KAS and IDEHPUCP 2017) recognising the relationship between gender, ethnicity and territorial protection. None of the analysed decisions explicitly affirmed concern with intersectionality and the protection of Indigenous women, even though in *Operation Genesis* there were specific claims from the victims in this regard. In *Xákmok Kásek*, the Court affirmed the importance of paying special attention to pregnant women, but the central concern was the rights of the children. The Court has specific case law regarding Indigenous women, recognising their special vulnerability and affirming specific state duties.[100] However, this perspective is still absent in territorial cases. The intersectional approach could be an essential improvement in the Court's case law.[101]

Undoubtedly the most considerable shortage of the Court's case law is the omission of self-determination as a guiding principle, promoting a level of protection lower than that in the international sphere. The recognition of self-determination for Indigenous peoples as an implicit right is an expansion of the Court's mandate that could be censured by states, allegedly for violating the state's sovereignty. However, self-determination could be, alongside cultural identity, a means of interpretation, promoting an interconnected approach

[99] By April 2021 the following states had ratified the Agreement: Antigua and Barbuda, Argentina, Bolivia, Ecuador, Guyana, Mexico, Nicaragua, Panama, Saint Vincent and the Grenadines, Saint Kitts and Nevis, Saint Lucia and Uruguay.

[100] *Fernández Ortega et al v Mexico*, Preliminary Objection, Merits, Reparations, and Costs, IACtHR Series C No 21 (30 August 2010); *Rosendo Cantú et al v Mexico*, Preliminary Objection, Merits, Reparations, and Costs, IACtHR Series C No 216 (31 August 2010).

[101] See IACHR. Indigenous Women and Their Human Rights in the Americas. OEA/Ser.L/V/II.Doc 44/17 (17 April 2017); Kuokkanen (2012).

to human rights. Self-determination and traditional territory are indivisible components that ensure Indigenous survival according to their own worldview. Therefore, rights to property, cultural identity and self-determination should be recognised as a complex and inseparable ensemble. This unique relationship between Indigenous peoples and land should be recognised and protected, shaping the nature and reach of human rights principles. The inclusion of self-determination as an interpretation mechanism leads to, simultaneously, three consequences: the expansion of the scope of the territorial protection; the review of the limitations to the traditional property and the strengthening of the safeguards for exploration of natural resources.

First, it promotes an expansion of the scope of the legal protection since it implies the recognitions of Indigenous and ethnic peoples as actors of their own development. The protection of the territory is expanded to encompass not only cultural and physical survival, but also the economic development and the environmental protection, guaranteeing the right of traditional peoples to freely pursue their economic, social and cultural development. Furthermore, the land protection should not overlook other fundamental aspects for Indigenous and ethnic peoples, ie the right to a dignified life and racial discrimination, which should be recognised in connection with the right to property. Second, the protection under Article 21 does not imply necessarily that the collective territory will have the same limitations as the private property. The possibility to deliver alternative lands or just compensation instead of the traditional territory is a limitation that mistaken the traditional territory for a private property, ignoring the singular relationship between traditional peoples and their communal land. When protecting the ancestral territory under the Article 21, but in an expanded interpretation by self-determination principle, the limitations are also reinterpreted: in case they are incompatible with the principle, they should be set aside. Lastly, regarding the safeguards for exploration of natural resources, the interpretation of Article 21 considering self-determination indicates the recognition of the right to free, prior and informed consent instead of the right to mere consultation. It also leads to the prevalence of the substantial safeguard (the absence of risk to the physical and cultural survival of the traditional people) over the procedural safeguards, guaranteeing an enhanced protection.

In conclusion, the Court has been extremely effective in developing international law in order to redress centuries of marginalisation and discrimination against Indigenous peoples. It created a complex ensemble of rights, ensuring that the traditional territories are protected by regional system. However, the decisions present some pitfalls, mostly by lack of reasoning and incoherencies. There are also some fields that could be approached by the Court, in order to provide an integral protection to Indigenous and ethnic peoples.

2

Reparations Regarding the Territorial Rights of Indigenous Communities

THE CONSTRUCTION OF the reparations system in territorial cases by the Inter-American Court was a considerable contribution in the struggle for the redress that Indigenous peoples had sought after centuries of dispossession. This was made possible through creative remedies, as well as through the provision of support for overcoming marginalisation and structural patterns of violation. It represented a breakthrough development of the jurisprudence, considered comprehensive, progressive and culturally adequate. This chapter analyses the effectiveness of the Court's norm development on the matter of reparations. The Court has focused on traditional land restitution and other non-monetary measures, even though compensation measures have also been a very important step in the redress that Indigenous peoples have sought. After a very brief quantitative analysis of the issued measures in territorial cases, each category of reparation measure is separately analysed. Considering the peculiarities of *Operation Genesis v Colombia* (2013),[1] which is a unique territorial case with deference to the state in terms of reparations, the case is analysed separately. The chapter concludes analysing the effectiveness of the measures and by offering suggestions for the improvement of the remedies ordered.

The 'reparatory activism' is not a singularity of Indigenous cases, since the Court has, over the years, developed a reparations methodology centred on the victims of human rights violation and based upon the principle of *pro personae* (Calabria 2019). The model has been considered extraordinary, forward-looking, extensive, sensitive and innovative, not only by researchers from across the world,[2] but also by victims of human rights violations (Beristaín 2009) as well as international courts and legislators.[3] Such a developed system is unique among

[1] *Comunidades Afrodescendientes desplazadas de la Cuenca del Río Cacarica (Operation Genesis) v Colombia*, Preliminary Objections, Merits, Reparations, and Costs, IACtHR Serie C No 270 (20 November 2013).

[2] But *cf* Cavallaro and Schaffer (2004); Cavallaro and Brewer (2008); Huneeus (2015).

[3] The jurisprudence of the Court on reparations was of central importance for the development of the 'Basic Principles and Guidelines on the Right to a Remedy and Reparation for Victims of Gross Violations of International Human Rights Law and Serious Violations of International Humanitarian Law', as recognised by the First Rapporteur of its draft, van Boen (2003).

regional systems and it must not be mistaken with the European system, as they have divergent objectives and tools.[4]

The American Convention on Human Rights (ACHR) foresees measures of reparation in Article 63.1, which is divided into two parts. First, it establishes that the Court shall order full restoration of the liberty and/or the right viola. Second, it states that the Court might rule, if appropriate, about compensation and other remedies. In addition to Article 63.1, the Court also argues that the reparations are based upon Articles 1.1 and 2, respectively the state's obligations to respect rights and to adapt the domestic legal system to conventional rights, and upon the principles restitution in integrum and pro personae, both assuring the centrality of the victim. The Court has also argued that reparations are a customary principle of international law.

The reparation must be integral, which means that the victim must be considered in each and all aspects of him/herself, re-establishing his/her condition to the situation before the violation, not only in material terms, but with full understanding of the complexity of the subjects (Nash Rojas 2009: 35). In some cases, the return to the previous situation would not provide the full enjoyment of rights, for example in cases of vulnerable groups, ethnic discrimination and extreme marginalisation. In those contexts, the Court has recognised that reparations are entitled to a transformative vocation aimed at overcoming the previous situation of the systematic denial of rights. The innovation leads to the incorporation of measures related to social, cultural and economic rights in measure to overcome structural patterns of exclusion and discrimination (Correa 2014: 838). In that sense, for Soley, integral reparations are an important tool for the transformative vocation of the Court. The Court is aware that 'behind every victim that accedes to the Inter-American system there are countless other suffering the same fate and for whom access is not possible', and it takes on, through its reparation system, a transformative mission. Even when repairing violations against individual victims, the Court was able to address reparations for multiple beneficiaries, aiming at a long-term systematic shift (Soley 2017).

It is important to note that the Court has been very sensitive to the special conditions of the victims, especially those in vulnerable situations, considering peculiarities and tending to their requirements as much as possible (Nash Rojas 2009: 75–6). Expert witnesses from a variety of fields have been of central importance, providing the Court with elements to comprehend the reach of the damage and, at the same time, offering a well-rounded perspective to remedy the situation (Beristaín 2009: 71–82).

[4] See Puente (2009); Schneider (2015).

Because of the thresholds developed by the Court, it has adopted a varied catalogue of applied remedies, separated into six categories, according to their main purpose: compensation; restitution; rehabilitation; satisfaction; non-repetition; and accountability measures. Compensation aims at restoring material and immaterial damaged caused by the violation, as well as any losses of earnings. Restitution measures are aimed at re-establishing the victim's state of affairs to their pre-violation state to the furthest extent possible. Rehabilitation is issued to promote the medical and psychological care for the victims, but it can also include educational measures. Satisfaction measures are the ones aimed at repairing immaterial damage through acts of public repercussion. Lastly, non-repetition measures have a transformative vocation, aimed at overcoming structural patterns of violation. Lastly, accountability measures include the obligation to investigate, prosecute and punish the perpetrators of the violation; a measure closely associated with justice and memory.

Reparations are conceived to be a process of deep transformation in a social and political order, promoting a change of culture in the relationship between victim and states. This visualisation of reparation as a transformative process is fundamental, as it implies that not only does the content of the reparations matter, but also how they are built and how they are implemented (Chiriboga and Donoso 2019). It is also important to note that some of the transformative processes inaugurated by the Court might last for generations, or even demand a new democratic chapter for the society (Ayala et al 2007: 1434). The understanding of reparations as a long-lasting process is relevant for an analysis of the compliance and implementation of the measures. Non-monetary remedies, in particular non-repetition measures, might take a long time for implementation and demand a permanent dialogue among the state, the victims and the Court. In that sense, while the recognition of violated rights stated a past situation of violation, the reparation design is a crucial moment for defining the future of Indigenous peoples. In other words, the factual realisation of the victims' rights on the future depends on a realistic and culturally adequate elaboration of the reparation measures. Since they usually last decades until final compliance, they also must be flexible to context alterations.

2.1. QUANTITATIVE OVERVIEW OF THE REPARATION MEASURES

The Court's reparatory system regarding territorial rights is characterised by a victim-centred perspective, the application of the principles of *pro personae* and integral reparation and a transformative approach. Furthermore, while considering the special vulnerability of traditional communities and their cultural peculiarities, the Court has been very sensitive when tailoring their measures, recognising the Indigenous cultural identity. In the 14 cases analysed, the

Court applied 114 reparation measures,[5] an average of eight measures per case. Restitution measures were the most applied type of reparation (50 measures), followed by non-repetition (21), satisfaction (20) and compensation (18). The least applied measures were accountability (4) and rehabilitation (1) (see Figure 2.1).

Figure 2.1 Reparation measures issued in territorial cases

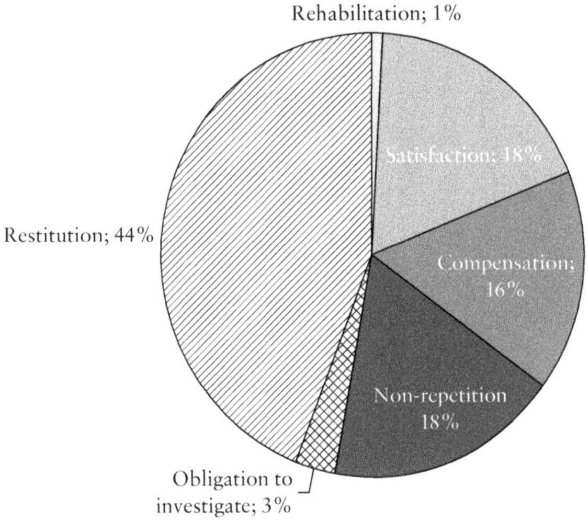

The Court has understood that, for Indigenous and ethnic peoples, the use and enjoyment of the traditional territory is the primary concern, considering their special cultural and spiritual bond with the ancestral lands, as well as their dependence on the land for physical survival. Therefore, among the reparatory measures, there is a clear prevalence of non-monetary measures, particularly ones of restitution, mostly related to the protection of the traditional territory (see Figure 2.2).

Two caveats regarding the analysis of the measures are pertinent. First, even though the classification of the reparation measures in categories facilitates a detailed analysis of each of the measures, understanding the coherence and complementarity among measures issued in a same case is fundamental, so that they are understood as a complex system of reparations that simultaneously allows the individual and collective victims in the cases to obtain redress, while transforming the structural patterns of marginalisation. A second caveat

[5] The quantification of the measures followed the number of operative paragraphs issued by the Court in each decision as much as possible, with small alterations for coherence purpose. The Court sometimes orders more than one measure in a single paragraph, and it sometimes divides a single measure into more than one paragraph. The research followed the majoritarian trend of the Court and adapted the distinguishable cases. It is rather concerning that reparation measures established in the reparation chapter are sometimes not included in the operative paragraphs, even in cases in which they represent measures of paramount importance. Even though they were not quantified, they are analysed considering their paramount importance.

Figure 2.2 Reparation measures issued per case

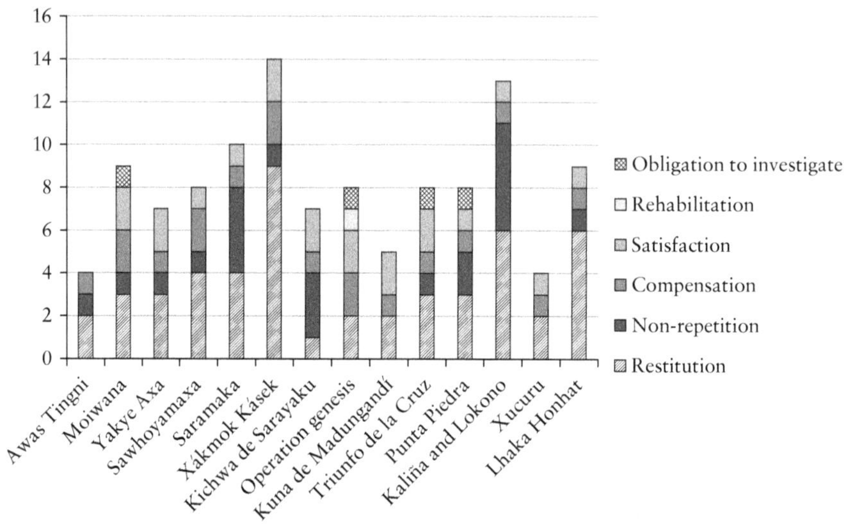

is the relationship between reparations and violated rights. Even though the reparation measures are presented in a different chapter than the recognition of violated rights, there is a clear connection between the evolutionary recognition of rights and the stipulation of adequate remedies. As the chapter demonstrates, the reparation's design is consistent with the recognition of rights.

2.2. RESTITUTION MEASURES

The Court ordered restitution measures in all cases; a total of 50 measures. In all cases, measures related to territorial rights were issued at least once, including the delimitation, demarcation and titling of the territory, provisional protection of the lands and the restoration of full use and enjoyment (see Table 2.1). The Court has applied the principle of *restitutio in integrum*, which foresees remedies aimed at the return to the situation before the violation occurred. Since all cases involve the violation of Article 21, it implied the recognition of historical dispossession and the guarantee of safe return to the ancestral lands, ensuring the full use and enjoyment of the territory and the natural resources thereon. In addition, the Court has gone further than mere restitution and has adopted a transformative approach. The tribunal has applied measures aimed at improving the social reality of the community, with the purpose of guaranteeing their right to a dignified life. Therefore, whenever the right to a dignified life was declared as having been violated, the Court also ordered the provision of public services and goods by means of a transformative approach.

Table 2.1 Restitution measures in territorial cases

Delimitation, demarcation and/or titling of the territory		13
Provisional protection of the territory	Guarantee that territory is not harmed	6
	Security guarantees	2
Restoration of full use and enjoyment of the territory	Settlement of conflict with nature reserve	3
	Rehabilitation of the area	2
	Cessation of activity initiated regardless of procedural safeguard	2
	Saneamiento	4
	General	1
Provision of public service	Provision of basic services and goods	7
	Communication system	2
	Registration and documentation program	2
Award of legal recognition to the community's association		2
Coordination among institutions regarding compliance		2
Recovery of mortal remains		1
Creation of fund for property purchase		1
Total		50

2.2.1. Protection of the Traditional Territory

For Indigenous peoples, the guarantee of the full use and enjoyment of traditional territories is the most pressing issue, as land is the essential threshold for their cultural and physical survival. Therefore, territory is considered by the Court to be indispensable ground for the realisation of several human rights, such as the right to a dignified life, to personal integrity and to cultural identity. Most of the Indigenous peoples litigating before the Court did not have the property titles of their lands, even though they had ancestrally occupied the territory and have maintained a strong cultural and spiritual bond with the land. In some of the cases analysed, the communities were dispossessed and living outside of the traditional territory (*Yakye Axa*, *Sawhoyamaxa*, *Xákmok Kásek*, *Moiwana* and *Operation Genesis*). In all those cases, the Indigenous members faced wretched living conditions and lacked access to basic services and goods. To ensure the cultural and physical survival of the traditional peoples, the protection of the territory had been guaranteed by a threefold model of integral restitution: the formal delivery of the territory; the provisional protection of the land and its resources; and the guarantee of full use and enjoyment.

2.2.1.1. *Formal Delivery of the Territory*

The main consequence of the recognition of the right to collective property under Article 21 is the state's duty to delimit, demarcate and title the territory, which should be effectuated through the adoption of all legislative, administrative and other measures that might be necessary. Demarcation should include the full participation of the communities and consider their customary law, values and customs. The measure to delimit, demarcate and title was ordered in 10 cases, three of which with two measures each.

In most cases, the Court did not specify the boundaries or the size of the property that was to be demarcated. Instead, it expressed the obligation to demarcate only in general terms, such as 'corresponding lands'[6] or 'said traditional territory'.[7] The Court has stated that it is the state's duty to identify the traditional territory, inasmuch as it is the state that 'has the technical and scientific means' to carry out the task. On the other hand, the Court reiterated the importance of the cultural memory of the community regarding the territory, which should be considered in any case.[8] Exceptionally, in *Xákmok Kásek*, the Court ordered the title of a specific area identified by the representatives. Similarly, in *Garífuna Triunfo de la Cruz*, the Court ordered the titling of the area called *Lote A1*, attaching to the decision a map of the territory.[9] In *Lhaka Honhat*, the Court ordered specific details regarding the land title. Not only the size and boundaries of the land were indicated, but also that the title should be a single one for all the communities, respecting the communal nature of the lands and autonomous administration and that 'this title cannot be taken away by proscription, seized or transferred, or subject to liens or attachments'.[10]

The vagueness is justified by the Court as the tribunal might not always have sufficient means of proof to determine the exact boundaries of the territory, aggravated when considering the peculiarities of Indigenous peoples (such as porous boundaries and the cohabitation of multiple peoples). Furthermore, this vagueness allows for a high level of deference for states and traditional peoples to establish the exact boundaries of the territory through negotiations. On the other hand, the lack of a clear definition of boundaries has in most of the cases hampered compliance with the judgment, as a common agreement between state, communities and in some cases third parties might be a difficult, long and extenuating process. It is important to bear in mind that the parties involved in

[6] *Mayagna (Sumo) Awas Tingni Community v Nicaragua*, Merits, Reparations and Costs, IACtHR Series C No 79 (31 August 2001) §164.

[7] *Yakye Axa Indigenous Community v Paraguay*, Merits, Reparations and Costs, IACtHR Series C No 125 (17 June 17 2005) §217.

[8] *Yakye Axa v Paraguay*, Interpretation of the Judgment of Merits, Reparations and Costs, IACtHR Series C No 142 (6 February 2006) §23.

[9] *Garífuna Triunfo de la Cruz Community and its members v Honduras*, Preliminary Objections, Merits, Reparations and Costs, IACtHR Series C No 305 (8 October 2015) §260 and Annex I.

[10] *Indigenous Communities of the Lhaka Honhat (our land) Association v Argentina*, Merits, Reparations and Costs, IACtHR Series C No 400 (6 February 2020) §327.

such negotiations have contrasting levels of bargaining power and a final agreement could be detrimental to the most vulnerable party, ie traditional peoples. Lastly, negotiations could take several years, prolonging the suffering of displaced communities that depend upon the final delivery of the territory to enjoy basic human rights. During implementation, the vagueness of the measures has been counterbalanced by an active role of the Court, acting as a mediator between the parties, even though, in most cases, it has not prevented long-lasting procedures. It would be desirable to establish an intermediary solution, in which the Court presents at least some general parameters for the demarcation of the territory, still leaving room for negotiation among the parties. Finally, only in *Yakye Axa* did the Court order the creation of a fund for the purchase of the private property, that is if the purchase was necessary, or for payment of compensation in the case of expropriation.[11]

2.2.1.2. Provisional Protection of the Territory

In the design of the restitution measures, the Court revealed concern beyond the formal aspect of the property, ordering measures for the provisional protection of the territory. Provisional protection was to be implemented immediately, guaranteeing the quality of the area and its natural resources. It is considered by the Court to be of foremost importance so that the long time spent during the demarcation's procedures does not lead to a loss of the characteristics of the land (Beristaín 2009). In six of the cases,[12] the Court ruled that, while the demarcation measure was not complied with, the state should 'abstain from acts which might lead the agents of the state itself, or third parties acting with its acquiescence or its tolerance, to affect the existence, value, use or enjoyment of the [traditional territory]'.[13] The protection reaches cultural sites and natural resources, including the protection of wooded areas.

The measure was ordered to last until the final delivery of the property. During the supervision of *Awas Tingni*, the Court decided that as soon as the traditional territory is finally delivered, the measure to abstain from harming the territory is also complied with. The provisional protection does not include an independent supervision, but is instead directly built around the measure to delimit, demarcate and title the territory.[14] As developed in chapter five, the provisional protection of the territory as it is currently designed has not been enough to protect traditional territories since non-compliance with the measure

[11] *Yakye Axa v Paraguay* (n 7) §218.

[12] The cases are *Awas Tingni*, *Saramaka*, *Xákmok Kásek*, *Kaliña and Lokono*, *Xucuru* and *Lhaka Honhat*. In the cases *Moiwana*, *Kuna de Madungandí y Emberá de Bayano*, *Garífuna Triunfo de la Cruz* and *Garífuna Punta Piedra*, the measure was mentioned in the reparation chapter, but it is absent from the operative paragraphs.

[13] *Awas Tingni v Nicaragua* (n 6) §164.

[14] ibid, Monitoring Compliance with Judgment, IACtHR (3 April 2009) §13.

does not have any consequence for states as far as it is temporarily linked to demarcation.

Another form of provisional protection of the territory is the issue of security measures. In two cases involving internal conflict and forced displacement (*Moiwana* and *Operation Genesis*), the Court ordered that specific security measures be put in place to guarantee the safe return of the community to their lands:

> [T]he State must send periodically – at least once a month – official representatives to the territories from which these persons were displaced … in order to verify the situation of public order and, consequently, they must meet with the communities or the designated representatives of the latter. If, during these monthly meetings, the inhabitants of the communities express concern about their safety, the State must take the necessary measures to guarantee this, and these measures must be designed in collaboration with the beneficiaries of such measures.[15]

In both cases, the measure was identical, except for the term: one year in *Moiwana* and five in *Operation Genesis*. Even though the measures are essential for a safe return, it is acknowledged by the Court and the representatives that the feeling of insecurity in the communities might last as long as the investigations and the prosecution of those who committed the violations are not concluded,[16] evidencing the relationship between the restitution and accountability measures.

2.2.1.3. *Restoration of Full Use and Enjoyment of the Territory*

In most of the cases, the traditional communities could not fully enjoy their territories because of the restrictions imposed either by states or by third parties with the state's acquiescence. There are three groups of restrictions on full use and enjoyment: the creation of wooded areas; third-party occupation and the exploration of natural resources. On three occasions – *Xákmok Kásek*, *Garífuna Triunfo de la Cruz* and *Kaliña and Lokono* – the full use and enjoyment of the territory had been prevented by declaration of a protected wooded area. In the former two, the Court ordered that the state should take any measure necessary to ensure that the decree establishing the wooded area would not be an obstacle to full use of the territory.[17] The Court did not order the full annulment of the decree, but it also did not enable restrictions on the collective property; instead, it established an intermediary solution, demonstrating the Court's comprehension of the compatibility between Indigenous rights and

[15] *Operation Genesis v Colombia* (n 1) §460.

[16] ibid; *Moiwana Community v Suriname*, Preliminary Objections, Merits, Reparations and Costs, IACtHR Series C No 124 (15 June 2005) §212.

[17] *Xákmok Kásek v Paraguay* (n 14) §§311–13; *Garífuna Punta Piedra Community and its members v Honduras*, Preliminary Objections, Merits, Reparations and Costs, IACtHR Series C No 304 (8 October 2015) §§280.

environmental protection. The compatibility is further developed in *Kaliña and Lokono* based upon international environmental treaties and the recognition of the sustainability of the Indigenous worldview. The Court ordered the state to guarantee the effective access, use and participation of the communities in nature reserves, and that any restriction to the Indigenous rights should 'comply with the requirements of legality, necessity and proportionality, and the achievement of a legitimate purpose'.[18]

A second group of restrictions refers to third-party occupation, in which the central concern of the Court was title clearance (*saneamiento*). In *Garífuna de Punta Piedra* and *Xucuru*, the demarcation and titling of the territory had already finished, but private persons still occupied the property. The Court ordered the state to perform *saneamiento*, removing any obstacle or interference over the territory. However, the Court permitted that, if performing a title clearance was impossible, states could offer alternative lands, after consultation with the communities.[19] In *Lhaka Honhat*, the Court ordered two measures for title clearance: the relocation of the peasants occupying the territory and the removal of fencing and livestock belonging to the peasants.

The third group of restrictions encompasses the exploration of natural resources. To guarantee full use and enjoyment, the Court has ordered two categories of remedies: the rehabilitation of the area and the cessation/review of harmful activities. In *Kichwa de Sarayaku* and *Kaliña and Lokono*, the Court ordered the rehabilitation of the damaged area. In *Kichwa de Sarayaku*, private companies had buried explosives throughout the territory because of its concession for oil exploration. When ordering the restoration of the territory, the Court revealed great concern towards technical information, outlining very specific and technical reparation measures.[20] The technicality of the measure has undermined cultural peculiarities and its specificity has hampered dialogue during supervision. As a result, implementation has been an extenuating process, as is developed in the next chapter. In addition to its concern regarding the explosives, the Court ordered that the area should be rehabilitated through the removal of 'any machinery, structures and non-biodegradable waste that have remained as a result of the oil company's activities', as well as the reforestation of the degraded areas.[21] Despite the clear importance of the measures, they are absent from the operative paragraphs and the Court has not specifically supervised these measures; it simply focused on the removal of explosives.

[18] *Kaliña and Lokono Peoples v Suriname*. Merits, Reparations and Costs, IACtHR Series C No 309 (25 November 2015) §286.

[19] *Garífuna Punta Piedra v Honduras* (n 18) §§323–26; *Xucuru v Brazil*, Preliminary Objections, Merits, Reparations and Costs, IACtHR Series C No 346 (5 February 2017) §§193–96.

[20] *Kichwa Indigenous People of Sarayaku v Ecuador*, Merits and Reparations, IACtHR Series C No 245 (27 June 2012) §294.

[21] ibid.

In *Kaliña and Lokono*, in order to overcome the harmful effects of bauxite mining, the Court ordered the outlining of a detailed action plan to remediate adverse effects and to reforest the area. The state should also monitor and supervise the execution of the rehabilitation by the company.[22] Both measures should be implemented within three years. There is a slight, but fundamental difference between the two cases. In *Kichwa de Sarayaku*, the Court ordered that the state itself should implement rehabilitation measures. In contrast, in *Kaliña and Lokono*, the rehabilitation should be implemented by the private company, following a plan prepared by the state and under its supervision. It is important to remember that *Kaliña and Lokono* was the first (and only) decision in which the Court cited the UN Guiding Principles on Business and Human Rights.

The second category of remedies was the review of concessions granted in disregard to the safeguards established by the Court. In *Saramaka*, the Court ordered the state to review the concessions 'in order to evaluate whether a modification of the rights of the concessionaires is necessary in order to preserve the survival of the Saramaka people'.[23] In *Garífuna de Punta Piedra*, the Court ordered the cessation of any activity performed without consultation with the community.[24] While in *Saramaka* the Court applied a substantial safeguard (the absence of risk), in *Garífuna de Punta Piedra* it applied a procedural safeguard (consultation). As discussed in chapter one, substantial safeguards are preferable to procedural ones since they avoid lenient restrictions to the collective territory and acknowledge the Indigenous peoples' self-determination.

In both cases there is a contradiction between the merits and the reparation stage, as the level of protection of the remedy was lower than the recognised right. When interpreting Article 21, the Court had recognised a substantive safeguard (absence of risk) and three procedural safeguards (consultation, benefit-sharing and prior environmental studies) for exploration of natural resources. When ordering the review of the harmful activities, the Court only mentioned one procedural safeguard in *Garífuna de Punta Piedra* (consultation) and the substantive safeguard in *Saramaka*.

In *Operation Genesis*, the Court was very vague when ordering the restoration of the full use and enjoyment of the Cacarica River Basin communities' territory. The Court ordered that the state should 'restore the effective use, enjoyment and possession of the territories recognised by law to the Afro-descendent communities assembled in the Cacarica Community Council'.[25] The vagueness

[22] *Kaliña and Lokono v Suriname* (n 19) §§290–91.

[23] *Saramaka v Suriname*, Preliminary Objections, Merits, Reparations, and Costs, IACtHR Series C No 172 (28 November 2007) §194.a.

[24] *Garífuna Punta Piedra v Honduras* (n 18) §327.

[25] *Operation Genesis v Colombia* (n 1) §459.

of the measure is related to the high level of deference present in the case, as analysed below in a separate section.

2.2.1.4. *Third-party Rights and Traditional Territorial Restitution*

The integral restitution of traditional territories to Indigenous peoples has, in most of the cases, conflicted, either directly or indirectly, with third-party rights to property. While third-party occupation is a problem both for the demarcation of the lands and for title clearance, the exploration of natural resources is a matter of concern both for the provisional protection of the territory and for the restoration of its full use and enjoyment. In all cases involving third-party rights, the Court has proposed direct or indirect expropriation, demonstrating a varied degree of precaution regarding the private owner's or investor's interests.

In cases involving concessions for the exploration of natural resources, the Court either ordered the annulment or the review of concessions in violation of safeguards. The Court did not mention third-party rights, such as compensation or due legal process, but merely ordered the indirect expropriation of investments. On the other hand, when analysing the direct juridical relationships between third parties and land property, the Court took two distinct positions according to the nature of the right. When a formal lawful private title exists, prior to the titling of the traditional territory to traditional peoples, the Court ordered either the purchase or the expropriation of the lands.[26] On the other hand, when the private title was posterior to the Indigenous title or in cases of mere third-party occupation (absence of title), the Court ordered the state to pay for improvements and reallocate the individuals.[27] In any case, if, for objective and well-founded reason, the expropriation and/or purchase was impossible, the state could offer alternative lands, chosen together with the community,[28] in accordance with its own decision-making and consultation procedures,[29] and thus guarantee that the alternative lands are in sufficient extension and quality in order to ensure the cultural and physical continuity of the community.[30] The alternative land should be contiguous to the already titled territory and, in some cases, an integral development plan should be established in agreement with the community.[31]

[26] *Yakye Axa v Paraguay* (n 7) §§217–18; *Sawhoyamaxa v Paraguay*, Merits, Reparations and Costs, IACtHR Series C No 146 (29 March 2006) §211; *Xákmok Kásek v Paraguay* (n 14) §284–86; *Garífuna Triunfo de la Cruz v Honduras* (n 9) §261; *Kaliña and Lokono v Suriname* (n 19) §280.

[27] *Xucuru v Brazil* (n 20) §194–95; *Garífuna Punta Piedra v Honduras* (n 18) §194. The division of these two categories is an attempt to clarify the Court's position, but it might oversimplify the criteria of the Court, which are not always entirely clear.

[28] *Yakye Axa v Paraguay* (n 7) §217.

[29] *Sawhoyamaxa v Paraguay* (n 27) §212.

[30] ibid.

[31] *Garífuna Punta Piedra v Honduras* (n 18) §325.

The alternative to delivering substitute lands represents a dangerous fragility in the Court's case law, as it offers insufficient protection for the guarantee of the cultural and physical survival of traditional peoples. First, property has a very specific meaning for Indigenous peoples, as they maintain cultural and spiritual bonds with ancestral territory that cannot be replaced. It means that property is a crucial threshold for traditional peoples, but it must encompass the same land that was occupied by their past generations and that is imbued with cultural and religious meaning. There is a clear distinction between the right to collective territory and the right to private property, even though both are protected under the same Article. Only in the second one can property be replaced without further damage to a right's protection, as is explored exclusively for economic purposes. Second, the Court has consistently recognised that the delimitation and demarcation of traditional lands is a declaratory proceeding, as the ancestral possession of traditional territories has the same effect as a formal property title. Following the Court's argumentation, it would not make a difference if the private property title had been issued before or after land demarcation, as the demarcation proceedings only declares a previous condition.

Third, specifically in two cases regarding title clearance (*Garífuna of Punta Piedra* and *Xucuru*) there is an even graver conflict with regards to the interpretation of the property right and the reparation measure. In *Xucuru*, the Court distinguished the duty of *saneamiento* from a possible conflict with private owners, asserting that the duty of title clearance emerges when property rights have already been guaranteed; on the other hand, in a conflict with a private owner prior to the titling, the conflict should be resolved case by case considering the elements of legality, necessity, proportionality, a legitimate objective in a democratic society and the absence of threats to the survival of Indigenous peoples. Still in the merits, the Court recognised that *Xucuru* was a case of *saneamiento* and, therefore, the reference to the balancing between private property and traditional territory would be inappropriate. The Court even recognised that the Brazilian domestic law ensures the prevalence of Indigenous rights over private property in cases of conflict. On the contrary, in the reparations section, the flexibility granted to the state regarding the final delivery of the territory (permitting the delivery of alternative lands) collides with the duty to perform *saneamiento*, as it questions the validity of the Indigenous property registration.[32]

Considering such elements, the alternative remedy to offering other properties instead of the traditional territory is in contrast with the Court's own interpretation of the collective right protected under Article 21, offering a protection lower than the reach guaranteed by the Court when interpreting the right.[33] The exception to this configuration was *Kuna de Madungandí y Emberá de Bayano*, the only occasion in which the Court ordered the state to

[32] *Xucuru v Brazil* (n 20) §125–27.
[33] ibid §§117–19.

annul (*dejar sin efecto*) the private title with no mention of expropriation or compensation.[34]

The Court has repeatedly affirmed that it should not act as a domestic court that resolves a conflict among two individuals, and therefore it would not analyse an eventual predominance of Indigenous rights over private property rights. According to the Court, its jurisdiction was exclusively to recognise human rights violations that are to the detriment of Indigenous peoples.[35] Despite arguing for self-restraint, the Court has detailed the path for states to solve the conflict between third parties and traditional peoples through a three-step solution: expropriation, purchase and alternative lands.[36]

Lhaka Honhat is a specific case, as the third-party occupants were poor peasants, whose livelihood also depended on the land. Recognising the rights of peasants, the Court established guidelines for relocation of the settlers: facilitate voluntary relocation; apply mediation or arbitral procedures when available; and guarantee that the relocation is implemented, safeguarding their rights.[37] It was the first time the Court proposed alternative dispute resolution methods, what is a considerable improvement to avoid conflicts and promote the rights of both involved parties.

2.2.1.5. Suggestions for the Improvement of Territorial Measures in Indigenous Cases

Territorial restitution is the central aim of traditional peoples, as it is the indispensable means to guarantee a collection of interdependent human rights, including the right to a dignified life, personal integrity, freedom of religion and expression, cultural identity and self-determination. However, the restitution of traditional lands has been insufficient. Some of the reparation measures' deficiencies are the consequence of an insufficient recognition of rights, discussed in the chapter one. In most cases, however, the protection guaranteed in the remedies is in contradiction with the Court's own interpretation of the right to property, offering a lower level of protection.

One central concern is the possibility of offering alternative lands in cases of conflict with third parties. The alternative conflicts with the purpose of guaranteeing the cultural and physical survival of traditional peoples. As the Court itself has recognised, it is not under the Court's jurisdiction to rule on a conflict between two private individuals, but instead to recognise a human rights violation and to order its cessation, ensuring that the victims are able to fully enjoy the right. If the lack of land demarcation and/or the impossibility to fully enjoy the natural resources thereon are recognised as a human rights violation, the

[34] *Kuna of Madungandí and Emberá of Bayano v Panama* §§138–45.
[35] *Sawhoyamaxa v Paraguay* (n 28) §136.
[36] ibid §138.
[37] *Lhaka Honhat v Argentina* (n 10) §329.

only adequate redress is the measure to cease the violation, restituting traditional lands and guaranteeing full access to the natural resources thereon.

A second concern is the provisional protection of the territory, timely bonded to the land demarcation and with no consequence in the case of grave harm to the territory and its natural resources after the decision. As developed later in this work, the territories have suffered considerable damage following the litigation, demonstrating the importance of the improvement of the provisional protection that was to be given. There are two paths for improvement: first, to consider the measure of no harming a separate reparation measure instead of being timely linked to the formal demarcation of the territory; second, in case of any harm caused to the territory or its natural resources, to impose monetary penalties and, if possible, rehabilitation of environmental damages caused. Another concern with regards to the exploration of natural resources is that the measure to provisionally protect the traditional territory is absent in the operative paragraphs of some cases.[38] It could be argued that such absence is indifferent, since they were described in the reparation chapter. However, in most of the cases in which the measure was absent from the operative paragraphs, it was not further supervised by the Court during the implementation stage.

A third concern is the insufficient application of the safeguards established for the exploration of natural resources. When interpreting Article 21, the Court has recognised three procedural safeguards (consultation, benefit-sharing and prior studies), as well as a substantive safeguard (absence of risk for the survival of traditional peoples). However, when applying the safeguards to the reparation measures, the Court has mentioned only one. In cases of natural resources exploration, all four safeguards should have been ordered in the reparation stage, and the absence of any of the safeguards should imply the revocation of all concessions, and not only their review. The situation is even graver in *Kaliña and Lokono*. Both the representatives and the Commission had claimed the review and revocation of concessions, but the Court did not order the measure. Instead, it ordered only a general provisional protection of the territory and non-repetition measures for future concessions.

The criticism presented above is related to incoherencies between the reparation and the merit chapters. Besides that, it is also possible to enhance the reparation chapter by enhancing the recognised rights. As developed in chapter one, the recognition of territorial rights by the Court could be improved by an interconnected approach to human rights in which both self-determination and cultural identity are considered indispensable means of interpretation for conventional rights. For restitution measures, it would mean an improvement in the measures related to the concessions for the exploration of natural resources in violation with the safeguards.

[38] The cases are: *Moiwana*, *Kuna of Madungandí y Emberá de Bayano*, *Garífuna Triunfo de la Cruz* and *Garífuna Punta Piedra*.

Another possible enhancement for the reparation measures would be the recognition and reinforcement of the responsibilities of business enterprises towards the protection of human rights and the design of reparation measures including the business duties to protect. The question has been overlooked by the Court so far, even though the relationship between foreign investment and Indigenous territorial rights has been present in multiple cases. The Court should better develop the relationship with private businesses considering their obligation to promote and respect human rights, particularly environmental and territorial rights. The recognition of business accountability through the approach of business and human rights could enhance the triple obligation to protect, respect and remedy, reinforcing the state's duty to make multinationals accountable for human rights violations. A first step for this approach was taken in *Kaliña and Lokono*, in which the Court mentioned the UN Guiding Principles for Business and Human Rights and ordered the rehabilitation to be performed by company under a plan created by the state and its supervision. The matter is later developed in chapter three.

2.2.2. Provision of Public Services

For communities that were experiencing marginalisation and extremely impoverished conditions, the Court has recognised the importance of a transformative approach, issuing restitution measures aimed at overcoming marginalisation. This approach was implemented in the Paraguayan trilogy (*Yakye Axa*, *Sawhoyamaxa* and *Xákmok Kásek*) and the *Lhaka Honhat* case.

The most common reparation issued is the supply of basic services and goods. In *Yakye Axa*, the Court ordered the supply of drinking water, regular medical care, food, latrines and bilingual material for the education of the children at school.[39] The same measures were issued in *Sawhoyamaxa*, even though they were characterised by a greater level of specification. Another innovative aspect in *Sawhoyamaxa* was the state's obligation to secure participation and informed consent by the victims regarding the implemented programmes.[40] In *Xákmok Kásek*, the measures were even more specific, and the Court ordered that the community should be consulted. The Court also ordered the establishment of a permanent health clinic.[41] In *Xákmok Kásek*, a study involving the quantity, frequency and manner of compliance of each public service was ordered. It should contain a high level of details, be prepared by experts and supervised by the state.[42]

[39] *Yakye Axa v Paraguay* (n 7) §221.
[40] *Sawhoyamaxa v Paraguay* (n 27) §233.
[41] *Xákmok Kásek v Paraguay* (n 14) §§201–306.
[42] ibid §303–04.

The growing level of specificity in each further case is consequence of accumulated experience from the supervision with past cases. When the Court presented the judgment in *Xákmok Kásek*, *Yakye Axa* and *Sawhoyamaxa* were already under the compliance supervision, and the Court was aware of the difficulty in evaluating the adequacy of the attempted compliance. Specificity in this case is an intricate matter. On the one hand, the vagueness of the measure guarantees deference for the state to implement the measure according to its domestic policies and consultation of the victims but, on the other hand, excessive vagueness creates a challenge for both the implementation and supervision of the measure, as detailed in chapter three.

The *Xákmok Kásek* design is repeated in *Lhaka Honhat*. The Court ordered the elaboration of two reports: the first to be delivered in six months and executed immediately, identifying critical cases of lack of access to food and water and the adequate action plan; the second to be delivered in one year, a report on how to conserve water and forestry resources, as well as to guarantee food security. The reports should be elaborated with specific technical expertise and in consultation with Indigenous peoples. The measure was not unanimous, as Judge Vio Grossi dissented.

One point of concern of the Court was the distance between the communities' settlements and the existing health centres, which was worsened by access limitations. As a remedy, the Court ordered the implementation of a communication system, allowing 'the victims to contact health authorities competent to address emergency cases'.[43] The measure was ordered in *Sawhoyamaxa* and *Xákmok Kásek*. Furthermore, also in *Sawhoyamaxa* and *Xákmok Kásek*, the Court realised that several community members did not have any official documentation. Therefore, the Court declared a violation of Article 3 of the Convention (right to a juridical personality) and ordered as a remedy the implementation, of a 'registration and documentation program, so that the members of the Community can register and obtain their identity documents'.[44]

For future cases, it is essential that, when ordering public services, the Court establishes an adequate level of specificity of the measures, facilitating the state's comprehension of its content and improving compliance with the measures, if possible by presenting specific indicators for compliance. Possible misinterpretation and conflicts about the meaning of the measures must be foreseen and avoided when possible. The specificities should include not only the measure itself, but also the way in which it should be developed. However, the measures might also leave room for adequacy to the domestic scenario, as well as an open dialogue with the communities. Considering the peculiarities of Indigenous peoples and in respect to their self-determination, all basic services may be implemented only after the free, prior and informed consent of Indigenous

[43] *Sawhoyamaxa v Paraguay* (n 27) §232; *Xákmok Kásek v Paraguay* (n 14) §306.
[44] ibid §307–38.

peoples, so they can become active actors in their overcoming of marginalisation, thus avoiding a paternalistic approach.

2.2.3. Other Restitution Measures

In some cases, the Court has applied specific remedies to tend to the peculiarities of the violation and of the communities. These measures are the consequence of the integral reparation principle, as they are complementary to the other restitution measures related to territorial protection. The Court has ordered the recognition of the communities as legal persons on two occasions (*Saramaka* and *Kaliña and Lokono*). The reparation measure is related to the violation of the right to juridical personality, as Suriname does not recognise collective juridical personality of Indigenous communities. According to the Court, recognition should be performed with the participation of interested communities and in accordance with their communal systems.[45]

The implementation of procedural mechanisms regarding compliance with the applied restitution measures was ordered on two occasions (*Garífuna de Punta Piedra* and *Kaliña and Lokono*) on very similar terms: the state must 'establish necessary mechanisms of coordination among decision-making institutions with jurisdiction in the matter, in order to ensure the effectiveness of the ordered measures'.[46] Even though the measure represented an innovation, the Court neither presented any justification, nor did it present any specification. It is also noticeable that, in similar cases that followed (*Garífuna Triunfo de la Cruz v Honduras* and *Xucuru v Brazil*), the Court did not apply the measure. The measure was neither claimed by the representatives nor by the Commission. Indeed, the lack of coordination among state organs has been labelled as a hindrance for the full compliance with judgments (Beristaín 2009; Krsticevic 2007; Vannuccini 2014). However, it is questionable as to whether such coordination should be imposed on the state by the Court. The measure to establish mechanisms of coordination is not a reparation measure per se, but a procedural mechanism of how to implement the reparation measures, which are primarily a state's decision according to its domestic system.[47]

One specific restitution measure issued only in *Moiwana* was the recovery of the mortal remains of the victims of the massacre that occurred in the traditional territory. On this occasion, the Court revealed great sensibility towards cultural peculiarities. The members of the community reported the existence of very specific burial rituals and, while the rituals would not be performed, all of the community's members would suffer from 'spiritually-caused illnesses'.

[45] *Saramaka v Suriname* (n 24) §194.b; *Kaliña and Lokono v Suriname* (n 19) §305.a.

[46] *Garífuna Punta Piedra v Honduras* (n 18) §328. Translated by the author, original in Spanish; *Kaliña and Lokono v Suriname* (n 19) §385.

[47] On the contrary, defending the measure, Vos (2013).

The recovery of the remains should include the completion of tests and analyses to prove their relation to the victims.[48]

2.3. SATISFACTION MEASURES

The satisfaction measures aim to repair immaterial damage through non-pecuniary measures. They are essential for increasing awareness about the facts and for countering stigmatisation of the victims. They also have an indirect preventative objective, as knowledge about the gravity of the violations and their consequences might educate and prevent future violations. (Beristaín 2009) The most common satisfaction measure ordered in territorial case law is the dissemination of the judgment, followed by the act of acknowledgment of responsibility and the construction of a memorial in honour of the victims (see Table 2.2).

Table 2.2 Satisfaction measures issued

Publication of the judgment	12
Act of acknowledgment of responsibility	7
Building of a memorial	1
Total	**20**

Publication of the judgment was ordered to take two forms: written and broadcast on the radio. Written publication, in turn, was ordered to use three outlets: in the *Official Gazette*, in a journal of national circulation and on the state's webpage. On some occasions, the Court has ordered the publication in Indigenous language, increasing the reach of the measure and promoting the Indigenous language (see Table 2.3).

Each type of publication has a different reach within the country, considering their respective means of access. Publication on the state webpage and in an *Official Gazette* depends on access to the internet, which is very scarce in poor rural areas where Indigenous communities usually live. Furthermore, the publications have a low reach throughout society, as access to them depends on active consultations with their sources. Therefore, publication in a nationally distributed newspaper is preferable, as it allows for easier access and has a wider impact, enhancing symbolic effects. Regarding the language of the publication, translations into a given Indigenous language is an important mechanism for the recognition and valorisation of Indigenous culture. It may be a delicate task, as the judgment contains technical vocabulary that might be absent from the Indigenous lexicon. Therefore, translations should count, with the active participation of Indigenous members.

[48] *Moiwana v Suriname*, Monitoring Compliance with Judgment, IACtHR (22 November 2010).

The Court has been very specific when ordering radio broadcast, indicating dates and time of the broadcast and previous communication to Indigenous peoples. The increasing specificity might be related to implementation failures in past cases, as discussed in chapter three. Broadcasting has a wider reach than written publication, as it is not dependent on literacy.[49] As portrayed in Table 2.3, the Court has an incommensurable logic for ordering and specifying the publication measures, considering the type and the language of the publication. Except for the publication on the state's webpage, which is always ordered in the state official language, there is no pattern in the other types of publication. For legal certainty, it would be desirable that the Court applied a more coherent criterion, or justified exceptions.

Table 2.3 Type of publication ordered by the Court

	WEBSITE	NEWSPAPER	GAZETTE	RADIO
Mayagna(Sumo) Awas Tingni	–	–	–	–
Moiwana	–	–	–	–
Yakye Axa	–	SL	SL	SL/IL
Sawhoyamaxa	–	SL	SL	SL/IL
Saramaka	–	SL	SL	SL/IL
Xákmok Kásek	–	SL	SL	SL/IL
Kichwa de Sarayaku	SL	SL/IL	SL/IL	SL/IL
Operation Genesis	SL	SL	SL	–
Kuna de Madungandí y Emberá de Bayano	SL	SL	SL	SL/IL
Garífuna de Punta Piedra	SL	SL	SL/IL	SL/IL
Garífuna Triunfo de la Cruz	SL	SL	SL	SL/IL
Kaliña and Lokono	SL	SL/IL	SL/IL	SL
Xucuru	SL	–	SL	–
Lhaka Honhat	SL	SL	SL	SL/IL

Type of publication ordered by the Inter-American Court in the territorial jurisprudence

The second most issued satisfaction order was the act of acknowledgment of responsibility. The measure is an important moment intended to mark a rupture

[49] As a consequence of centuries of marginalisation and poverty, the illiteracy rate among indigenous peoples is considerably high. As an example, in Paraguay, the rate is 33.3% and, in Brazil, it is 32.3% (among the indigenous who live on indigenous territories). DGEEC, 'Principales Resultados Encuesta Permanente de Hogares 2016 Encuesta Permanente de Hogares 2017 Población Indígena' (2018) 15; IBGE, 'Estudos especiais, O Brasil Indígena, característica socidemográficas e domiciliares' (2010).

with the situation of the violation, as states have the opportunity to show a commitment to changing their behaviour towards the communities, as well as to re-establish trust between the parties (Beristaín 2009). The Court has specified several details of the act: it should be attended by 'high rank states agents' and by the communities' leaderships; it should be widely publicised in the national media; the details should be decided after consultation with the community; the act should be carried out in the state's official language and in the respective Indigenous language; and the act should respect cultural peculiarities and traditional customs.[50] In cases of systematic violation against human rights or structural patterns of exclusion, the act might have a wider reach than victim. In fact, most of the Indigenous cases that arrive before the Court are representative of multiple similar cases of dispossession and the denial of rights. In this scenario, the act of acknowledgement could be designed to tend to multiple similar cases, representing a wider commitment of the state to the Indigenous peoples (Beristaín 2009: 200; Beristaín, 2010). Lastly, in *Moiwana*, considering the gravity of the massacre that had occurred in the community, the Court ordered the construction of a memorial in a public location. Both the design and the location should be designated in consultation with the community.[51]

The satisfaction measures need to be tailored to each specific situation, analysing specific characteristics of the traditional people involved. The adequacy needs to be present both in the moment of the judgment and during the implementation process, so that the community becomes an active subject of its own redress. Each type of satisfaction has a different reach and should be carefully chosen by the Court. Taking into account levels of marginalisation, illiteracy, access to internet and the importance of widespread awareness, the radio broadcast in both the official and Indigenous languages is the most effective measure and should be the rule for cases involving Indigenous rights. It is essential that the victims are able to take part in the planning of the measure's implementation, as the process might have as much importance as the final object. Additionally, social and cultural aspects must be carefully considered, in order to respect and include the victims' social organisation (Beristaín 2009).

Two cases arose concerning low levels of protection of the measures of satisfaction. In *Operation Genesis*, a severe internal conflict led to forced displacement. The representatives had claimed very specific measures, including memorials and cultural and social programmes, but the Court believed the written publication was sufficient. Considering the peculiarities of the case and the Colombian context, the satisfaction measures could have been expanded to permit a more effective redress. In *Xucuru*, as a measure of satisfaction, the Court only ordered the publication on the state's webpage and in the

[50] *Moiwana v Suriname* (n 18) §216–17; *Yakye Axa v Paraguay*; *Xákmok Kásek. v Paraguay* (n 14), §297; *Kichwa of Sarayaku v Ecuador* (n 21) §305; *Operation Genesis v Colombia* (n 1) §447; *Kuna of Madungandí and Emberá v Panama* §219; *Garífuna Triunfo de la Cruz v Honduras* (n 9) §274.

[51] *Moiwana v Suriname* (n 18) §218.

Official Gazette in the official language, not only offering a lower protection level than former cases, but also insufficient redress for the Indigenous peoples.

2.4. COMPENSATION MEASURES

Compensation measures are monetary remedies aimed at covering material and immaterial, individual and collective, damage caused by the violations. They have been issued in virtually all cases before the Court, but in territorial cases, due to cultural peculiarities, they have presented singularities. The remedy was ordered in all 14 cases, with a total of 18 measures. Considering the collective dimension of traditional peoples' territories, collective damage has been recognised in all cases, while individual damage has been recognised only in cases in which, besides dispossession, members of the community had died. To verify the effectiveness of the compensation, this section will separately analyse collective and individual compensation, followed by the analysis of some possibilities for the improvement of the Court's parameters.

2.4.1. The Evaluation of the Collective Damage

One of the most innovative singularities of the compensation in Indigenous cases is the recognition of a collective damage, both material and/or immaterial. The compensation for collective damage is derived from the recognition of the violated rights' collective nature as well as from the promotion of the Indigenous collective worldview. There is no pattern for recognition of material or immaterial damage (see Figure 2.3). Considering the sum issued, the average value of the damage has been approximately US$1,100,000.

Figure 2.3 Value of collection compensation in Indigenous territorial cases

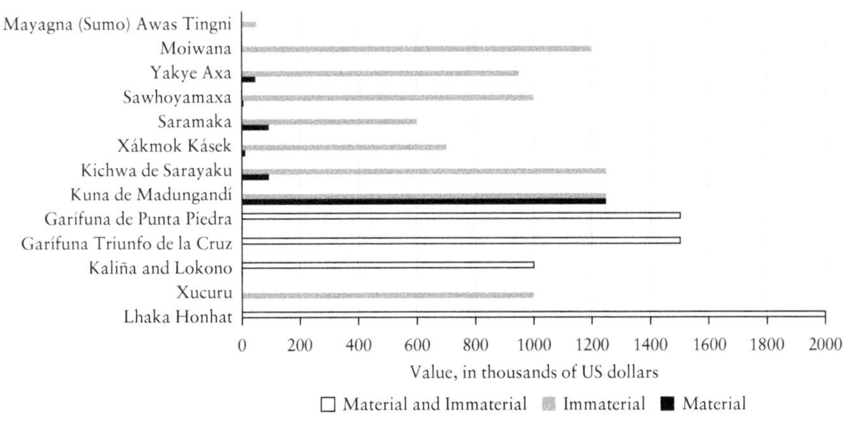

The collective immaterial damage has been evaluated based upon prudency, equity and fairness, considering that it is not susceptible of a precise evaluation. According to the Court, compensation must be an amount sufficient to 'encompass both the suffering and sorrow caused to the direct victims and their relatives, detriment to very significant values of individual persons, as well as non-pecuniary alterations in the conditions of existence of the victim or his family'.[52] The Court has considered that the loss of the traditional territory represents to traditional communities a denial of highly significant values, endangering their lives, identities and cultural heritage.[53] Even though the criteria in all the cases are very similar, the value of the compensation for immaterial damage differs greatly. Even in very similar cases, such as the Paraguayan trilogy, the values vary and the Court presents no further justification.

Material damage has been evaluated considering more precise aspects that include the 'loss of or detriment to the victims' income, expenses incurred due to the facts, and pecuniary consequences that have a causal link with the sub judice case'.[54] In *Yakye Axa*, *Sawhoyamaxa* and *Xákmok Káse,k*[55] the damage was evaluated by the Court through fairness, and included the (mostly travel-related) expenses for requesting the property title. In none of the three cases did the representatives present receipts. However, very distinct values were stipulated (respectively, US$45,000, 5,000 and 10,000). The representatives had also requested compensation for lost earnings, considering the impossibility to engage with traditional economic activities, but the Court denied the request. In *Saramaka*, the Court affirmed that compensation should include damage caused by logging and it was evaluated on equitable grounds.[56] Even though the Court recognised a 'legacy of environmental destruction', as the traditional territory had been deforested by a logging company, the stipulated value was considerably low: US$75,000.

In *Kichwa de Sarayaku* the Court demanded robust evidence for material damage. The representatives had presented a study with the value of lost earnings, considering the impossibility of planting and offering touristic services. Explosives had been buried all over the traditional territory and access to some areas had been denied. They also alleged environmental damages (deforestation, contamination of rivers and the destruction of special sites) and presented a substantial amount of proof.[57] The Court asserted that, in order

[52] *Yakye Axa v Paraguay* (n 7) §199.

[53] *Sawhoyamaxa v Paraguay* (n 27) §§121–23.

[54] *Yakye Axa v Paraguay* (n 7) §193.

[55] ibid §§194–95; *Sawhoyamaxa v Paraguay* (n 27) §§217–18; *Xákmok Kásek v Paraguay* (n 14) §§315–18.

[56] *Saramaka v Suriname* (n 24) §199.

[57] *Kichwa of Sarayaku v Ecuador*, Escrito Autónomo de Solicitudes, Argumentos y Pruebas, IACtHR (10 September 2019).

to measure the damage, 'the parties must provide clear evidence of the damage suffered, as well as the specific relationship between the pecuniary claim and the facts of the case and the violations alleged'.[58] The Court considered that the 'probative elements submitted are not sufficient or specific enough'. Even so, the Court established US$90,000 as compensation, not specifying how it determined the final value.

In *Garífuna de Punta Piedra*, *Kaliña and Lokono*, *Garífuna Triunfo de la Cruz* and *Lhaka Honhat*,[59] the Court established only one compensation amount for both categories of damage, ie material and immaterial. In *Garífuna de Punta Piedra* and *Lhaka Honhat*, there is a total lack of justification of the stipulated value, while in *Garífuna Triunfo de La Cruz* the Court reaffirmed its precedents based upon lost earnings and the deep sorrow caused by the lack of demarcation, following the analysis of testimonials presented before the Court. Lastly, in *Kaliña and Lokono*, the Court briefly mentioned the harm caused to representative values of the community.

2.4.2. Collective Compensation and Forms of Payment

The Court has ordered as collective compensation, in most of the cases, the creation of a development fund with a specific destination. Table 2.4 specifies the management of the fund and their destination. The three Paraguayan cases (*Yakye Axa*, *Sawhoyamaxa* and *Xákmok Kásek*) are peculiar, as the compensation for the collective material damage was to be delivered directly to the communities' leaders, while only the collective immaterial damage was destined to go to the development fund. In all other cases, there was no differentiation between the payment of material and immaterial damages.

Considering the destination of the fund, even though the list was broadened in each subsequent case, it still represents an undue interference in the management of the fund, judicially imposing constraints upon a decision that should be taken exclusively by the traditional people, according to their self-determination (Antkowiak 2014). In more recent cases the Court seems to have understood the limitations of the development fund and it has only presented a list of recommendations, followed by the generic expression 'and others that the … peoples consider pertinent'. Furthermore, in the most recent case, *Xucuru*, the Court did not mention any specific destination. In *Lhaka Honhat*, however, the destination is very specific.

[58] *Kichwa of Sarayaku v Ecuador* (n 21) §314.

[59] *Garífuna Punta Piedra v Honduras* (n 18) §§331–36; *Garífuna Triunfo de la Cruz v Honduras* (n 9) §§289–98; *Kaliña and Lokono v Suriname* (n 19) §295–99.

Table 2.4 Collective compensation in territorial cases

Case	Management of the compensation	Destination
Mayagna (Sumo) Awas Tingni v. Nicaragua	State	Works or services of collective interest
Moiwana v. Suriname	Development fund managed by tripartite Committee	Health, housing, and educational programmes
Yakye Axa v. Paraguay	Development fund managed by tripartite Committee	Health, housing, educational and agricultural programmes
Sawhoyamaxa v. Paraguay	Development fund managed by tripartite Committee	Health, housing, educational, agricultural, and sanitation programmes
Saramaka v. Suriname	Development fund managed by tripartite Committee	Health, housing, educational, agricultural, sanitation and eletricity programmes
Xákmok Kásek v. Paraguay	Development fund managed by tripartite Committee	Health, housing, educational, agricultural, and sanitation programmes
Kichwa de Sarayaku v. Ecuador	Direct delivery for association	As the people see fit
Kuna de Madungandí y Emberá de Bayano v. Panama	Direct delivery for representatives	As the people see fit
Garífuna de Punta Piedra v. Honduras	Development Fund managed by State's agent	Agricultural productivity, infrastructure, reforestation and others
Garífuna Triunfo de la Cruz v. Honduras	Development Fund managed by State's agent	Agricultural productivity, infrastructure, reforestation and others
Kaliña e Lokono v. Suriname	Development Fund managed by State's agent	Health, education, food security, resource management and others
Xucuru v. Brazil	Development fund	
Lhaka Honhat v Argentina	Development fund managed by tripartite Committee	Recovery of the indigenous culture

2.4.3. Individual Damage

The Court recognised individual damage in cases in which community members had been personally harmed (*Moiwana*, *Sawhoyamaxa*, *Xákmok Kásek* and *Operation Genesis*). Even though the damage was individual, cultural identity has played an essential role in the recognition of the reach of the damages. In *Moiwana*, individual compensation was established for material and immaterial damage because of years of impunity following the massacre that was committed against the community, as well as the forced displacement and the impossibility of returning to their traditional lands. Despite gravity of the harm, the Court established a material damage of US$3,000 to each of the 130 victims and immaterial damage of around US$10,000 each. As Antkowiak states, individual compensation in Moiwana was 'manifestly disproportionate to their moral travails and to the Inter-American jurisprudence' (Antkowiak 2008: 398–99).

In *Sawhoyamaxa* and *Xákmok Kásek*,[60] the wretched living conditions of the community caused the death of several community members. In *Sawhoyamaxa*, the Court established US$20,000 for each of the 19 deceased, to be paid to the next of kin. In the second case, US$260,000 was to be delivered to the leader of the community in compensation for 13 deaths. Finally, in *Operation Genesis*, regarding the death of a community leader by paramilitary forces who acted with the support and acquiescence of the state, the Court ordered compensation for immaterial damages. The compensation consisted of US$70,000 to the companion of the victim, US$35,000 to each of his children and US$10,000 to each sibling.[61]

2.4.4. Suggestions for the Improvement of the Compensation Measures

The Court has adopted a non-monetary focus for reparation in territorial cases. The approach is undoubtedly laudable, but it must be accompanied by sufficient compensation for damages, guaranteeing integral reparation. This section reveals, however, that the Court has been reluctant to fixate adequate monetary compensation in Indigenous cases, overlooking the claims and evidence presented by the victims' representatives. Regarding collective compensation, the case law has lacked clarity in the evaluation of damages, both material and immaterial. Additionally, it has offered a paternalistic method of payment, underestimating the capacity of self-management possessed by the Indigenous peoples. With respect to individual compensation, the problem is related to cases with multiple victims in which the damage was under-evaluated and did

[60] *Sawhoyamaxa v Paraguay* (n 27) §§226–27; *Xákmok Kásek. v Paraguay* (n 14) §325.
[61] *Operation Genesis v Colombia* (n 1) §476.

not include the sorrow of the family. Each of the points will be presented below, followed by a presentation of suggestions for the improvement of the compensation measures.

The first point of concern is the evaluation of the collective damage, both material and immaterial. The criteria considered by the Court for the evaluation of the damage are not clear, nor is the necessary means of proof to be provided by the representatives. In the first cases no robust evidence of damage was presented and the damage was evaluated by equity. The value was considerably distinct, even though some cases had very similar factual background. *Saramaka* is the gravest case of discrepancy in terms of the value of compensation. A logging company had, with state approval, deforested a very large area of the traditional territory, irreparably eliminating the means of survival of the traditional community. The market value of the timber extracted was valued at US$10,000,000, according to an expert witness before the Court, and the damage to the property was considered by the Court to be a 'legacy of environmental destruction' (Antkowiak 2014). The Court recognised the magnitude of the damage and the importance of wooded areas for the traditional people's physical and cultural survival. It has also confirmed the deep sorrow caused to the individuals by the logging concessions. The damage was presented with the help of large amounts of evidence: affidavits, documents, expert witnesses and witnesses' testimonials. Even so, the stipulated value was considerably low: US$75,000. Similarly, in *Kichwa de Sarayaku*, the Court demanded a greater amount of evidence than former cases and concluded that the multiple evidence presented by the representatives was insufficient, establishing low value for compensation of the material damage.

One point that deserves further clarification by the Court is the recognition and evaluation of environmental damage, as the criteria that has been applied until now is not yet clear. The subject is contested in international law and there is not a single methodology for its evaluation, but instead several proposals.[62] *Saramaka* was the first time the Court recognised ecological damage, but the evaluation of the amount of damage by means of equity resulted in a considerably low value. Environmental damage was a part of the factual backgrounds of other cases but the Court has not analysed the matter sufficiently enough, losing the opportunity to propose a clearer form of methodology and advance in international law.

It seems that the Court has established a standard value of compensation (development fund between one and one-and-a-half million dollars) and it has

[62] See eg *Costa Rica v Nicaragua*, International Court of Justice, Compensation owned by the Republic of Nicaragua to the Republic of Costa Rica (2 February 2018). For a brief analysis of the case, see Desierto (2018). See also the separate opinion of Judge Cancado Trindade in the case, defending the application of the principle integral reparation to environmental damage and the necessity of non-monetary orders. For an overview on the methodologies of evaluation of environmental damage, see Bowman and Boyle (2002).Beristaín (2010).

applied the standard for all litigating traditional communities, despite the singularities present in each case. Since the very first case took place, the Court has resorted to equity and fairness in the analysis of both material and immaterial damages. However, in the most recent cases, the justification of the value of compensation is nearly inexistent, with no overview of the criteria or analysis of the evidence.

The equity parameter as the only justification might not be enough, as different evaluations of similar damages might generate the sentiment of discrimination. The Court should, in addition to equity, analyse objective criteria in the evaluation of collective damage, promoting adequate compensation for the singularities present in each case. The criteria presented below are suggestions for improving the evaluation of the material damage They do not intend to propose a completely objective method, but instead to propose some parameters to assist in the evaluation of the damage, reinforcing the legitimacy of judicial argumentation. Equity and fairness could remain as fundamental yardsticks, facilitating the complex burden of evaluating the damages.

First, it would be of fundamental importance to distinguish cases in which the community is currently occupying the traditional territory from the ones in which they had been forcefully dispossessed. In the cases in which the community occupies the territory, but full use and enjoyment is hampered by the exploration of natural resources, the Court could estimate the compensation based upon the market value of the extracted resources, the environmental damages caused, and the cost and time necessary for the restoration of the area. In cases of third-party occupation with state acquiescence, the Court could consider the extension of the occupied area, the market value of the land and the duration of the occupation. In both cases, estimated lost earnings caused by the incapacity to use the land could be evaluated based upon the economic evaluation of the traditional use of the lands. In cases of dispossession, particularly in the long-standing ones, it might be harder to evaluate the damage, as several uncertainties arise, such as the exact boundaries of the property and what the traditional use would be. Even so, evaluation could be based on the lapse of time of the dispossession, existence and intensity of conflicts, state's behaviour towards the community and the living conditions of the community members (including access to basic services and goods).

There are, however, two important caveats for the proposed evaluation. These economic criteria should not undermine the spiritual and cultural importance of the territory to Indigenous peoples, and for that purpose equity remains a central parameter. Furthermore, the proposed thresholds should not enhance the level of evidence demanded from the victims' representatives. Considering the vulnerability of Indigenous communities, the production of robust amounts of evidence could represent a burdensome undertaking. Instead, 'the Court should show more willingness to presume material damages in indigenous group cases' (Antkowiak 2014: 73–74). Another possibility could be the Court itself to require evidence that it considers necessary, including requesting information for chosen entities or organs.

The method of payment of the compensation has also been subject to much criticism, considering the paternalistic approach of the development fund (Nash Rojas 2009; Dulitzky 2010; Antkowiak 2014; Robles 2018). The Court's remedy is considered to be inadequate, as it underestimates the capacity of Indigenous communities to manage the money on their own.[63] There are also discrepancies between the development funds and the recognition of the principle to self-determination, as it prevents the full enjoyment of the traditional peoples' right to freely pursue their social, economic and cultural development. In addition, territorial cases are characterised by a great amount conflict between the communities and the state. The participation of the state in the management of the fund might worsen such conflicts. The safeguards established by the Court to protect Indigenous peoples (consultations and the designation of representatives to the committee) might not be sufficient to guarantee the communities wishes, particularly considering the difference in bargaining power of both parties. In the end, compensation might be invested in services that are not adequate for the self-determination of the traditional peoples, as detailed in the next chapter.

The supervision of compliance with the compensation measures has revealed grave conflicts with regards to the management of the fund, including the misappropriation of the money in the Paraguayan cases.[64] Even so, the Court did not adapt its parameters and maintained a flawed mechanism of payment. The Court does not present any justification that could explain the use of the fund and its management by the Commitee. In *Kaliña and Lokono*, the victims' representatives claimed a different method of payment than in *Saramaka* and *Moiwana* to guarantee the peoples' discretion. They presented detailed information about conflicts that arose in the management of the funds in past cases and described experiences of the communities in managing monetary funds.[65] The Court dismissed the claim with no further justification.

At last, there is a worrisome doubt regarding which moment should be considered as the final step in compliance. If, on the one hand, the Court uses expressions indicating compliance in one such action, such as 'create the fund' and 'pay the compensation', on the other hand, it also provides specific instructions for the management and application of the fund, suggesting that compliance supervision lasts until the final disbursement of the fund. To avoid

[63] In *Yakye Axa*, for example, the payment of the compensation for collective material damage was equitably distributed among the members of the community, without any conflict, demonstrating their capacity for management of monetary reparations. Beristaín (2009: 259).

[64] 'Extitular del Indi, Rubén Quesnel, condenado a 10 años de cárcel' *Ultima Hora* (28 August 2018).

[65] *Kaliña and Lokono v Suriname*, Pleadings, Motions and Evidence of the Victim' Representatives (24 April 2014); *Kaliña and Lokono v Suriname*, Final Written Argument of the Victims' Representatives (5 March 2015).

misappropriations or the inappropriate application of the fund, the Court should indeed maintain supervision until the final disbursement of the whole fund. In that case, it would be more adequate if the Court ordered the remedies using expressions that denoted continuous implementation, such as 'create and implement a development fund'. Clearly, if the compensation was directly delivered to the community as suggested here, the moment of compliance would not be a question.

With regards to individual compensation, a matter of concern lies in the fact that, in cases with multiple victims, the value of compensation has been considerably low. Unfortunately, it is a frequent occurrence in the Court's general case law to set lower values in cases with multiple victims, avoiding lump sums with which the state would not comply (Beristaín 2009). The Court's rulings on the recognition of Indigenous rights to traditional territory was ground-breaking. However, when not sufficiently repaired, rights are diminished. As Antkowiak stated,

> [T]he Court's historic affirmation of indigenous peoples as communal property owners is compromised. Rather than receive their due payment for lost, damaged, or co-opted property, they receive a nonthreatening fund to redress moral harm – when they have actually suffered from both moral and material perspectives (Antkowiak 2014: 79).

Even though the Court adopts a non-monetary approach towards reparation, compensation for Indigenous and ethnic peoples is fundamental for enabling the improvement of living conditions and/or the restitution and reforestation of the territory and could be considerably improved.

2.5. NON-REPETITION MEASURES

Non-repetition measures intend to avoid future violations similar to the case *sub judice*. They are the Court's ultimate instrument for a transformative approach and for widespread impact in the society. The Court issued non-repetition measures in 11 territorial cases, detailed in Table 2.5.

Table 2.5 Non-repetition measures in territorial cases

Adaptation of the domestic legal system	17
Application of procedural safeguard for future restrictions within the territory	2
Mandatory course on indigenous and tribal peoples' rights	2
Total	**21**

The obligation to adapt the domestic system is a consequence of Article 2 of the Convention (duty to adopt domestic instruments) and it is related to the recognition of the incompatibility between domestic legislation with the conventional order. The measure to adapt the legal system to guarantee the right to collective property is present in 10 cases. In eight of them (*Awas Tingni*, *Moiwana*, *Yakye Axa*, *Sawhoyamaxa*, *Saramaka*, *Xákmok Kásek*, *Kaliña y Lokono* and *Lhaka Honhat*) the measure was as follows: 'the state must adopt … administrative, legislative or any order measure necessary to create an effective mechanism for the delimitation, demarcation, and titling of the property of indigenous communities'.[66] The measure should be carried out while respecting Indigenous peoples' customs, uses and culture. In *Moiwana* and *Saramaka*, the order was more specific, as the novel legislation should be aimed at guaranteeing the rights of the *Moiwana* and the *Saramaka* communities to their traditional territories. The level of detail was bigger in *Xákmok Kásek*, in which the Court ordered specific details of the legislation to be adopted, including that it should foresee a judicial authority to solve eventual conflicts.[67] *Saramaka*, *Kaliña and Lokono* and *Lhaka Honhat* were the only cases in which the Court ordered that the legislative adaptation should be carried out through prior, effective and fully informed consultation with the communities, despite the importance of consultation with Indigenous peoples in matters affecting their interests.

In both Garífuna People cases, the Court considered the domestic registration system to be imprecise and indicated that it was the cause for overlap between private property titles and the collective title to the traditional territory. The Court ordered the state to regulate the registry of properties with the purpose of avoiding overlap titling over the Indigenous territory.[68] The measure has a high level of vagueness as there is no orientation or further outline of how it should be implemented. The registry failure was alleged neither by the Commission nor the representatives.[69] The measure to adapt the registry of property is, in both cases, questionable considering the lack of claim from the parties, the lack of reasoning and the lack of parameters for compliance. Furthermore, it is not clear as to whether improvements in the property registries will avoid non-repetition of the violations, as the overlap of property titles was caused by the indeterminate borders of the property or the absence of a final title to the ancestral territory.

The Court also ordered the adoption of a legislative framework regarding procedural safeguards for restrictions on the traditional property in *Saramaka*, *Kichwa de Sarayaku*, *Garífuna de Punta Piedra* and *Kaliña and Lokono*. When interpreting Article 21, the Court recognised that states shall restrict full use

[66] *Awas Tingni v Nicaragua* (n 6) §164.

[67] *Xákmok Kásek v Paraguay* (n 14) §309–10.

[68] *Garífuna Triunfo de la Cruz v Honduras* (n 9) §282; *Garífuna Punta Piedra v Honduras* (n 18) §347.

[69] *Garífuna Triunfo de la Cruz v Honduras*, Escrito de solicitudes, argumentos y pruebas and Escrito de Sometimiento del Caso por la Comisión; *Garífuna Punta Piedra v Honduras*, Escrito de solicitudes, argumentos y pruebas and Escrito de Sometimiento del Caso por la Comisión.

and enjoyment of collective property, as long as three procedural safeguards are met: consultation, benefit sharing and social and environmental impact assessment. The Court has further stated that restrictions to the property might not risk the cultural and physical survival of traditional people. In *Saramaka*, the Court ordered the adoption of benefit-sharing and consultation within the legislative framework. In *Kichwa de Sarayaku* and *Garífuna de Punta Piedra* only the regulation of consultation was ordered,[70] and in *Kaliña and Lokono* the regulation of the three procedural safeguards was ordered. Despite recognising four safeguards on the merits, when tailoring the non-repetition measure, the Court has placed emphasis on the regulation of the right to free, prior and informed consultation, the only safeguard present in all four cases. In both *Saramaka* and *Kaliña and Lokono*, the safeguards were to be adopted in all investment projects in the traditional territory, with the distinction that, in the first case, the measure should reach the *Saramaka* people and, in the second, all Indigenous and ethnic peoples of Suriname. In *Garífuna de Punta Piedra*, the measure was specifically in respect to the Mining Code.

A third group of ordered adaptation of the domestic legal system is the adoption of necessary resources to guarantee collective access to justice, ordered in *Saramaka* and *Kaliña and Lokono*.[71] The remedy is a consequence of violations against the right to juridical protection the right to information. While in *Saramaka* the measure was general, in *Kaliña and Lokono*, the Court specified detailed information about the remedy, as the access to justice should be accessible, simple and adequate to Indigenous and tribal peoples. The details include, among others, interpreters during the legal proceedings, legal assistance and physical accessibility to the juridical institutions.[72] Lastly, the Court ordered the state exclusively in *Kaliña and Lokono* to 'take necessary measures to recognise the collective juridical personality of Indigenous and tribal peoples' as a consequence of the violation of Article 3 (right to juridical personality), in combination with Articles 1.1 and 2.

Besides alterations in the domestic system, the Court has also issued non-repetition measures specifically aimed at the victims of the case, imposing the adoption of procedural safeguards to future restrictions in their traditional territories. The measure relates to the recognition of the right to property and was very similar in both decisions, *Saramaka* and *Kichwa de Sarayaku*. The Court ordered that the implementation of any further concessions for the exploration of natural resources should comply with free, prior and informed consultation and the performance of environmental and social impact assessments.[73]

[70] *Saramaka v Suriname* (n 24) §194.d; *Kichwa of Sarayaku v Ecuador* (n 21) §301; *Garífuna Punta Piedra v Honduras* §345; *Kaliña and Lokono v Suriname* (n 19) §305.d.

[71] *Saramaka v Suriname* (n 24) §194.f; *Kaliña and Lokono v Suriname* (n 19) §305.a–c.

[72] *Kaliña and Lokono v Suriname* (n 19) §251.

[73] *Saramaka v Suriname*, Interpretation of the Judgment on Preliminary Objections, Merits, Reparations and Costs, IACtHR Series C No 185 (12 August 2008) §194e; *Kichwa of Sarayaku v Ecuador* (n 21) §300.

Exclusively in *Saramaka*, the Court also ordered the state to 'implement adequate safeguards and mechanisms in order to minimise the damaging effects such projects may have upon the social, economic and cultural survival of the Saramaka people'.[74]

The measures related to future investment projects might be considered redundant and unnecessary. First, the Court had also ordered a more general remedy, ie the adoption of legal measures to domestically enforce the procedural safeguards established by the Court. This reasoning could be set aside once we realise that legislative measures usually take a long time to be adopted and both the communities were under imminent risk of new concessions in their territories, justifying the necessity for the specific non-repetition measure. The second argument is that the Court interpreted the Convention recognising a right to protect Indigenous traditional territory, including protection through the safeguards in cases of natural resources exploration. The Court's case law is binding, so the recognition of the territorial right compels states to respect the communal property. The reparation measure is unnecessary, as it only reiterates a general duty already asserted in the merits. The third argument is that it is not clear as to the moment of compliance with the measure, as the measures were established in general terms. This could signify that the supervision of compliance would last indefinitely.

Finally, the Court ordered the implementation of permanent mandatory courses on Indigenous and tribal rights in *Kichwa de Sarayaku* and *Kaliña and Lokono*. The measure should be implemented with the respective budgetary provisions and should be aimed at law enforcement officials and those whose functions relate to the subject at hand.[75] It is a measure of difficult compliance supervision, as it does not specify details for the training, such as hours of the course, content of the lessons and the method of its application.

Non-repetition measures are a valuable innovation of the Court, guaranteeing not only integral restitution for the victims but also expanding the protection of rights to society as a whole, in an attempt to avoid future violations. The Court is aware that the cases that finally hear the judgment of the Court are usually representatives of broader structural patterns of violation that reach multiple victims throughout the country (Soley 2017; Schonsteiner 2007; Nash Rojas 2009). Through non-repetition measures, the tribunal intends to offer wider solutions aimed at overcoming the marginalisation of Indigenous and ethnic peoples. On the other hand, non-repetition measures have been criticised, mostly by states, for constituting an undue interference in the domestic sphere, as well as an excessive extension of the Court's mandate. The states believe that socioeconomic policies should be defined by the states themselves (Correa 2014: 838–41; Huneeus 2015).

[74] *Saramaka v Suriname*, Interpretation of the Judgment §194e.
[75] *Kichwa of Sarayaku v Ecuador* (n 21), §302; *Kaliña and Lokono v Suriname* (n 19) §309.

Despite such criticism, the Court's mandate to issue non-repetition measures is an explicit outcome of the Convention. First, Articles 1.1 and 2 prescribe the obligation to respect rights and the duty to domestically adopt all necessary measures to guarantee conventional rights. The non-repetition measures are merely the application of both articles to a concrete case. Second, Article 63.1 establishes that the Court shall ensure to the victims full enjoyment of the rights violated. In some cases, the full enjoyment of rights is only possible through legislative alterations, conforming the domestic system to conventional standards. One point of concern, however, is that the Court has under its analysis only individual cases that might not always consider all of the information regarding the structural patterns of the violation. The Court must be aware of such limitations and only award broader measures when the evidence of the case reveals sufficient corroboration of a structural pattern, as well as its content. As Antkowiak stated, 'the Court must strive for proportionality so that its authority is not ultimately undermined' (Antkowiak 2008: 396).

It is fundamental to establish a mid-term goal regarding the level of specifics of the ordered measures. If, on one hand, vague outlines with ambiguous language have very little chance of being complied with, on the other hand, some flexibility is desirable, enabling states to adapt the Court-ordered measures to their respective domestic socio-political scenario and to the democratic debate (Antkowiak 2014). Furthermore, context might change in the long term until full compliance is achieved, and the measure needs to be adaptable to new circumstances. Consequently, the Court must present some guidelines regarding compliance with the measure and at the same time leave room for democratic deliberation in the domestic sphere. In territorial cases, the level of specification in non-repetition remedies has been considerably low, with only few exceptions. As developed in detail in the next chapter, vagueness of the remedies impairs compliance, as states usually struggle to comprehend the extent of the necessary adaptation of the domestic system. It also hampers the supervision of the measures, as the parameters for evaluation are not clear.

A possible solution for the Court could be the consultation with experts from different disciplines in respect to reparation measures, either following the claims from the parties or *ex officio* (Rules of Procedure, Article 46). Before the delivery of the decision, the consultation would promote a precise evaluation of structural patterns of violation and the most adequate non-repetition measures. During the supervision of compliance, the consultation could provide input for the analysis of the compliance with non-repetition measures (Beristaín 2009). It is also relevant to bear in mind that the adaptation of legislation and programmes offering human rights courses are relevant measures, but in most cases, they might not be enough to render complete guarantee of non-repetition. Non-repetition depends on structural changes which rely upon a multiplicity of factors, as developed further in chapter five. Furthermore, even in cases closed due to full compliance, the Court's decision cannot prevent further regressive changes in the legislation.

In another perspective, the territorial non-repetition measures have presented an insufficient level of protection. First, as already criticised in chapter one, when ordering regulation of restrictions to Indigenous property, the Court has placed undue emphasis on procedural safeguards instead of favouring the material safeguard, ie the absence of risk for the physical and cultural survival of the community, offering insufficient protection to the right to property. The insufficiency is worsened in the reparation, as not only does the Court not mention the material safeguard, but it is also inconsistent in terms of ordering which procedural safeguards should be regulated. The Court has placed emphasis on the regulation of the right to free, prior and informed consultation; the only safeguard present in all four measures, in detriment to the social and environmental impact assessment and benefit-sharing. The absence of the safeguards is not justified by the Court. Furthermore, the Court could have gone further and ordered not only consultation, but free, prior and informed consent, according to the right to self-determination and the *corpus iuris* of international Indigenous law. Second, consultation should have been considered relevant not only in the substance of the measures, but also in its creation. There should have been an emphasis on free, prior and informed consultation with Indigenous and ethnic peoples in the establishment of all issued non-repetition measures.

To sum up, non-repetition measures are an excellent outcome of the Court's mandate and contribute towards overcoming the centuries of exclusion that Indigenous peoples had to endure. However, the Court must be careful with regards to its ruling, using an adequate level of specificity and consulting experts when necessary. Even though the measures might propel positive changes in the domestic system, their effectiveness hangs upon a multiplicity of factors of difficult compliance. Finally, the Court has been inconsistent with regards to the regulation of the safeguards to restrictions to the property, offering an insufficient level of protection.

2.6. ACCOUNTABILITY AND REHABILITATION MEASURES

The obligation to investigate, prosecute and punish was ordered in *Moiwana* (in relation to the massacre), *Operation Genesis*, *Garífuna de Punta Piedra* and *Garífuna Triunfo de la Cruz* (all three in relation to murders of the communities' leaders).[76] There is a strong relationship between the right to traditional territory and the impunity of crimes against Indigenous peoples. In *Moiwana*, witnesses explained that the community could not return to their traditional land until justice was served and the perpetrators of the massacre were punished. In the cases of the Garífuna People, the leaders were killed as they acted in defence of

[76] *Moiwana v Suriname* (n 18) §202–07; *Operation Genesis v Colombia* (n 1) §439–40; *Garífuna Punta Piedra v Honduras* (n 18) §352–53; *Garífuna Triunfo de la Cruz v Honduras* (n 9) §265–67.

their traditional territory following land conflicts, caused by the state's omission to protect the territory. The measure is similar in all cases, as the Court ordered the use of all necessary means to continue or to start investigations effectively and with the greatest possible diligence, as well as to individualise, prosecute and eventually punish all those responsible for the violations. The measure to investigate is related to the violation of the right to a fair trial and the right to judicial protection and it has been declared even in cases in which a violation of the right to life was not declared.

One absent aspect of fundamental importance is the participation of the victims during the investigation, ensuring a victim-centred perspective. In order to guarantee their right to truth, it is important that community members are informed about the investigation steps, re-establishing a relationship of trust and respect between victims and states. In the general case law of the Court, mostly during its early years, accountability measures were one of its fundamental contributions when it came to consolidating the transition to democracies in Latin America. This guaranteed the right to truth and the redress of massive and systematic human rights violations committed during dictatorships.[77] In more recent cases, the Court has recognised the obligation to investigate in cases involving vulnerable groups and human rights defenders.[78]

The implementation of accountability measures is lengthy and complex, as it simultaneously involves multiple state organs and relates to deep-rooted structural deficiencies (Basch 2007; Huneeus 2011). In most of the cases, investigations are impaired by a multiplicity of elements, such as lapse of time, domestic legal restrictions, corruption and the involvement of high rank authorities. The Court has declared that the obligation is one of best-efforts, but it still lacks the parameters to evaluate the implementation of measures adopted during the investigation (Beristaín 2009: 350ff). Considering the multiple difficulties hindering the implementation and supervision of accountability measures, the measure should be restricted to cases involving either gross human rights violations or systematic patterns of impunity against vulnerable groups. In the territorial cases, *Moiwana* and *Operation Genesis* are part of the first group, while both *Garífuna* cases are part of the second group.

As already stated, violence against human rights defenders and Indigenous leaderships has greatly increased over the last decades because of increased pressure for natural resources and land. The violence has been accompanied by the impunity of its perpetrators and the absence of preventive public policy.

[77] See, in particular, cases *Barrios Altos v Peru*, Reparations and costs, IACtHR, Series C No 87 (30 November 2001); *Bámaca Vélasquez v Guatemala*, Reparations and costs, IACtHR Series C No 91 (20 December 2002); *Molina Theissen v Guatemala*, Reparations and costs, IACtHR Series C No 108 (3 July 2004).

[78] See, eg, *Bulacio v Argentina*, Merits, Reparations and Costs, IACtHR, Series C No 100 (18 September 2003); *Yarce y otras v Colombia*, Preliminary Objection, Merits, Reparations, and Costs, IACtHR Series C No 325 (22 November 2016).

The region is the most dangerous on the planet when it comes to defending land rights, increasing the need for specific measures on the matter, both fighting against impunity and guaranteeing security measures (Global Witness 2019). This context highlights the meaning of accountability measures in the territorial disputes, suggesting its importance for free exercise of territorial rights through tackling rising levels of violence against Indigenous and ethnic peoples.

In the Court's case law, it is common to grant rehabilitation measures in cases related to gross human rights violations in which traumatic psychological impacts on the victims are present, such as massacres, forced disappearances and summary executions. The rehabilitation is ensured through the psychological and medical treatment offered to the victims and their relatives. In the territorial cases, these rehabilitation measures were only ordered in *Operation Genesis*, because of traumatic consequences of years of internal conflict and forced displacement, even though it could also have been relevant in *Moiwana*, enabling psychological redress for the multiple victims of the massacre and the ensuing forced displacement. The measure in *Operation Genesis* presents several details, such as the inclusion of the provision of medicine and the fact that the rehabilitation was to be provided with collective, family and individual treatment as agreed with each of the victims.[79]

The Court opted to order rehabilitation through the public health system. The measure might generate some problems, as public services face several difficulties, including cultural and linguistic barriers, distance to remote communities and the lack of knowledge and adequacy of traditional practices (Antkowiak 2014). In order for the rehabilitation to be effective, Indigenous and ethnic traditional healthcare systems must be included in the rehabilitation phase, and cultural elements should be carefully considered as an adequate form of treatment (Gómez 2008; Ruiz and Donoso 2014). Additionally, partnerships with NGOs holding a relevant amount of expertise in the subject could guarantee adequacy to the peculiarities present as well as efficient for of treatment (Antkowiak 2014).

2.7. *OPERATION GENESIS*: APPLICATION OF DOMESTIC COMPENSATION

Operation Genesis is the only case in which the Court did not establish any compensation for the victims, but instead referred to the Domestic Restitution Program (DRP).[80] The Court was also very brief when ordering restitution measures, referring generically to the DRP measures. The case represents part of the most recent turn on the Court's case law. Since the very first cases, the Court had stated that the regional reparations are independent from eventual

[79] *Operation Genesis v Colombia* (n 1) §452–53.
[80] See Sandoval (2018).

domestic reparation, as the Convention guarantees full jurisdiction to the Court in matters regarding the establishment of compensation (Nash Rojas 2009). However, from 2013 onwards, the Court shifted its position in some cases and adopted DRPs when ordering reparations, particularly in cases from Chile and Colombia. However, this has been inconsistent and has generated uncertainty, as the Court has adopted different justifications in similar cases (Sandoval 2018).

The situation in Colombia is one of very peculiar circumstances, as the country hosts the world's largest internally displaced population as consequence of decades of internal conflict[81] and the DRP was established in 2011 within a process of transitional justice (Colombia 2011a, 2011b, 2011c; Forero-Nino 2017; Rojas 2016). In *Operation Genesis*, the Court recognised and appreciated the progress made by Colombia regarding reparations to the victims of the internal armed conflict. To analyse the adequacy of the DRP, the Court presented several criteria: legitimacy; adoption in good faith; reasonableness and proportionality; degree of social inclusion; and distribution criteria (including the position of women and the succession order).[82] The principle of complementarity (Preamble of the ACHR) was also mentioned.

The Court decided 'to acknowledge the compensation granted at the domestic level and to abstain from ordering reparations in this regard, when this is pertinent' and ordered the state to guarantee that all the recognised victims of the judgment 'have priority access to the said administrative reparations, and that it proceed to pay them, as soon as possible, irrespective of the time frames that domestic law may have established for this, avoiding obstacles of any type'.[83] Regarding restitution measures, the Court was very broad when ordering the restitution of the full use and enjoyment of the traditional territory to the communities and it ordered further restitution to be established according to the DRP. In the words of the Court,

> domestic reparation programs refer specifically to housing programs and to land restitution mechanisms, as well as to other measures of rehabilitation, satisfaction and non-repetition. Consequently, the victims in this case should also have access to these other forms of reparation.[84]

Even though not a confirmed turn, the designation of the DRP instead of the establishment of compensation is a setback in the rulings, as the regional tribunal is denying the victims not only a just compensation but also restitution of their territorial rights. The context of the DRP is understandable; the Court is sensitive towards transitional justice and it shows concern with regards to the compliance with its decisions. However, the absence of compensation and vague restitution measures creates discrimination between the present Colombian case

[81] UN Human Rights Committee, 'Global Trends: forced displacement in 2017' (2018).
[82] *Operation Genesis v Colombia* (n 1) §§470–74.
[83] ibid.
[84] ibid §461.

and the other territorial cases decided by the Court. Even worse, the lack of a clear justification and incoherence with other cases involving transitional justice generate uncertainty about future decisions.

2.8. THE NORM DEVELOPMENT EFFECTIVENESS OF REPARATIONS

The reparation system created by the Court in the territorial cases has been a laudable effort in redressing centuries of dispossession, as well as providing support for overcoming marginalisation and structural patterns of violation. The Court has adopted a multidimensional approach based upon the principle of integral reparation, which is focused on non-monetary remedies and sensitive to cultural peculiarities. Through decades of evolutionary case law, the Court was able to achieve three different levels of protection, ie individual rights, collective claims and protection of society as a whole, which is an impressive outcome considering it only rules on individual cases (Tigroudja 2010).

Even though the Court already recognises cultural identity as a means of interpretation for reparations, self-determination has been overlooked. The recognition of the principle represents for Indigenous and ethnic peoples an opportunity to overcome the position of victims and to lead their way as actors of their own development. The reparation chapter of the rulings must be understood as a bridge that connects the recognition of violation of rights to the transformation of factual situation of marginalisation and exclusion. One central improvement of the recognition of the self-determination principle is the order to obtain consent from traditional peoples during the implementation processes of the remedies, guaranteeing that the measures tend to their own development plans. In several cases, the peoples' representatives have claimed for a wider control of the reparation measures, but the Court has ignored such demand, concentrating the decisions about implementation within the state. Wider participation of traditional peoples would promote not only their self-determination, but also more adequateness of the measures in a victim centred perspective (Antkowiak 2014; Chiriboga and Donoso 2019).

The most pressing issue for Indigenous and tribal peoples, not only in LAC but throughout the whole world (Gilbert 2007), is the guarantee of full use and enjoyment of their traditional territory, as land is an indispensable component for their cultural and physical survival. As an answer to that claim, restitution measures have been the central concern of reparations ordered by the Court. To promote integral restitution, the Court has ruled not only on the formal delivery of the property, but also provisional protection of the territory and its natural resources, the creation of peace mechanisms and the restoration of environmental damages. However, the possibility of delivering alternative lands might impair the full effectiveness of the measure. Another visible concern is the incoherence when ordering provisional protection of the territory, caused by two shortfalls: temporarily linking them to the demarcation remedy, and excluding them from the operative paragraphs in some cases. Lastly, an approach that includes the responsibility of business corporations for the protection of human rights was suggested, according to the threefold rule to respect, protect and remedy.

The measures of satisfaction, rehabilitation and accountability are non-pecuniary measures with a very important role when seeking redress, increasing awareness about rights and promoting the right to truth and justice. In the measures of satisfaction and rehabilitation, the Court has been careful with regards to cultural peculiarities and thus ordered the adequacy of Indigenous and ethnic uses and customs. The same level of adequacy and participation could have been applied to the accountability measure, guaranteeing a victim-centred approach. Despite the focus on non-monetary remedies, the Court has also issued pecuniary compensation. The collective compensation has been, however, fragile, both regarding evaluation of the damage (incoherent and imprecisely justified) and to the method of payment (paternalistic and potentially contentious). According to the self-determination of Indigenous peoples, the compensation should be directly delivered to the community instead of delivered through a development fund with specific destination. Failures are also present in individual compensation, as they have ignored the sorrow of next of kin and have been set at low values. Finally, the most controversial measures of the Court are the non-repetition measures, mainly the adaptation of the domestic legislation. The measures allow for carrying out the duty to amend the domestic system to conventional parameters (ACHR, Article 2) and are an attempt to overcome structural patterns of violation.

Reparations are an essential aspect in the struggle for justice. Not only does the recognition of the violation matter; a just and effective redress is fundamental for the strengthening of such rights. Considering the peculiarity of Indigenous and ethnic peoples and their rights to cultural identity and self-determination, special attention should be given to the reparation stage, ensuring its effectiveness and adequacy. The reparations are the inauguration of a new phase in the struggle for Indigenous and ethnic peoples' rights, and not only a final point of destination after years of litigation. Compliance with the reparations entails a complex and lengthy process, and it is essential that the Court's remedies reflect this understanding. During this process, it is fundamental that community members become leading actors of their own redress, overcoming marginalisation and exclusion to assume a position of agents of their own development. Participation, and in some cases consent, is a mandatory element in the process of reparation, just as well as the adequacy of the measures to their cultural identity. (Gómez 2008; Beristaín 2009: 440; Donoso 2009; Antkowiak 2014: 56; Ruiz and Donoso 2014). Furthermore, the cases involving traditional territory are usually very conflicting, both between Indigenous peoples and the state, and between Indigenous peoples and third parties. If the conflicts are not seriously considered, the reparations might not offer an adequate response or may even worsen the conflict. Lastly, it is of great value to have in mind the diversity among Indigenous and ethnic people and consider special peculiarities in each case, avoiding having a generic position on Indigenous peoples, bearing in mind that culture is volatile and thus might change. Both the use of stereotypes and essentialisation might be discriminatory, leading to an inadequate redress for Indigenous communities (Beristaín 2009; Citroni and Osuna 2008).

3

The Implementation of Reparation Measures: The Court's Point of View

THE REPARATORY SYSTEM inaugurated by the Court in the matter of traditional lands consubstantiated a creative and forward-looking attempt to guarantee not only redress for traditional peoples, but also a path towards the transformation of a long-endured condition of radical deprivation. However, the Court's decision does not represent the final step for redress, as the struggle for restitution of the lands might last for years after the victory, in an extenuating process involving multiple actors and elements. This chapter analyses the process of implementation[1] of the reparation measures, quantitatively analysing the compliance and qualitatively describing the case-specific effectiveness. It concludes by analysing elements involved in compliance, and suggests improvements for enhanced implementation.

Territorial case law is a unique field of the Court, characterised by a large expansion of recognised rights and a comprehensive programme of reparations. It involves peculiar parties that overcome the standard dispute between individuals and states, with the emergence of new actors with very distinct bargaining power, such as Indigenous peoples and multinational companies. Lastly, they involve mostly economic, social and cultural rights, contrary to the majority of the Court's decisions, which is focused on civil and political rights. The sum of these peculiarities triggers different implementation processes, demanding a careful analysis of the elements involved in compliance to comprehend the elements that have triggered or hampered full compliance with the Court's measures.

In order to present a broad overview of the implementation, the first section quantitatively analyses compliance with the reparation measures, comparing it with the general case law of the Court. The main source of the research is the supervision orders issued by the Court, which were available online on the tribunal's website until December 2023. The *Kaliña and Lokono* case is excluded from analysis in this chapter since it has no supervision order yet.

[1] Compliance is defined as 'full execution of the action (or complete avoidance of the action) called for (or prohibited) in one or more court rulings', while implementation is the domestic process leading to compliance: Kapiszewski and Taylor (2013).

The Court has adopted a proactive role in supervision procedures, actively engaging in multiple innovative procedures to foment compliance. It has even interpreted and clarified the reparation measures whenever necessary, indicating to states possible paths to promote compliance. Supervision is regulated in the Court's Rules of Procedure and it is carried out mainly through reports presented by the state, observations from the victims and their representatives and observations from the Commission. The Court can convene the parties and the Commission at a hearing (either public or private), require information from other sources, including expert opinions, proceed with on-site visits and issue supervision orders. In the territorial cases under analysis, the most common procedures used by the Court include requiring information from the state and the issuing of supervision orders. The Court has issued 45 supervision orders on territorial cases. It is not possible to perceive a pattern in the issuance of supervision orders, as the quantity and frequency vary considerably among cases and among time.

Hearings were carried out at least once in all the analysed cases, except for *Xucuru* and *Lhaka Honhat* (most recent cases). *Kichwa de Sarayaku, Sawhoyamaxa, Garífuna de Punta Piedra* and *Garífuna Triunfo de la Cruz* were the only cases with public hearings; all others were private. The visits are a recent innovation of the Court and, so far, they have contributed considerably to compliance supervision, simultaneously pressuring states towards compliance, enabling the obtainment of first-hand information and initiating dialogue among multiple state organs and victims. They occurred in Panama and Paraguay. The Court has in some cases adopted the joint supervision of similar cases against the same state. It has been adopted in the Paraguayan trilogy and in the cases against Honduras. Regarding Colombia, the Court has analysed the implementation of rehabilitation measures issued in several cases, including Operation Genesis, in a joint supervision.

The active role of the Court during implementation is atypical among international courts and so far, it has triggered implementation and promoted the adequateness of the reparation measures to cultural peculiarities, in an attempt to guarantee a victim-centred perspective. The Court's efforts and the relation with domestic politics is described below, organised by country.

3.1. QUANTITATIVE ANALYSIS OF THE COMPLIANCE

The compliance analysis was separated in two ways. First, each specific measure was classified as 'complied with', 'pending compliance' or 'partially complied with'. Partial compliance is applied by the Court when the state has taken some steps towards compliance, but has not yet completely fulfilled the measure. The criteria for considering partial compliance are not always evident, though, and a 'partial compliance' classification will be critically assessed in the implementation sessions.[2] Second, the cases can also be classified as 'complied' (all reparation measures complied with), 'partially complied' (at least one reparation measure complied with) and 'non-complied' (all measures pending compliance).

Figure 3.1 Quantitative analysis of the compliance

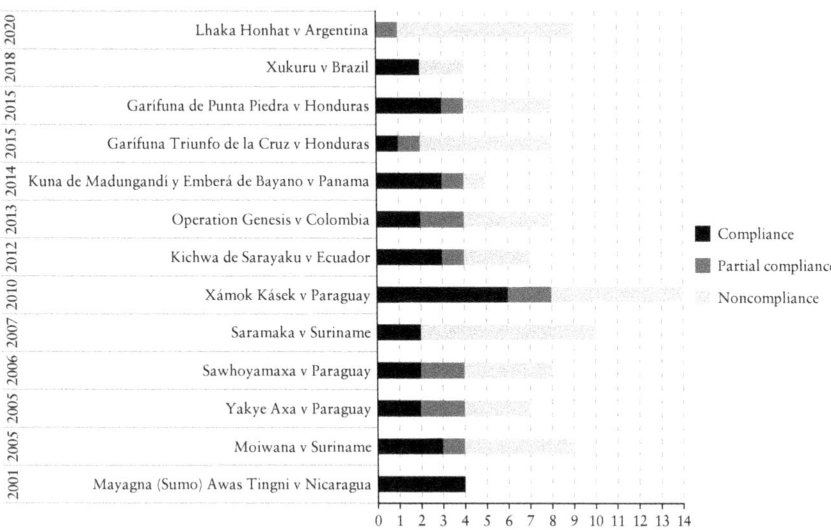

Among the 13 cases analysed, only one was filed due to compliance: the first case, *Mayagna (SUMO) Awas Tingni v Nicaragua* (2001). Partial compliance prevails, as in all other cases states complied at least with satisfaction measures (see Figure 3.1). No state has overtly contested Court decisions: even though states accept the content of the decisions, implementation is a troublesome and complex matter. Further, almost all involved states already enshrined Indigenous rights constitutionally (with the only exception of Suriname) and the recognised violations were a matter of domestic effectiveness of rights and not legal recognition. This previous recognition could explain the lack of open contestation against the Court. It also indicates that the Court is reinforcing the domestic rule of law in the matter of territorial rights, strengthening constitutional guarantees.

Of the 101 reparation measures issued by the Court, only 33 were fully complied with, while 14 have been declared partially complied with and 54 are still pending compliance. Compliance rates are greater among satisfaction and compensation measures. Accountability and rehabilitation measures have

[2] For a critical view of the use of the category partial compliance, see Hillebrecht (2009).

Figure 3.2 Percentage of compliance per type of measure

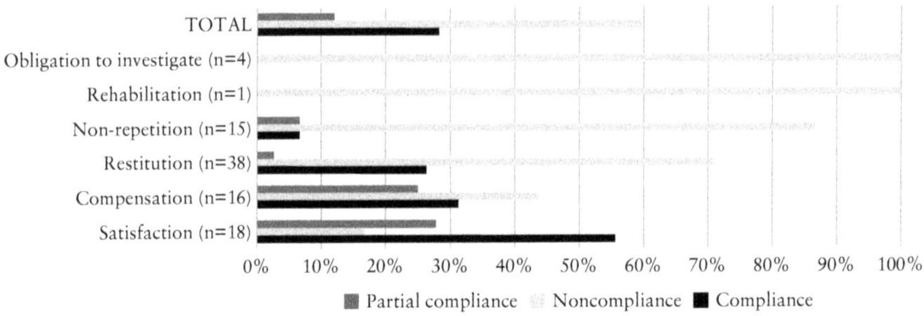

never been complied with. Low compliance is observed in restitution and non-repetition measures (see Figure 3.2).

Comparing the rates of compliance of territorial cases with the general case law of the Court[3] (see Table 3.1), compliance in territorial cases is lower than general cases. There is a considerable contrast among accountability and non-repetition measures. Satisfaction and compensation measures have a similar rate of compliance. The only category in which the compliance rate is greater in territorial cases than in general case law is individual measures (including the categories restitution and rehabilitation).

Table 3.1 Percentage of complied measures

Type of measure	General cases	Territorial cases
Compensation	55	31
Symbolic/Satisfaction	58	56
Accountability	14	0
Nonrepetition	23	7
Individual/Restitution and rehabilitation	16	26
Total	34	28

Several elements might explain lower compliance rates in territorial rulings. Regarding non-repetition measures, particularly the alteration of the domestic legal system, generally have low rates of compliance, as they are vague, highly dependent on political will and usually in charge of the legislature. However, lower rates of compliance in territorial cases could reveal structural patterns of discrimination against Indigenous and ethnic peoples, as well as the influence of economic power within the legislature.

[3] Comparison using data from Hillebrecht (2014). The comparison should be analysed with caution, considering different years and classification criteria.

Accountability measures are vague and dependent on the behaviour of several state branches, which summed up to specific elements of the case (legal barriers, a prolonged lapse of time and incomplete processes of transitional justice) justifies low rates of compliance and delayed delivery, both in general and territorial cases. Specifically in territorial cases, however, the low rate of compliance follows a pattern of impunity in murders committed against human rights defenders in Latin America and the Caribbean (LAC).[4] Furthermore, accountability measures in general case law were a consequence of decisions on mass atrocities and transitional justice in LAC. Although still early to confirm, it could be that domestic actors in new democracies trying to repair past dictatorships might be more forthcoming when it comes to complying with accountability measures than when investigating individual cases of murder, even when committed against vulnerable groups (Sandholtz et al 2018; Soley and Steininger 2018).

Time is a relevant element for the analysis of the compliance, as states usually take a long time to fully comply with the decisions.[5] Delayed compliance has been used by states as a strategy for limiting the effects of a decision domestically but avoiding frontal defiance. The average time between final judgment and declaration of compliance (full or partial) is 75.4 months. Compliance time varies according to the complexity of the measure issued as it is higher among restitution measure (almost 81 months) and lower in satisfaction measures (around 50 months) (see Table 3.2).

Table 3.2 Compliance time, in months

Restitution	80,9
Satisfaction	50,1
Non-repetition	63,5
Compensation	88,6
Average	75,4

The Court fixes in each judgment a term for compliance, which is usually between six and 12 months.[6] This term is frequently disrespected by states, as compliance takes longer than the term ordered by the Court. There is, however, no consequence for complying with a measure after the ordered term, except for

[4] IACHR 'Hacia una política integral de protección a personas defensoras de derechos humanos' (29 December 2017) OEA/Ser.L/V/II. Doc 207/17; UNHRC, 'Visit to Honduras, Report of the Special Rapporteur on the situation of human rights defenders' (11 January 2019) A/HRC/40/60/ Add.2.

[5] For an analysis of expected time of compliance with reparation measures, see Pérez Liñán et al (2019).

[6] The exceptions are the non-repetition orders and the accountability measures, usually ordered for compliance in a 'reasonable time'.

pecuniary compensation in which the state shall pay interest in case of arrears.[7] The Court considers delayed compliance as full compliance. Considering the reiterated disrespect to the fixated term, the Court could adopt two possible responses. First, it could order more realistic terms, considering the structural difficulties of implementation with the measures. Second, it could adopt a new classification during supervision measure, classifying the measures in 'complied' and 'complied with delay'. One last observation on compliance time: it cannot be interpreted separately from the levels of compliance. For example, non-repetition measures have a short time of compliance, what could give the impression that it is easily implemented by states. However, it has a very low compliance rate. On the contrary, satisfaction measures have simultaneously low compliance time and high rates of compliance, confirming that the measures are easily complied with.

The quantitative data presents a general pattern, but full comprehension of compliance in territorial cases can only be assessed by careful analyses of the path taken towards compliance, since implementation is a very complex process involving multiple elements and actors, both within the state and civil society.

3.2. FULL COMPLIANCE IN *MAYAGNA AWAS TINGNI*

The first case, *Mayagna (Sumo) Awas Tingni v Nicaragua* (2001), is so far the only territorial case filed due to compliance.[8] The dispute involved concessions for logging in the traditional territory and the state was held responsible for violating the rights to collective property, judicial protection and the obligation to respect rights. The Court had ordered four reparations: the delimitation, demarcation and titling of the traditional territory; the adoption of legislation measures to create a procedure of land demarcation; pecuniary compensation; and the measure not to harm the territory until its final demarcation.[9]

The state presented regular reports clarifying the steps toward compliance. Full compliance took almost eight years. The first measure complied with was the adoption of a legislation creating an effective mechanism for the delimitation, demarcation and titling of the property of Indigenous communities, implemented by the adoption of Law 445 on 23 January 2003.[10] The legislation was quickly approved since its draft was already under discussion in the legislature even before the Court's merits decision, as a result of a conditioning

[7] Except in *Xákmok Kásek*, in which the Court established a monthly fine in case of late compliance with demarcation of the lands.

[8] As ch 4 aims to develop further aspects of the impact that the decision had in Nicaragua, this section briefly introduces the path towards compliance.

[9] *Mayagna (Sumo) Awas Tingni Community v Nicaragua*, Merits, Reparations and Costs, IACtHR Series C No 79 (31 August 2001).

[10] *Awas Tingni v Nicaragua, Monitoring Compliance* (7 May 2008) §13.

imposed by the World Bank for a loan. The legislation and its approval are detailed in the next chapter.

In March 2003, the compensation measure was complied with. The Court had ordered an investment totalling US$50,000 in works or services of collective interest for the benefit of the community. In consultation with the community, the state built a student hostel in Bilwi, Puerto Cabezas. Even though building was completed after a four-month delay, there was no dispute regarding compliance.[11] Consultation with the community was essential for adequately implementing the measure, as the state proposed the construction of a highway or toilets, while the Community refused the offer, considering that the proposed services were already a state obligation and proposed instead the construction of the hostel (Beristaín 2009).

Despite considerably fast compliance with compensation and non-repetition measures, Nicaragua struggled to comply with the restitution measure. Several difficulties had to be overcome, most of which were related to conflicts with neighbouring communities. In May 2008, considering the difficulties hindering compliance, the Court celebrated a private hearing that was acclaimed by the judges as 'extremely useful', considering the goodwill and spirit of cooperation of the involved parties.[12] The most important commitment assumed during the hearing was an agreement with compromises and terms assumed by the state regarding the restitution measure.

On 4 December 2008, the state finally titled the land of the community. The Court declared the case filed due to compliance on April 2009, but reaffirmed that the further implementation of Indigenous rights was very important.[13] Regarding the measure not to harm the traditional territory and its natural resources, as a consequence of the delay in the demarcation, third-party occupation escalated, threatening the territory with the exploitation of natural resources, and thus causing massive environmental damage and the escalation of violence (Alvarado 2007). When analysing compliance with the measure not to harm, the Court reiterated that 'the duty regarding abstention remains in force as long as the active obligation to delimit, demarcate and title has not been done, for which reason once the latter is discharged, the former lapses'.[14] Therefore, the measure was considered complied with by the Court, as the duty to demarcate the territory was fulfilled, despite the harm provoked.

Contrary to all future territorial cases, compliance in *Awas Tingni* represented a successful case in terms of land demarcation. A favourable political scenario prompted the implementation domestically, as well as the active participation of the Court as a mediator during the private hearing. The Court did not analyse the title clearance, even though third-party occupants remained in

[11] ibid.
[12] ibid §7.
[13] *Awas Tingni v Nicaragua, Monitoring Compliance* (3 April 2009) §§15–16.
[14] ibid §13.

the territory. However, as analysed in chapter four, compliance was not enough to guarantee the full enjoyment of rights.

3.3. SLOW AND HAMPERED COMPLIANCE IN SURINAME: *MOIWANA* AND *SARAMAKA*

Suriname featured in territorial cases before the Court on three occasions: *Moiwana* (2005), *Saramaka* (2007) and *Kaliña y Lokono* (2015). The most recent case has no supervision measure and is therefore excluded from the present analysis. *Moiwana* refers to a massacre in a village of the *N'Djuka* people in 1986, which was followed by forced displacement and a lack of investigation into the facts. The Court declared that the state violated the rights to access to justice, judicial protection, property, personal integrity and freedom of movement. As reparation measure, the state should demarcate the traditional territory, perform an act of acknowledgment of responsibility, build a memorial, pay individual compensation, establish a development fund, investigate the facts related to the massacre, restore mortal remains of the victims and adopt legal measures guaranteeing territorial rights.[15]

The most salient feature in the supervision procedure in *Moiwana* is the high level of interdependence among the remedies ordered. Due to security concerns, the community could only return to the territory once justice was served and those involved in the massacre were punished. It was also considered to be essential to identify the mortal remains of the deceased and to perform burial rituals to re-establish harmony in the community. On the other hand, the demarcation of the territory is fundamental for an efficient implementation of the development fund, to establish the adequate location for the implementation of housing, education and health services. In turn, demarcation is only possible when legal measures are adopted creating a procedure with such purpose. Lastly, compensation and satisfaction measures only achieve their aim of repairing the victims when they are followed by a change in the state's attitude toward the community characterised by full compliance with other orders.

In *Saramaka*, the dispute regarded concessions for logging on the traditional territory, which had caused massive deforestation. According to the Court, the state violated the rights to access to justice, judicial protection, property, legal personality, obligation to respect rights and self-determination. The remedies ordered were: the creation of a development fund; publication of the judgment; provisional protection and demarcation of the traditional territory; and the adoption of several legal measures to guarantee the Saramaka people territorial rights.[16]

[15] *Moiwana v Suriname, Preliminary Objections*, Merits, Reparations and Costs, IACtHR Series C No 124 (15 June 2005).

[16] *Saramaka v Suriname, Preliminary Objections*, Merits, Reparations, and Costs, IACtHR Series C No 172 (28 November 2007).

In both cases, the measures of satisfaction and compensation were complied with considerably fast: 21 months in *Moiwana* and 25 in *Saramaka*, while compliance with restitution and non-repetition measures are far from being achieved. The percentages of complied measures are 33 per cent in the first case and 20 per cent, in the second. The cases have two supervision orders each. In *Moiwana*, two hearings were performed and in *Saramaka*, one.

Regarding satisfaction, in *Moiwana*, the acknowledgment act was performed in 2006 with the presence of the President of the Republic and families of the victims. The measure was declared complied with in 2007.[17] The following year, a memorial was inaugurated in honour of the victims.[18] According to one of the Moiwana's leaders, the monument was a 'visible symbol of the beginning of the healing process', strengthening the collective memory of the massacre.[19] The *Saramaka* decision was published in Dutch and Saramaka language in a newspaper, in the *Official Gazette* and broadcast on the radio in 2010.[20]

Individual compensation was paid in *Moiwana* in 2006.[21] The *Moiwana* development fund was created in 2006 through the institution of a foundation for its management and the payment was parcelled over the following years. However, controversies remained regarding the management and application of the fund. According to the community leader, the management process has been sluggish and time-consuming, generating frustration among the victims.[22] At first, the state refused to pay for travel expenses of the community's representatives to take part in the decision-making. In 2010, the Court ordered the state to ensure the foundation had funds to perform all necessary operative and logistical matters of its mandate, including the community representative's travel expenses. In 2012, the state declared that 20 houses had been constructed with the development fund, but the representatives alleged that they were built without consultation, outside the traditional territory and caused conflict with neighbouring communities. There was no investment on education and health, allegedly because the community had not yet returned to their lands, according to the state. The Court demanded more information regarding the exact location of the houses and the level of participation of the victims in the decision-making process.[23] The *Saramaka*'s development fund was created in 2010 and declared complied with in 2018. The Court did not analyse the management of the fund.[24] If in *Moiwana* only the full and adequate investment of the fund was considered for compliance, in *Saramaka* the mere payment into the fund was considered sufficient.

[17] *Moiwana v Suriname*, Monitoring Compliance (21 November 2007) §§6, 7 and 9.
[18] *Moiwana v Suriname*, Monitoring Compliance (22 November 2010) §§41–4.
[19] Stanley Rench, interviewed by Beristaín, in Beristaín (2009: 229).
[20] *Saramaka v Suriname, Monitoring Compliance* (23 November 2011) §§31–38.
[21] *Moiwana v Suriname* (n 17) §§10.b, 11.c and 19.
[22] Stanley Rench, interviewed by Beristain, in Beristaín (2009).
[23] *Moiwana v Suriname*, Monitoring Compliance (21 November 2018) §§34–43.
[24] *Saramaka v Suriname*, Monitoring Compliance (26 September 2018) §§9–11.

Despite the above-mentioned compliances, domestic implementation in both cases has virtually stopped since 2010. The state has presented a lack of goodwill, not presenting reports or presenting inaccurate reports. It has also overtly expressed the impossibility of compliance with the non-repetition measures, as they allegedly are contrary to domestic legislation. The Court has attempted different approaches, such as hearings, reports and a proposed visit, but so far, they have been unsuccessful. The participation of the victims during supervision has been essential, as the state has alleged compliance with the measures and the representatives have detailed the failure of the adopted steps.

In both cases, in the matter of land demarcation, very few steps were taken. The state reported conflicts between traditional groups over the *Moiwana* territory, while the representatives alleged that they were not consulted.[25] In *Saramaka*, the state reported several attempts to start compliance, all of which were refuted by the representatives. The Court determined that the state had taken no steps to comply and in the 2010 order demanded precise information on the actions undertaken, reiterated again in 2018.[26]

The state of Suriname was unable to guarantee the security in the traditional territory ordered in *Moiwana*. The Court had ordered very specific security measures[27] and the state responded with general security actions. The state reported the construction of police stations, but the Court asserted that it was not enough to guarantee security in the traditional territory. Based upon the representatives' reports, the Court reiterated the existing relationship between investigation of the massacre and the perception of safety by the victims. Since 2007 the state has stuck to this argument and the Court has refused the allegation repeatedly in all measures.[28]

A central concern in *Saramaka*, besides demarcation, is the preservation of natural resources. The Court ordered the review of former concessions for logging (restitution measure) and the duty to perform prior environmental studies before the implementation of any further concession for exploration of natural resources (non-repetition measure). According to the representatives, the concessions were not reviewed and new concessions had been granted without respect to the safeguards established by the Court, causing severe environmental damage. The state did not report on the matter despite the Court's reiterated request for detailed information.[29]

[25] *Moiwana v Suriname* (n 18) §§15–18; (n 23) §§21–25.

[26] *Saramaka v Suriname*, Monitoring Compliance (20 April 2010) §§8–11; (n 20) §8; (n 24) §§19–22.

[27] The Court ordered: 'the State shall send representatives every month to Moiwana Village during the first year, in order to consult with the Moiwana residents. If the community members express concern regarding their safety during those monthly meetings, the State must take appropriate measures to guarantee their security, which shall be designed in strict consultation with said community members': *Moiwana v Suriname* (n 15) §212.

[28] *Moiwana v Suriname* (n 17) §14; (n 18) §§29–33; (n 23) §§35–37.

[29] *Saramaka v Suriname* (n 20) §§13–21; Monitoring Compliance (4 September 2013) §§18–25; (n 24) §§21–23.

In 2013, the representatives requested a provisional measure, considering the state had given a concession for mining within the traditional territory in breach with the Court's safeguards, endangering the survival of the *Saramaka* people. Even though the representatives presented considerable evidence of the concession, including information about its potential risks, the Court denied the provisional measure. It alleged the tribunal would continue to analyse the question during monitoring with compliance. The Court ordered the state to present updated information about mining concessions.[30] The demarcation of the *Saramaka* traditional lands was related to the legal recognition of the *Saramaka* people, restitution measure ordered by the Court. The state had not informed about it in any of the presented reports, so the Court repeatedly demanded detailed information.[31]

The state has presented little information regarding the adoption of legal measures (regulation of the right to consultation, access to justice and land demarcation), and the Court has repeatedly required precise reports.[32] In 2013, the state argued that it was impossibile to comply with the measures as they conflicted with the Surinamese domestic legal system. The Court affirmed that states could not invoke internal legal aspects to avoid compliance with international obligations because of the principle of *pacta sunt servanda*. The Court asserted continued violation of the Convention and ordered the state to present updated information.[33]

The state took no effective steps to investigate the 1986 massacre. It has blamed the massacre survivors for the lack of investigation, as they allegedly refuse to testify, fearing retaliation. The Court has repeatedly stated the importance of the investigations.[34] In 2012 an Amnesty Law was approved, which temporally included the Moiwana massacre. The Law includes an explanatory note affirming it is not applicable to the *Moiwana* investigations, with explicit reference to the Court's decision. However, the juridical force of such declaration is unclear. The Law was declared unconstitutional by the Surinamese Constitutional Court in June 2016 (ICJ, 2017). In the 2018 supervision order, the Court affirmed the contrariety of self-amnesty laws to conventional rights, citing consolidated precedents from the Court in the matter. The analysis of the specific Surinamese legislation was not pursued considering lack of information of its reach.[35]

Another measure with limited compliance was the recovery of mortal remains in *Moiwana*. In December 2008, some remains were found by a simple

[30] *Saramaka v Suriname*, Request for provisional measures and monitoring compliance with judgment, IACtHR (4 September 2013) §§18–25.

[31] *Saramaka v Suriname* (n 26) §§12–15; (n 20) §§27–30; (n 24) §§43–45.

[32] ibid §§16–19; (n 20) §§27–30; (n 24) §§34–35; *Moiwana v Suriname* (n 18) §§24–28; (n 23) §§28–32.

[33] *Saramaka v Suriname* (n 24).

[34] *Moiwana v Suriname* (n 23) §20.

[35] ibid §11.

solicitation made by the General Attorney to the police. In February 2009, the victims performed burial ceremonies in the location, but later stated that they were not sure the remains were indeed those of the massacre victims. In the 2010 order, the Court demanded information regarding the technical means applied by the state to confirm the remains as belonging to the victims of the massacre. The request was reiterated in 2018.[36]

The distinction of two moments in the supervision stage is clear. Between the final judgments and 2010, the state presented detailed reports and demonstrated concern in complying with at least compensation and satisfaction measures. From 2010, the state did not report any effort towards compliance. In fact, the 2018 orders are virtually a reiteration of the 2010 orders, stating the missing points of compliance, their importance for redress and ordering the state to provide information. The abrupt behaviour change is concomitant to government alteration. In August 2010, Desiré Bouterse was elected President of the Republic. During the 1980s he was head of the military government after the 1980 *coup d'état*, governing during the period the Moiwana massacre occurred. He was re-elected in 2015 and was recently condemned as being behind summary executions and torture during the 1980s.[37]

Even though the state promptly complied with satisfaction and compensation measures, the most central remedies for the communities remain far from complied with. Investigation of the massacre in Moiwana and review of the logging concessions in *Saramaka* are unavoidable measures to guarantee the physical and cultural survival of the traditional peoples, and while they are not implemented, the state continues to violate human rights. Despite the struggle and mobilisation of the victims, and despite the Court's attempts to actively promote compliance, the lack of domestic political will prevails, hampering compliance. Even though the state has not directly contested the decision, it has consistently alleged the presence of domestic obstacles for compliance, such as the contrariety of the non-repetition measures with the domestic legislation, or the necessity to provide development for the majority of the population.

In the specific case of Suriname, the design of the measures seems to influence less than the role of domestic actors. The measure to pay the development fund, for example, is vague and, even so, it was promptly complied with in *Saramaka*. On the other hand, the duty to guarantee security in the *Moiwana* traditional lands had a very specific outline, but no steps were taken towards compliance. The state has presented a total lack of political will to comply, hampering completely the implementation of the decisions. In *Saramaka*, the violation of human rights has been promoted with abetment of a multinational company that acquired logging concessions in disrespect of the rights to property and consultation. The lack of mechanisms to make multinational companies

[36] *Moiwana v Suriname* (n 18) §§15–18; (n 23) §§21–25.
[37] See also Ramsoedh (2016); Ramsoeh (2017); Veenendaal (2019).

accountable for the violation, or even to consider them as compliance partners, is a troublesome matter and it should deserve more careful attention.

Considering the failure of the Court's attempt to promote compliance, the application of Article 65.2 of the American Convention was considered. The Article establishes that the Court shall report to the General Assembly of the Organization of American States about states' non-compliance with the Court's decisions. As it is the most extreme measure taken by the Court, it has been applied only in cases of express refusal of the state with regards to compliance. In the territorial cases, the mechanism was never applied, even though it was discussed during *Saramaka*. In 2011, Judge Vio Grossi presented a concurring opinion defending the inclusion of the case in the annual report of the Court presented to the OAS General Assembly. He argued that it was an unavoidable duty of the Court to report all cases of non-compliance and stated that it was inappropriate to consider the mechanism of monitoring compliance as an unlimited extension to comply with the judgment. On the other hand, Judge García-Sayan stated that the application of Article 65 is possible only when 'faced with a state's express refusal to fully or partially comply with that ordered, in addition to the failure of all means of supervision possible'; elements that were not present in the situation. The majority of the judges followed suit.

3.4. THE PARAGUAYAN TRILOGY

There have been three territorial cases against Paraguay: *Yakye Axa* (2005), *Sawhoyamaxa* (2006) and *Xákmok Kásek* (2010).[38] The Indigenous communities were displaced in the twentieth century and their territories sold to private estates. The communities occupied provisional settlements in very precarious conditions, with no access to sources of water and food. Several Indigenous members, mostly children, died because of malnutrition and a lack of healthcare. The Court recognised a violation of the rights to property, cultural identity, dignified life, personal integrity, obligation to respect rights and access to justice. It ordered the demarcation of the traditional lands, the supply of basic services and goods, publication of the judgment, performance of an act of acknowledgment of responsibility, the modification of the Paraguayan land demarcation law, individual compensation and the creation of a development fund. During supervision, the Court has been very active, editing 15 supervisions orders, performing six hearings and visiting the country in 2017.

The percentages of compliance in the cases are 29 in *Yakye Axa*, 25 in *Sawhoyamaxa* and 43 in *Xákmok Kásek*. Since the decisions were issued almost two decades ago, the Paraguayan trilogy is an example of how time is

[38] This section briefly exposes the path towards compliance. In ch 4, the study will be deepened by the analysis of the domestic political context, the influence of further international organs and the current situation of Indigenous peoples in Paraguay.

a determinant for compliance with structural reparation measures, as well as the challenges faced in the interim by the victims. The state has contributed to the supervision, presenting regular reports and slowly adopting steps towards compliance. These efforts, however, are far from sufficient considering the extreme vulnerability of the communities. The long duration of the compliance has been recognised by the Court as a continuous violation of the rights to a dignified life and personal integrity, and domestically it represents a permanent struggle of power.

In *Yakye Axa*, a first attempt to acquire the traditional lands through an expropriation law was frustrated in 2011 by an adverse political scenario, when the community instead accepted alternative lands. In 2014, the state acquired a property, an isolated piece of land among private properties with no accessible path (Correia 2019a). The community refused to move as long as a road was not built. The construction of the road started in 2017 and was halted for two years waiting for expropriation of the lands (Correia 2019a). In December 2019, an expropriation law was approved guaranteeing the road, but in 2020 it was discovered that the law wrongly identified the area to be expropriated,[39] so it was replaced by a law approved in September 2020. The road construction started and the state claimed it was nearly ready, but the representatives contest the adequacy of the road.[40] The acquired lands still lack formal title since they allegedly overlap with another Indigenous land. The Court reinforced the importance of titling and demanded celerity in the process.[41] The Court had ordered the creation of a fund for acquisition of the property. It was created in June 2006[42] and money was transferred in 2010, but in 2013 a considerable sum of money was diverted.[43] In 2015, the state declared it would investigate the diversion and replace the amount.[44] In the 2019 order, the Court declared the measure complied with as the state had already acquired the property.[45] As of June 2022, part of the community still occupied the provisional settlement in very precarious conditions, while the other part occupied the acquired lands despite the absence of an access road.[46]

In *Sawhoyamaxa*, negotiations to buy the lands were unsuccessful until, in 2013, the community occupied the territory. The private landowners

[39] Ministerio de Relaciones Exteriores, 'Presidente Abdo promulgó la ley para el ingreso de la comunidad Yakye Axa a sus tierras ancestrales' (12 October 2019), www.mre.govpy/index.php/noticias-de-embajadas-y-consulados/presidente-abdo-promulgo-la-ley-para-el-ingreso-de-la-comunidad-yakye-axa-sus-tierras-ancestrales.

[40] *Yakye Axa v Paraguay*, Monitoring Compliance (24 June 2022) §§7–8.

[41] ibid.

[42] *Yakye Axa v Paraguay*, Monitoring Compliance (14 December 2007) §§13–17.

[43] The former public servant Rubén Darío Quesnel was sentenced to 10 years of prison for diverting the money. 'Diez años de cárcel para Rubén Quesnel' ABC Color (28 August 2018).

[44] *Yakye Axa, Sawhoyamaxa and Xákmok Kásek v Paraguay*, Monitoring Compliance (24 June 2015) §§41–45.

[45] *Yakye Axa v Paraguay*, Monitoring Compliance (14 May 2019) §§21–31 and §§38–39.

[46] ibid.

(a multinational company) submitted civil and criminal lawsuits against the community and its members, and a ranch house in the property continued to be occupied by the company.[47] One year later, an expropriation law was approved through which the state acquired the property. Three lawsuits were proposed against the expropriation law. The first two were decided by the Supreme Court in favour of the expropriation law. The third one is pending appeal. While the litigation does not end, the state cannot title the land in the name of the community and proceed with the formal delivery of the territory.[48] Both in the 2015 and in the 2017 supervision orders, the Court appreciated the efforts taken by the state regarding the demarcation, despite the large delay.[49] In the 2019 and the 2023 orders, the Court ordered the state to present detailed information about the judicial proceedings and about third-party occupation in the territory, alleged by the representatives.[50] The community currently occupies the territory.

The measure to restore traditional lands in the *Xákmok Kásek* was composed of several elements. The state should title the provisional settlement; delimit, demarcate and title the ancestral territory; annul the effects of a decree that created a natural reserve within the traditional territory; and guarantee no harm to the property before the land demarcation. In September 2011, the state titled the temporary settlement of the community. There was no dispute concerning the compliance, which was declared complied with in 2017.[51] In relation to the Decree that recognised the lands as protected wooded area, it expired in January 2013 and the Court declared the measure complied with in 2019.[52]

The measures to assure demarcation of the ancestral lands were initiated only in 2014 through negotiation with the private owners of the property and the recognition of the community as a legal entity. In the 2015 order, the Court showed concern with the protection of the natural resources within the territory, reminding the state of its obligation not to harm the territory until final demarcation.[53] In 2015, the community occupied the territory and in 2016 a considerable part of the territory (almost 70 per cent) was acquired by the state through purchase and in 2022 it was titled. Despite the advance, the remaining territory is titled to a private company and has undergone severe deforestation. According to the representatives, 'all natural resources were razed'. The lands lost value for the community, which accepted instead alternative lands. In 2020, state and Indigenous peoples reached an agreement regarding the location of alternative lands, but in 2022, considering the state's delay to acquire the lands, the community demanded the original territory instead. Information about the

[47] *Sawhoyamaxa v Paraguay*, Monitoring Compliance (14 May 2019); Correia (2018).
[48] ibid §§16–19.
[49] *Yakye Axa, Sawhoyamaxa and Xákmok Kásek v Paraguay* (n 44) §§17–27; *Yakye Axa, Sawhoyamaxa and Xákmok Kásek v Paraguay*, Monitoring Compliance (30 August 2017) §§7–8.
[50] *Sawhoyamaxa v Paraguay* (n 47) §§20–23.
[51] ibid §§26–27; *Sawhoyamaxa v Paraguay*, Monitoring Compliance (21 March 2023) §§7–11.
[52] *Xákmok Kásek v Paraguay*, Monitoring Compliance (14 May 2019) §§29–32.
[53] *Yakye Axa, Sawhoyamaxa and Xákmok Kásek v Paraguay* (n 44) §§33–40.

attempts to acquire the lands from 2022 onwards are imprecise.[54] The Court recognised the state's efforts towards compliance, but asserted the state's omission to protect the territory and its natural resources, which led to irreparable environmental damage.[55] The Court ordered compensation for delays to the delivery of the property, but so far, the state has not paid such compensation.[56]

In all three cases, displacement from the traditional territories is directly related to the grave situation of vulnerability experienced by the communities, a concerning point in the compliance supervision. The Court ordered the supply of basic goods and services as long as the communities remained landless. However, the state has adopted insufficient steps towards compliance; until 2019 the supply had been sporadic and insufficient, leading to a permanent emergency situation recognised by the state.[57] In at least two of the cases (*Yakye Axa* and *Sawhoyamaxa*), deaths of Indigenous members have been reported because of the state's omission. The Court, through its secretary, had demanded very specific information about the quality and quantity of the provided services and goods, but information provided by the state was still too vague.[58] During the Court's visit in 2017, the grave situation of the communities was considered precarious and dangerous.[59] In the 2022 and 2023 reports, however, there is a considerable improvement on the reported basic services and goods. The state built houses in *Xákmok Kásek* and *Sawhoyamaxa*, has offered regular medical assistance, built latrines and a rainwater reservoir, has donated monthly food kits and created schools. The representatives contest some aspects of the services, such as the inadequacy of the houses and water reservoirs, the absence of emergency health transportation, the insufficiency of the food provided, and the lack of education on the traditional language. The situation is graver in the *Yakye Axa* community, as none of the services are accessible for the members that moved to their newly acquired territory.[60]

One difficulty common to all three cases is the lack of standards under which the compliance with the provision of public services should be analysed. Details of the emergency services, such as amount of water or quality of the sanitation system, were not specified in the judgment and were not known by the representatives or by the state, hindering compliance and supervision (Beristaín 2009). When tailoring the reparation measures, the Court learned from past cases and in subsequent judgments ordered a more precise level of specification regarding basic services and goods. It might seem, though, that it was not decisive for

[54] *Xákmok Kásek v Paraguay*, Monitoring Compliance (19 April 2023) §§7–10.

[55] *Xákmok Kásek v Paraguay*, Monitoring Compliance (n 52) §§12–28.

[56] *Xákmok Kásek v Paraguay*, Monitoring Compliance (n 54) §12.

[57] *Yakye Axa v Paraguay* (n 45); *Sawhoyamaxa v Paraguay*, (n 57); *Xákmok Kásek v Paraguay* (n 52).

[58] ibid, Monitoring Compliance (8 February 2008) §12.

[59] *Yakye Axa v Paraguay*, Monitoring Compliance (n 42) §§8–12.

[60] *Xákmok Kásek v Paraguay* (n 54); *Sawhoyamaxa v Paraguay* (n 51); *Yakye Axa v Paraguay* (n 40).

compliance with the measures, as the state still struggled to comply, despite the specificity of the remedies ordered. In *Xákmok Kásek*, the Court tried to overcome the problem by ordering the state to prepare, with support from experts, a detailed report on the required services and goods, but the state did not comply. A similar claim was made in the *Sawhoyamaxa* supervision order, also pending compliance. In the most recent supervision order, the Court convened an on-site public hearing, so it could obtain first-hand information on the implementation. There is no data on whether the hearing occurred.[61]

The implementation of a system for emergency communication was ordered in *Sawhoyamaxa* and *Xákmok Kásek*, and compliance was analysed only in the former. After receiving information about its installation and operation in 2008 the Court declared compliance.[62] However, in 2009, the representatives were informed that no one was in charge of answering the calls at the local hospital.[63] In the same year, the Court ordered the state to present more information in that matter,[64] but in posterior orders this point was not analysed. Paraguay implemented a documentation and registration programme in November 2017, establishing regular campaigns in the three litigating Indigenous communities aiming to provide birth certificates and identity card,s and the Court declared the measure complied with in 2019.[65]

The measure to pay collective compensation through the creation of a development fund is characterised, in all three cases, by reiterated delay and partial compliance. The state started to pay into the fund in 2019 and paid the following quotas in the subsequent year, but the representatives contested the exchange rate. A tripartite committee for fund management was created in each case. In 2019 the Court declared partial compliance.[66] Specifically in *Yakye Axa*, in 2019 the Court considered it grave that instead of applying the fund on its permanent lands, the community would have to use it to attend the emergency situation in which they were living.[67] As the situation persisted into 2022, the Court ordered the state to reimburse the expenditures that tended to 'situations of imperative need, which do not coincide with the purposes envisaged in the decision'.[68]

Individual compensation was ordered in *Sawhoyamaxa* and *Xákmok Kásek*. In the first, the amount was deposited in 2007 and the Court declared partial compliance in 2008 (because of controversies regarding an interest in arrears) and full compliance in 2023. In the second, the amount was deposited in 2017 and declared complied with in 2023. It is concerning that the representatives

[61] ibid.
[62] *Sawhoyamaxa v Paraguay*, Monitoring Compliance (8 February 2008) §§36–39.
[63] *Sawhoyamaxa v Paraguay*, Monitoring Compliance (20 May 2009) §§27–28.
[64] ibid.
[65] *Xákmok Kásek v Paraguay* (n 52), §§33–37; *Sawhoyamaxa v Paraguay* (n 52) §§33–36.
[66] *Yakye Axa v Paraguay* (n 45) §§42–49; *Sawhoyamaxa v Paraguay* (n 49) §§26–30; *Xákmok Kásek v Paraguay* (n 52) §§38–46.
[67] *Yakye Axa v Paraguay* (n 45) §§42–49.
[68] *Yakye Axa v Paraguay* (n 40).

alleged, after receiving the monetary compensation, that some state employees were refusing assistance, saying they should use the compensation to acquire basic goods and services by themselves.[69] It is a clear misunderstanding regarding the reparative aim of the compensation and the state's duties to provide basic services.

The Court ordered the same non-repetition measure in the three cases, ie the adaptation of domestic legislation in order to guarantee Indigenous peoples ownership rights over traditional territory. Information about compliance is scarce. The representatives alleged that the state had not taken any steps and the Court had repeatedly requested further information.[70]

The act of acknowledgement of international responsibility was ordered in *Yakye Axa* and *Xákmok Kásek*. In the former, the act was performed in the community, in August 2006; in the second, the Court affirmed in 2023 that the state had not presented enough information.[71] An act was celebrated in 2019 with the presence of the President of the Republic, in which the payment of the first instalment of the development fund was delivered, but it is not clear whether it was the act of acknowledgment of responsibility.[72] In *Sawhoyamaxa*, even though the act was not ordered, in June 2019 the state delivered part of the development fund in a public act with the presence of the community and the President of the Republic (MRE, 2019).

In all three cases, the judgment was published in the *Official Gazette* and none were published in a newspaper with national circulation. The measure was declared partially complied with in 2008 (*Sawhoyamaxa*[73]) and 2017 (*Yakye Axa* and *Xákmok Kásek*).[74] The radio broadcast of the judgments of *Yakye Axa* and *Sawhoyamaxa* was took place in 2009 and the measure was declared complied with in 2017.[75]

Despite advances, the long duration of the supervision and the maintenance of the communities living in wretched conditions years after the judicial victory highlights the challenges faced domestically. Demarcation of the lands, a central reparation measure, depended on the legislature (expropriation law) and the judiciary (easement lawsuit and actions against the expropriation law). The state is aware of the emergency endured by the communities and the distressing delay cannot be merely attributed to bureaucratic malfeasance, but instead, as

[69] IACtHR. Resolución de la Presidenta de la Corte Interamericana de Derechos Humanos de 20 de Mayo de 2009, op cit, §§14–16.

[70] *Xákmok Kásek v Paraguay* (n 54); *Sawhoyamaxa v Paraguay* (n 51); *Yakye Axa v Paraguay* (n 40).

[71] *Yakye Axa*, *Sawhoyamaxa* and *Xákmok Kásek v Paraguay* (n 49) §§23–25; *Xákmok Kásek v Paraguay* (n 54).

[72] *Xákmok Kásek v Paraguay* (n 52) §§38–46.

[73] *Sawhoyamaxa v Paraguay* (n 62) §§48–51.

[74] *Yakye Axa, Sawhoyamaxa and Xákmok Kásek v Paraguay* (n 49) §7. In the *Yakye Axa* case, despite the late declaration of compliance, the implementation was timely, but the state did not present the Court sufficient evidence.

[75] *Yakye Axa, Sawhoyamaxa and Xákmok Kásek v Paraguay* (n 49) §§8–11.

affirmed by Correia, it reproduces racialised structural violence, in which the Indigenous people are in a state of liminality as 'rights-bearing subjects who are subject to the abandonment of their rights' (Correia 2018).

Just as in *Saramaka*, the lack of accountability mechanisms regarding private business has been a hindrance for compliance, as in all three cases the private companies that owned the territories refused to collaborate by negotiating the properties. In *Yakye Axa*, the conflict also expanded to private properties through which the access road would be built. The *Xákmok Kásek* seems to be in an even graver situation, as it has been alleged that the company deliberately deforested the area in order to avoid expropriation.

The development of compliance strategies of all involved actors has been a very interesting turning point. The state has created domestic mechanisms for implementation of the decisions (an interdisciplinary commission and an online software with international recommendations), the Indigenous peoples have consolidated important partnerships with international NGOs, and the Court has stimulated compliance through visits, hearings and joint supervision.

3.5. PROMPT, BUT PARTIAL: COMPLIANCE IN THE CASES AGAINST PANAMA AND ECUADOR

Kuna de Madungandí y Emberá de Bayano v Panama (2014) focuses on third-party occupation and illegal logging in the traditional territory, as well as the lack of official land titles. The state was held responsible for violating the rights to collective property, judicial protection, access to justice and the obligation to respect rights. As a form of reparation, the Court ordered the publication of the judgment, the performance of an act of acknowledgment, restitution of the traditional territory and payment of collective compensation. The Court visited the country in 2015 and published two supervision orders. The case was the one with the shortest compliance time among all Indigenous territorial cases (approximately 11 months), as well as the case with highest rate of compliance (60 per cent of fully complied measures).

The written publication of the judgment was published in the *Official Gazette* in May 2015 and in a journal with national coverage in April 2015. The decision is also available on the website of the Ministry of Foreign Affairs. The judgment was broadcast between August and October 2015 on national radio. The representatives contested the broadcast, as it was late in the evening. The Court declared the measure complied with, as there was no specific detail in the reparation measure regarding the time of the broadcast.[76] The act of acknowledgment of responsibility was performed on 13 October 2015, with the presence

[76] *Kuna of Madungandí and Emberá of Bayano v Panama*, Monitoring Compliance (23 May 2017) §§8–11.

of the President of the Republic and other high-ranking ministers. The ceremony was executed simultaneously in Spanish and in Indigenous languages, was covered by the media, and the victims and its representatives were present. The representatives complained that they were not consulted regarding the date, and several members could not participate on the day chosen by the state. However, the Court declared the measure complied with.[77] The act of acknowledgement also marked the delivery of the collective compensation ordered by the Court. The payment was undisputed.[78]

The Court's 2015 visit to the communities was considered essential to obtain first-hand information on the challenges to and proposals for compliance on territorial restitution, demonstrating the state's goodwill towards Indigenous peoples.[79] The Emberá de Ipeti's traditional territory was titled in 2015 and, since the measure was uncontested, the Court declared partial compliance. The territories of the communities Ipetí and Piratí Emberá had not even been demarcated and the Court was able to identify, during the visit, third-party occupation of the traditional lands, increasing concern about the compliance delay. Regarding an overlapping private title within the Emberá's territory, purchase of the property failed. As strategy against the expropriation, the private owner had divided and sold the estate. The state expropriated the land, but a lawsuit contesting the value of the lands halted the proceedings. The Court recalled the importance of land titling for the community and ordered the state to inform on further progress.[80]

A similar pattern of prompt and partial compliance is observed in *Kichwa de Sarayaku v Ecuador* (2012). The case regards oil exploration concessions in traditional lands. The state was held responsible for violating rights to collective property, judicial protection and access to justice, life, personal integrity and the obligation to respect rights. As a form of reparation, the Court ordered the publication of the decision, the performance of an act of acknowledgment of responsibility, the payment of monetary compensation, the removal of explosives buried throughout the territory, the adoption of legislation measures to guarantee the right to consultation, the implementation of mandatory courses in Indigenous rights and the guarantee that no further project affecting the traditional territory would be undertaken without procedural safeguards. The Court issued one supervision order and performed one public hearing, both in 2016.

Ecuador has presented a great amount of effort towards achieving compliance with the case, as it has a comparatively high rate of compliance (43 per cent of complied measures), with an average time of compliance of two years. The state alleged it had implemented, between 2012 and 2014, courses on the collective rights of peoples of Ecuador. The representatives, however, argued there was not enough evidence to support the adequacy and the continuity

[77] ibid §§12–17.
[78] ibid §§19–20.
[79] ibid §§4 and 18.
[80] *Kuna of Madungandí and Emberá of Bayano v Panama* (n 76) §§5–20.

of the programme.[81] Even though the Court recognised the adequacy of the content of the course, it considered that there was not enough evidence regarding the compulsory requirement and the permanence of the courses. The Court requested more information from the state and declared the measure partially complied with.[82]

Regarding satisfaction measures, two acts of acknowledgment of international responsibility were performed. The first was performed in November 2013 and transmitted on a national TV station. The Court had been consulted about the definition of 'senior state authorities', explaining that the participation of the President of the Republic could be replaced by state ministers. The act was celebrated by the Justice Minister, who not only accepted responsibility, but also apologised to the *Kichwa* people. The Commission and the representatives disputed the compliance with the act. In October 2014, following a consultation with the community, a second act was performed inside the Sarayaku territory. The state apologised to the Sarayaku people and to the 'protector beings of the living forest'. The act was performed in both Spanish and *Kichwa*. The representatives still disputed compliance, pointing out, among other things, the absence of the President of the Republic and the content of the speech. The Court, however, considered the measure complied with.[83] The judgment was published in the *Official Gazette*, in a national newspaper and on the state's websites.[84] The radio announcement was broadcast in September 2014 on four different stations in Spanish, *Kichwa* and *Shuar* after consulting with the people.[85] The Court declared the measure complied with, but asserted that it would have been useful if the representatives had been previously informed about the exact time of the announcement. The payment of monetary compensation was made in July 2013 and, as there was no dispute regarding compliance, it was declared complied with.

Despite this progress, the most pressing issues for the victims, regarding full restitution of the territory, have not been implemented, generating suspicion and insecurity. The measures to restore full use and enjoyment of the territory (through the removal of explosives buried on the territory), as well as the non-repetition measures to consult with the community and to adopt legislation measures, are still pending compliance. On the 2016 hearing, the state alleged that the safer method to deal with the explosives would be to leave them buried so they would naturally decompose, while the victims' representatives alleged the permanence of the explosives to be a violation of their right to collective property. The Commission highlighted the lack of evidence regarding the security of the explosives. With regards to the obligation to consult the community in any future concessions in the territory, as well as to perform prior

[81] *Kichwa of Sarayaku v Ecuador, Monitoring Compliance* (22 June 2016) §§7–8.
[82] ibid §§10–14.
[83] ibid §§16–25.
[84] ibid §§27–29.
[85] ibid §30.

environmental studies, the representatives announced that, in 2016, 91 per cent of their traditional territory was currently impacted by oil extraction concessions, which had not been preceded by consultation. Besides, the Commission explained that the interested companies, instead of the state, had performed prior environmental studies in violation of the Court's parameters.[86] On the matter of the non-repetition measure, the regulation of prior consultation, in July 2012 (only one month after the decision), the state adopted Decree 1247, regulating the right to free, prior and informed consultation in cases involving oil concessions. The Ecuadorian Indigenous peoples were not consulted before its adoption and the victims' representatives alleged that the Decree did not follow the Court's standards on consultation.

In conclusion, even though Ecuador has promptly complied with compensation and satisfaction measures, demonstrating recognition and concern with the Court's authority, the most central measures, related to full use and enjoyment of the territory, are still pending compliance and there is not even agreement on the strategies for implementation. It seems likely that conflicts in the matter of oil concessions in the Sarayaku territory will remain an intricate conflict, thus postponing compliance. In November 2019, the victims' representatives proposed a lawsuit before the Ecuadorian Constitutional Court, claiming compliance with the three remaining reparation measures through an implementation action foreseen in the 2008 Ecuadorian Constitution, Article 93. In December 2023, a decision was published, which considered the Court's reparation measures clear, explicit and enforceable, as well as recognising the state's non-compliance. The decision ordered the Ministry of Women and Human Rights to coordinate compliance with the removal of the explosives and the obligation to consult. It also ordered the National Assembly to systematise and consolidate the draft laws on free, prior and informed consultation. Finally, it ordered as a satisfaction measure the issuance of public apologies for the delayed compliance, which should be affixed in public buildings and on the state's webpage. The orders should be complied with within six months.[87]

3.6. FIRST STEPS TOWARDS COMPLIANCE: COLOMBIA, HONDURAS, BRAZIL AND ARGENTINA

Operation Genesis v Colombia reveals the difficulties of compliance in a context of transitional justice. This case involves internal conflict and the

[86] IACtHR, '116 Período Ordinario de Sesiones – Del 21 de noviembre al 2 de diciembre de 2016; Audiencia pública de supervisión de cumplimiento de sentencia: Entre las 14:30 a las 16:00 del 2 de diciembre se celebrará una audiencia pública sobre la supervisión de cumplimiento de sentencia en el caso Pueblo Indígena Kichwa de Sarayaku Vs. Ecuador' (online video).

[87] Sentencia 60-19-AN/23. *Mirian Liduvina Cisneros et al v State of Ecuador*, Corte Constitucional de Ecuador, 20 December 2023.

forced displacement of Afro-Colombian communities, as well as the murder of the community leader, followed by a lack of investigation. Colombia was held responsible for violating rights to collective property, judicial protection and access to justice, life, personal integrity, the obligation to respect rights, rights of the child and freedom of movement. As a measure of reparation, the Court ordered an investigation into the facts, publication of the decision, act of acknowledgment of responsibility, rehabilitation, individual compensation for the next of kin of the murdered leader, inclusion of the victims in the domestic restitution program, restoration of full use and enjoyment of the territory and security guarantees in the territory. So far, the Court has issued three supervision orders and held two supervision hearings.

The measure to publish the judgment was complied with in 2014. The representatives did not present any dispute and the Court declared the measure complied with in 2016.[88] Besides written publication, both parties presented the intention to further publicise the measure by audio-visual and oral media, as well as locally, even though this was not ordered by the Court. A broadcast of the judgment occurred on a local radio station.[89] An act of acknowledgment of responsibility was performed in March 2023 and the measure was declared complied with in August 2023.[90] In 2023 the Court recognised the lack of substantive advances on the investigation and the lack of due diligence by the state. Regarding rehabilitation, the state had included the victims on a national programme of psychological assistance, but the representatives alleged it did not comply with the Court's criteria. The Court recognised the non-compliance and indicated for the state a series of actions to be taken in an effort to adequately comply with the decision. The restitution of full use and enjoyment of the territory is proceeding according to the Decree 4635/2011, that regulates the restitution of property within the national transitional justice. Even though the state has initiated the process, the representatives allege the advances are insufficient. The security of the region remains a complex matter. The victims have returned to part of their territory, but have denounced increasing insecurity caused by armed groups (*neo-paramilitares*). The insecurity is aggravated by the omission from the armed forces to implement the security plan. The Court reiterated the importance of the measure for securing the life of the community members.[91]

In 2015 the state paid the stipulated compensation to the widow of the victim, and in 2023 the Court ordered more information regarding the payment to the victim's siblings and children. The Court declared partial compliance. Lastly, the Court had ordered the payment of collection compensation via the domestic

[88] *Operación Génesis v Colombia*, Monitoring Compliance (20 October 2016) §§5–9.
[89] ibid §8.
[90] *Operación Génesis v Colombia*, Monitoring Compliance (30 August 2023).
[91] ibid.

reparation programme, in deference to the transitional justice process. However, the parties disputed the domestic legislation applicable: the state claimed the land restitution law is applicable (Decree 4800), while the representatives alleged the decree on reparation for traditional people was applicable (Decree 4635). The representatives brought forth a domestic judicial decision in their favour. Despite the deference given by the Court to the state for payment, during the supervision the Court had to decide which domestic law was applicable. It ordered the state to present more detailed information on the controversy. There were also some incongruencies regarding the name of the victims: the state said it had rectified some errors, but it did not include all corresponding documents. The state demonstrated it had paid almost half of the victims' compensation, so the Court declared partial compliance.[92]

The case *Xucuru v Brazil* (2018) has two supervision orders, issued in 2019 and 2023. The case regards third-party occupation of Indigenous territory. The Court declared violation of the rights to collective property, judicial protection and access to justice, and the obligation to respect rights, ordering the state to publish the decision, implement a development fund, perform title clearance and provisionally protect the territory. The decision was published in the *Official Gazette* and on the state website on 2018, and the Court declared the measure complied with.[93] The state and the Indigenous association reached a compensation agreement in November 2019. The compensation would be directly transferred to the association and it would be applied according to an activities plan. The money was transferred in January 2020. The parties involved altered the form of compliance of the measure, which should be through a development fund. The Court decided to respect the celebrated agreement and declared the measure complied with. However, it stated that the agreement should not restrict the Indigenous right to self-determination, nor impose strict accounting measures upon the community.[94] The restitution of the territory remains pending compliance and the Court has not manifested on the matter.

In Honduras two cases involve the Garífuna people (*Garífuna de Punta Piedra* and *Garífuna Triunfo de la Cruz*), both decided in 2014. Both cases are concerned with the restoration of full use and enjoyment of the lands, which had been hampered by third-party occupation, mining concessions and protected wooded areas, and had caused extreme violence related to land disputes. In both cases, Honduras was held responsible for violating rights to collective property, judicial protection and access to justice and the obligation to respect rights.

In both cases, the Court ordered the publication of the judgment, an investigation into the murders of community leaders, compensation through development fund, full restitution of the ancestral lands and a non-repetition

[92] ibid.
[93] *Xucuru v Brazil*, Monitoring compliance (22 November 2019) §§5–7.
[94] ibid (26 June 2023).

measure to adapt the property registration system. In *Triunfo de la Cruz*, the Court also ordered the performance of an act of acknowledgment of responsibility. In *Punta Piedra*, the Court ordered the reform of the mining code. The Court issued one supervision order in each case in 2019 and two joint supervision orders in 2021. Additionally, a private hearing was performed in 2021.

A first step towards compliance was the publication of the judgments, ordered in both cases in written media and on the radio. Written publication took place in 2016 and the decision was broadcast in the same year on a local radio station. The representatives argued that the community had not consented with the details of the publication, while the Court explained that only information was necessary, not consent. There was controversy regarding the way the decision was translated into the Garífuna language, since the representatives alleged that the translation was incomprehensible. In 2019, the Court considered that compliance with the measure entails a good faith effort to translate the order, and that the translation should be understandable to the community.[95] After information presented by the state, the Court declared the measure complied with in 2023.[96] Regarding pecuniary compensation, in both cases the state created a trust fund in 2016, but the community refused to receive the funds as long as the title clearance was not concluded. In 2020, the state confirmed that it had paid almost half of the compensation. The Court declared the measure partially complied with.[97]

In 2016, the state created the Inter-Institutional Commission for Compliance with International Decisions (CICSI) by order of Decree 01/2016, complying with the measure to coordinate domestic implementation of the decisions. The representatives questioned the measure, alleging that, since the reparation measures had not yet been complied with, the coordination mechanism was ineffective. The Court dismissed the question, alleging that the measure was to create the coordination mechanism and not its effectiveness, and declared the measure complied with.[98]

The central measures ordered – restitution of the territories – are pending compliance and have been the cause of intense conflicts. While the state alleged difficulties with full compliance, the representatives reported that very few effective steps had been taken. The only effective advance in the protection of the traditional lands is related to mining concessions in the *Garífuna de Punta Piedra* territory that was not consulted upon; the Court had ordered the cessation of mining activity. The concession was annulled in February 2017.

[95] *Garífuna Triunfo de la Cruz v Honduras*, Monitoring Compliance (14 May 2019) §§34–39; *Garífuna Punta Piedra v Honduras*, Monitoring Compliance (14 May 2019) §§32–37.

[96] *Garífuna Triunfo de la Cruz and Garífuna Punta Piedra v Honduras*, Monitoring Compliance (30 April 2021).

[97] ibid §§7–8.

[98] *Garífuna Punta Piedra v Honduras* (n 95) §§21–30.

Even though the representatives had contested compliance, as the decree could still be reviewed judicially, the Court declared the measure complied with.[99]

Particularly regarding title clearance in both cases, in 2017, a timetable was established after consultation with the communities and, in the same year, negotiations started with third-party occupants. The private occupants were hostile towards the public evaluation of the properties and announced that they were unwilling to leave the lands. Specifically in *Triunfo de la Cruz*, the state initiated an evaluation of the lands for expropriation, estimating a preliminarily value of more than US$100,000,000. Considering the high amount, the state offered the representatives alternative lands instead. The representatives criticised the long delay and the lack of effective steps taken by the state. They also contested the method of evaluation and affirmed that the high value of the lands was not an excuse for the violation of human rights, thus refusing alternative lands. They further explained that the state had been acquiescent with regards to continuous harm in the traditional lands caused by third-party occupation. With regards to the demarcation and title to the Punta Piedra territory, in 2018, the measurement of the area started. The Court recognised some of the advances, but criticised the delay. The state had argued that the delay was due to controversies regarding boundaries of the territory. In answer to this, the Court reiterated that it was the state's duty to identify and demarcate the traditional lands, which should be carried out with maximum diligence.[100] In both cases, the Court reiterated that title clearance is the central measure to obtain redress for the victims, and that alternative lands should be offered exclusively in case of an 'objectively justified impossibility'. The Court considered that the state had not used all available possibilities to obtain the property, but instead had merely adopted procedural actions. It also recognised that non-compliance generates internal crisis in the community and increases conflicts such as threats and violent acts.[101] The 2023 order reiterates the 2019 arguments and the Court reinforces the urgency of the land demarcation and title clearance considering the escalating violence and the permanent violation of rights.[102]

In *Triunfo de la Cruz*, full use and enjoyment of the lands had been hampered by the declaration of a protected wooded area. The state presented a project for the management of protected wooded areas in traditional territories, alleging it had been prepared in consultation with the community. On the other hand, the representatives alleged that they had not been consulted and the project ignored traditional knowledge of the Garífuna people. They also announced that access to the protected area had been denied and that land titles within the territory had been granted. The Court recognised the progress made and the importance

[99] ibid §§17–19.
[100] ibid §§6–12.
[101] *Garífuna Triunfo de la Cruz v Honduras* (n 95) §§7–25; *Garífuna Punta Piedra v Honduras* (n 95) §§13–15.
[102] *Garífuna Triunfo de la Cruz and Garífuna Punta Piedra v Honduras* (n 96).

of the project, but suggested that the state should work in consultation with the traditional people. The Court requested more information regarding the community's access to the lands.[103]

Regarding the non-repetition measures, the Court had ordered, in both cases, the adaptation of the property registry system in order to avoid overlapping titles to property. The state affirmed that it had adapted the registration system and improved cooperation among state's organs on the matter. The Court recognised the importance of the alterations and the steps taken, but required more information on the matter.[104] Exclusively in *Punta Piedra*, the Court had ordered the adaptation of the Mining Code to guarantee the right to free, prior and informed consultation. The state informed three measures on that matter: in November 2015, the Preliminary Draft Law on Free, Prior and Informed Consultation with Indigenous and Afro-Descendent Peoples was approved; the National Congress discussed changes in the Mining Code; and in 2017, the Supreme Court of Justice had declared that some articles of the Mining Code unconstitutional, applying international standards in the matter of consultation with traditional peoples. Even though the Court recognised these advances, it considered that the current state of the legislation and the effect of the unconstitutionality decision upon traditional peoples' right to consultation were still not clear. The Court declared that the measure was pending compliance and demanded more information about each of the elements informed by the state.[105]

In *Punta Piedra*, the state and the representatives agreed to perform the act of acknowledgment of responsibility only when at least some of the other remedies were complied with, but the Court stated that both parties should agree to perform the act as soon as possible.[106] Lastly, the Court had ordered an investigation into and the prosecution and punishment of the murder of Indigenous leaders in both cases. According to the state, the public prosecution had created a task force to investigate the murders and proceeded with conducting a preliminary investigation. The state also announced that prison was ordered by decree against any suspect of the murder, while some other suspects had been murdered. The representatives alleged that the steps taken were very preliminary and no considerable advance was observed. The Court reiterated that the investigation was to follow all available mechanisms, thus avoiding any omission. The Court suggested that the investigations should consider the existing land conflict, urging the state to conclude the investigations in a reasonable amount of time. The 2023 order reiterates the 2019 order.[107]

[103] *Garífuna Triunfo de la Cruz v Honduras* (n 95) §§44–48; *Garífuna Triunfo de la Cruz and Garífuna Punta Piedra v Honduras* (n 96) §§40–42.

[104] *Garífuna Triunfo de la Cruz and Garífuna Punta Piedra v Honduras* (n 96) §§43–47.

[105] ibid §§9–11.

[106] ibid.

[107] *Garífuna Triunfo de la Cruz v Honduras* (n 95) §§27–32; *Garífuna Punta Piedra v Honduras* (n 95) §§53–56.

Honduras has complied with compensation and satisfaction measures, but it has taken very few steps on the most substantive measures, restitution and accountability. The only considerable measure complied with was the annulment of mining concessions in *Punta Piedra*, as all other steps have been disputed by the representatives and questioned by the Court. The prompt creation of a domestic commission for implementation could be considered a sign of good faith towards compliance, but it is merely a procedural measure with no direct impact upon the Garífuna's land situation. While the substantive measures are not complied with, violence in the region has increased. Between 2019 and 2020 alone, five Garifuna leaders were killed, including one from Punta Piedra. In 2020, five members from Triunfo de la Cruz, including a community leader, were abducted at gunpoint by men in police uniform. Despite the Court issuing precautionary measures in their defence in August and September 2020, the representative NGO alleges very little was done to investigate the violent acts and to protect the members of the community. The Court recognised the correlation between the lack of compliance with the case and the extreme gravity and urgence of the violent outbreak in the communities. The Court insisted that, if the grave state omission persisted, it could apply Article 65 of the Convention.[108]

Lastly, *Lhaka Honhat v Argentina* (2020) is the most recent case issued and has only one supervision order. The case involves third-party occupation of traditional territory and it was the first time the Court recognised the direct justiciability of social rights within the territorial cases. So far, the only measure declared partially complied with is the publication of the decision. The written publication was complied with within the six-month term, but there is not enough information about radio transmission in the Indigenous language. One very peculiar aspect of the case is that in 2022 the parties reached an agreement for the implementation of the decision, containing detailed goals for compliance with some of the measures. The Court celebrated the efforts and dialogue undertaken, and homologated the agreement.[109]

3.7. WHY DO STATES COMPLY WITH TERRITORIAL CASES?

The analysis of the implementation in territorial cases must be complemented by an understanding of the elements that fomented and hindered compliance in order to highlight success strategies that could be used in other cases, as well as to avoid elements that delayed the implementation process. Past research has developed multiple theories on why states comply with the Inter-American case law, but so far, no study has analysed specifically the applicability of these elements to territorial cases.

[108] ibid.
[109] *Lhaka Honhat v Argentina*, Monitoring Compliance (7 February 2023).

The reasons why states comply with decisions issued by international courts can be divided into four areas: features of the measure issued; domestic laws and institutions; engagement of domestic actors; and the Court's role. In the first area – features of the issued measure – some categories of measures (compensation and satisfaction) have superior rates of compliance, while measures with a higher cost and/or grater complexity for the state have low compliance, for example accountability measures (Basch et al 2010; Hawkins and Jacoby 2010; Hillebrecht 2014; Gonzalez-Salzberg 2017) and structural measures (Huneeus 2015). Compliance varies according to which domestic organ(s) is (are) in charge of implementation, since 'the more separate state branches or institutions an injunctive order involves, the less likely its implementation becomes' (Huneeus 2011). Lastly, vagueness of remedies can provoke delays, resistance and outright defiance (Staton and Romero 2019).

In the second area, the existence and consolidation of domestic laws and institutions aimed at complying with international decisions are seen as a central factor for compliance (Krsticevic 2007; Ayala et al 2007; Baluarte and Vos 2010; Rodríguez-Garavito and Kauffman 2015). In contrast, however, Torelly (2017) argues that constitutional architecture alone does not influence the impact of international adjudication, and Anzola et al (2014) asserts that legal factors do not explain contrasting levels of compliance among cases against the same country.

Third, domestic actors are a central factor of compliance, both within the state and from civil society. In relation to the former, states are not monolithic structures and international litigation reinforces domestic organs that work in the protection of human rights, thus boosting compliance (Vos 2013; Soley and Steininger 2018; Engstrom et al 2016; Parra-Vera 2019). Particular attention has been given to domestic courts when implementing international decisions. (Huneeus 2011; Skaar 2013; Torelly 2017; Kunz 2019). Non-governmental organisations play a very important role in compliance, as they have used strategic litigation in the IAS to achieve collective goals, boosting constitutional change domestically and mobilising society around a specific political agenda (Cavallaro and Brewer 2008; Cavallaro and Schaffer 2006; Gonzalez-Salzberg 2017; Soley 2019). Hillebrecht, evaluating the influence of domestic political actors such as NGOs, independent judiciaries and political parties, pursued a comprehensive study regarding compliance and domestic politics. The author identifies three mechanisms of compliance: signalling a commitment to human rights, both to the state's constituents and to the international community; setting and advancing domestic human rights agenda according to preferences or as a political cover in difficult policies reforms; and begrudging compliance through long-standing democratic preferences (Hillebrecht 2014).

The last block is the role of the international court, both during the supervision procedure and beyond it. During the supervision, the realisation of hearings has been a considerable improvement, enabling dialogue with the parties (Baluarte and Vos 2010; Huneeus 2014; Rodríguez-Garavito and Kauffman 2015;

Engstrom et al 2016) as well as the on-site procedures and the joint supervision of cases (Baluarte and Vos 2010). Beyond the supervision procedure, the Court engagement with domestic actors could transform them into compliance partners, including the national justice system (Huneeus 2011), social movements (Cavallaro and Brewer 2008; Engstrom and Low 2019), or widely disseminating of the decisions among the society (Gómez 2008).

The qualitative study on selected cases within a specific area revealed that a complex bundle of specific actors and structures influences compliance on different levels, according to the subject of the decisions and the parties involved. The territorial cases decided by the Court are not only at the forefront of the international protection of Indigenous peoples; they also constitute part of a recent turn of the Court in the protection of vulnerable groups through a transformative approach, recognising social and economic rights. The case law portraits multiple unique features considering parties involved, factual background, recognised rights and expansive reparation measures. This distinctiveness imposes different processes of implementation, with the emergence of new elements as well as the adjustment of those presented above. The understanding of the influent factors provides elements for the development of more adequate and improved strategies for litigators, social movements and civil society in defending territorial rights and, more broadly, socio-economic rights. It also enables international tribunals and bodies to reevaluate their strategies in protecting social, cultural and economic rights.

One caveat before analysing the cases: almost all states involved (except Suriname) have already constitutionally guaranteed the Indigenous rights to collective property and the right to cultural identity. This means that the implementation of the decision is a matter of implementation of the domestic legislation, and some variables involved in compliance with the international decision might be the same ones hindering domestic effectiveness of territorial rights. In other words, the roots of the violation are, simultaneously, the cause of the lack of compliance with the Court's reparation measure. This relationship must be considered when analysing each of the variables indicated.

Considering their application to the territorial case law, it was possible to divide the influent factors presented into three categories: blocking, constricting and enabling. While enabling factors favour full and prompt compliance, constricting factors promote delayed and partial compliance. None of the elements in the two categories are decisive for compliance and the observed result is a counterbalance of multiple factors, promoting unique and complex implementation processes. On the contrary, blocking factors are the ones that, by themselves, are decisive for non-compliance, even if multiple enabling factors are present. In the present study, the identified enabling factors include: the consolidation of legal and institutional mechanisms aimed at compliance; political low-cost reparation measures; the active role of the Court; the consolidated networks in civil society; and the existence of domestic thresholds for the implementation of Indigenous rights. On the other hand, constricting factors include: the involvement of multiple state powers; vagueness in reparation measures; and the relationship between private actors and human rights accountability. Lastly, the only blocking factor observed was incomplete transition to democracy.

Regarding the existence and consolidation of legal and institutional mechanisms in the domestic system aimed at compliance with international decisions, the Paraguayan cases reveal that domestic institutions indeed facilitate implementation, even though they alone were not a determinant factor. The creation of state organs for implementation[110] was followed by improvements in the implementation of the decisions, facilitating dialogue with victims and among state branches, evidencing the importance of domestic institutions for the coordination of the implementation. However, the creation of both organs itself shows a previous commitment of the state to compliance, which was only facilitated after their constitution, but not determined by them. The creation of the institutions is simultaneously an impact of the Court's orders and a cause of improvement on compliance.

The Court itself has recognised this contribution, demanding in two subsequent territorial cases against Honduras and Suriname the implementation of 'the necessary inter-institutional coordination mechanisms in order to ensure the effectiveness of the measures established'.[111] Honduras implemented the SIMOREH[112] and created a CICSI, which assumed a leading role in implementation, coordinating the steps towards compliance. However, in both of the Honduran cases, the creation of the CICSI was indicated by the victims' representatives as merely preliminary procedural steps towards compliance, with no real impact on the communities' territorial condition.

A generally low level of compliance with non-repetition and accountability measures is perceived among the territorial cases, as they involve multiple and separated state organs. The element can also be perceived in the protection of the traditional territory, as detailed in the Paraguayan cases: the involvement of the judiciary and of the legislature has halted the delivery of the ancestral lands in *Yakye Axa* and *Sawhoyamaxa*, even when the judiciary was not directly in charge of implementation (the constitutionality lawsuit in *Sawhoyamaxa*, and easement actions in *Yakye Axa*, both regarding the restitution measures). Similar judiciary involvement is also present in *Kichwa de Sarayaku* and *Kuna de Madungandí*, even though in the former the judicial decision could propel compliance.

It has been stated that compensation and satisfaction measures are easily complied with, as they represent low political costs for the state (Hawkins and Jacoby 2010), are usually clear (Staton and Romero 2019) and are usually

[110] Comisión Interinstitucional para el Cumplimiento de las Sentencias Internacionales (CICSI) and Sistema de Monitoreo de Recomendaciones (SIMORE).
[111] *Garífuna Punta Piedra v Honduras*; *Kaliña and Lokono v Suriname*, Merits, Reparations and Costs, IACtHR Series C No 309 (25 November 2015).
[112] Honduras, SIMOREH, simoreh.sedh.gob.hn/buscador/home.

implemented directly by the executive (Huneeus 2011). Indeed, satisfaction measures have been complied with, at least partially, in all cases in which they were ordered. However, the territorial case law states that there should be a differentiation between compensation through the development fund and direct delivery of the payment. Collective compensation through the development fund is a peculiarity of Indigenous cases, as they have been barely ordered in other judgments. The problems observed during the implementation processes of development funds should be a strong argument against their use. Among all territorial cases, *Saramaka* is the only case in which the measure was complied with and, even so, the Court analysed the mere payment instead of its implementation and management. *Xucuru* was also declared complied with, but through direct payment to the community, not through the development fund. *Moiwana* is an exemplary case of the complications involving the management and application of the fund, as the state did not consult the community and invested the money in measures ineffective for the victims' redress. The representatives allege that houses were built outside the territory, causing conflicts with neighbouring communities, in a context in which the victims refused to return to their lands as long as the investigations were not concluded. On the other hand, individual compensation was paid, at least partially, in all analysed cases. In addition, in the two cases in which collective compensation was ordered to be delivered directly to the community (*Kichwa de Sarayaku* and *Kuna de Madungandí*), the measures were fully and promptly complied with.

The territorial reparations are characterised by a high degree of vagueness. The provision of basic services and goods is exemplary, as the lack of clear criteria has been indicated as problematic both by the state and by the Court during supervision (Beristaín 2009). In *Xákmok Kásek*, the Court attempted to overcome this by ordering the state to perform a study specifying the necessary services, but the problem remained, since the state did not present such a study. The public services that were ordered with more specific details, ie a system for emergency communication and a registration programme, were implemented more promptly than the vague remedy to provide basic goods and services.

The restitution of the traditional territory is another example of this lack of clarity. In most cases, the Court ordered it in general terms ('said territory', or 'corresponding lands'), but in others, the Court ordered specific details about the property, ie in *Xákmok Kásek* ('the State must return to the members of the Xákmok Kásek Community the 10,700 hectares it is claiming') and in *Garífuna Triunfo de la Cruz* ('the State must … grant the Garífuna Triunfo de la Cruz Community the title to communal property of the delimitated and demarcated area called Lote A1', including a map of the area). When exclusively considering the lack of clarity, a greater amount of compliance in the two cases with higher specificity would be expected. However, both the territories remain untitled. Delimitation of the ancestral lands is a delicate task, involving conflicts with neighbouring communities, private estates and third-party occupants. It also demands a good amount of multidisciplinary knowledge about geography, anthropology, sociology, etc. In fact, the same elements that caused the violations in the first place remain as hindrances to compliance with the decisions even after the Court's rulings. The study suggests that compliance with territorial restitution takes place regardless of the specificity of the area to be titled.

On the other hand, *Kichwa de Sarayaku* exemplifies the problems that entail an excessive amount of technicality and specificity in the design of the remedies. As detailed in chapter two, the Court ordered very specific measures to rehabilitate the territory regarding the removal or deactivation of buried explosives. During supervision, it became clear that the technical measure did not tend to the requests of the Indigenous people, and that the very detailed measure had hampered the dialogue between the parties during implementation.

The three examples above demonstrate different results from this lack of clarity: vagueness as a hindrance to compliance (public services remedy); level of vagueness indifferent for compliance (territorial restitution); and excessive details as a hindrance to compliance (removal of explosives). The Court should, as best as possible, present clearer parameters for the implementation of the measures, including indicators for analysing compliance. However, some level of deference is also desirable, allowing for the construction of reparation measures through dialogue between the victims and the state, which would be mediated by the Court during hearings on implementation. Vagueness is not a determining factor for compliance, and it should be evaluated in the context of the case. Lastly, the Court has overcome uncertainties generated by vagueness during supervision, in which it solves doubts proposed by the parties. Some examples are the definition of 'high rank state authorities' in the act of acknowledgement; the conditions to deliver alternative lands; and the participation of the community during management of the development fund.

Moving on to the next area, an active role of the Court during supervision has stimulated compliance. New mechanisms of supervision (private hearings and visits) have presented substantial contributions for compliance and have facilitated an approximation between the Court and relevant domestic actors, including NGOs and the domestic justice system. In *Awas Tingni*, the private hearing was a fundamental opportunity to settle compromises and establish compliance agreements, which was followed by full compliance with the case. Similar progress is observed in the Paraguayan cases, as concrete agreements were established in the 2017 hearings, thus boosting compliance. The visit was an essential milestone for the cases, as it enabled the better understanding of hindrances for compliance (eg the construction of the path to the Yakye Axa lands and the titling of the Emberá territory). In some cases, national actors visited the communities for the first time, which promoted considerable awareness about their wretched living conditions. In *Yakye Axa*, for example, the state installed water storage tanks in the community the day after the visit, at the request of one of the Indigenous leaders.[113]

[113] *Yakye Axa v Paraguay* (n 45) §16, footnote.

There are two instruments available to the Court that have not yet been applied in territorial cases and which could prompt compliance, particularly in cases of open defiance. The first is the request of information from other sources, including expert opinions and national public institutions. It could be an opportunity for the Court to engage with different state organs that could domestically prompt compliance, such as the public prosecution or the ombudsman offices. The second mechanism is the application of Article 65.2 in cases of reiterated non-compliance, considered in *Saramaka* and the Garífunas cases.

Regarding the active involvement of social movements and NGO networks, the victims were represented by NGOs in all territorial proceedings before the Court. Human rights organisations also participated actively as *amici curiae*, demonstrating the importance of civil society in litigations. Furthermore, during the implementation of the measures, there were multiple examples of partnerships and networking among national and international organisations, which are exemplary of successful strategies. In the Paraguayan cases, the domestic NGO Tierraviva represented *Yakye Axa* (in partnership with the international NGO CEJIL), *Sawhoyamaxa* and *Xákmok Kásek*. During post-litigation, Tierraviva established important partnerships with multiple international NGOs in order to foment compliance (Amnesty International, Survival International, Cultural Survival, ESCR-net and OXFAM). This consolidated network was very important to exert pressure on the state, thus propelling compliance. A similar network is also present in the Surinamese cases in which the communities were represented by an international NGO (Forest People Programme – FPP) in partnership with a local organisation.

On the other hand, even if all enabling factors are present, compliance can be paralysed if there is a total lack of political will, which is worsened in incomplete transitions to democracy. The Surinamese cases are representative of the difficulties in implementing human rights decisions in countries with incomplete transitions to democracy, as well as the lack of political will to prosecute perpetrators of human rights violations when these are still in power. In such scenarios, compliance seems to be hampered no matter the design of the reparation measure, the active role of the Court or even the formation of coalitions between victims and international NGOs. The approval of the Amnesty Law in 2012, along with the complete paralysis of the investigation into the Moiwana massacre, reveals the state's lack of compromise with accountability for mass violation of human rights. The paralysis in the implementation of the Surinamese cases is the reason why an incomplete transition to democracy was classified as being a blocking factor. It is no surprise that *Saramaka* was the only territorial case in which the application of Article 65.2 was discussed, as all attempts to boost compliance in the case had failed. However, even the blocking element can be temporary, following the alteration of domestic politics. In 2020, President Bouterse was condemned for multiple murders committed during his dictatorship and lost the presidential election. The new elected president, Chan Santokhi, was involved in the investigations that led to Bouterse's incrimination. The effects of the election to the cases are still to be observed.

Besides the presented elements, compliance with territorial cases is also influenced by the relationship between business and human rights, and the lack of strategies to make companies accountable for violations against territorial rights. In the three Paraguayan cases, the property had been sold to private companies that refused to collaborate with the implementation of the decision. In *Xákmok Kásek*, the situation was even graver, as the company deforested a considerable area as a strategy against the expropriation of the lands. In *Saramaka* and *Kichwa de Sarayaku*, logging and mining companies acquired concessions in violation of human rights, threatening the lives and the culture of the traditional peoples.

The relationship between business and human rights has increasingly captured the attention of international scholars and legislators (Ruggie 2007; Ruggie 2011), both in private and public international law, considering the lack of effective instruments to make multinational corporations accountable for human rights violations. In 2011, the UN Human Rights Council adopted the 'Guiding Principles on Business and Human Rights', thus establishing, for the first time, standards for addressing human rights violations related to business activities. The matter has also been approached by the Inter-American System, which, in 2019, issued the report 'Business and Human Rights', presenting the Inter-American standards on the matter.[114]

The Inter-American Court has jurisdiction *rationae personae* to impose remedies exclusively on the state, recognising its obligation to protect citizens from a third party's harmful action. However, in cases in which private companies are responsible for the violations, they could become compliance partners, assisting in the compliance with the reparation measures. For that purpose, the recognition of the relationship between business and human rights is an important advance in the Court's case law and could improve the implementation of the decisions. In the 2018 case *Kaliña and Lokono v Suriname*, the Court mentioned the UN guiding principles on business and human rights to reaffirm the obligations of private companies with traditional peoples' rights. As a measure of reparation, the Court ordered the state to prepare, with participation of the private company, a plan for the rehabilitation of the environmental damage. The state should also 'monitor and supervise the execution of the rehabilitation by the company'.[115] In contrast to all previous cases, in this decision, while imposing an obligation to protect on the state, the Court involved the private company as a compliance partner. Instead of ordering the state to rehabilitate the area directly, the Court ordered the state to supervise the company's rehabilitation work. The Court has not yet issued a supervision order with respect to the case but it seems that the private company is complying with the restitution measure to rehabilitate the territory, following a consultation with the

[114] CIDH, 'Informe Empresas y Derechos Humanos: Estándares Interamericanos' (1 November 2019) OEA/Ser.L/V/II CIDH/REDESCA/INF.1/19.

[115] *Kaliña and Lokono Peoples v Suriname*, Merits, Reparations and Costs, IACtHR Series C No 309 (25 November 2015) §290.

Indigenous peoples. According to the victims' representatives, the company Sucralco visited the affected territory in 2018 accompanied by Indigenous representatives and experts in environmental rehabilitation to develop a rehabilitation plan. In fact, Surinamese Indigenous peoples have resorted to direct dialogue with mining companies on past occasions in Suriname, considering the state's omission (Jong 2011).

Another factor is the pre-existence of state organisations in the matter of Indigenous rights, including the domestic recognition of the rights. Suriname is the only country among those analysed that does not recognise any Indigenous and ethnic people's rights. It has not ratified ILO 69 and it voted against the UNDRIP before the UN General Assembly. It has no specialised institution on territorial rights and the Government has even openly challenged territorial rights, seeing them as discriminatory towards the non-Indigenous population (Koorndijk 2019; Rombouts et al 2016). Such absence of protection of traditional peoples' rights domestically represented a hindrance to compliance with the Court's decisions, as the state did not even have minimum thresholds or experience in implementing territorial rights. However, as other cases demonstrate, the pre-existence of an Indigenist structure is only an enabling factor. Even in the countries that are viewed as having advanced legislation on territorial rights and consolidated state Indigenist institutions (ie Ecuador and Colombia), compliance has been delayed for several years.

In an overall analysis of the supervision proceedings, the study reveals that the supervision stage should be understood as a distinctive moment of the Court's work. While, during the merit proceedings, the Court is bound to the alleged facts and to the strict limits imposed by the Convention, during supervision, it has a wider discretion to perform. This discretion is foreseen by the own Convention and the Rules of Procedure through the use of an open language, including terms as 'when it deems it appropriate' or 'relevant information' (Rules of Procedure, Article 69). The territorial cases spent an average of two years before the Court until final judgment, which is a considerably less time spent compared, on average, to that spent on supervision (almost 20 years in *Yakye Axa*, for example). During the supervision process, the Court had acted strategically with great discretion, deciding the best strategies and identifying potential compliance partners. It has also partially altered the ordered reparation measures, by clarifying their meaning and altered terms for compliance

It has been argued that the Court should strategically use the judgment in order to have a broader impact, since the decision would be more effective when embedded in the domestic context (Cavallaro and Brewer 2008). Building upon this argumentation, and going one step further, the present research recognises that the Court should be aware of the domestic context not only during the judgment, but even more so during the supervision stage. Therefore, the performance of hearings and visits during the supervision stage would give the Court the opportunity to analyse contextual elements and to enhance domestic social movements towards the effectiveness of the violated rights. The recognition of distinctive phases before the Court during the merits proceedings and the supervision stage is relevant for the victims' and their representatives' strategies. Since the merits proceedings are a technical phase, the victims would benefit from professional legal NGOs that have great amounts of experience in international litigation, like CEJIL and FPP. During supervision, however, the victims could benefit from partnerships with politically engaged representatives, with experience in naming-and-shaming campaigns and with awareness-raising strategies among civil society. In the supervision stage, proximity to domestic political centres might as well be beneficial, as it simultaneously promotes pressure on specific actors and increases knowledge about specific domestic procedures for compliance.

Despite the contributions presented in this chapter, there are still some fields that demand more thorough analysis. There is a considerable interplay among international organs and the Court, and it might play a determining role in compliance in territorial cases. One central element that propelled full compliance in *Awas Tingni* was incentives by the World Bank (Alvarado 2007), and the same influence seems to be present in the Panamanian case.[116] Similarly, the agreement for compliance in the *Lhaka Honhat* case mentions financing by the Inter-American Development Bank (IDB). In both the Surinamese and the Paraguayan cases, several UN organs (CERD, HRC CESCR, among others) have issued reports calling for compliance with the Court's decision, and their role in influencing compliance is not yet quite clear. Similar influence towards compliance seems to be present from the UN programme for the mitigation of carbon emissions through the reduction of deforestation and forest degradation (UN REDD+). In Suriname, in order to obtain the benefits from the UN REDD+ programme, the state committed itself towards adopting national safeguards for Indigenous rights. These safeguards include the respect for Indigenous rights foreseen in the UNDRIP and affirmed by the Court in the three Surinamese cases, ie free, prior and informed consultation and property rights to the land. In addition to the safeguards, Indigenous protection is also the subject of some of the UN REDD+ projects, which include regulating land tenure, sharing benefits and incorporating traditional knowledge into the projects. In 2013, Suriname was granted US$3.8 million for readiness activities regarding the programme, along with an additional US$2.65 million in 2018.[117]

[116] Since 2018, the World Bank has approved of an innovative project for Indigenous peoples in Panama, including a loan of US$80 million to support the implementation of the Comprehensive National Plan for Indigenous Peoples of Panama (World Bank, 2018). Panama, 'Support for the National Indigenous Peoples Development Plan Project' (English) (World Bank Group, 2018).

[117] Government of Suriname, 'Forest Reference Emission Level for Suriname's REDD+ Programme' (2018). Detailed information about the projects, the safeguards and their implementation are available online at sis.surinameredd.org.

Similar relationships between REDD+ and Indigenous rights has already been studied in Guiana (Laing 2018) and in Paraguay.

Lastly, the present research focused on legal and institutional elements, but socio-economic conditions have a deep influence on compliance, especially in the territorial restitution measures, thus demanding further analysis. As mentioned above, almost all countries had already recognised territorial rights even before the international litigation began, and the causes of the human rights violations remain present after the Court's decision, thus hampering compliance. Some specific elements of territorial cases that should be considered are deep-rooted racial discrimination, long-lasting colonialist approaches, increased pressure regarding natural resources and unequal land distribution (Correia 2019b, 2018; Koorndijk 2019; Wetterslev 2020).

3.8. FINAL CONSIDERATIONS ON COMPLIANCE

The Court has developed a proactive approach committed to altering factual circumstances of marginalisation and vulnerability, both during and after litigation. It is undeniable that territorial case law had a positive impact on the victims' situations and on the general recognition of territorial rights. The active supervision of the Court is unique in international law and has proved fundamental for boosting the effectiveness of Indigenous peoples' rights, even though full compliance with the cases is still far from being achieved. As the quantitative research has revealed, there are concerningly low compliance rates in territorial cases. States usually delay compliance for several years, while the Indigenous communities struggle with wretched living conditions. This chapter has also detailed, through qualitative analysis of the implementation of territorial cases, elements of domestic resistance to Inter-American territorial case law, detailing incentives and hindrances to full compliance with the decisions. The research reveals that implementation is a complex process that involves multiple factors and actors. Each territorial case presented peculiarities that influenced time, rates and the manner of compliance.

To comprehend general elements that influenced implementation, the previous section indicated and categorised possible influent factors. Then, it analysed the applicability of such elements to territorial cases, confirming their applicability and suggesting some original elements. An original classification of the factors was presented, dividing them into blocking, enabling and constricting. The results of the study regarding influent elements indicated by scholars and original elements are summarised in Table 3.3.

The research demonstrated general patterns in terms of compliance with territorial cases, but it also suggested that compliance is mostly a domestic matter that relies on the socio-political context of each country, influenced by very specific actors and factors. The Court can influence compliance, but only inasmuch as it facilitates the domestic context for implementation, thus

Table 3.3 Compliance elements in territorial case law

Court's behaviour	Active role during supervision	Enabling
Measure's design	Low political cost Vagueness	Enabling Constricting/Enabling
Domestic elements	Active network of NGOs	Enabling
	Pre-existence of indigenist institutions and regulations	Enabling
	Consolidation of legal and institutional mechanisms for implementation	Enabling
	Involvement of multiple state organs	Constricting
	Lack of accountability of private companies	Constricting
	Incomplete transition from dictatorship	Blocking

reshaping domestic human rights policies (Hillebrecht 2014; Stiansen 2019). The identified ways in which the Court influenced compliance include: transforming domestic actors into compliance partners (ie multinational companies, NGOs, domestic public organs); establishing clear criteria and indicators for the implementation of reparation measures; and initiating dialogue between the parties through hearings and visits. As Hillebrecht concluded, complying with reparation measures is integrated in the context of domestic politics, becoming the result of political manoeuvring among domestic actors. Based on domestic political calculations, states engage in 'a la carte compliance', choosing parts of international rulings with which they will comply (Hillebrecht 2014: 136–37).

The central measure issued in territorial cases, ie the restitution of traditional lands (including the measures to demarcate and title properties, to perform title clearance and to guarantee full use and enjoyment), has been fully complied with on only very few occasions: the land demarcation in *Awas Tingni*; the annulment of a decree creating protected wooded areas throughout parts of the *Xákmok Kásek* traditional territory; and the revocation of mining concessions throughout parts of the *Garífuna de Punta Piedra* territory. In terms of structural measures, the most central non-repetition measures ordered, ie the adoption of necessary measures to regulate the right over traditional territories (including land demarcation and safeguards for natural resources exploration), issued in 10 of the 13 cases, has been fully complied with only once, in *Awas Tingni*. It is also concerning that the development fund, ordered in eight cases, has only once been fully paid, in *Saramaka*, and the Court did not analyse the implementation and management of the fund. The development fund could have been an important way to overcome the marginalisation endured by Indigenous peoples, or at least a mechanism to attenuate the grave consequences of uprootedness in cases of the displacement of traditional territories.

Non-compliance has hazardous effects in the everyday life of the Indigenous and ethnic communities. During the years following the judicial victory, Indigenous peoples continue their struggle for redress, in some cases enduring the same wretched living conditions as those prior to the litigation. The death of several Indigenous members in the Paraguayan cases *Yakye Axa* and *Sawhoyamaxa*, massive deforestation of the *Saramaka* traditional lands and the escalation of violent conflicts in the Honduran cases are concerning consequences of a lack of compliance.

The present research analysed influent factors on compliance with international courts, but the results obtained could also applied to effectiveness of domestic territorial rights. Further research could expand the results presented here to analyses of implementation of domestic legislation on territorial rights. The elements' influence of multiple and separated state organs, lack of accountability of private actors and consolidation of NGO network might impact not only compliance with international decisions, but also influence the domestic effectiveness of territorial rights. Furthermore, even though the present research focused on territorial rights, future research could investigate whether the results could be expanded to cases that include multiple victims (massacres, for example) or cases involving the individual rights of Indigenous peoples.

One last caveat is necessary in the matter of compliance. One could argue that the pessimistic scenario would represent a lack of authority of the Court's decisions. However, there are at least two reasons to continue to affirm the Court's authority in matters of territorial case law. First, even if compliance is low, case law has an impact that is greater than compliance, ie it influences the domestic legal system. This embeddedness will be analysed in chapter four. Second, some of the structural measures ordered by the Court might take years to reach final compliance and the lack of full compliance is not equivalent to the total lack of implementation. The Paraguayan trilogy (*Yakye Axa*, *Sawhoyamaxa* and *Xákmok Kásek*) reveals this very clearly: even though restitution of the traditional territories is pending in those three cases, the state has indeed taken considerable steps towards compliance over the years and has acquired the three properties.

In order to perceive the effects of case law that are not covered by compliance, the next chapter will focus on domestic audiences, analysing how they have reacted to the Court's rulings, which, in some cases, led to adopting the Court's parameters for Indigenous peoples.

4

Territorial Protection in Nicaragua: From Full Compliance to Open Defiance

THE NEXT THREE chapters will analyse the embeddedness of the decisions issued by the Inter-American Court in territorial cases, describing the after-effects of strategic international litigation within the country, beyond compliance with reparation orders. In other words, the chapters present the extent to which the Inter-American Court influenced domestic legal systems in order to remedy potential treaty violations and avoid future international litigation. It also analyses the variables that have promoted or hindered wide impact of the decisions, demonstrating possible paths for an increased effectiveness of territorial rights. The chapters focus on case study of three countries, Nicaragua, Paraguay and Brazil. The three countries are representative of the Latin American situation of territorial rights protection, as all of them have a consolidated legislative framework recognising Indigenous and ethnic territorial rights, but lack implementation of such rights, demonstrated by increased pressure over natural resources and third-party occupation. They also have similar level of opening towards the Inter-American System, as in the three countries regional treaties on human rights have a special hierarchical position, just as in most of Latin America. In that perspective, the choice of countries is representative of Latin America and the results could be expanded for litigation in other countries. One of the elements for the choice of the countries was the time between the research and the decision. While Nicaragua and Paraguay were the first cases issued by the Court in 2001 and 2005, Brazil was condemned in one of the most recent cases. Furthermore, the cases present contrasting rates of compliance (full compliance in *Awas Tingni v Nicaragua* and initial compliance steps in the three cases against Paraguay) and could demonstrate different patterns of embeddedness.

The research on the domestic legal system was based mainly on primary sources, including legislation, debates on national organs, judicial decisions, recommendation from international organisations and reports from local and international NGOs. Secondary sources were also consulted, mostly to guarantee an interdisciplinary approach, resorting to researches from geography, anthropology, sociology and political science. The research includes documents published until the first semester of 2023.

This chapter demonstrates the embeddedness effectiveness in Nicaragua, demonstrating how the Court impacted the state and strengthened social movements in their struggle for land protection, even though they were not sufficient to transform the factual situation of indigenous and ethnic peoples. It also analyses the contradictions in the territorial protection of Nicaragua, characterised by high level of legal recognition of rights, but reiterated violation of territorial rights. Nicaragua is the only country with full compliance with territorial rights decided by the Inter-American Court, demonstrating high level of case-specific effectiveness. The ancestral lands of the *Awas Tingni* community were demarcated and titled, and the non-repetition order was fulfilled. Besides that, Nicaragua has one of the most advanced legislation on indigenous rights in Latin America, guaranteeing autonomy and self-government to indigenous peoples. After the Court' 2001 decision, the Nicaraguan National Assembly has approved laws extending indigenous and ethnic rights and the state has prompted a wide process of land demarcation.

Despite the advances, traditional peoples in Nicaragua still struggle with grave threats to their territorial rights in the last few years. The most pressing issue is the lack of title clearance, as most territories have been occupied by irregular settlers, increasing violence against indigenous peoples and their representatives. The state, aware of such violence, has taken no action to protect human rights defenders or to investigate the violence, a fact that has been considered a violation of conventional rights by the Inter-American Court in the cases *Acosta and others v Nicaragua* (2017) and *Pobladores de las Comunidades del Pueblo Indígena Miskitu de la Region Costa Caribe Norte* (2016).

Aggravating the scenario, from 2018 onwards, the country experienced a grave political crisis as the state violently repressed and criminalised political protests. After the re-election of President Ortega in 2021, the state was labelled an authoritarian regime, characterised by press censorship, persecution and criminalisation of political opponents and the closure of the civic space. The Inter-American System has played a very central role in the supervision of human rights situation, ordering multiple precautionary measures and elaborating regular reports. Between only August 2018 and December 2023, the Court issued 27 provisional measures against Nicaragua, almost one-quarter of all provisional measures issued by the Court.

In order to comprehend the advances and limitations of the territorial rights in Nicaragua, this chapter will present the advances on legislation and land demarcation, followed by an analysis of how the lack of title clearance hinders indigenous peoples in their enjoyment of their territorial rights. The political crisis of 2018 is presented, demonstrating how the grave violations of human rights affected indigenous and ethnic peoples, and the role of the Inter-American System in the conflict. Lastly, the megaproject of the transoceanic canal is presented, analysing the violation of indigenous rights and the use of the IAS as the last resource for social movements.

The Nicaraguan Constitution affirms the full validity (*plena vigencia*) of the American Declaration, the San Salvador Pact and the American Convention, what for some scholars would mean the adoption of the treaties as part of a constitutional block (Sierra Cadena 2016: 567), even though the jurisprudence of the Constitutional Court is not clear on the matter (Góngora Mera 2014). In November 2021, President Ortega denounced the OAS Charter, informing the exit of the country from the IAS in a two-year term. Nicaragua has been held responsible for rights violations by the Court on six occasions: *Genie Lacayo* in 1997 (extrajudicial execution);[1] *Awas Tingni* in 2001 (indigenous territorial rights);[2] *YATAMA* in 2005 (indigenous political rights);[3] *Acosta and others* in 2017 (human rights defenders rights);[4] *VRP and VPC* in 2018 (lack of investigation of child abuse);[5] and *Roche Azana and others* in 2020 (police violence).[6] The two first cases have been fully complied with, while in *YATAMA* and *Acosta and others* the state complied with the satisfaction and compensation measures, but overtly refused to comply with the non-repetition measures, not even participating in the supervision hearings ordered by the Court.[7] In both *VRP and VPC* and *Roche Azana and others*, the Court issued a supervision order, reaffirming its mandate to supervise the compliance and expressing concern with the total non-compliance with the decision. According to the 2005 national census, eight Indigenous peoples live in Nicaragua, comprising approximately 8.6% of the national population. The social condition of Indigenous peoples is considerably more vulnerable than the rest of Nicaraguan society. According to a report elaborated by the UN Development Program in 2013, the Human Development Index of the Autonomous Region of the Caribbean is 0.466 (North) and 0.454 (South), but for the country the index is 0.639 (CIDH 2023A).

4.1. ADVANCES IN THE REGULATION: ADOPTING THE COURT'S FRAMEWORK

During the years that followed the *Awas Tingni* decision, Nicaragua experienced a considerable advance in the legal recognition of Indigenous and Afro-descendant rights. Most of the decisions were unanimously approved,

[1] *Genie Lacayo v Nicaragua*, Merits, Reparations, and Costs, Inter-American Court of Human Rights Series C No 30 (29 January 1997).

[2] *Mayagna (Sumo) Awas Tingni Community v Nicaragua*, Merits, Reparations and Costs, Inter-American Court of Human Rights Series C No 79 (31 August 2001).

[3] *Yatama v Nicaragua*. Preliminary Objection, Merits, Reparations, and Costs, Inter-American Court of Human Rights Series C No 127 (23 June 2005).

[4] *Acosta et al v Nicaragua*, Preliminary Objections, Merits, Reparations and Costs, Inter-American Court of Human Rights Series C No 334 (25 March 2017).

[5] *VRP, VPC et al v Nicaragua*, Preliminary Objections, Merits, Reparations and Costs, Inter-American Court of Human Rights Series C No 350 (8 March 2018).

[6] *Roche Azana and others v Nicaragua*, Preliminary Objections, Merits, Reparations and Costs, Inter-American Court of Human Rights Series C No 350 (3 June 2020).

[7] *Yatama v Nicaragua*, Monitoring Compliance with Judgment, Inter-American Court of Human Rights (20 November 2015). Despite non-compliance with the non-repetition orders, the Indigenous party YATAMA managed to participate in the elections and celebrated in 2006 an agreement with the situation party, guaranteeing political engagement in the Government. Sierra Cadena (2016).

demonstrating a great commitment with regulation of traditional peoples' rights. Furthermore, there is an evident concern with adequacy between domestic system and international law on Indigenous peoples, as international treaties have been repeatedly mentioned, including soft law and binding conventions, both from regional and UN level.

In the 2001 decision *Awas Tingni*, the Court ordered the state to adopt the legislative, administrative, and any other measures necessary to create an effective mechanism for the delimitation, demarcation and titling of Indigenous property. The law was adopted in December 2002 under the name Ley de Régimen de Propiedad Comunal de los Pueblos Indígenas y Comunidades Étnicas de las Regiones Autónomas de la Costa Atlántica de Nicaragua y de los ríos Bocay, Coco, Indio y Maíz (Law 445). A first draft of the bill had been presented to the National Assembly in October 1998 under the name Anteproyecto de Ley Orgánica que regula el Régimen de la Propiedad Comunal de las Comunidades Indígenas de la Costa Atlántica y BOSAWAS. The presentation of the draft was a condition imposed by the World Bank for a loan in the project Corredor Biológico del Atlántico. The first proposed bill was elaborated without consultation with Indigenous peoples and it did not count with demarcation procedures, relegating it for further regulation by a Decree (Acosta 2006). In the letter of submission of the draft, it is prominent that the intention is far from self-determination and autonomy. It asserted that the project intended to guarantee the population of the Atlantic Coast participation in the wealth of the lands, peacefully and orderly. It also stated the law should not be interpreted as lack of authority of the Government over the complete national territory, as Nicaragua was a country 'united and indivisible'.[8]

In order to promote consultation and to foster the project among the civil society, the Commission for Coordination of Demarcation and Titling was established, composed by multiple representatives of social movements and traditional peoples. With financing from the above-mentioned World Bank project, the Commission pursued wide consultation. As a result, in 2000 it presented an improved project (Jarquín 2003). In December 2002, the legislation was discussed in the National Assembly in a swift debate. None of the deputies presented any disagreement with the legislation, which was approved unanimously. Among the arguments used by the Assembly to defend the Law, ILO Convention 169, the Indigenous customary law, the marginalisation and impoverishment of traditional peoples and the lack of basic public services offered to these people were mentioned.[9]

Law 445 has a specific territorial range: the Atlantic Coast and the basins of the rivers Bocay, Coco, Indio and Maíz. To this day the Pacific Coast and

[8] Asambleia Nacional de Nicaragua, Diário de Debates, Anteproyecto de Ley Orgánica que regula el Régimen de la Propiedad Comunal de las Comunidades Indígenas de la Costa Atlántica y BOSAWAS, 13 Deember 2002. Original in Spanish, translated by the author.

[9] Asambleia Nacional de Nicaragua, Diário de Debates, 13 December 2002.

the Northern region do not have a law on demarcation of traditional lands.[10] The law stipulated the procedure for ancestral lands demarcation and created authorities in charge of the demarcation. The demarcation is divided into five stages: presentation of the demand; conflict settlement; measurement; titling; and *saneamiento*. The law also establishes safeguards to concessions for exploration of natural resources, including prior consultation, benefit-sharing and compensation in case of damages. Finally, the law regulates representative organs of traditional peoples, coordinating their work with municipal, regional and national authorities. Even though Law 445 does not mention the Court's decisions, nor was it mentioned during the debates in the National Assembly, involved actors have affirmed that the decision was an important instrument in the political struggle exercised by interested traditional communities (Jarquín 2003; Acosta 2006; Wiggins 2002; Alfred-Cunningham 2011). Furthermore, Law 445 paraphrases in Article 44 the operative paragraph 3 of the decision (Isa 2017) and it has adopted the Court's parameters for land demarcation and consultation rights.

Following Law 445, Nicaragua approved several other bills in the matter of traditional peoples' rights, advancing in the protection of traditional territories. In 2008, the National Assembly issued a declaration recognising the importance of the UN Declaration on the Rights of Indigenous Peoples and its compatibility with the Nicaraguan constitutional rights. The Assembly committed to reframe the domestic legal system to the UNDRIP parameters, and urged the Executive to take all necessary measures to implement the treaty.[11] The ILO Convention 169, the most important treaty in the matter of territorial rights, was ratified in 2010 by the Decree no 5934, which specifically recognised the application of the convention to Indigenous peoples and to the Nicaraguan Afro-descendant peoples and communities, Rama and Kriol (Article 2). There is considerable equivalence between the IACtHR's parameters for territorial protection, ILO Convention 169 and the UNDRIP, such as the right to communal property, the right to consultation and non-discrimination, as the Court has used both treaties to interpret the American Convention.

In 2011, the Law on dignified and equitable treatment to Indigenous and Afro-descendant peoples (Law 757) was approved, which sought to guarantee equitable opportunities of access to labour market, specifying rights for members of traditional peoples and establishing duties for employees, including a quota reserved for Indigenous and Afro-descendent members. In favour of the legislation, multiple international treaties were mentioned, including the American Convention on Human Rights and ILO Convention 169.[12] In the

[10] There is a draft law on the rights of the Indigenous peoples of the region, but it stalled in the National Assembly in 2007. Acosta (2012).

[11] Asamblea Nacional, Declaración AN no 001-2008 (11 March 2008).

[12] Asambleia Nacional de Nicaragua, Diário de Debates, Ley de Trato digno y equitativo a pueblos indígenas y afro-descendientes, 2 March 2010.

same year, the Law on Ancestral Medicine (Law 759) was approved, establishing mechanisms to protect and promote traditional practices of traditional medicine of Indigenous and Afro-descendent peoples, articulating the national health system with traditional practices. The bill also regulated traditional knowledge, recognising the right to free, prior and informed consent for use of resources associated to traditional knowledge. In 2014, Law 886 was unanimously approved, declaring the Garífuna culture immaterial cultural heritage of Nicaragua. The explanatory statement mentions a plurality of international treaties on cultural heritage and Indigenous rights, including the UNDRIP.[13] The most recent legislative decision on the matter of traditional peoples' rights is the ratification of the Regional Agreement on Access to Information, Public Participation and Justice in Environmental Matters in Latin America and the Caribbean (the Escazú Agreement),[14] approved through the Decree AN no 8629 in December 2019. The treaty is a binding agreement that regulates access to justice in the matter of environmental rights, including rights of Indigenous peoples to participation and protection of human rights defenders in environmental matters.

Besides the approved legislation, some decrees are also worth mentioning: Decree 25-2014, approved in 2014, regulates Law 759/2011 (Law on Ancestral Medicine); Resolution 04-03-11-2010 approves the policy for gender equality in the context of Indigenous peoples and ethnic communities of the autonomous region of the north Atlantic – RAAN; Decree no 5154-2007 creates the National Day of Nicaraguan Indigenous Peoples; and Decree no 37-2006 creates the Garífuna National Day. The legislation presented above enlarges Indigenous and ethnic peoples' rights, promoting implementation of constitutional guarantees and international rights. It demonstrates the embeddedness of the Court's parameter for land demarcation, consultation and non-discrimination, as even if the Court is not directly mentioned, the legislation consolidates international parameters within the domestic system. However, the absence of a legislation for territorial rights for the Pacific Coast and the Northern region is a concerning hindrance (CIDH 2023A).

4.2. ADVANCES IN LAND DEMARCATION

Between 2005 and 2017, 23 Indigenous territories were demarcated and titled, representing a total extension of 32 per cent of the national territory and almost

[13] Asambleia Nacional de Nicaragua, Diário de Debates, Ley de declaración de la cultura Garífuna como patrimonio cultural inmaterial de la nación, 29 October 2014.

[14] The Agreement was negotiated under the UN's Economic Commission for Latin America and the Caribbean (ECLAC) and opened for signatures in March 2018, entering into force when upon receiving 11 ratifications. It was signed by 22 countries and ratified by 15 states. See: Stec and Jendrośka (2019); Médici Colombo (2018).

55 per cent of the Caribbean Coast (Macdonald and Wetterslev 2019). Some very few ancestral territories remain untitled, mostly those located in the Pacific, Centre and North regions (Alianza de Pueblos Indígenas y Afrodescendientes de Nicaragua 2017; del Cid 2019; CONADETI 2013). Land demarcation was prompted by an outstanding agreement reached between the Sandinista Party (FSLN) and the indigenist party, YATAMA, in 2006. The agreement emphasised the importance of land demarcation and titling, signalling a commitment of both parties with implementation of Law 445. The agreement also mentioned the *Awas Tingni* decision and the importance of full compliance (Gonzalez 2016). The land demarcation process was mostly financed by international funding, including support from multilateral and bilateral donors, and loans by the World Bank (Acosta 2011). The financing has been consistent and long-lasting, even across different political administrations, demonstrating international long-term interest in land regularisation in the country (Brook 2016). Since 2003, the World Bank has financed a specific project aimed at land regularisation, the PRODEP.[15]

Demarcation was a complex and long-lasting process. The most difficult stage was the conflict settlement, as the Law 445 foresaw exclusivity in the ownership of the lands, contrary to customary traditional law of porous and unstable boundaries and pacific co-habitation (Macdonald and Wetterslev 2019). Despite the efforts of the legislation to bind the commons, demarcation process intensified disputes among Indigenous groups and between Indigenous and Afro-descendant communities (Brook and Offen 2009; Brook 2016). Furthermore, conflicts were also present in the representation level, as

> the decision over which communities would join which territories was sometimes hotly contested, with competing interests among communities and between communities and regional indigenous leaders; at stake was control over territory and natural resources as well as political power, with many communities questioning the goals of leaders at multiple levels (Larson et al. 2016).

The *Awas Tingni* demarcation is exemplary of the disputes created and/or aggravated with the demarcation process. The knowledge of the Indigenous community was forced to fit in a legalistic language and since there were contrasting definitions of the disputed place from the state officials and from the claimants, the process heightened a production of contested space, intensifying long-standing racial and economic disputes (Brook and Offen 2009). The territory was disputed between the *Awas Tingni* community and two *Miskito*

[15] The first Project on Land Administration (PRODEP) lasted between 2003 and 2011, with the specific aim of regulating property rights. In 2012, it approved the PRODEP II, aimed at strengthening institutions related to land demarcation, land regularisation and demarcation of protected areas. Finally, in 2018 it announced the PRODEP III, with a focus on the central region of the country. Specifically in relation to demarcation of ancestral territories, the project does not mention title clearance.

villages, *Tasba Raya* and *Diez Comunidades*. In the first conflict, the states split the conflicted area in half, and in the second it favoured the *Mayagna* community, to the detriment of the *Miskito*. It generated intense conflicts between the communities, with the emergence of violent threats against the *Awas Tingni* (Brook and Offen 2009). The final title of the community, issued in December 2008, contains explicit mention to the regional Court's decision, on a clear recognition of the Court's authority.[16]

Despite the expansive land demarcation, tenure insecurity remains, as the last stage foreseen in Law 445, *saneamiento* of the lands, has not even started for most of the communities. Third-party occupation has generated intense conflicts and a legacy of environmental destruction. The Government has remained inert to the demands of Indigenous peoples, as presented below.

4.3. LACK OF TITLE CLEARANCE OF TRADITIONAL PEOPLES' LANDS

The most pressing issue for Indigenous and Afro-descendent people in Nicaragua is the lack of title clearance. Indigenous leaders expressed frustration with the slowness and the lack of political will to finish the last stage foreseen in Law 445 (Sylvander 2018), as they appointed title clearance as vital for protection of the natural resources and exercise of the self-government (CADPI and Mairena 2014). According to the NGO CEDUJHCAN (2019), out of 23 demarcated traditional territories, at least 21 suffer from illegal occupation by third parties, even though each community has its peculiarities.

The legislation stipulates that after land demarcation, the community shall start the title clearance of the area in relation to third-party occupants. The bill, however, does not define *saneamiento*, causing insecurity and doubts (Bonilla Toruño 2013). Bonilla (2013: 7) defined *saneamiento* as the state's duty to solve 'the situation of third party, natural or juridical, distinct from the community, that allege property rights and that are legally or illegally occupying an ethnic or indigenous territory'.[17] There are considerable unsolved issues in the matter of title clearance. First, it is not clear what should be the expected behaviour towards third party, as some communities expect the eviction of settlers, while others aim at pacific co-living rules. Furthermore, the concept of 'third-party' encompasses a wide range of actors, from peasants to cattle estates and land traffickers, each of whom should receive different treatment, but are treated equally by the legislation. Lastly, regarding the institutions in charge of the *saneamiento*, the lack of financial, personal and institutional resources has been labelled as concerning hindrances, as well as considerable unawareness of the

[16] República de Nicarágua, Comisión Nacional de Demarcación y titulación – CONADETI, Título de propiedad comunal no 007-13-12-2008, Territorio Awas Tingni Mayangnina Sauni Umani – AMASAU (13 December 2008) según diário numero 5297, tomo 015, fls 92-5.

[17] Original in Spanish, translated by the author.

specificities of Indigenous and Afro-descendent legislation. Bonilla (2010) identified that most actors in charge of the stage were unaware of their duty or of the necessary procedures. Besides that, the obligation of *saneamiento* falls in the local communities, often unprepared to deal with such delicate duty (Sylvander 2018). The lack of *saneamiento* has been aggravated by an accelerated migration movement of peasants from the Pacific region to the Caribbean Coast, intensified by climate change (Kumari Rigaud et al 2018). Usually trying to escape poverty and in the search for more fertile lands, these groups occupy the Indigenous and ethnic territories, some of them backed by false titles or illegal contracts of land sale (CEJIL 2019: 23).

Third-party occupation is usually followed by a concerning rise in violence. Between 2015 and 2018, 36 Indigenous persons were murdered, 36 were kidnapped and four have disappeared. There are multiple reports of criminal arsons in houses, plantations and wooded areas (CIDH 2023a). Furthermore, non-Indigenous occupation has led to massive deforestation. Between 2011 and 2018, Nicaragua lost the equivalent of 20 per cent of its wooded areas. Consequently, it deeply affects the livelihood of Indigenous peoples, considering the importance of fishing and hunting for their food security. Lastly, it might also affect the quality of the available water, reducing already scarce access to drinkable water sources (CIDH 2023a).

Specifically regarding the *Awas Tingni* territory, since the titling in 2008 there has been a considerable growth in third-party occupation, even though since 2009 the community has presented multiple demands to the authorities requesting the *saneamiento*. In 2011, the community elaborated a detailed report about the situation of the territory, identifying 424 families occupying the territory, with a claim of property of more than 67,000 hectares, or 91 per cent of the ancestral territory. Some occupants alleged they were backed by the local government, which would have affirmed the lands were national property and were available (Comunidad Mayagna de Awas Tingni and Gobierno Territorial Amasau 2012). The report also recognised a considerable threat to the natural resources caused by deforestation, contamination by waste disposal, poaching and cattle farming. The construction of basic infrastructure without consultation was seen as a facilitator for increase in illegal mining and logging operations. The report demanded immediate actions should be taken, both to stop intrusion by third parties, as well as to evict the illegal settlers (Comunidad Mayagna de Awas Tingni and Gobierno Territorial Amasau 2012; Wetterslev 2021).

In 2019, state and community estimated that more than 800 family settlers occupied the territory (part of it is inaccessible due to the presence of armed groups), outnumbering the 200 Mayagna families that occupied the territory and are now surrounded by the settlers (Macdonald and Wetterslev 2019; Wetterslev 2020). There are some indications of illegal sales of the lands by Mayagna leaders, generating conflicts within the community (Wetterslev 2020). The community members share a sense of abandonment, since full implementation of the decision remains unfulfilled, despite the declaration of full compliance by the Court (Isa 2017). Community leaders alleged that the cultural survival of the community is endangered, even more now than before the international litigation (Macdonald and Wetterslev 2019). The community established some rules for pacific cohabitation with poorer settlers, but it still struggles to obtain state support to protect their territory (Macdonald and Wetterslev 2019). In 2019, an arson occurred in the office of the territorial government, destroying not only the building and equipment, but also files with maps, statistics and documents. Indigenous leaders have related the arson to the tenure insecurity in the territory, despite the lack of official investigation (Wetterslev 2020b).

The prospect for future action is concerning, as the two central elements that prompted fulfilment of land demarcation are not present in relation to *saneamiento* of the lands. First, the political agreement between YATAMA and FSLN is since 2016 broken, as the Miskito party alleges grave election fraud (Gonzalez 2016). Furthermore, land demarcation was widely financed by international aid, and the central form of financing, the World Bank project PRODEP, does not mention *saneamiento* (Bonilla Toruño 2010). The lack of political will and the scarcity of resources might be the central barriers to the effectiveness of territorial rights, hindering full effectiveness of Law 445.

One grave case of lack of title clearance is the *Miskito* case, provisional measure analysed by the Court in 2016 and supervised in the subsequent years. It regards illegal third-party occupation of the Miskito ancestral territory, generating multiple violent acts (among others, thefts, fires, rape, murder and threat).[18] The state had been completely inert in offering protection, even though aware of the situation. In the provisional measure order, the Court affirmed the state should take all necessary measures to eradicate violence and to protect the Indigenous members, and create an institution to investigate the violence's source and to offer possible solutions. All measures should be implemented with participation of the community and the state should present detailed reports. In subsequent orders, the Court expanded the reach of the measure to other communities and emphasised the gravity and urgency of the situation.[19] According to the victims' representatives, Nicaragua has taken insufficient steps to protect the communities and their representatives, as the communities still endure the same wretched conditions since 2015. The NGO's CEJIL and CEJUDHCAN estimate that 30 per cent of the communities' members were forcefully displaced, living either in neighbouring cities or in Honduras. Between 2016 and 2018, three murders were committed and more than 15 acts

[18] For a detailed list of the violent acts committed against the community, see CEJIL (2019) See also UNHCHR (2015).

[19] Matter of Members of the Miskitu Indigenous People of the North Caribbean Coast regarding Nicaragua, Request for Provisional Measures, Orders of the Inter-American Court of Human Rights (23 November 2016); (22 August 2017); (23 August 2018); (6 February 2020); (14 October 2021); (27 June 2023).

of violence, all of them still unpunished. The displacement has deep impacts in the cultural life of Indigenous peoples, considering their peculiar bond with the territory. Furthermore, during the displacement, they did not receive any humanitarian aid and were facing lack of health and education services and food insecurity (CEJIL 2019).

4.4. THE RISE OF AUTHORITARIANISM IN NICARAGUA AND OPEN DEFIANCE AGAINST THE COURT

The already fragile situation of Indigenous and ethnic peoples due to the lack of title clearance is aggravated by the eruption of a grave political crisis in 2018, which led to the consolidation of an authoritarian regime. NGOs acting in the defence of Indigenous and Afro-descendent peoples were considered illegal, several human rights defenders (HRD) went into exile after receiving multiple threats, armed groups have attacked traditional communities and Indigenous leaderships have been prosecuted and incarcerated (Acosta 2019). The crisis is considered the apex of an already ongoing process of des-democratisation (Martí i Puig 2016), meaning that for Indigenous and ethnic peoples it only exacerbates ongoing violations: land encroachment, violence and persecution of HRD.

The political crisis erupted with social protests in early April 2018 denouncing the state's insufficient response to control a bush fire in a Kriol territory, but these intensified and became national against a proposed reform in the pension system. The protests were largely peaceful, but the state responded with strong repression.[20] The state's violence changed the demands of the protests, which became revolutionary, demanding the renounce of President Ortega and denouncing the grave human rights violations (Martí i Puig 2019b; Cabrales 2019). Up to 2021, the conflicts occasioned 355 deaths, 2000 arbitrary imprisonments (160 people are still imprisoned) and the forceful migration of 250,s000 Nicaraguan to neighbour states (CIDH 2023b). A peculiar repression strategy has been the suppression of the civic space by the massive arbitrary cancellation of juridical personality of civil society organisations and the seizure of their assets.[21] In 2023, 3390 organisations had been impacted (CIDH 2023b).

According to the Inter-American Commission, the state's violence had the specific aim of dissuading participation in the protests and suffocating political dissent, characterised by a pattern composed of the following elements: a) excessive and arbitrary use of police force; b) use of paramilitary groups or chock

[20] UN High Commissioner for Human Rights, 'Human rights violations and abuses in the context of protests in Nicaragua, 18 April–18 August 2018' (August 2018).

[21] The conflict was approached by the Court in the case *Matter of the Nicaraguan Center for Human Rights and the Permanent Commission of Human Rights (CENIDH-CPDH) regarding Nicaragua*, Adoption of Urgent Provisional Measures, Order of the President of the Inter-American Court of Human Rights (12 July 2019).

groups with the acquiescence and tolerance of the state's authorities; c) obstacles in access to emergency health attention for the injured; d) arbitrary detention of adolescents that participated in the protests; e diffusion of stigmatisation campaign and propaganda, direct and indirect censorship; f) harassment and threats against social movement leaders; and g) lack of diligence in the investigation of the murders and injuries committed.[22] The repression to the protests was followed by criminalisation of individuals involved in the demonstrations, including students, human rights defenders and journalists, as they faced trial for terrorism and organised crime. The trials occurred in disrespect of the due process of law.

The Commission created two specific mechanisms to supervise the human rights situation. The Interdisciplinary Group of Independent Experts (GIEI) was created in June 2018 and presented its report in December 2018.[23] The Follow-up Mechanism for Nicaragua (MESENI) started its activities in June 2018 with the aim of following the Commission's recommendations and monitoring the human rights situation.[24] The presence of MESENI was suspended by Nicaragua in December 2018 and the monitoring continued remotely. The Commission had a very active role during the crisis, and until 2019 presented 67 press releases, collected almost 16,000 testimonials, offered 27 capacitation courses and issued 76 precautionary measures.[25] In fact, considering the number of precautionary measures ordered by the Commission, Nicaragua represented 45 per cent of the total issued in one year in the whole Latin America.

The political crisis has been considered the apex of a long process of deterioration of the rule of law, so perspectives on overcoming the crisis are pessimistic. The current violence in Nicaragua is a reflex of systemic erosion of human rights over the years, demonstrating the fragility of the rule of the law. The political crisis is the apex of what has been called the des-democratisation process, which is characterised by the development of tactics to remove the democracy of electoral questions. Ortega's regime has been characterised by the concentration of power in a family circle, as well as a populist government with centralisation of power (Martí i Puig 2019a, 2019b; Gori 2018). The 2021 elections were characterised by intense repression, persecution of opponents, censorship against the press and allegations of fraud. Seven candidates for the presidency were arrested, and two political parties had their juridical personality cancelled (CIDH, 2021). The crisis has affected considerably the Indigenous and ethnic communities of Nicaragua. The Commission has reported a proliferation of violence

[22] Inter-American Commission of Human Rights, 'Graves violaciones a los derechos humanos en el marco de las protestas sociales en Nicaragua' (21 June 2018) OEA/Ser.L/V/II. Doc 86 §58.

[23] GIEI Nicaragua, Informe sobre los hechos de violencia ocurridos entre el 18 de abril y el 30 de mayo de 2018 (21 December 2018).

[24] CIDH, 'CIDH instala el Mecanismo Especial de Seguimiento para Nicaragua (MESENI)') Press release 135 (25 June 2018).

[25] Inter-American Commission of Human Rights, 'Mecanismo especial de seguimiento para Nicaragua, Boletin Noviembre–Deciembre 2019' (20 December 2019).

(threats, kidnapping, harassment and territorial deprivation) committed either by third parties with state acquiescence or directly by the state after the political crisis against Indigenous and ethnic leaderships.[26] Furthermore, some of the NGOs acting in defence of territorial rights have been persecuted by the state (Alianza de Pueblos Indígenas y Afrodescendientes de Nicaragua 2017).

After the crisis, Nicaragua adopted a hostile posture against international organs, rescinding diplomatic invitations to a team of the Office of the High Commissioner for Human Rights and to the Commission mechanism. In November 2021, President Ortega denounced the OAS Charter, but the definitive exit will only occur after a two-year term. The Inter-American Court maintains jurisdiction over the country and has issued provisional measures and decisions, as well as supervised compliance with the decisions. The first act of open defiance against the Court occurred in 2019, during supervision with the case *Acosta and others* (2017). The case relates to violence against human rights defenders and the lack of accountability for murder.[27] In order to follow the implementation, a public hearing was celebrated in March 2019. The state submitted a brief stating it would not take part in the procedure and openly refusing to comply with the accountability measures. The Court considered the brief a demonstration of grave unawareness about the duties emerging from the Court's decision and from the conventional state's duties. The lack of attendance in the hearing was considered a gross affront to the supervision procedures.[28] The Tribunal also reaffirmed the state's obligation to comply with the Court's orders, a consequence of the principle *pacta sunt servanda*. The refusal to comply with the measure configured not only a frontal defiance to the Court, but also an international violation of conventional rights.[29] Despite open defiance against the accountability measure and the lack of effective steps taken to implement the non-repetition measure, Nicaragua partially complied with the satisfaction measure and fully complied with the monetary compensation.[30] In its supervision of *Roche Azana and others* (2020) the state was even more aggressive towards the Tribunal, not recognising at all the Court's mandate. According to the state, the decision 'is nothing more than guidelines of the interventionist and human rights violating policy, exercised by the rulers of the United States of America'. The Court sustained the position of reinforcing its jurisdiction and condemning the state's declaration.[31] Since November 2021, the state has not responded to the Court, either in reports or hearings.

The democratic erosion in Nicaragua has led to the intensification of human rights violations against vulnerable groups. Despite a substantial advance in

[26] ibid.

[27] *Acosta and others v Nicaragua* (n 4).

[28] *Acosta and others v Nicaragua*, Monitoring Compliance with Judgment, Inter-American Court of Human Rights (22 November 2019) §§7–9.

[29] ibid §§20–27.

[30] ibid §53.

[31] *Roche Azana and others v Nicaragua*, Monitoring Compliance with Judgment (17 November 2021).

the recognition of rights and consolidation of institutions, the current political situation has promoted reiterated threats against human rights of Indigenous and tribal peoples. The already fragile situation of territorial rights due to the lack of title clearance is aggravated in an authoritarian context characterised by persecution and criminalisation against land defenders. If on one hand it could indicate that the Court has failed in its aim to induce deep transformations within the situation and strengthen democracy, on the other hand civil society still relies deeply on the IAS as a last resort to protection of their rights. The high number of provisional and precautionary measures issued by the IAS is a clear indicator of the trust that Nicaraguan civil society still has in the system.

4.5. FUTURE STEPS: *RAMA Y KRIOL V NICARAGUA*

The ongoing case of *Pueblos Rama y Kriol, Comunidad de Monkey Point y Comunidad Negra Creole Indígena de Blue Fields y sus miembros* (*Rama y Kriol*) is representative of the insufficient territorial protection in Nicaragua and illustrates the trust civil society has in the IAS. The case regards the megaproject of a 287-kilometre transoceanic canal cutting the country in two. The project imposes expropriation of Indigenous and ethnic territories and gravely impacts the livelihood of multiple communities. It has not been preceded by free, prior and informed consultation. The total sum of investment is estimated in US$50 billion. The project also foresees multiple subprojects, including airport, ports, roads and touristic complexes (Academia de Ciencias de Nicaragua 2015: 7).

The project started in 2012 with the approval of Law 800 (Law of the juridical regime of the Nicaraguan Grand Canal). It specifically mentions social environmental concerns, including the elaboration of environmental impact assessments and the right to free, prior and informed consultation with Indigenous and ethnic communities, following international parameters for restriction to Indigenous and ethnic territories (ILO Convention 169, UNDRIP and the Court's jurisprudence). The concession for the construction was approved in June 2013 by Law 840. In contrariety with Law 800, the project did not contain any viability survey or socio-environmental study and the information about the contract were not transparent. The debate, both within general society and in the National Assembly, was swift and accelerated, lacking consultation and information. Regarding traditional peoples' consultation, it was alleged that it had been fulfilled since the Regional Council of the Autonomous Region of South Atlantic had approved the project (Resolution 703, 23 May 2013),[32]

[32] Nicaragua, Asamblea Nacional, Comisiónde infraestructura y sevicios públicos, Dictamen (10 June 2013), presented in the Second Ordinary Session of the National Assembly, XXIX Legislature, Diário de Debates, Ley especial para el desarollo de infraestructura y transporte nicaraguense atingente al canal, zonas de lbre comercio e infraestructuras asociadas (13 June 2013).

but the Indigenous and ethnic communities had not been informed about the proceedings (Acosta 2016).

Despite the importance and complexity of the project, the approval of Law 840 was discussed for only three hours in the National Assembly. The opposition drew multiple arguments against its approval, including the socio-environmental impact, lack of consultation, necessity of a referendum, loss of sovereignty and economic insecurity. The Inter-American parameters for development projects were cited and the congresspersons acknowledged its binding character. On the other hand, the majority of the Congress voted for the Law, arguing the importance of the canal for economic growth, as well as the long national dream of building a canal.[33]

The environmental and social impact assessment (ESIA) was elaborated on only in 2014 by a company hired by the concessionary. The company announced it had consulted 5,000 people (approximately four per cent of the affected population),[34] but civil society and press reported access to the meetings had been denied (Amnesty International 2017). The content of the studies were made available only after their conclusion, in July 2015 (Amnesty International 2017). The insufficiency of the consultation is recognised by the ESIA, which states that 'additional efforts are needed to help stakeholders better understand the Project and the extent to which they and other resources of interest would be affected by the Project'.[35] The constructions started one year later, in December 2014. Between 2014 and 2018, the project moved slowly, focused mostly on studies (McCall and Taylor 2018). From 2018, the concessionary faced multiple financial difficulties and the work stalled (Muller 2019).

It has been argued that, if accomplished, the project will have an enormous economic impact on the country, immediately generating 50,000 jobs within construction alone. It could double Nicaragua's gross domestic product as well as promote a growth of 122 per cent in tax revenue, increasing investments in social programmes.[36] However, the viability of the project has been contested on political, social and environmental grounds (Márquez Domínguez and Díaz-Diego 2016). Law 840 permits the expropriation of any property necessary for the construction of the canal, including communal lands of traditional peoples, without foreseeing any mechanism of consultation. The canal zone passes

[33] Second Ordinary Session of the National Assembly, XXIX Legislature, Diário de Debates, Ley especial para el desarollo de infraestructura y transporte nicaraguense atingente al canal, zonas de lbre comercio e infraestructuras asociadas (13 June 2013).

[34] ERM; HKND Group; Canal de Nicaragua Environmental and Social Impact Assessment, Executive Sumara (July 2014); ERM; HKND Group, Nicaragua Canal public consultations overview (20 August 2014).

[35] ibid.

[36] Nicaragua, Asamblea Nacional, Comisiónde infraestructura y sevicios públicos, Dictamen (10 June 2013), presented in the Second Ordinary Session of the National Assembly, XXIX Legislature, Diário de Debates, Ley especial para el desarollo de infraestructura y transporte nicaraguense atingente al canal, zonas de lbre comercio e infraestructuras asociadas (13 June 2013).

through or near 282 communities (Márquez Domínguez and Díaz-Diego 2016) and will displace 120,000 people from their lands (McCall and Taylor 2018; Alexander von Humboldt Centre 2014). Specifically considering traditional communities, 52 per cent of the proposed route is located within ancestral territories, and the impacts in these communities are not yet clear. One affected community is the Indigenous Creole Black Community of Bluefields (CNCIB). The community has demanded demarcation of its traditional lands under Law 445 since 2006, but the official title was obtained late in 2016 and only seven per cent of their ancestral territory was recognised, leaving the remaining area available for the construction of the canal (Acosta 2017). In the matter of environmental protection, the project has been considered catastrophic. Several scientists have appointed the indispensability to perform further environmental studies to assess the impact on lakes, rivers, forests, wetlands and coastal ecosystems, as it has been grossly underexplored (Huete-Perez et al 2015). The canal will deforest around 400,000 hectares of rainforest and wetlands, and the impact in Lake Nicaragua is still unknown. The canal will also impair surrounding natural reserves and impact the animal population, putting at peril territorial, marine and freshwater biodiversity (Meyer and Huete-Pérez 2014).

Law 840 violates the rights of Indigenous peoples over their lands by foreseeing expropriation and by neglecting their right to free, prior and informed consent, violating the Constitution, Articles 180 and 181; Law 28 (Autonomy Statute, Articles 4, 8 and 9); Law 445 (Law of the Property Regime, Articles 4, 5, 12 and 31); the ILO Convention 169; the UN Declaration on the rights of Indigenous Peoples; and the American Convention, Article 21, with the interpretation given by the Court. It also impacts the livelihood of Indigenous and ethnic peoples, considering their deep relationship with natural resources. The environmental damage could impact food security and access to fresh water, violating the rights to a dignified life, cultural identity and healthy environment.

Nicaraguan civil society has resorted to multiple actions against the project. In April 2016, it submitted a Draft Law of Popular Initiative to the Nicaragua's National Assembly signed by almost 7,000 citizens, proposing the derogation of Law 840. Besides expressing concern over political, social, environmental and economic impacts, the proposed legislation specifically mentions the impact upon the traditional communities and their rights recognised in the Constitution, in Laws 28 and 445, in the UNDRIP and the ILO Convention 169.[37] The Secretary of the Assembly refused the proposal, alleging lack of jurisdiction. A lawsuit (*amparo*) was proposed against the decision and the Supreme Court of Justice in January denied the demand by alleging the lawfulness of

[37] Nicaragua, Asambleia Nacional, 'Iniciativa Ciudadana de Ley para la derogación de la ley especial para el desarrollo de infraestructura y transporte nicaraguense, atingente a el canal, zonas libres de comercio e infraestructuras asociadas (Ley 840), acuerdos y resoluciones conexas' in Baltodano (2017).

the Assembly's decision.[38] Furthermore, 32 unconstitutionality lawsuits were proposed before the Supreme Court of Justice in 2013. The Nicaraguan Court denied all in December 2013, alleging incompatibility of the Law and the Constitution, as well as the importance of the project to the Nicaraguan development.[39] Specifically regarding the lack of free, prior and informed consent with the traditional communities Rama and Kriol, seven lawsuits were proposed ('*amparo*'). All of them were dismissed, demonstrating the lack of an effective remedy to protect the territorial rights of traditional peoples in Nicaragua (Alianza de Pueblos Indígenas y Afrodescendientes de Nicaragua 2017: 87).

In 2014, Indigenous leaders, represented by the NGO CALPI, submitted before the Commission a requirement for information, a petition for violation of rights (P 912-14) and a precautionary measure (MC 495-14).[40] The Commission presented the merits report in 2020 (385/20) with recommendations to the state, considering the violation of multiple human rights. Considering the state's lack of response, the case was submitted to the Court in January 2022. The Commission highlighted four elements for the recognition of the rights violations: the lack of demarcation and titling of the Bluefields community; the lack of title clearance of the Rama and Kriol territories; the lack of free, prior and informed consultation for the construction of the canal; and the interference in the traditional decision-making process. The state allegedly violated the rights to property, political rights, equal protection before the law, judicial guarantees and the right to a healthy environment established in Articles 8, 21, 23, 24, 25 and 26 of the American Convention. In the public hearing held in February 2023, the representatives stated that the case does not relate to the lack of recognition of rights, but instead the state's omission to implement them. They also denounced the harassment the victims and their representatives were suffering as a reprisal against their activities in the defence of the land.

As of 2023, the construction remains stalled and uncertainties regarding the implementation of the concession remain. The case illustrates how the Inter-American System has played a important role in the struggle against the canal. During the debates in the National Assembly regarding the approval of Law 840, three congresspersons mentioned the Inter-American Court's parameters for development projects in Indigenous territories. Furthermore, activists and human rights organisations have repeatedly mentioned such parameters when presenting human rights violations. Lastly, the ongoing case before the Court,

[38] Corte Suprema de Justicia, Sala Constitucional, Sentencia n. 648 (31 January 2017) in Baltodano (2017).

[39] Corte Suprema de Justicia, Sala Constitucional, Sentencia n. 30 (18 December 2013) in Baltodano (2017).

[40] CIDH, Press Release, Report on the 154th Session of the IACHR (19 June 2015). Hearing available at www.youtube.com/watch?v=oOxVVwrKnBc&feature=youtu.be. See also: Argumento de las organizaciones peticionarias ante na Comision Interamericana de Derechos Humanos (16 March 2015) in Baltodano (2017).

brought forth by an Indigenous association, demonstrates the use of the IAS as strategic litigation in the struggle against rights violations.

4.6. FINAL CONSIDERATIONS

One interesting point about Nicaragua is the scarcity of UN reports and recommendations in regard to Indigenous peoples' rights. The most recent review of human rights conditions is the Universal Periodical Review of 2019, which set out very conservative recommendations regarding Indigenous and ethnic peoples – one recommendation to improve land demarcation and one to protect their cultural identity and property regime.[41] The most recent report from a UN treaty body is the 2008 concluding observations from the Committee on Eradication of Racial Discrimination (CERD). The CERD recommended the state adopt legislation for the Indigenous Peoples of the Pacific, Central and Northern Regions of Nicaragua and comply with the *Awas Tingni* decision before the IACtHR, as well as improve access to justice for Indigenous peoples.[42] Since the ratification of ILO 169, the ILO has supervised compliance with the Convention. In the most recent report, in 2019, the Expert Committee noted the IACtHR decision in the *Miskito* case, issuing recommendations very similar to the Court (prevention of violence, accountability and participation of the victims). It also required information about land demarcation, resolution of conflicts between Indigenous and third-parties, and participation in the World Bank project of land regularisation.[43]

On the matter of embeddedness analysis, during the first decade that followed the *Awas Tingni* merits decision, Nicaragua observed a concrete enhancement in the legislative framework of protection of Indigenous and ethnic peoples. Among the multiple advances in the domestic legal system, Law 445 represented the adoption of international parameters in matters of territorial rights, guaranteeing the right to collective property in the terms foreseen in the Court's interpretation and in the UNDRIP. The ratification of ILO 169 and of the Escazú Agreement are fundamental milestones in the acceptance of international law of Indigenous peoples, even more so as they represent binding rules for the domestic system. The concurrence of beneficial political arrangement and multiple incentives from international financial organisations and development programmes propelled the fulfillment of demands from the civil society and social movements, leading to a wide process of land demarcation and the creation of public organs to attend such demands.

[41] HRC, 'Report of the Working Group on the Universal Periodic Review Nicaragua' (5 July 2019) A/HRC/42/16.

[42] CERD, 'Concluding observations of the Committee on the Elimination of Racial Discrimination Nicaragua (19 June 2008) CERD/C/NIC/CO/14.

[43] ILO, CEACR, Observations Indigenous and Tribal Peoples Convention, 1989 (No 169) – Nicaragua (Ratification: 2010).

The legal innovation, added to the existent Nicaraguan Constitution and Autonomy Law (Law 28), ensured Nicaragua has some of the most advanced legal protections of Indigenous and ethnic peoples in Latin America. The practice, however, has demonstrated a concerning implementation gap as violation of territorial rights is a constant pattern, both caused by third parties or directly by the state. Despite some examples of peaceful cohabitation, the occupation has generated violence and forced displacement. A common element in all cases is the state's omission to protect traditional territories, even when ordered to take action by international organisations. The Transoceanic Canal project is exemplary of the lack of effectiveness of territorial protection. The construction has barely started, but Law 840 has already violated the rights to property, free, prior and informed consent, cultural identity and self-determination. The attacks against human rights defenders and organisations defending territorial rights against the canal are a concerning violation of the rights to freedom of expression and of association. Lastly, considering the grave political crisis experienced since July 2018 and its impact on Indigenous and ethnic peoples, the prospects of overcoming the implementation gap in a short term are very low.

Specifically regarding the *Awas Tingni* community, while chapter three described the path towards full compliance, this chapter has demonstrated how compliance has not been enough to guarantee full use and enjoyment of the property and its natural resources, as illegal occupation increased after the final title. In 2004, 41 families occupied the territory (Universidad de Arizona, Programa de derechos y políticas indígenas 2004), while in 2019 it was estimated that 1,000 families were illegally settled (Macdonald and Wetterslev 2019), comprising around 91 per cent of the total area, endangering the environment and the traditional Indigenous way of life. The feeling of despair and abandonment can be noted by the testimony of an aciant of the community, Grandfather Solomon:

> When we received the Title, it was a sign or a symbol of joy, especially for us, the Elderly, who have fought for this. We thought that with this title we secured the future of these children of the coming generations. We thought the land would be intact. But today we know that the AMASAU territory is full of people, occupied by other people. Totally invaded. It really causes me to feel sad. Even as I am ill, and old, it really causes me discomfort and preoccupation. It is really preoccupying, and mostly it leaves me feeling disappointed. That after so much struggle, the land has been occupied by other people, and not by us. It is sad (Wetterslev 2020).

The rise of violation of territorial rights in Nicaragua is simultaneous to deterioration of democratic institutions and, consequently, of the rule of the law. The Inter-American System becomes, for Nicaraguan civil society, the last hope of justice, as domestically all attempts of obtaining redress, politically and judicially, have been frustrated. The territorial social movements demonstrate awareness of the rights recognised by the Court and are willing to try all available options to guarantee their rights, including litigation to the regional system. In that sense, it is fair to say that the Inter-American Court's jurisprudence has strengthened Nicaraguan civil society's struggle for their rights, even though it was not enough to guarantee effectiveness of territorial rights in a context of des-democratisation.

More than 20 years separate the cases *Awas Tingni* and *Rama y Kriol* going before the Court. During this period, the country completed a full circle on the protection of Indigenous rights. It starts with the lack of regulation on Indigenous rights, impairing land demarcation and violating the territorial rights. It evolves to full domestic recognition of Indigenous rights and a massive process of Indigenous land titling. However, the lack of title clearance hinders full use and enjoyment of the territory and the 2018 democratic rupture closes the civic space for Indigenous peoples. The violation of territorial rights in Nicaragua returns to the Court in the expectation of achieving final redress. As discussed in chapter one, *Awas Tingni* was the leading case on communal property of traditional territories and *saneamiento* was not a concern in the decision. Additionally, chapter two demonstrated the fragility of the reparation order not to harm the territory, temporarily linked to final demarcation of the lands. In that way, chapter three described how the *saneamiento* of the lands was not analysed for declaration of full compliance in *Awas Tingni*, even though full use and enjoyment of the territory has been impaired by third-party occupation. *Rama y Kriol* could become an opportunity for the Court to face the shortfalls highlighted in the previous chapters and further develop the case law, including the concern with title clearance in the recognition of rights, the reparation measures and the supervision orders.

On the other hand, the full circle also indicates the failure of the Court in its mandate to promote the non-repetition of human rights violations and to transform factual scenarios of discrimination. In the chapter three's analysis of *Suriname*, it was explained how the absence of democracy blocks the implementation of the Court's decisions. This chapter has demonstrated that embeddedness is also affected by authoritarian governments, since the Court's further impact on the country has been hindered by the lack of democratic institutions.

5

Setbacks in the Brazilian Domestic Protection

BRAZIL HAS A consolidated framework of protection of Indigenous and Afro-descendant people. The 1988 Constitution guarantees the rights to juridical personality, ancestral territory and cultural identity to Indigenous peoples and the right to property over territories occupied by *quilombos*.[1] The organs responsible for land demarcation are the National Foundation of Indigenous Peoples (FUNAI) and the National Institute for Settlement and Agrarian Reform (INCRA). However, the period that followed the *Xucuru* decision before the Court is simultaneous with the dilapidation of human rights policies in the country and aggravation of already-in-course setbacks on traditional peoples' rights. The grave setbacks have been in course at least since 2016 (OHCHR 2017); however, from 2019 onwards, President Bolsonaro took office strongly supported by the agribusiness sector and neo-Pentecostal churches, with an open discourse against traditional peoples' rights and environmental protection.[2] The strong threats to Indigenous rights were opposed by active resistance of civil society, human rights state organs and, to some extent, the judiciary. In this context, the Court's decision in 2018 strengthened the domestic struggle and offered legal arguments for the defence of territorial rights.

Xucuru People v. Brazil[3] was the first territorial decision issued against Brazil, decided in 2018. Brazil has been considered responsible for human rights violations by the Inter-American Court 10 times, in cases related to human rights defenders (*Sales Pimenta*), violence against women (*Barbosa de Sousa and others*), work-related accidents and discrimination (*Employees of the*

[1] *Quilombos* are traditional ethnic communities with historical roots related to black ancestry and the struggle against racism. They are usually composed of the descendents of enslaved people, with peculiar traditions, customs and religion.

[2] Some of the polemic statements given by President Bolsonaro are: 'there will be no demarcation of indigenous lands under my government'; 'the indian is gradually evolving; he is becoming a human being like us'; 'most of our indians are condemned to live as prehistoric men in our own country. This has to change. The indian wants to produce, to grow, he wants the benefits and marvels of science, technology. We are all Brazilians' IWGIA (2020: 362–72).

[3] *Xucuru Indigenous People and its members v Brazil*, Preliminary Objections, Merits, Reparations and Costs, Inter-American Court of Human Rights Series C No 346 (5 February 2017).

Santo Antônio de Jesus Fireworks Factory), summary execution (*Herzog et al*[4]), forced labour (*Workers of the Farm Brasil Verde*[5]), massacres (*Guerrilha do Araguaia*[6] and *Favela Nova Brasilia*[7]), forced disappearance (*Garibaldi*[8]), mistreatment in a mental institution (*Ximenes Lopes*[9]) and illegal telephone interceptions (*Escher and others*[10]). So far, Brazil has fully complied two cases, *Escher and others* and *Ximenes Lopes*, while in all other cases it has complied with satisfaction and compensation measures, pending non-repetition, restitution, rehabilitation and accountability measures. Brazil has been considered a latecomer to the IAS, with the importance of the system increasing only recently, both in the domestic mentions to the Court as in the number of petitions submitted to the Commission (Engstrom and Low 2019; Cavallaro 2002).

In order to understand the contributions of the *Xucuru* case to the strengthening of domestic institutions, this chapter starts by analysing the current threats to territorial rights, including the lack of land demarcation, the increasing dilapidation of the state organs in charge of territorial protection and the approval of deleterious regulation. Next, the resilience of domestic institutions, despite the grave attacks to the territorial rights, is presented, demonstrating how the Court's jurisprudence has provided legal arguments on the protection of territorial rights. Lastly, two recent Brazilian cases before the Court are analysed, indicating a possible refocus of the federal government. The chapter concludes by demonstrating that, in the context of grave domestic setbacks against territorial rights and in a short period of time, the Court's standards for Indigenous and Afro-descendant rights strengthened domestic institutions and social movements in their resistance against the most serious threats to human rights since the Brazilian re-democratisation.

5.1. CURRENT LIMITATIONS TO THE EFFECTIVENESS OF TERRITORIAL RIGHTS

Brazil has a consistent regulation of land demarcation for Indigenous peoples and *quilombolas* communities. Brazil is home to immense ethnic diversity, with

[4] *Herzog et al v Brazil*, Preliminary Objections, Merits, Reparations and Costs, Inter-American Court of Human Rights Series C No 353 (15 March 2018).

[5] *Hacienda Brasil Verde Workers v Brazil*, Preliminary Objections, Merits, Reparations and Costs, Inter-American Court of Human Rights, Series C No 318 (20 October 2016).

[6] *Gomes Lund et al ('Guerrilha do Araguaia') v Brazil*, Preliminary Objections, Merits, Reparations, and Costs, Inter-American Court of Human Rights, Series C No 219 (24 November 2010).

[7] *Favela Nova Brasília v Brazil*, Preliminary Objections, Merits, Reparations and Costs, Inter-American Court of Human Rights Series C No 333 (16 February 2017).

[8] *Garibaldi v Brazil*, Preliminary Objections, Merits, Reparations, and Costs, Inter-American Court of Human Rights Series C No 203 (23 September 2009).

[9] *Ximenes Lopes v Brazil*, Merits, Reparations and Costs, Inter-American Court of Human Rights, Series C No 149 (4 July 2006).

[10] *Escher et al v Brazil*, Preliminary Objections, Merits, Reparations and Costs, Inter-American Court of Human Rights, Series C No 200 (6 July 2009).

252 Indigenous peoples living in the country, speaking 274 different languages and dialects (ISA, 2020).[11] Currently, 487 Indigenous lands are demarcated and homologated, representing 137 per cent of the national territory. In the 2022 census, almost 1.7 million people declared themselves Indigenous, representing 0.83 per cent of the population. Despite advances in land demarcation, 237 Indigenous lands still await regularisation. The situation is graver for Indigenous peoples outside the Amazon region: although 98 per cent of the demarcated area is in the Amazon region, 46 per cent of Indigenous people live outside the Amazon (ISA 2020). The demarcation process virtually stopped between August 2016 and January 2023 (ISA 2020a). Regarding *quilombolas* land demarcation, the situation is even graver. Despite recognising 2,847 *quilombos* as certified communities, only 241 of them have land title and there are 1,716 pending processes of recognition of *quilombos* (ISA 2019b).[12] The annual budget for land demarcation of *quilombolas* communities has drastically decreased (93 per cent in 10 years) (Schramm 2019), and since 2018 no property has been expropriated for guaranteeing *quilombolas* land demarcation (INCRA 2020).

There has been a deterioration of the indigenist organ, the FUNAI, since 46 per cent of all workplaces are unoccupied and the budget has decreased over the years: between 2010 and 2019, it reduced 25 per cent (ISA 2019a). Even worse, in 2021 only half of the planned budget was actually invested (Lunelli and Silva 2021). The foundation occupies only around 1,500 people, who have responsibility for all Indigenous lands. The aggravation of public policies through the destruction of the organs in charge of their appliance has been called institutional harassment. In the case of FUNAI, a ethnographic research demonstrated the lack of institutional support and the harassment suffered by FUNAI employees at work, aggravating already fragile conditions (Lunelli and Silva 2022). As Rufino stated, 'the asphyxiation of the indigenist agency has been a practical and effective method, requiring little bureaucracy, for paralyzing the state actions and its constitutional obligations to demarcation' (Rufino 2022).

Furthermore, the regularisation of traditional lands has not been enough to guarantee the effectiveness of the right to property, since exploration of natural resources is a continuing threat. There are currently numerous demands for mining in Indigenous lands, covering 25 per cent of the total area of Indigenous lands. In 33 territories, the mining area covers more than half of the Indigenous land (ISA 2020b). Increasing deforestation in Indigenous lands is also concerning. In 2019 10,000 km^2 were deforested only in the Amazon region, an increase of around 34 per cent in 2018, and the variation in 2017–18 had already been eight per cent greater (INPE 2020). In April 2020, the preliminary deforestation

[11] The numbers of indigenous peoples, as well as the number and situation of indigenous lands, vary according to the source. This work adopts the consolidation elaborated by the NGO ISA. See also FUNAI (2020); IBGE (2010).

[12] The number of *quilombolas* communities and the situation of their territory varies according to the source. See also Terra de Direitos (2020); INCRA (2020).

alerts were around 64 per cent greater than the same period in 2019, demonstrating a worrying growth in the 2020 deforestation rate (INPE, DETER 2020). Considering exclusively the deforestation in Indigenous lands, in 2019 490 km^2 were deforested, an increase of 102 per cent in relation to the previous year and 608 per cent in relation to 2015 (INPE, PRODES 2020).

As a consequence of the lack of land regularisation, violence against Indigenous peoples and *quilombolas* has increased rapidly over the years, a tendency aggravated in 2019 with the aggressive discourse of the President against traditional peoples. During Bolsonaro's Government, between 2019 and 2022, 795 murders of Indigenous people were reported, representing an increase of 54 per cent in relation to previous governments. In 2022 alone, 416 cases of violence were reported against Indigenous people, including 180 murders and 28 attempted murders. There is a particular concern for Indigenous people in voluntary isolation, since 36 Indigenous lands occupied by these people have been invaded and attacked (CIMI, 2022). Regarding *quilombolas* communities, the most recent data available refers to 2017, when there was an increase of 350 per cent in the number of murders compared to previous years, with 18 cases (CONAQ and Terra de direitos 2018). Violence against Indigenous and *quilombolas* is included in a context of rising land conflict in Brazil: in 2019, 1,206 conflicts over the land were identified (46 per cent of them against Indigenous people and *quilombolas*) and 489 cases of conflict over water access (Canuto et al 2020). Violence against traditional peoples has assumed very different forms, eg massacres (Della Barba and Junqueira 2020), fumigation by agrochemicals (Della Barba 2019; Grigori 2020), arson fire (Oliveira 2019) and restricted access to sacred places (Barros 2019).

The paralysation of the land demarcation processes and the weakening of the institutions and the regulatory framework were considered concerning elements in the Brazilian implementation of ILO Convention 169 by the ILO supervision mechanism, which requested the state to follow up in the very near future with all pending processes on land demarcation and to provide information on the human and material resources allocated in the FUNAI and in the INCRA related to their mandate (ILO, CEACR 2019).[13]

Another concerning issue on the limitations of the territorial rights is the lack of regulatory framework on the right to consultation.[14] Some traditional peoples have adopted their own protocol of consultation, some of them with support from state organs such as the FUNAI, the DPU and the MPF. However, the status of these protocols and their compulsory adoption by entrepreneurs and by the public sphere is not clear. In fact, there are examples of the state

[13] ILO, CEACR, 'Observation, Indigenous and tribal peoples Convention, 1989 (n 169) – Brazil', adopted 2019, 109th ILC session (2020).

[14] ibid.

ignoring the protocols, approving infrastructure projects without consultation (Silva, Liana Amin Lima da 2017).[15]

The shortfalls demonstrate a concerning implementation gap in Brazil: there are several Indigenous and *quilombolas* lands pending demarcation; even demarcated lands suffer threats from exploration of natural resources; and there is a worrying rise in the violence against Indigenous peoples and land defenders. Despite having a consolidated legislative and institutional framework for protection of Indigenous peoples, it has not been enough to guarantee effectiveness of territorial rights.

5.2. SETBACKS IN THE REGULATION OF TERRITORIAL RIGHTS

The apex of Indigenous rights consolidation in Brazil was the 1988 Constitution, approved in the context of re-democratisation and the outgrowth of intense Indigenous mobilisation. However, from 2000 onwards, there were considerable attempts to diminish the Indigenous protection. A 2018 study demonstrated that there were 33 ongoing legislative propositions against Indigenous rights, either altering the land demarcation process or enabling natural resources exploration in Indigenous lands. Some of the draft bills are still pending deliberation as they face considerable resistance in the congress, mostly as result of the Indigenous mobilisation (Cavalli 2018).

Since 2019, the strategy of Bolsonaro's Government to dismantle Indigenous protection has been to edit executive orders that, while not extinguishing rights, limit the practice of Indigenist organs. One of the first measures adopted by the Government was the approval of a Provisional Measure[16] restructuring the public administration and submitting the FUNAI to the Ministry of Agriculture, instead of the Ministry of Justice (MP 870). The measure was altered in the Congress, which maintained the former structure of the FUNAI. During deliberations, Joenia Wapichana, the first Indigenous woman elected to the Congress, proposed the amendments 191–198, arguing against the alteration by mentioning the ILO 169 and the UNDRIP.

The Government also intended to considerably alter the Indigenous health system, extinguishing the national secretariat for Indigenous health (SESAI) and

[15] MPF, 'Protocolo de Consulta Prévia dos Povos Indígenas e Comunidades Tradicionais', www.mpf.mp.br/atuacao-tematica/ccr6/documentos-e-publicacoes/protocolos-de-consulta-dos-povos-indigenas.

[16] Provisional measures are a vestige of the authoritarian regime in Brazil and characteristic of hyper-presidentialism. They can be adopted by the President with force of law in cases of emergency and should be confirmed by the Congress within 60 days (renewable once) or they lose validity. Despite exceptional provision in the Constitution for urgent and relevant situations, they have been widely used to regulate matters with resistance in the Congress, such as labour rights (MP 905), environmental protection (MP 901), pension systems (MP 871), university autonomy (MP 914 and 979), student movement (MP 895) and union membership (MP 873).

charging the municipalities with the Indigenous health instead. The proposal was strongly resisted by the Indigenous movement, which obtained support in the Congress (Angelo 2019a). Considering the resistance within the legislative organ, the Government approved Decree 9795,[17] integrating the SESAI to the municipal health system (SUS), extinguishing organs and reducing Indigenous participation on health policies (Jucá 2019; Angelo 2019b). In the same direction, the Decree 9759 extinguished multiple councils of participation of Indigenous peoples in the Indigenous policies.[18]

On November 2019, the FUNAI edited an administrative act deciding it would provide public policies exclusively to Indigenous living in homologated territories,[19] excluding one-third of Indigenous peoples from basic public services such as food and water supply. Even though the Indigenist organ argued the decision was based on budget cuts, it has been argued that it is actually a strategy to force Indigenous disoccupation of contested lands (Shalders 2020). The Federal Prosecution Office (MPF) and the Federal Public Defender issued a recommendation reaffirming the Indigenous rights to public policies even if occupying non-titled lands, citing the ILO Convention 169, the UNDRIP, the ADRIP and other international treaties on the matter of Indigenous rights.[20]

Recent measures have also stimulated land-grabbing in traditional lands. A first attempt was the Provisional Measure 910/2019, awarding amnesty and land regularisations for occupants of public lands. Even though it does not explicitly mention Indigenous properties, the land regularisation would be based on self-declaration of occupants and on the Rural Environmental Registry (CAR), which does not correspond to land title. In 2019, 4.5 million hectares of registered properties in the CAR overlapped with homologated Indigenous land and integral conservation areas, and at least 500 properties overlapped Indigenous areas inhabited by Indigenous peoples in voluntary isolation (Sparovek et al 2019; Fonseca and Oliveira 2020). The PM 910/2009 was refuted by scientific studies, ascertaining its impact to environmental protection, the aggravation of rural conflicts, the lack of transparency and problems with the self-declaration methodology (Sparovek et al 2019; Sauer et al 2019; Brito et al 2019). Also, the MPF issued a technical note presenting multiple unconstitutionalities of the measure and recommending its refusal by the Congress.[21] Several civil society organisations expressed concern with the measure.[22] It was proposed in December 2019,

[17] Decree 9795, Aprova a Estrutura Regimental e o Quadro Demonstrativo dos Cargos em Comissão e das Funções de Confiança do Ministério da Saúde, remaneja cargos em comissão e funções de confiança, transforma funções de confiança e substitui cargos em comissão do Grupo-Direção e Assessoramento Superiores – DAS por Funções Comissionadas do Poder Executivo – FCPE (17 May 2019) Arts 40–43.

[18] Decree 9759, extingue e estabelece diretrizes, regras e limitações para colegiados da administração pública federal (11 April 2019). See also ISA (2019c); Guajajara (2020).

[19] FUNAI, Despacho SEAV/COGAB/PRES/2019 (25 November 2019).

[20] MPF; DPU, Recomendação Conjunta No 01/2019/6CCR/DPU (2 December 2019).

[21] MPF, Nota Técnica no 1/2020/PFDC/MPF (3 February 2020) PGR-00032061/2020.

[22] Terra de Direitos, 'Nota Técnica' (12 May 2020), terradedireitos.org.br/noticias/noticias/7-razoes-para-nao-aprovar-a-mp-da-grilagem/23306; CIMI, 'Se aprovada, MP 910 irá legalizar esbulho

but since it was not deliberated by the Congress, it lost validity in May 2020. It was followed by the draft bill 2633/2020, with the same content, which is still pending deliberation. On the same matter, the FUNAI edited in April 2020 the Normative Instruction no 09/2020 (IN 09/202), regulating the certification of Indigenous lands. Contrary to former regulation, the IN 09/2020 obliges the indigenist organ to certify merely homologated Indigenous lands, leaving 33 per cent of Indigenous lands unprotected. The Normative Instruction has suffered strong resistance within the Congress,[23] civil society,[24] the MPF[25] and in the judiciary.[26] Only one month after editing the measure, the FUNAI certified 72 properties in non-homologated Indigenous lands (Fonseca and Oliveira 2020), aggravating land conflicts and violence against Indigenous leaders.

In 2021, FUNAI edited a normative resolution regulating the hetero-identification of Indigenous peoples and establishing criteria to evaluate who should be considered Indigenous.[27] The resolution violated the principle of self-identification established by multiple international organs, such as the ILO Convention 169 and the Inter-American Court's case law. The resolution was suspended by the Supreme Court a few months later, who considered it unconstitutional and unconventional. In the same year, FUNAI edited a resolution about economic exploration of Indigenous lands by non-Indigenous people through partnership. Both resolutions were revoked in 2023. In 2022, Bolsonaro edited the Decrees 10966 and 10965, instituting a programme for artisanal and small-scale mining, with a focus on the Amazon region. The decree facilitated the licensing process for mining and excluded traditional communities from participating on the procedures. Indigenous associations denounced the absence of free, prior and informed consultation and the possible impacts on Indigenous lands. The decree was revoked in 2023.

e grilagem de terras públicas' (15 May 2020), cimi.org.br/2020/05/se-aprovada-mp-910-ira-legalizar-esbulho-e-grilagem-de-terras-publicas; ISA, 'Sumário Executivo Sobre a Medida Provisória No 910/2019' (20 April 2020), www.socioambiental.org/pt-br/noticias-socioambientais/isa-divulga-nota-tecnica-contra-a-mp-da-grilagem.

[23] Draft laws were proposed in order to suspend the effects of the Normative Instruction (PDL 174/2020, PDL 170/2020, PDL 247/2020 and PDL 166/2020), still pending deliberation.

[24] CIMI, 'Nota do Cimi contra a Instrução Normativa no 09/2020 da Funai' (29 April 2020); ABA, 'Nota da ABA de repúdio à Instrução Normativa No 9/2020 da FUNAI, que desconsidera parte maciça dos processos de regularização fundiária do próprio órgão indigenista, acentuando os riscos aos povos indígenas e a seus territórios no País' (30 April 2020); INA, 'Nota Técnica: a Instrução Normativa da Funai no 09/2020 e a gestão de interesses em torno da posse de terras públicas' (20 April 2020); ISA, 'Funai edita medida que permite ocupação e até venda de áreas em Terras Indígenas' (24 April 2020).

[25] MPF, Procuradoria da República em Mato Grosso, Ofício de Populações Indígenas e comunidades tradicionais, Recomendação n. 13/2020 (29 April 2020) PR-MT-00015076/2020.

[26] STF, ADPF 679, rel Min Fux, dismissed on 6 May 2020 for inappropriateness of the chosen procedural mean; TRF1, 3a. Vara Federal Cível da SJMT, ACP 1007376-21.2020.4.01.3600 (8 June 2020). The judge ordered a precautionary measure suspending the effects of the IN until the final decision; TJDFT, 16 Vara Federal de Brasília, Ação Popular 1026656-93.2020.4.01.3400, pending decision.

[27] FUNAI, Resolução Normativa 4 (22 January 2021).

The overall scenario is of worrying setbacks in the regulation of Indigenous rights, mostly through executive orders. Some of the setbacks have been reverted or diminished through active resistance of state powers and civil society, but they have intensified violent conflicts, land-grabbing and deforestation. If before 2019 the effectiveness of territorial rights was in jeopardy because of the implementation gap, since 2019 it has been aggravated by attempts to diminish territorial rights or the structure for their implementation. The existence of the rule of law has partially halted the threats, demonstrating that even weak democracies are vital in guaranteeing stability in the protection of socio-economic rights.

5.3. THE FEDERAL SUPREME COURT TOWARDS CHANGE

The Brazilian Federal Supreme Court (STF) has maintained an ambiguous relation with the conventionality control and the applicability of the Court's standards on human rights (Daly 2017). In 2008, the Court decided that the American Convention has a supra-legal status in the Brazilian system, infra-constitutional but above the domestic legislation.[28] The jurisprudence of the Court has been cited in multiple themes, including press freedom,[29] provisional execution of criminal decisions,[30] LGBTI+ rights,[31] and positive action against discrimination.[32] Most of the decisions were issued as of 2018, demonstrating a rising dialogue between the Court and the STF.[33] However, regarding the validity of self-amnesty law in relation to crimes committed during the military dictatorship, the STF has ignored the application of the Court's jurisprudence, affirming the validity of the domestic legislation,[34] even though the country had already twice been held responsible for human rights violations.[35] Brazil is the only country in Latin America that has not reviewed the amnesty law, promoting the impunity of mass atrocities committed during the dictatorship.

Specifically in respect to territorial rights, the Court also presents a contradictory case law, even though it is possible to perceive a growing tendency on the strengthening of Indigenous rights. The Court has recognised the significance

[28] STF, Pleno, RE: 466343 (3 December 2008). See Maues (2013). Despite the recognition of the supra-legality, mentions to the ACHR have been applied only to confirm an already consolidated interpretation of the Constitution, only ratifying a former understanding. Magalhães et al (2017).

[29] STF, Pleno, RE 511961 (17 June 2009).

[30] STF, Primeira Turma, ARE 1092362 (20 August 2019); and AgR HC 171891 (9 August 2019).

[31] STF, Pleno, RE 670422 (15 August 2018) separate opinion of Justice Rosa Weber; ADI 4275 (01 March 2018) separate opinion of Justice Edson Fachin.

[32] STF, Pleno, voto Min. Edson Fachin, ADI 5617 (15 March 2018).

[33] For a detailed analysis of some of the cases, see Maues (2018).

[34] STF, Pleno, ADPF 153 (29 April 2010). The STF does not even mention the Inter-American jurisprudence and the case is decided merely based upon domestic legislation. See Bernardes (2011); Bernardi (2017); Schneider (2011); Souza et al (2019).

[35] *Gomes Lund and others v Brazil* (2010) and *Vladmir Herzog v Brazil* (2018).

of Indigenous communal property in some cases,[36] but it has also applied the timeframe theory to invalidate land demarcation decrees in others.[37] There are also multiple decisions pending final decision, some for several years.[38] One worrying aspect of the cases is that the Indigenous peoples are not party to the procedures, since according to the Brazilian legislation they are not owners of the lands, but the state is. In most of the cases, Indigenous peoples have not even participated in the proceedings. It has generated in recent years the proposition of rescissory actions to void judicial proceedings that occurred without Indigenous participation.[39]

In the reasoning of the decisions, only recently international treaties and jurisprudence were cited. The first time the Inter-American Court was cited was in February 2018, a few days after the Court's decision in *Xucuru*. The ADI 3239 is a paradigmatic decision that recognised the constitutionality of Decree 4887/2003, which regulates the right to communal property of *Quilombolas* communities.[40] The decision mentions the Court's cases *Moiwana* and *Saramaka*, recognising the protection of Afro-descendant people's traditional territory under the right to property. In 2019, the STF decided a lawsuit analysing access to justice and the importance of functional coherence among state branches in charge of Indigenous policies. The *Xucuru* case is mentioned, specifically the obligation of due process of law during land demarcation.[41] When analysing the statute of limitations regarding environmental damage on Indigenous territory, the STF cited *Kichwa de Sarayaku*, reinforcing the interdependence between environmental protection and Indigenous rights.[42] In the context of the 2020 pandemic, the STF issued the decision ADPF 709-MC Ref, ordering positive state actions to be taken to protect the rights of Indigenous peoples during the COVID-19 pandemic. The tribunal cited multiple treaties from the inter-American system and decisions issued by the Court.[43] Similarly, the Court is also cited in a lawsuit regarding the right to health of *quilombolas* communities during the pandemic.[44]

[36] STF, Pleno, PET 3388 (19 March 2009); ACO 312 (2 May 2012); ACO 362 (16 August 2017); ACO 366 (16 August 2017).

[37] STF, 2 Turma, RMS 29087116 (16 September 2014); RMS 2954230 (30 September 2014); ARE 803462 (09 December 2014); ARE 984335 (24 April 2018); STF, Mon Dias Tofoli, ARE 1038545 (29 August 2017); STF, Mon Rosa Weber, ARE 1.181.112 (1 February 2019).

[38] STF, ACO 204, ongoing process since 1981; MS 26853, ongoing process since 2007; MS 28541, ongoing process since 2009; ACO 2323, ongoing process since 2014; RE 1017365 ongoing process since 2016; AR 2686, ongoing process since 2018; AR 2750 ongoing process since 2019; AR 2751 ongoing process since 2019 and AR 2756 ongoing process since 2019.

[39] STF, AR 2750, AR 2756 and AR 2751.

[40] STF, Pleno, ADI 3239 (8 February 2018).

[41] STF, Pleno, ADI 6062-MC Ref (1 August 2019).

[42] STF, Pleno, RE no 654833/AC (20 April 2020).

[43] STF, Pleno, ADPF 709 – MC Ref (5 August 2020).

[44] STF, Pleno, ADPF 742 – MC Ref (24 February 2021). See also Navarro and Calabria (2023).

Another novelty in recent cases has been the mention to the ILO Convention 169 as reasoning for the protection of the Indigenous right to property. In the cases AR 2750 and AR 2756, precautionary measures were issued in order to review past judicial decisions in which the Indigenous peoples were not party in the processes. The reporting justices Carmen Lúcia and Rosa Weber cited the ILO Convention 169 to recognise the right to collective personality.[45] Furthermore, in the MS 3450, regarding revision of a land demarcation decree, the reporting Justice Celso de Mello dismissed the lawsuit for lack of procedural requirements, but mentioned the ILO Conventions 169 and 107 *ad argumentum tantum*.[46]

In 2023, the STF made one of its most paradigmatic decisions, regarding the 'timeframe' theory (*marco temporal*). For decades, this has been one of the most worrying limitations on territorial rights. According to the theory, Indigenous peoples have the right to land demarcation only if they were occupying the traditional territory by the time the 1988 Constitution was approved. The exception is cases of forcefully displacement when the community can prove its persistent resistance against the forced eviction.[47] It was first conceived by the Supreme Court in 2009 in the paradigmatic decision *Raposa Serra do Sol*[48] and later adopted by the executive through binding opinion 01/2017 of the Attorney General of the Republic (AGU Parecer 01/2017) in 2017. After the 2009 decision, the Supreme Court repeatedly applied the timeframe theory to invalidate land demarcation decrees[49] and the executive halted and revised multiple land demarcation processes. In January 2020, the Justice Ministry returned 17 land demarcation processes to the FUNAI, arguing they should be adjusted to the timeframe theory. The processes were in the last stage of land demarcation, only pending the final homologation (Valente 2020).

The timeframe theory had been strongly rejected by civil society and the Indigenous movement,[50] by the National Council on Human Rights[51] and by

[45] STF, Mon Rosa Weber, AR – MC 2750 (1 October 2019); STF, Mon Rosa Weber, AR – MC 2756 (5 March 2020).

[46] STF, Mon. Celso de Mello, MS – MC 34250 (14 June 2018).

[47] Silva and Souza Filho (2016); STF, PET 3388-4 (19 March 2009); STF, ED PET 3388.4 (23 October 2013).

[48] STF, PET 3388-4 (19 March 2009); STF, ED PET 3388.4 (23 October 2013); Silva (2018); Yamada and Villares (2010); Starck and Bragato (2020).

[49] STF, 2 Turma, RMS 29087116 (16 September 2014), referent to the Indigenous Land Guyraroka; RMS 2954230 (30 September 2014), regarding the indigenous land Porquinhos dos Canela Apãnjekra; ARE 803462 (9 December 2014), regarding the indigenous land Limão Verde; STF, Mon Alexandre de Moraes, MC ACO 2323 (26 March 2018), regarding the indigenous land Morro dos Cavalos; STF, Mon Luiz Fux, MC ACO 2224 (6 November 2013); STF, Mon Dias Tofoli, ARE 1038545 (29 August 2017); STF, Mon Rosa Weber, ARE 1.181.112 (1 February 2019). However, see MC MS 31901 (11 March 2014) regarding the indigenous land Kayabi, and MC ACO 1100 regarding the indigenous land Ibirama Laklaño (20 February 2020).

[50] Mobilização Nacional Indígena, Pela inconstitucionalidade do Parecer 01/17 e o reconhecimento do direito originário / povos indígenas às suas terras (19 May 2020); APIB, Nossa história não começa em 1988! Marco Temporal não! (3 August 2017).

[51] CNDH, Nota pública de repúdio ao parecer 01/2017 da AGU que viola o direito dos povos indígenas aos seus territórios (27 September 2017), mentioning as arguments for land protection the

the Prosecution Office.[52] Internationally, it had been refuted by the ILO supervision mechanism[53] and by the UN Special Rapporteur on Indigenous Rights.[54] An unconstitutionality lawsuit was proposed against the applicability of the AGU Parecer 01/2017 before the Supreme Court, decided in September 2023. The lawsuit was one of the longest ever seen in the Court, lasting 11 sessions. It involved 72 *amici curiae* from Indigenous peoples, national and international NGOs, public organs and political parties. The tribunal considered several arguments to refute the theory. First, Indigenous lands are constitutionally protected in Brazil since 1934 and since then forceful displacement was not sufficient reason for loss of the right over the lands. Second, the theory violates multiple international treaties that recognise the Indigenous property even in cases of dispossession (ILO Convention 169, UNDRIP and ADRIP), as well as the interpretation of international organs and courts in the matter, including the jurisprudential construct of the Inter-American Court. Third, the timeframe theory interprets the Constitution from an individualistic perspective, applying concepts of the Civil Code to the collective Indigenous property, ignoring the specificities of the protection of Indigenous territories. Fourth, the land demarcation is merely declaratory of a former situation, which is, the relationship between Indigenous peoples and their ancestral territory. The decision also established the possibility of monetary compensation to private owners of territories identified as Indigenous, which has been considered a significative hindrance for land demarcation.

It is possible to perceive a gradually and non-consolidated expansion both in the recognition of rights and in the reasoning applied by the STF on the matter of territorial rights. Since 2018, the STF has invoked international treaties and jurisprudence to recognise territorial rights, and has presented an increased tendency to expand the rights of Indigenous peoples (Prado Jr and Scotti), dismissing the applicability of the timeframe theory and recognising the collective juridical personality of Indigenous peoples. The expansion of the reasoning to intentional treaties follows a pattern in the general decisions of the STF, as demonstrated above. In times of accelerated threats to the rule of law, in general, and to the territorial rights, specifically, the STF has assumed a resilient posture against setbacks, issuing forward-looking decisions that protect vulnerable groups (women, racial minorities, LGBTI+ people, incarcerated people, etc) and reinforce the rule of law (Melo 2019). This increased consolidation

international recognition of territorial rights in the ILO Convention 169, the International Convenant for Econominc, Social and Cultural Rights and the American Convention.

[52] MPF, 6CCR, Enunciados no 37, 38 and 39, www.mpf.mp.br/atuacao-tematica/ccr6/copy_of_enunciados/enunciados; MPF, 6 CCR, Notá Técnica 02/2018/6 CCR (20 March 2018) PGR-00067386/2018; MPF, Nota técnica 1/2020/6ª CCR/MPF (11 May 2020).

[53] ILO, CEACR, Observation, Indigenous and tribal peoples Convention, 1989 (n. 169) – Brazil. Adopted 2019, 109th ILC session (2020).

[54] HRC, Report of the Special Rapporteur on the rights of indigenous peoples on her mission to Brazil (8 August 2016) A/HRC/33/42/Add.1; Dolce (06/26/2020 09:47:31).

to affirm Indigenous rights is accompanied by additional references to international treaties and decisions, demonstrating how the tribunal instrumentally uses international sources to reinforce its evolutional jurisprudence.

5.4. STRENGTHENING DOMESTIC HUMAN RIGHTS INSTITUTIONS

The Court's jurisprudence in territorial law has strengthened domestic institutions in the struggle for human rights, offering valuable arguments and parameters in the interpretation of territorial rights. One of the institutions to have gained prominence in the protection of Indigenous rights is the Ministério Público Federal (MPF).[55] According to the 1988 Constitution, the MPF not only has the prosecution prerogative, but also has responsiblity to 'judicially defend the rights and interests of indigenous population' (CF, Articles 127 and 129 V). The organ has an active role in issuing recommendations and technical notes, but it also proposes judicial class actions (*ação civil pública*) in the defence of Indigenous rights. It counts with a specialised secretary for Indigenous and traditional peoples affairs.

Recent agreements between the MPF and the IASHR have been celebrated, strengthening of the relationship between the institutions. The first covenant celebrated was between the MPF and the Court in 2016 aimed at promoting 'technical and cultural interchange, through visits, documents exchange …, training of members and employees in the thematic of their respective jurisdiction and implementation of other activities of mutual interest'.[56] In 2018, the MPF celebrated an agreement with the IACHR, with the very same object.[57] In the same year, the Federal Council of the MPF made an agreement with the IACHR specifically aimed at promoting the use and application of the IASHR's parameters and recommendations.[58]

The MPF has gradually incorporated the Inter-American standards into its legal framework for Indigenous protection. Before the *Xucuru* decision in 2018, the MPF had mentioned the Court's jurisprudence on a few occasions, but as of 2018, it has cited the Inter-American standards in multiple occasions. The MPF published two handbooks that include a chapter dedicated to the Inter-American case law: *Recognition of Quilombolas Communities' Territorial Rights* (MPF 2018) and *Handbook on Indigenous Rights Jurisprudence* (MPF 2019).

[55] On the impact of the MPF in other human rights areas, see Engstrom and Low (2019).

[56] MPF and IACtHR, 'Memorando de entendimento que entre si celebram o Ministério Público Federal da República Federativa do Brasil e a Corte Interamericana de Direitos Humanos' (6 June 2016).

[57] MPF and IACHR, 'Memorando de entendimento que entre si celebram o Ministério Público Federal da República Federativa do Brasil e a Secretaria-Geral da Organização dos Estados Americanos através da Comissão Interamericana de Direitos Humanos' (5 November 2018).

[58] MPF and IACHR, 'Acordo de cooperação que entre si celebram a Secretaria-General da Organização dos Estados Americanos e o Conselho Nacional do Ministério Público' (5 November 2018).

When acting in non-contentious cases, the MPF issued in 2018 a technical note refusing the AGU Parecer 001/2017 regarding the timeframe theory, citing multiple cases in the Court in the matters of consultation, property and access to justice.[59] In 2019, a technical note was issued analysing the concession of a military area for spatial exploration without consultation to the traditional peoples that ancestrally occupy the area. The cases *Saramaka v Suriname* and *Kichwa de Sarayaku v Ecuador* were cited in respect of the right to consultation.[60] In 2020 the MPF issued a recommendation against the FUNAI's normative instruction IN 09/20, citing *Awas Tingni* to reinforce the communal property right.[61] Lastly, the MPF has also acted in judicial processes regarding Indigenous rights, proposing lawsuits or offering non-binding opinions. The Inter-American Court has been cited by the MPF in some recent class actions in order to protect territorial rights, including against illegal mining in Indigenous lands,[62] against the FUNAI normative instruction 09/2020[63] and demanding positive actions during the COVID-19 pandemic.[64] The MPF presented non-binding opinions before the STF in cases pending decisions and it has mentioned the Court's jurisprudence on two occasions: in ACO 2323 and in RE 1017365.[65]

A second human rights institution with a significant role in the protection of territorial rights is the Federal Public Defender Office (DPU). The DPU in Brazil has constitutional jurisdiction to defend individual and collective rights of 'needy citizens' (*necessitados* or *hipossuficientes*), according to Article 134 of the Constitution.[66] The DPU has a secretary who specifically represents the DPU before the Inter-American System, the Coordination of Support to the Practice in the Inter-American System of Human Rights and a specialised working group on Indigenous peoples. The DPU has acted as *amicus curiae* in multiple cases before the Court, not only against Brazil,[67]

[59] MPF, 6 CCR, NOTA TÉCNICA No 02/2018-6CCR (20 March 2018) PGR-00067386/2018.

[60] MPF, NOTA TÉCNICA No 03 /2019-6CCR (30 September 2019).

[61] MPF, Procuradoria da República em Mato Grosso, Ofício de Populações Indígenas e comunidades tradicionais, Recomendação n. 13/2020 (29 April 2020) PR-MT-00015076/2020.

[62] TRF1, Justiça Federal em Altamira, Ação civil pública 1002918-56.2019.4.01.3903, petição inicial (26 November 2019); TRF1, 9ª Vara Federal Ambiental e Agrária da SJPA, Açao civil pública 1014306-62.2019.4.01.3900, petição inicial (27 November 2019); TRF1, Vara Federal Cível e Criminal da SSJ de Castanhal-PA, Ação civil pública 1006591-54.2019.4.01.3904, petição inicial (28 November 2019).

[63] TRF1, 3a. Vara Federal Cível da SJMT, ACP 1007376-21.2020.4.01.3600, petição inicial (15 May 2020).

[64] 19 Procuradoria da República em Roraima, MPF vai ao TRF1 para garantir plano emergencial de combate à covid-19 na Terra Indígena Yanomami (30 May 2020), www.mpf.mp.br/rr/sala-de-imprensa/noticias-rr/mpf-vai-ao-trf1-para-garantir-plano-emergencial-de-combate-a-covid-19-na-ti-yanomami.

[65] MPF, PGR, ACO 2223, parecer da PGR (13 November 2018); MPF, PGR, RE 1017365, parecer PGR (3 September 2019).

[66] See Leite (2014).

[67] *Favela Nova Brasília v Brasil* (n 7) and *Xucuru People v Brasil* (n 3).

but also in advisory opinions.[68] The DPU is also *amicus curiae* in several cases before the STF, defending Indigenous rights.

5.5. BRAZIL BEFORE THE COURT: *ALCANTARA* AND *YANOMAMI*

Since *Xucuru*, Brazil has been involved in two other territorial cases before the Court. *Comunidades Quilombolas de Alcâtara* is a contentious case submitted to the Court in 2022 regarding the lack of consultation with traditional peoples for the construction of an aerospace facility. The case *Yanomami, Ye'kwana and Munduruku Indigenous peoples* (*Yanomami*) is a provisional measure regarding violence and mining on Indigenous territory. The cases are representative, on one hand, of the continuous violation of territorial rights even after *Xucuru* and, on the other hand, a possible change of behaviour after 2023.

Comunidades Quilombolas de Alcântara relates to the right to property over traditional territory of 152 *quilombolas* communities. They were displaced in the 1980s for the construction of an aerospace facility and relocated to agro-villages inadequate for their traditional way of life. The settlement impacted the socio-economic condition of the communities, reducing access to water and food sources. Over subsequent decades, the facility was expanded, imposing increased restrictions on the traditional territory. Both the construction and the expansion were not preceded by consultation. The communities demanded the titling of their traditional territory and respect to free, prior and informed consultation, both via administrative and judicial mechanisms. Despite the long lapse of time, the state has not tended to their demands. The case was proposed before the Commission in 2001 and only in 2022 did the Commission submit it to the Court. In 2023, the Court held a hearing, during which the state acknowledged responsibility for the rights violations, offered public apologies and proposed reparation measures, including the titling of the territory and monetary compensation. By December 2023, the Court had still not presented the final decision, and it is uncertain whether it will accept the acknowledgment of responsibility.[69]

Yanomami was first analysed by the Court on May 2022, following submission by the Commission. The Indigenous land, already titled by the state, had been invaded by thousands of people working in illegal mining. The invasion was followed by intense violence against the Indigenous communities, including threats, armed attacks, sexual violence and forced displacement. The state had

[68] Opinión Consultiva 24, Identidad de Género, e Igualdad y No Discriminación a Parejas del Mismo Sexo, Inter-American Court of Human Rights Serie A no 24 (24 November 2017) and Opinión Consultiva 25, La Institución del Asilo y su Reconocimiento Como Derecho Humano en el Sistema Interamericano de Protección Inter-American Court of Human Rights Serie A no 25 (30 May 2018).

[69] CIDH, Caso no 12.569 *Comunidades Quilombolas de Alcântara v Brasil*, Carta de submissão à Corte Interamericana de Direitos Humanos; Merits report OEA/SER.L/V/II.176 Doc. 202 (14 June 2020).

been repeatedly informed about the grave situation and did not take any action to counter the violence. Furthermore, the Indigenous representatives alleged a grave health emergency caused by pollution of the rivers by mining, food insecurity considering the lack of access to traditional means of survival, and a lack of basic medical assistance and medications. The Court considered the situation urgent and grave and ordered provisional measures to protect the lives and the personal integrity of the Indigenous peoples. The Court took into consideration that the situation had worsened even after decisions issued by the Commission and by the Brazilian Supreme Court.[70]

Between 2018 and 2021, 570 Indigenous children died of evitable causes, an increase of one-third compared to the same period. The estimate is that six out of 10 children suffer from malnutrition (Machado et al 2023). The mining activity increased by 46 per cent in 2021 and 30 per cent in 2022, in total an increase of 3,350% between 2016 and 2022 (Hutukara Associação Yanomami and Associação Wanasseduume Ye'kwana 2022). After the Court's decision, the state did not take any substantial action to protect the Indigenous people and the situation only worsened. In January 2023, the new federal Government took power and initiated a series of actions in the *Yanomami* Indigenous land. It declared a Public Health Emergency of National Importance, created a commission for coordination of the actions, sent military forces to counter illegal mining and rescued people who were gravely ill. In only one week, 1,000 Indigenous peoples were rescued and sent to hospitals (G1 RR 2023). The situation in the Indigenous lands is extremely complex and demands continuous action. However, the change in commitment from the Government is clear and has already positively impacted the livelihood of the Indigenous communities.

On one hand, these cases demonstrate the continuous threats to territorial rights in Brazil. Despite an advanced legislation on territorial rights, there is a clear implementation gap and the territories of *quilombolas* and Indigenous peoples are not protected according to the legislation. *Yanomami* also exemplifies how the actions, omissions and discourse of an extreme-right government can impact the daily lives of traditional communities. On the other hand, the cases also indicate a possible change in Brazil's behaviour towards international decisions. The emergency operation on Yanomami lands occurred only a few days after the new Government took power, indicating a definitive change of perspective.

5.6. FINAL CONSIDERATIONS

Just as Nicaragua and Paraguay, despite having a consolidated legislation on territorial rights and specialised organisations for their implementation, the

[70] Matter of individuals of the Indígenas Yanomami, Ye'kwana and Munduruku indigenous peoples in relation to Brasil. Provisional Measures. Resolución de la Corte Interamericana de Derechos Humanos (1 July 2022).

institutional framework has not been enough to guarantee the effectiveness of Indigenous and *quilombolas* rights in Brazil. Furthermore, from 2016 onwards, Brazil has also experienced the greatest setbacks in Indigenous regulation since the military dictatorship. Violation to territorial rights can be observed in the lack of implementation of the legislation, in the adoption of administrative measures that undermine the protection (restricting rights or restricting the organs in charge) and in the judicial revision of land demarcation through the timeframe theory. In this domestic context, it would be expected that *Xucuru v Brazil* had only a small impact in the country, especially considering the short period of time from the publication of the decision.

However, the Court's decision has been adopted by social movements, Indigenous associations and human rights state bodies as a strengthening argument against the setbacks and in the struggle for effectiveness of territorial rights. One of the most important battles in the defence of territorial rights was the judgment of the RE101765 by the STF, definitely considering the timeframe theory void. Analysing the Court's authority (Helfer et al 2018) in the country in respect to territorial rights, it is possible to say that the Court has intermediary and extensive authority, with its decisions being cited and applied by a wide range of domestic audiences and new cases being proposed to the Commission in the field, such as *Guarani Kaiowa* and *Belo Monte*.

One peculiarity of Brazil is the high level of heterogeneity in the state. The political system has been characterised as a coalition presidentialism (Abranches 2018), in which the xecutive must establish coalition with very diverse political groups within the Parliament in order to approve desired policies. Furthermore, the Brazilian federalism also creates different levels of jurisdiction. Among prominent political groups, the agribusiness sector holds strong political power, represented in the legislature by the Agriculture Parliamentary Front (FPA), in 2020 with 251 deputies (from a total of 513) and 40 senators (from a total of 81).[71] The FPA has historically opposed Indigenous and environmental rights in the Congress, officially endorsing legislative setbacks in the field, ie the timeframe theory, the land-grabbing executive measure and the liberation of mining in Indigenous lands. As noted by Reis, in order to understand the impact of the Court's decisions, one should recognise the internal balance of power of political groups and the coalition-building process among them. Domestic groups struggling for human rights implementation resort to the IAS in order to rearrange the domestic power balance, setting an agenda with interested pro-rights recommendations (Rocha Reis 2019). In this scenario, international litigation is a strategic tool to strengthen domestic HRO and NHRI and reinforce the human rights-based agenda.

[71] FPA, fpagropecuaria.org.br.

Violation of Indigenous and environmental rights plays a central role in the contemporary Brazil's international relationships, considering the centrality of agribusiness in the Brazilian exportation and the rise of an international conservationist and sustainable discourse. The Indigenous movement is aware of this and has internationally denounced the setbacks and the continuing violations. In this scenario, two multilateral agreements are particularly important. The first is the free trade agreement between the European Union and the Mercosur (European Commission 2019) reached in June 2019, which has suffered intense resistance from European countries allegedly opposed to the lack of protection of the Amazon forest in Brazil.[72] The second is the Brazilian attempt to integrate the OECD: negotiations started in 2017, but the negative to comply with environmental standards might impair the approval of the country (Boadle 2019). In 2019, an Indigenous delegation visited 12 European countries for the campaign 'Indigenous blood: not a single drop more', aimed at pressuring the Brazilian Government and agribusiness companies to comply with internationally committed treaties in Indigenous and environmental rights (APIB 2019). In the same year, a delegation headed by the prominent Indigenous leader Raoni obtained important support from the French President Emmanuel Macron (Le Monde avec AFP 2019).

Comparing Brazil with Nicaragua, the importance of the rule of law is noticeable. Despite having a government that overtly opposed Indigenous rights, the country was able to counter the setbacks and to resist. The resilience has many elements, such as constitutional design, the strength of social movement and the consolidation of national human rights institutions. Many of the measures imposed during Bolsonaro's Government were later overturned, either judicially or by the new Government, reaffirming the protection of Indigenous rights. Of course, some of the damage caused is irreversible or might take decades to revert, but the reaffirmation of the rule of law might provide an example for other countries facing the same challenge.

[72] France, Ireland, Slovakia and Austria have already openly refused the trade. Oltermann (2019); SME.sk (8/28/2019); BBC News (2019).

6

Territorial Protection in Paraguay: Defending Indigenous Rights in an Agribusiness State

PARAGUAY HAS BEEN held responsible for violation of rights by the Court three times in Indigenous cases (*Yakye Axa*, 2005; *Sawhoyamaxa*, 2006; and *Xákmok Kásek*, 2010), which until 2020 represented 50 per cent of cases pending compliance before the Court against the country. The state has fully complied with one case (*Ricardo Canese*, 2004), regarding freedom of expression and due process of law. The cases *Instituto de Reeducación del Menor* (2004; lack of adequate infrastructure in a detention centre for children and adolescents), *Goiburú and others* (2006; forced disappearance during the dictatorship), *Vargas Areco* (2006; forced recruitment of children for military purpose), *Nogueira and other* (2020; forced recruitment of children for military purpose), *Ríos Avalos and other*, *Nissen Pessolani* (2021 and 2022; both regarding illegal destitution of civil servants) and *Leguizamón Zaván* (2022; murder of a journalist) are pending compliance, and the state has paid monetary compensation and complied satisfaction measures. On the other hand, measures of rehabilitation and accountability have never been complied with.[1]

The country has adopted a posture of goodwill towards international recommendations. UN bodies have provided multiple reports and recommendations regarding human rights, and the country has attempted to demonstrate concern towards full compliance. Furthermore, there is an active network of international organisations, including NGOs, development agencies and financial institutions, aimed at stimulating human rights effectiveness in the country. Despite the state's apparent efforts to make human rights effective, many challenges remain. The substantial and continuous economic growth of the last decade has not altered the precarious human development indicators of the country, as it remains one with the worst social indicators in the region, with high inequality levels and low Human Development Index (United Nations Development Program 2022).

[1] Information obtained from the IACtHR website, www.corteidh.or.cr.

Specifically regarding Indigenous peoples, the country has developed a robust mechanism for Indigenous protection. It has a specialised body for Indigenous peoples (INDI) and a specific legislation for land demarcation (Law 904/81), but Indigenous protection is also considered a transversal theme, and multiple specific state organs also has a secretary for Indigenous peoples. The national Constitution guarantees Indigenous rights, including the rights to self-government, property over ancestral lands and social rights (Articles 62–67). Finally, the country is a signatory of the ILO Convention 169 since 1993. Notwithstanding the legal protection, there is a considerable implementation gap, as the violation of Indigenous rights remains a concerning issue, with land evictions and violence increasingly being denounced.

In order to analyse the embeddedness of territorial rights in Paraguay, this chapter will start by analysing the relationship between the UN system and the regional system on territorial rights, followed by an analysis of the advances in the recognition of Indigenous rights in the legislature and in the judiciary. Afterwards, it demonstrates how the advance in the adoption of legislative parameters was not enough to guarantee effectiveness of territorial rights. The implementation gap is presented though analysis of census data and is related to institutional deficiencies and the economic model adopted by Paraguay. Lastly, the cases of the three communities before the Court are analysed, as example of the hindrances faced in land demarcation.

6.1. DIALOGUE AMONG UN BODIES AND THE IASHR REGARDING INDIGENOUS RIGHTS

Paraguay has demonstrated goodwill towards international supervision of human rights standards, presenting a considerable spirit of collaboration with the UN system bodies. It is also up to date to all its reports to the treaty bodies, as recognised by the Working Group on the Periodical Universal Review, which congratulated the state's will to engage in dialogue and to cooperate at the international level to improve the promotion and protection of human rights.[2] It has received multiple reports and visits from UN system bodies in the last decade, and a frequent concern in the reports has been the vulnerability within Paraguayan Indigenous peoples. On that matter, there has been a considerable dialogue in UN bodies' recommendations and the Inter-American parameters for territorial rights, making it essential to comprehend the interrelation in order to clarify the further effects of strategic litigation in Paraguay.

[2] UNHRC 'Report of the Working Group on the Universal Periodic Review' (12 April 2016) A/HRC/32/9 §§4–6.

Table 6.1 Recommendation from UN bodies regarding Indigenous peoples in Paraguay

		UNPFII	SR poverty	HRC	CESCR	SR indigenous	CERD	UPR	SR food	SR slavery
		2009	2011	2013	2015	2015	2016	2016	2017	2018
Adopt legislative framework	non discrimination law		■	■	■	■	■	■	■	
	right to consultation			■	■	■	■	■		
	land demarcation and protection					■	■	■		
	environmental protection		■			■			■	
Regulate impact of soy production			■		■	■	■			■
Perform prior environmental studies							■			
Strengthen indigenous organ		■		■		■	■	■		
Protect indigenous peoples in isolation						■	■			
Protect human rights defenders				■			■	■	■	
Guarantee access to justice		■			■	■	■	■		
Counter forced labour		■			■					■
Counter deforestation		■	■			■			■	
Ensure land demarcation and protection		■	■		■	■	■		■	

Sources: CERD: Committee for Elimination of Racial Discrimination;[3] CESCR: Committee on Economic, Social and Cultural Rights;[4] HRC: Human Rights Committee;[5] SR poverty: Special Rapporteur on Extreme Poverty and Human Rights;[6] SR slavery: Special Rapporteur on contemporary forms of slavery, including its causes and consequences;[7] SR food: Special Rapporteur on the right to food;[8] SR indigenous: Special Rapporteur on the rights of indigenous peoples;[9] UNPFII: UN Permanent Forum for Indigenous Issues;[10] UPR: Universal Periodical Review.[11]

[3] UN Committee on the Elimination of Racial Discrimination, 'Concluding observations on the combined fourth to sixth periodic reports of Paraguay' (4 October 2016) CERD/C/PRY/CO/4-6.

[4] UN Committee on Economic, Social and Cultural Rights, 'Concluding observations on the fourth periodic report of Paraguay' (5 March 2015) E/C.12/PRY/CO/4.

[5] UNHRC, 'Observaciones finales sobre el tercer informe periódico de Paraguay, aprobadas por el Comité en su 107º período de sesiones' (29 April 2013) CCPR/C/PRY/CO/3.

[6] UNHRC, 'Report of the Special Rapporteur on extreme poverty and human rights, Magdalena Sepúlveda Carmona, Addendum, Mission to Paraguay' (3 April 2012) A/HRC/20/25/Add.2.

[7] UNHRC, 'Report of the Special Rapporteur on contemporary forms of slavery, including its causes and consequences, on her mission to Paraguay' (20 July 2018) A/HRC/39/52/Add.1.

[8] UNHRC, 'Report of the Special Rapporteur on the right to food on her mission to Paraguay' (27 January 2017) A/HRC/34/48/Add.2.

[9] UNHRC, 'Report of the Special Rapporteur on the rights of indigenous peoples, Victoria Tauli-Corpuz, Addendum, the situation of indigenous peoples in Paraguay' (13 August 2015) A/HRC/30/41/Add.1.

[10] UNHRC, 'Report of the Working Group on the Universal Periodic Review' (12 April 2016) A/HRC/32/9.

[11] Foro Permanente de las Naciones Unidas para Cuestiones Indígenas, 'Misión a Paraguay, Informe y Recomendaciones' (31 August 2009).

Table 6.1 synthesises the recommendations issued by UN bodies and experts, aimed specifically at Indigenous peoples in Paraguay. There is an observable prevalence in the concern around Indigenous territory, including demarcation, land protection and conservation of natural resources, which includes recommendations for adoption of legislative frameworks as well as implementation of public policies. There has been a particular concern with national policies of favouring soybean monoculture for exportation, and the adoption of stricter rules of regulation, as well as the implementation of the already existent framework have been suggested. Procedural elements related to the protection of territorial rights have also been appointed, including the independence of the judiciary, respect of Indigenous customary law and system of justice, Indigenous rights awareness-raising courses for justice officials, introducing an effective remedy to claim for territorial rights, and creation of specialised justice units. Another important procedural aspect has been the protection of human rights defenders, particularly the ones acting in the defence of land rights, as well as the investigation and prosecution of threats and acts of violence against them.

There is a considerable compatibility between the recommendations from the UN system and the reparation orders issued by the Court in the cases against Paraguay. The Court's reparation orders are stricter, as it is restricted to cases *sub judice*, while the UN system recommendations analyse human rights effectiveness as a whole. In *Yakye Axa*, *Sawhoyamaxa* and *Xákmok Kásek*, the Court ordered Paraguay to improve its legislative framework regarding land demarcation in order to promote an effective remedy for Indigenous peoples' demands, just as recommended by the CERD, the Special Rapporteur on the Rights of Indigenous Peoples and by the UPR. Furthermore, there is compatibility between the order to demarcate and title the Indigenous lands in *Yakye Axa, Sawhoyamaxa* and *Xákmok Kásek* and the recommendation to ensure land demarcation issued by the UNFPII, the CERD, the CESCR and the Special Rapporteurs on the Right to Food and on the Rights of Indigenous Peoples. Furthermore, recommendations to adopt legislation on the right to prior consultation, to protect human rights defenders and to perform prior environmental studies is compatible with territorial cases decided by the Court against other countries, such as *Saramaka v Suriname, Garífuna Triunfo de la Cruz v Honduras* and *Kichwa de Sarayaku v Ecuador*. Lastly, the decisions issued by the Court against Paraguay have been explicitly mentioned in the reports of the UNPFII, the CERD and the Special Rapporteurs on the Right to Food, on Extreme Poverty and on the Rights of Indigenous Peoples, all of them strongly recommending compliance with the Inter-American cases.

The UN system has also presented an active role in financing and coordinating projects in Paraguay in defence of Indigenous peoples' rights. The projects encompass varied areas, such as food security (Ramos 2014), participation and consultation (Valina 2014), education (UNICEF and MEC 2012), rural development (FIDA 2015; FIDA 2017) and environmental protection (FAO 2020). However, it has been recognised that temporary projects in specific areas without systematisation might not be enough to tackle the central issue, ie the guarantee of territorial rights for Indigenous peoples, including demarcation, titling and title clearance of the lands and free, prior and informed consultation and consent (Ramos 2014).

The cooperation of Paraguay with international human rights bodies is also observable through the creation of internal mechanisms to prompt compliance with the recommendations. One such mechanism is SIMORE, online software for the systematisation and diffusion of international human rights recommendations, including information on the body in charge of compliance and the actions that have been taken to implement it. The system was developed with technical cooperation from the UNDP and the UN High Commissioner for Human Rights. It became an example of good practice and was adopted by several Latin-American countries and by the Inter-American Commission.[12] The second mechanism was the Inter-Agency Commission on the Enforcement of International Judgments (CICSI), created by Decree 1595/2009 and expanded by Decree No 4367/2015, with jurisdiction to follow-up all international recommendations issued against Paraguay, from either the UN system or the Inter-American system. The Commission has engaged with the victims and visited interested communities to implement international recommendations.

Specifically considering the Inter-American system, one reflex of the triple condemnation against Paraguay in Indigenous cases has been an increased promptness of the country to celebrate friendly settlements when the litigation is still before the Commission, avoiding future litigation before the Court. In the matter of territorial rights, the first celebrated friendly settlement agreement was in 2011, and concerned a petition proposed by the Indigenous community *Kelyenmagategma* in 2004, which denounced forced displacement of their ancestral lands and lack of minimal conditions for a dignified life. The community was partially titled in 2011 during a working visit of the Commission to Paraguay (IACHR 2011), and in 2019 the state established a development fund for the community (IACHR 2019), which was delivered in a public act of acknowledgment of responsibility. Some of the remaining measures to be complied are title of part of the territory; construction of an access path; construction of houses; and payment of the totality of the development fund (STP 2019; MRE Paraguay 2020).

The second friendly settlement refers to the Indigenous people *Ayoreo Totobiegosode*. In 2016, the Commission issued a precautionary measure, responding to a demand for violation of the rights to life, property, personal integrity, cultural identity and access to justice caused by third-party intrusion on traditional lands and deforestation. Some Indigenous communities were in voluntary isolation and the invasion of their territories posed a grave and urgent threat to their rights. The Commission recommended that the state counter deforestation in the traditional territory,create a mechanism to avoid third-party

[12] See UNHCHR 2015 and Pompeu, Lima 2018.

invasion, create specific protocols for the protection of Indigenous peoples in isolation, and adopt all necessary measures to protect life and the personal integrity of Indigenous people.[13] Besides the demand for precautionary measures, the victims presented a petition in 2015 (petition no 850-15). In 2017, the Commission started negotiations between the victims and the state to promote an agreement of friendly settlement, and the UN Office in Paraguay was chosen to mediate the negotiations (GAT 2017). Several meetings were regularly celebrated (Ministerio de Justicia 2018; Ultima Hora 2017) and in 2018 the state adopted the Protocol for performance, prevention and contingency regarding Indigenous peoples in isolation and/or at initial contact in the national cultural and environmental heritage Ayoreo Totobiegosode – PNCAT, located in the Departments Alto Paraguay and Chaco Paraguayo.[14] In 2019 the ancestral territory of the *Ayoreo Totobiegosode* was partially titled after the state purchased 18,000 hectares from a private company (Ultima Hora 2019; Corte Suprema de Justicia 2019).

In 2019, Paraguay was held responsible for violating the rights of an Indigenous community by the Human Rights Committee. *Portillo Cáceres and others v Paraguay* regards the contamination of water sources in Indigenous territory by pesticides used on a neighbouring farm. The contamination deeply impacted the community, which could not perform traditional rituals on the river and did not have access to clean water. It also provoked the death of an Indigenous member and the hospitalisation of several others. The HRC declared a violation of the rights to life, to a family life and to juridical remedy, ordering the state to complete the criminal and administrative proceedings against the persons responsible and to fully repair the victims. The state was also to take measures to prevent similar future violations from occurring.[15] Similar circumstances were considered in *Benito Oliveira Pereira and others* (2022) in which the country was considered responsible by the HRC for violating the rights of a dignified life of the members of an Indigenous community. One peculiarity of the case is that besides recognising the violation of the right to life, the HRC also recognised violation to the right to a dignified life, affirming the state's 'obligation to adopt the necessary positive measures to ensure the effective exercise of this right'. Other rights recognised as violated were the rights to cultural identity, consultation and to juridical remedies.[16]

Despite the state's efforts to demonstrate commitment to international law, civil society has determined that such behaviour might be mere rhetoric,

[13] CIDH, Medida Cautelar no 54-13 Asunto comunidades en aislamiento voluntario del pueblo Ayoreo Totobiegodsode respecto de Paraguay (3 February 2016) Res 04/2016.

[14] Ministerio de Justicia, Protocolo de actuación, prevención y contigencia para pueblos indígenas en situación de aislamiento y/o en situación de contacto inicial en el patrimonio natural y cultural Ayoreo Totobiegosode – PNCAT, situado en el departamento de Alto Paraguay, Chaco Paraguayo (April 2018). See Ministerio de Justicia 2018.

[15] UNHRC 'Views adopted by the Committee under article 5(4) of the Optional Protocol, concerning communication No. 2751/2016' (20 September 2019) CCPR/C/126/D/2751/2016.

[16] UNHRC 'Views adopted by the Committee under article 5(4) of the Optional Protocol, concerning communication No. 2552/2015' (21 September 2022) CCPR/C/132/D/2552/2015.

intending to strengthen Paraguayan diplomacy within international bodies, while internally adopting regressive measures that question the authenticity of the internationally reached commitment (Alonso and Caceres 2018: 510; Caceres 2017). The criticism is valid, but the influence of international bodies in Paraguay is visible through the adoption of legislation in Indigenous rights and the regulation of access to justice regarding Indigenous peoples. Paraguay has adopted international parameters of human rights protection, in some cases directly citing international norms. The advances in both spheres are presented in the following sections.

6.2. ADVANCES IN LEGISLATION

The recognition of Indigenous rights in Paraguay has advanced considerably in the last few years. In the matter of the right to education, in 2007 Law no 3231 was approved, creating a general directorate of Indigenous education, and in 2014 Law 5347 improved access to university for Indigenous peoples through the creation of quotas. Further, Law 6279/2019 created quotas in the public service, establishing the obligation of hiring Indigenous members in public institutions. In the field of the right to health, in 2015 Law 5469 was approved, known as the Indigenous Health Law. This was a proposal by Indigenous organisations based upon the principles of participation and interculturality. The draft of the law referred to multiple international treaties, such as the ILO 169 and the UNDRIP.

One area that has seen considerable advances is the regulation of the right to consultation, an obligation foreseen in the ILO 169, in the UNDRIP and in the Court's jurisprudence regarding the exploration of natural resources within Indigenous lands. A first step in recognising the right to consultation was resolution no 2039/2010 edited by the Indigenist body INDI. The resolution foresees that INDI shall intervene in all processes affecting Indigenous communities and mentions explicitly the ILO 169. However, resolution 2039 did not foresee consultation with Indigenous peoples and their institutions, but merely the state body's participation, not fulfilling the right to free, prior and informed consultation prescribed in the ILO 169 (Paola Canova 2018; Valina 2014).

The problem was redressed with the adoption of Decree no 1039 in 2018, creating the consultation protocol. The protocol had been proposed in 2013 by the Indigenous organisation Federation for the Self-Determination of Indigenous Peoples (FAPI), in a project financed by the UNDP (UNDP 2011), after consultation with multiple Indigenous associations and leaderships and discussion in two workshops.[17] During the debate, recommendations from multiple UN bodies were considered, including the HRC, the CERD, the UPR, the ILO Expert

[17] ILO, CEACR, Observation (adopted 2017, published 107th ILC session 2018), Indigenous and Tribal Peoples Convention, 1989 No 169, Paraguay.

Committee and the UN Special Rapporteur on the rights of Indigenous Peoples. The debate concerned the importance of respect to Indigenous peoples' traditions and customs, including timing of discussions, authorities to be consulted, availability of information and the participation of the whole community (Valina 2014; Valina et al 2014), recommending their inclusion in the regulation.

The adopted protocol mentions the ILO 169, the UNDRIP, the American Convention on Human Rights, the Convention for Eradication of Racial Discrimination, the Paraguayan Constitution and the Law 904. It establishes in the preamble that the

> procedure of free, prior and informed consultation and consent shall be applied in all cases in which local, departmental and national governments, companies, international financial institutions and other entities public, private and indigenous as project proponent, have interest in working in Paraguay and executing activities that could affect the rights to land, territory, life and traditional means of living of the indigenous peoples.

The protocol encompasses a wide range of situations, considering the project proponents, the content of the activity and the content of the procedures, including consultation and consent. Despite not citing directly the Inter-American Court jurisprudence on the right to consultation, the Court's parameters are present in the protocol, as consultation should be carried on with good faith, free from coercion, preceded by socio-environmental studies, followed by benefit-sharing and respecting the Indigenous peoples' laws, values and customs.[18] The protocol is a considerable effort to promote Indigenous rights and demonstrates the state's determination that the domestic system satisfies international parameters of Indigenous rights.

The protocol, however, was adopted as a decree and could be withdrawn by any future government. The adoption of a law could have guaranteed more juridical security. A draft law (*expediente* D-1326050) was proposed before Congress by the Ombudsman (*Defensor del Pueblo*) in 2013. It was refused from the Commission of Indigenous Affairs of the Deputy Chamber in 2014 and since August 2018 has awaited deliberation from the Deputy Chamber. The terms of the draft are less encompassing than the adopted protocol and the draft was not preceded by consultation with Indigenous peoples. In fact, Indigenous peoples have suggested the dismissal of the draft, considering the lack of consultation (Valina 2014; Valina et al 2014).

Moving on, and specifically regarding the rights of Indigenous peoples in isolation, in 2018 the Protocol for performance, prevention and contingency regarding Indigenous peoples in isolation and/or at initial contact in the national cultural and environmental heritage Ayoreo Totobiegosode – PNCAT, located

[18] *Saramaka People v Suriname*, Preliminary Objections, Merits, Reparations, and Costs, Inter-American Court of Human Rights Series C No 172 (28 November 2007).

in the Departments Alto Paraguay and Chaco Paraguayo was approved.[19] The protocol is an inter-agency compromise intended to ensure the rights of the *Ayoreo Totobiegosode* in voluntary isolation. It recognises multiple international and regional treaties on Indigenous rights, including the jurisprudence of the Commission and the Court. For the implementation of the protocol, an inter-agency commission and a monetary fund were created.[20]

Besides the regulation of Indigenous rights, 2019 saw multiple legal recognitions of the emergency situation endured by the Paraguayan Indigenous peoples. In May, intense flooding led to the adoption of the Laws 6301, 6306 and 6308, recognising emergency in the regions Boquerón, Presidente Hayes and Alto Paraguay for the term of 90 days in the first case, and 120 days in the second. In June, Congress edited Law 6319 declaring an emergency situation in all Paraguayan Indigenous communities, urging effective action in providing public services.[21] The Law does not expand the reason for the emergency situation, but it is observable in the Draft Law, which mentions the state's obligation to provide public services under ILO 169, as well as the report from the UN Special Rapporteur recognising the poverty of Indigenous peoples and land insecurity in several communities, all aggravated by the floods.[22] In September, the western region was suffered major bush fires; in response, Congress approved Law 6373/19 declaring an emergency situation for 60 days.[23]

The lack of public services and the Indigenous peoples' fragile land situation have been severely aggravated by environmental disasters. The absence of adequate roads and poor emergency healthcare caused the deaths of Indigenous members during the flood, as well as grave respiratory problems during the fires. The impact of the fires was even more harmful for Indigenous groups in voluntary isolation, as it destroyed ecological corridors used by the groups for dislocation (CODEHUPY 2020: 89–91). Despite the fatalities and the emergency declaration, the state's response has not been enough to guarantee minimal rights for Indigenous peoples, and the emergency situation persists (CODEHUPY 2020: 81–85).

One central issue still pending in the Paraguayan regulation of Indigenous rights is the creation of an effective mechanism for land demarcation. The measure was ordered by the Court in the three cases (*Yakye Axa*, 2005; *Sawhoyamaxa*, 2006; and *Xákmok Kásek*, 2010), as the tribunal considered the

[19] Ministerio de Justicia (n 14).

[20] The protocol is directly related to a precautionary measure ordered by the Inter-American Commission in 2016 regarding the Ayoreo Totobiegosode people, analysed supra.

[21] Ley no 6319, que declara en situación de emergencia a las comunidades indígenas que conforman los diecinueve pueblos diseminados en varios departamentos del territorio nacional (7 July 2019).

[22] Proyecto D-1951223, Dip Marlene Ocampos (7 May 2019).

[23] Ley 6373, que declara en situación de emergencia ambiental los departamentos Alto Paraguay y Boquerón en la región occidental afectados por los incendios forestales registrados (4 September 2019).

Paraguayan legislation to be ineffective to guarantee the demarcation of ancestral territories.[24] In *Sawhoyamaxa*, the Court identified three major flaws in the Paraguayan legislation: the possibility expropriating only non-productive properties; the inexistence of a procedure within the INDI to settle disputes over property in cases where there is an unwillingness to negotiate; and the absence of technical studies regarding the identification of Indigenous lands.[25] There is not even a draft proposal on the matter before the Congress for deliberation (Barreto 2017). The persistence of the problem has been highlightedd by Paraguayan NGOs and Indigenous leaderships as a central hindrance for the effectiveness of territorial rights in the country (FAPI and FPP 2015b; CODEHUPY 2013). Without an effective mechanism for land demarcation that overcomes the failures appointed by the Court, the right to communal property in Paraguay remains unfulfilled (FAPI and FPP 2015a).

Another failure in the Paraguayan legislation is the lack of an anti-discrimination law, what has been recommended by several UN bodies (CERD, CESCR, UPR, HRC and Special Rapporteurs on the Right to Food, on Extreme Poverty and on the Rights of Indigenous Peoples). There have been two draft laws before the Paraguayan Congress on the matter. The first was *expediente* 74805, proposing a general anti-discrimination law,[26] which was presented in 2007 but refused by the Senate in 2014. During the debate, international recommendations and treaties were cited, as well as the importance of regulating the Constitution and the factual situation of discrimination. On the other hand, it was argued that the law does not define sufficiently the terms and creates unjustified privileges. During the debates, there was a clear concern with gender identity, and religion was frequently cited.[27] A second project was presented in 2015 by a national NGO (*Red Contra Toda Forma de Discriminación*).[28] It mentions multiple international treaties and recommendations from international bodies. Since 2016 the project has awaited deliberation, and civil society has observed this lack of legislation to hinder denouncements, persecution and reparation before discrimination cases.[29]

[24] *Yakye Axa Indigenous Community v Paraguay*, Merits, Reparations and Costs, Inter-American Court of Human Rights Series C No 125 (17 June 2005) §§92–98; *Sawhoyamaxa Indigenous Community v Paraguay*, Merits, Reparations and Costs, Inter-American Court of Human Rights Series C No 146 (29 March 2006) §§102–11; *Xákmok Kásek Indigenous Community v Paraguay*, Merits, Reparations and Costs, Inter-American Court of Human Rights Series C No. 214 (24 August 2010) §§309–10.

[25] *Sawhoyamaxa Indigenous Community. Paraguay* (ibid) §§102–11.

[26] Expediente 74805, Proyecto de Ley contra toda forma de discriminación, presentado por los senadores Miguel Abdón Saguier y Carlos Filizzola (24 May 2007).

[27] Camara do Senado, Diario de sessiones (13 November 2014), silpy.congreso.gov.py.

[28] Expediente S-157013, Proyecto de Ley 'Contra Toda Forma De Discriminación', Presentado Por Los Senadores Carlos Filizzola, Miguel Abdón Saguier, Adolfo Ferreiro y Blanca Fonseca (23 November 2015).

[29] CODEHUPY, Informe Alternativo de la CODEHUPY para consideración del Comité de Derechos Humanos §12.

Indigenous organisations also suggest other possibilities to improve the Paraguayan legislation on territorial rights: inclusion of the terms 'territory' and 'people' in the Indigenous legislation; legislation on the rights of cross-border peoples, including cooperation with bordering countries; participation of Indigenous peoples in the management of environmentally protected areas; recognition of the right to water as a human right (Valina et al 2014); recognition of Indigenous peoples as juridical personalities instead of recognition merely of communities; and protection of the cultural heritage of Indigenous peoples, including the lack of protection of immaterial heritage (FAPI and FPP 2015a).

Beyond regulation, the legislature plays a very important role in land demarcation; in cases where the ancestral territory is owned by private individuals or companies and it is not possible to negotiate purchase of the lands, the legislature has to approve an expropriation law. In some cases, the expropriation law has been promptly approved, for example Law 3209 in 2007[30] and Law 4304 in 2011.[31] In other cases, the draft bill stalls for several years without justification, as is the case with *expedientes* D-1223886[32] and D-1223695,[33] proposed in 2012 and still pending. In some cases, the expropriation is refused, for example in the draft law 70427[34] in 2011 and the *expediente* S-08538 in 2009.[35] It is not possible to perceive a pattern in the behaviour of the Congress, and the debates in the

[30] Ley 3209, que declara de interese social y expropia a favor del Instituto Paraguayo del Indígena (INDI), el inmueble individualizado como finca nº 5967, del distrito de Mariscal Estigarribia, departamento de Boqueron, para destinarlo al asentamiento de la comunidad indígena Ebetogue perteneciente a la etnia Ayoreo (10 May 2007).

[31] Ley 4304, que desafecta del dominio de la secretaría del ambiente y transfiere en forma gratuita a la comunidad indígena Kuetuvy Ko'etí de la etnia Ache Guayakí, la finca no 470, situada en el lugar denominado caí cué del distrito de Curuguaty, departamento Canindeyú (09 August 2011).

[32] D-1223886, proyecto de ley que declara de interés social y expropia a favor del Estado paraguayo Instituto Paraguayo de Indígena (INDI), un inmueble individualizado como finca no 473, ubicado en el lugar denominado Puerto Bertoni del municipio los Cedrales, para su posterior transferencia a título gratuito a sus actuales ocupantes indígenas de la parcialidad Ava Guarani.

[33] D-1223695, que declara de interés social y transfiere a titulo gratuito a favor del Instituto Paraguayo del Indígena (INDI), para posterior trasferencia en forma gratuita a las comunidades indígenas de Joyvy Iri y 8 de diciembre de la parcialidad Aba Guarani, las fincas nos.8.516, 8.523, 6.438, 6.426, 6.439 y 9.442, ubicados en el distrito de presidente franco del departamento de Alto Parana. There has been no deliberation since 2016.

[34] 70427, mensaje no 733 del Poder Ejecutivo, vía Ministerio de Educación y Cultura, de fecha 20 de setiembre del 2007, por el cual remite el proyecto de ley *que declara de interés social y expropia una superficie de quinientos (500) hectáreas seiscientos quince (615) metros cuadrados, desprendimiento del inmueble individualizado como finca nº 65, del departamento de Caaguazú, a favor del Instituto Paraguayo del Indígena (INDI), para asiento definitivo de la comunidad indígena Joyvy de la etnia Mbya Guaraní, rejected by the Senate on 9 June 2011. It was alleged the draft was obsolete as it had been offered in 2007.

[35] S-08538, mensaje nº 48 – Ministerio de Educación y Cultura, de fecha 20 de noviembre de 2008, por el cual remite el proyecto de ley que declara de interés social y expropia a favor del instituto paraguayo del indígena Yakye Axa del pueblo Enxet, las fincas nos 15.179, 15.180 y 15.181 del distrito de Villa Hayes, (Pozo Colorado), departamento de Presidente Hayes, perteneciente a la firma agroganadera Loma Verde S. A. en cumplimiento del punto resolutivo número 6 de la sentencia recaída contra el estado paraguayo ante la Corte Interamericana de Derechos Humanos (CORTE IDH).

plenaries are usually swift and do not offer any explanation.[36] The unpredictability and long delays within the expropriation process has been recognised by a former president of the INDI, Augusto Fogel, who related it to racist and colonialist bias against Indigenous peoples (Beristaín 2009: 435; 445). The legal reasonings justifying the draft laws are usually the same – Law 904/81 and the Paraguayan Constitution – so the unwillingness to adopt the expropriation law might be related to political grounds rather than technical or juridical issues. For example, specifically regarding the approval of Law 4304, expropriating the ancestral territory of the Ache people, a thorough research on the demand process demonstrated the victory of a strategy based on constructing networks of political alliance and strengthening a discourse of sustainability and productivity of the Indigenous lands (Correia 2019c). The unwillingness to adopt the laws and the delay in analysing them demonstrates a considerable fragility within the demarcation procedure, as it submits the demarcation of ancestral territories to the political game, widely dominated by agribusiness interests.

6.3. ADVANCES IN ACCESS TO JUSTICE

Inter-American parameters hold considerable influence over the Paraguayan judiciary at the regulation level, with the adoption of protocols that aim to increase access to justice for Indigenous peoples. However, in contentious cases, there has been a low level of protection of territorial rights with a persistent denial of the legal parameters established by the Inter-American Court, even though the conventionality control is widely accepted for several issues.

Considering the regulation of access to justice for Indigenous peoples, in 2010 Paraguay adopted the '100 Brasilia's rules for access to justice of people in vulnerability'. The document was elaborated by the Iberoamerican Judicial Chamber and approved in 2008 by the Plenary Assembly.[37] The rules protect vulnerable people who '[meet] special difficulties to fully exercise before the justice system the rights recognized', including for ethnic and cultural reasons. It foresees that judiciaries should guarantee a justice administration respectful of Indigenous peoples' dignity, language and cultural tradition (Articles 6 and 9). The rules also stipulate multiple measures to guarantee that procedures and procedural requirements are more accessible, such as gratuity, unwritten procedures, priority and use of alternative means of conflict resolution. The agreement does not cite explicitly the American Convention, nor the Inter-American Court's jurisprudence, but it adopts the same parameters established

[36] Exceptions are the expropriation draft law of the cases decided by the Court, *Yakye Axa* and *Sawhoyamaxa*. They are analysed in detail below.

[37] XIV Cumbre Judicial Iberoamericana, 100 reglas de Brasilia sobre acceso a la justicia de las personas en condición de vulnerabilidad. Revista Jurídica, v 1, n.1, 111–32 (2013). See Ribbota (2012).

by the Court regarding access to justice. Furthermore, in the manual of application of the rules, also elaborated by the Iberoamerican Judicial Chamber, the dispositions are analysed in light of the Court's case law (Martín 2019). The international treaty was internalised in Paraguay through *Acordada* no 633 adopted in June 2010. The *Acordada* mentions the state's obligation to comply with international treaties and the importance of improving access to justice for vulnerable groups. It also creates a commission within the human rights ministry in charge of enforcing compliance with the treaty.[38]

In order to specify the application of the 100 Rules, in 2016 the Paraguayan Judiciary adopted the Performance Protocol for an Intercultural Justice, which is based upon the recognition of Indigenous procedural rights and the peculiarities of each people, offering specific procedures and tools in order to promote adequate access to justice. The protocol recognises multiple international treaties as sources of Indigenous rights, such as the ILO Convention 169, the UNDRIP and the American Declaration on Indigenous Rights. It mentions the international jurisprudence on the field, including cases from the Inter-American Court and from the UN treaty body system. It acknowledges the right to cultural identity and establishes as parameters mutual respect, transparency, participation and equity, among others (Prieto 2016).[39] The protocol has been disseminated among the judiciary during several meetings: in 2018 four meetings were held, with 150 participants; and in 2019, two were held, including 40 judges and 45 Indigenous members.[40] Furthermore, the Supreme Court of Justice (CSJ) edited the handbook 'Hechakuaa – Recommendations for inclusive language use in relation to people in situation of vulnerability', which aims to provide adequate language for dealing with vulnerable people (including Indigenous peoples), considering the principles of non-discrimination, access to justice and equality. Lastly, the concern with access to justice is also present in the CSJ's 2016–2020 Strategic Plan. The plan proposes a specific line of action to facilitate access to justice, identifying critical issues in cases involving Indigenous peoples and proposing the development of judicial policies specialised for vulnerable groups.[41]

In 2015, the CSJ held a conference on Indigenous rights (*Ciclo de conferencias La Protección de la Persona Humana. El Caso Indígena*), which considered multiple themes such as history of Indigenous rights, Indigenous education and Indigenous customary rights. This was considered by the CSJ to be of great

[38] Paraguay, Corte Suprema de Justicia, Acordada no 633 (10 June 2010).

[39] The protocol was financed by the German development agency Deutshce Geselschaft für Internationale Zusammenarbeit (GIZ), for more information about the GIZ project, see: GIZ (2020).

[40] CSJ, Datos estadísticos – Dirección de derechos humanos (2019); CSJ, Datos estadísticos – Dirección de derechos humanos (2018).

[41] CSJ, Plan Estratégico Institucional Corte Suprema de Justicia 2016–2020, https://www.pj.gov.py/contenido/1397-plan-estrategico-institucional-csj-2016-2020/1397. The plan was financed by the US American development fund USAID.

institutional importance (resolution 5656/2015) (Astigarraga 2019: 211–15). Furthermore, the Human Rights Directorate of the CSJ has promoted multiple activities related to the dissemination of Indigenous rights among judicial clerk, judges and law students, including courses, educational material, visits to communities, etc (Astigarraga 2019: 217–37). The CSJ has published specialised books on the rights of Indigenous peoples, citing the Inter-American jurisprudence and international treaties on the matter (Astigarraga 2019; Paiva Godoy 2016; CSJ 2010; CSJ 2012; CSJ 2003).

Access to justice was also promoted by the creation of the Ethnic Rights Directorate within the Public Prosecution Office (*Ministério Público*) created in 2009 through Resolution 3918. This body intervenes in processes involving Indigenous peoples, offers consultation and guarantees the application of Indigenous rights, including those foreseen in ILO Convention 169 and in other international treaties. It also provides counselling to Indigenous communities about their rights.[42]

In the matter of judicial decisions, the CSJ has repeatedly adopted conventionality control when deciding contentious cases, applying the Inter-American parameters of human rights established by the Court in multiple decisions. The CSJ has a programme to incentivise the conventionality control regarding access to justice, including promotion of the ILO Convention 169.[43] Promotion of conventionality control is a priority line of action in the CSJ Strategic Plan 2016–2020.[44] Among many decisions, in the *Acuerdo y sentencia* 608, decided on July 2018, the Supreme Court performed a thorough analysis, explaining the concept of conventionality control and citing multiple cases from the Inter-American Court. The judges stated 'the Inter-American Court is a supranational justice organ whose jurisprudential decisions are binding for the countries that accept the supranational jurisdictional authority'.[45] The conventionality control is increasingly applied, as knowledge about Inter-American case-law increases

[42] Ministério Público, Dirección de Derechos Étnicos, ministeriopublico.gov.py/direccion-de-derechos-etnicos-.

[43] CSJ, Dirección de derechos humanos, Programa Acceso a la justicia, www.pj.gov.py/contenido/135-direccion-de-derechos-humanos/1515.

[44] CSJ, Plan Estratégico Institucional Corte Suprema de Justicia 2016-2020 no 184.

[45] CSJ, Acuerdo y sentencia 608, Consulta Constitucional en la R.H.P. del abog. Martin Almada en: Martin Almada Cl Estado Paraguayo S/ Indemnizacion Danos y Perjuicios (31 July 2018). See also CSJ, Acuerdo y sentencia 522, Acción de inconstitucionalidad ES S.A. c/ el art 10 de la Ley 4333/2011 (12 July 2018) no 1697 OC 6/86; CSJ, Acuerdo y sentencia 609, Consulta Constitucional en la R.H.P. del abog. Martin Almada en: Martin Almada Cl Estado Paraguayo S/ Indemnizacion Danos y Perjuicios (31 July 2018); CSJ, Acuerdo y sentencia 1070, Acción de inconstitucionalidad en el juicio: Antonio Zacarias D'Ecclesis Peralta c/ Estado Paraguayo S/ Indemnización de Daños y Perjuicios por Responsabilidad Extracontractual (21 November 2018); CSJ, Acuerdo y Sentencia no 1306 Daniel Vargas Tellez a la Municipalidad de San Lorenzo, Acción de Inconstitucionalidad en el Juicio, Defensoría del Pueblo c/ Municipalidad de San Lorenzo s/Amparo, no 1.054 (15 October 2013); CSJ, Sala Penal de la Corte, Acuerdo y Sentencia n. 556 (13 July 2005); CSJ, Centro Interdisciplinario de Derecho Social y Economía Política (CIDESP), *Aplicación del Pacto de San José de Costa Rica por órganos jurisdiccionales de la República del Paraguay* (2005).

and more bodies include the parameters in their frameworks, as affirmed by the former president of the CSJ, Torres Krimser (Torres Kirmser 2014).

However, in the matter of territorial rights, the CSJ has only mentioned the Court's jurisprudence on decisions related to *Sawhoyamaxa*. Most of the Indigenous cases before the CSJ are related to precautionary measures aimed at avoiding damage to the Indigenous territory while the legal procedures for land demarcation are ongoing. Despite legal provision for the issuance of the measure (Law 1372/88, Article 4), compatibility with the ILO Convention 169 and with the Inter-American Court's jurisprudence, the CSJ has consistently denied the precautionary measures, arguing only by citing the civil procedure code.[46] The lack of award of precautionary measures is a worrying hindrance for territorial rights, as they have been appointed as fundamental instruments to ensure land protection in the face of long procedural delays and high levels of deforestation (FAPI and FPP 2015a). Aside from analysing precautionary measures and excluding the *Sawhoyamaxa* decisions, the CSJ has decided only one case regarding Indigenous lands. When analysing the constitutionality of Law 4304/2011 (expropriation of territory belonging to the *Aché* people), the CSJ considered the demand of *Ava Guarani* people, alleging they were ancestral from the territory and had not been consulted. Based upon the ILO Convention 169 and the Paraguayan Constitution, the CSJ declared Law 4303 unconstitutional as it violat the right to free, prior and informed consultation.[47]

This book analyses exclusively decisions from the CSJ, but the lack of implementation of Indigenous rights is also present in first instance and provincial courts, revealing a racist and discriminatory judiciary.[48] Current reports of violations might also demonstrate a discriminatory pattern within the judiciary system; for example: judicial orders to eviction affronting Indigenous titles; criminalisation of Indigenous leaderships; lack of redress in cases of forced eviction for the construction of dams; and lack of investigation and prosecution of wrongful appropriation of lands followed by acts of violence (Tierraviva a los pueblos indígenas del Chaco 2014; Miranda 2018, 2017).[49]

[46] CSJ, Acuerdo y Sentencia No 1385, Acción de Inconstitucionalidad en el Juicio: 'Instituto Paraguayo del Indígena S/ Medidas Cautelares' (6 October 2004) ADI 928 2001; CSJ, Acuerdo y Sentencia 243, Acción de Inconstitucionalidad en El Juicio: 'Instituto Paraguayo Del Indígena S/ Medidas Cautelares' (13 May 2008) ADI 253 2005; CSJ, Acuerdo y Sentencia 1079, Acción de Inconstitucionalidad: 'Compulsas Comunidad Ava Guarani (Paso Cadena) S/ Amparo Constitucional' (14 November 2018) ADI 925 2015; CSJ, Acuerdo y Sentencia 1080, Acción de Inconstitucionalidad: 'Compulsas Comunidad Ava Guarani (Paso Cadena) S/ Amparo Constitucional' ADI 818 2015. Exceptionally, see CSJ, Acuerdo y sentencia 2123, Acción de Inconstitucionalidad Comunidad Indigena M'byA Guarani De Ka Atymi S/ Medidas Cautelares y copia de Titulo de Propiedad (6 December 2012) ADI 3103 2012, alleging the precautionary measure is unavoidable in order to protect the Constitution and the ILO Convention 169.

[47] CSJ, Acuerdo y sentencia 1526, Acción de inconstitucionalidad contra la Ley 4304/11 (28 October 2016) ADI 1098 2011.

[48] UNHRC (n 9).

[49] See also UNHRC (n 9) §31.

In conclusion, the Paraguayan judiciary has adopted a very advanced framework regarding Indigenous peoples' access to justice. The adoption of protocols, handbooks and rules of procedure demonstrates coherence with international parameters of the due process of law regarding litigation of Indigenous rights and it was followed by wide dissemination among judicial clerks and judges. However, regulatory advances were not adopted in the resolution of contentious cases, as the CSJ has repeatedly denied Indigenous rights when analysing precautionary measures. It demonstrates that regulation of access to justice and dissemination of the applicable legislation are not enough to overcome the implementation gap in territorial rights.

6.4. INDIGENOUS LAND REGULARISATION

Every 10 years Paraguay conducts a very detailed census of Indigenous communities, gathering important information on land regularisation and housing situations. The most recent data, the 2012 census,[50] identified a considerable increase in the number of Indigenous lands regularised, as 86 per cent of the Indigenous community had registry of juridical personality, a first step for land regularisation, and 72 per cent had demarcated ancestral lands, even though a small percentage of them (four per cent) still lack an official title. Considering the Indigenous communities without property title, the majority of them occupy state properties (40 per cent), while a considerable number of communities occupy lands owned by private persons, companies or estates (20 per cent) (STP-DGEEC, 2012). There is a considerable improvement in the Indigenous land tenure situation when compared to the 2002 data: then, only 54 per cent of the communities had title of their lands, 22 per cent occupied the territory but without title, and 23 per cent were landless (FAPI and FPP 2015b). However, this comparison should be analysed with caution, as the 2002 census underestimated the number of Indigenous communities (disregarding those living outside demarcated lands), meaning different numbers of communities and communities without demarcated lands were identified in the 2012 and 2002 censuses (FAPI and FPP 2015b).

In relation to third-party occupation in traditional lands, in 2012 almost 37 per cent of the communities affirmed they lease the lands, even though according to the Paraguayan laws the Indigenous property is non-transferable and inalienable. Several communities highlighted problems with land tenure, including conflicts regarding the leasing (47 communities), invasion by private companies (42 communities), invasion by *campesinos* (31 communities) and overlapping titles (23 communities), in a total of 29 per cent of the communities. Despite the concerning data, the situation in 2012 was better than 2002, when the percentage of land usurpation was 38 per cent (STP-DGEEC, 2012).

[50] Only preliminary data from the 2022 census is available and could not be used in this research.

The number of communities affected by environmental problems is alarming. In 2012, of 493 communities, 134 declared a considerable decrease in the number of wild animals, 109 declared fumigation by agrochemicals and 101 reported water contamination. The supply of basic public services is another concerning statistic, as only 34 per cent of the communities have health clinics and only 70 per cent have a local school, half of them without electricity and adequate furniture (STP-DGEEC, 2012). As a consequence of the lack of infrastructure, in 2017, the level of illiteracy was considerably high (33.4 per cent among people older than 14 years old) and the average number of years in school was 3.4. There was a considerable improvement in the illiteracy rate: in 2002 it was 51 per cent and the average number of years in school was 2.1; and in 2012 the illiteracy rate as 37.6 per cent and average number of years in school was 3.4 (DGEEC 2002; DGEEC 2018; STP-DGEEC 2012). In relation to the housing, in 2017 running water was available to 56.5 per cent of Indigenous houses and almost 60 per cent have electricity, another considerable improvement: in 2002, only 2.5 per cent of Indigenous houses had access to running water and 9.7 per cent had access to electricity; in 2012, 15 per cent of the Indigenous houses had running water and 30 per cent had access to electricity (DGEEC 2002; DGEEC 2018; STP-DGEEC 2012).

6.5. CONSTANT VIOLATIONS: WHEN LAND TITLES ARE NOT ENOUGH

Despite considerable advances in the recognition of rights and in the land demarcation process, Indigenous territorial rights in Paraguay are continually declining. This is caused by two main elements. First, a failed mechanism for land demarcation, aggravated by structural discrimination within the INDI, which results in a property titles being delayed, in fewer areas and in discordance with cultural aspects. Second, the rising power of agribusiness and its interference in national politics has generated violent conflicts and accelerated the privatisation of communal natural resources.

The first element to be considered is the failures of the regulation and institutionally available mechanisms. Considering the size of the titled land, several communities have a demarcated area insufficient to guarantee the physical and cultural survival of the community, especially considering that virtually all communities still practice hunting, fishing and gathering, relying on wide areas of forest or basic activities. The Indigenous lands in Paraguay are demarcated on an agrarian bias, demarcation parameters around peasant colonies, and not as territory, respecting culturally adequate frontiers (Marcelo Bogado et al 2016). While the Constitution states that the communal land should be demarcated 'in enough extension and quality to guarantee the conservation and development of their [Indigenous peoples'] way of life' (Article 64), Law 904/81 defines Indigenous lands as the one currently occupied by the people, and Law 1379/88 establishes as minimal area for Indigenous lands 20 hectares per family in the western region and 100 hectares per family in the eastern (FAPI and FPP 2015a). The legislation ignores the ancestrality criteria established by international law. Some examples of Indigenous properties titled with minimal areas are the Mbyá-Guaraní community Ka'aguy Pa'u, with 164 ha, the Ava Guaraní community Tres Nacientes, with only 23 hectares, the Paĩ Tavyterã communities Pirity with 75 hectares (FAPI and FPP 2015b: 20–1) and the Rio Apá, with 55 hectares (Caceres 2020).

Furthermore, the borders of the property usually follow linear frontiers with neighbouring estates, ignoring the peculiarities of Indigenous lands and potentially excluding culturally significant sites. This is frustrated by the Indigenous communities' lack of participation in the demarcation process, as well as a lack of anthropological technical study (FAPI and FPP 2015b). Lastly, the constant violation of the reasonable term for demarcation and titling of Indigenous lands is concerning, in some cases lasting for 30 years and increasing Indigenous communities' vulnerability to violence and the dilapidation of natural resources (Caceres 2020). As a recent study demonstrated, one-third of Indigenous lands pending demarcation in 2018 have been waiting since at least the 2002 census (Rodrigo Villagra Carron 2018).

The Indigenist body, INDI, presents several troublesome shortfalls that prevent the adequate protection of Indigenous peoples. One concerning issue is the insufficient allocation of financial resources, with a substantive decrease in the budget in recent years (Rodrigo Villagra Carron 2018). Furthermore, there is a considerable lack of personal resources, as the body does not employ anthropologists and sociologists (Gómez Bote 2019). The body has also been investigated by corruption, for example in the case of misappropriation of funds for the purchase of the *Yakye Axa* lands (ABC Color 2018; Marcelo Bogado et al 2016). Lastly, it sustains an underprivileged position in the state structure, and the discriminatory bias against Indigenous peoples is also aimed towards the INDI, as recognised by a former director of the body (Beristaín 2009: 448). Although there is a draft bill to convert the INDI into a ministry, which would give it a higher position in the hierarchy, it has been refused by Indigenous organisations considering the lack of consultation and the increase in the bureaucratic burde (Caceres 2020: 73), even though Indigenous organisations have recognised the importance of moving the body higher up the hierarchy (Valina et al 2014: 29; 70–71).

Despite the inadequacies of the legal procedure for land demarcation foreseen in the Paraguayan legislation and the deficiencies within the INDI, the implementation gap on territorial rights cannot merely be attributed to lack of technical mechanisms; instead, it is widely related to socio-economic elements. Paraguay has adopted a development model focused on agro-exportation and monoculture, promoting land concentration, hierarchical social structure and an elite-oriented political sphere. In this context, the ineffectiveness of Indigenous rights emerges as a systematic pattern of broader structural discrimination (Rodrigo Villagra Carron 2018).

The biggest threat to Indigenous territorial rights comes from the increase in agribusiness (mostly soy production) within the state, leading to land encroachment, pollution by agrochemicals, deforestation and increased violence (WWF 2016). Paraguay is the most unequal country in land distribution, with a Gini index of 0.93,: 91.4 per cent offarmers have less than 50 hectares, concentrating only 6.3 per cent of the territory, while one per cent of the landowners own 71.3 per cent of the arable lands (Guerena 2016; Grupo Banco Mundial 2018). Agribusiness accounts fo the most common use of the lands, representing 94 per cent of the cultivated lands, in opposition to six per cent of the lands used for family farms. In the last decade, there has been a continued growth in agribusiness, followed by a decrease in peasant farming. In 2017, peasant agriculture reduced by 33 per cent and it is estimated that between 1995 and 2005, 90,000 peasant families were expelled from their lands (García and Ávila 2019). The principal field of agriculture is the production of soy for exportation, representing one-third of the country's export value, with an expanding area of production of 36 per cent between 2009 and 2018 (García and Ávila 2019) and occupying 62 per cent of the country's arable lands in 2019 (CAPECO 2020).

The increased area for soy production was accompanied by massive use of genetically modified (GM) seeds and pesticides. The uncontrolled use of agrochemicals is a concerning issue in Paraguay: in 2019 it imported 6.2 per cent of all agrochemicals in the world. Between 2012 and 2018, the importation of agrochemicals increased almost 75 per cent and in 2018, 44 per cent of the agrochemicals imported were extremely dangerous, according to international levels of toxicity (García and Ávila 2019). This is an even greater cause for concern considering Paraguay lacks a system of control for food contamination by agrochemicals (Apipé 2019). The fumigation of pesticides usually does not respect legal parameters, reaching schools (Rodriguez and Peralta Victoria 2019), Indigenous communities (Bassi 2018) and peasant settlements (Manzoni 2020). The pesticides have health effects in short term, including intoxication, headaches, nausea and skin lesions, but the worst effects might be observable only in the long term, including miscarriage, foetal malformation, cancer and tumours (García and Ávila 2019). There are suspicions that pesticide fumigation has been used as a chemical weapon against Indigenous peoples, forcing them to lease or leave the lands (Bassi 2018).

The unequal land distribution and the severe effects of soy agribusiness was followed by a rise in protests by *campesinos* and Indigenous peoples. Between 2008 and 2018, there were 106 land occupations in Paraguay. Only 10 of them received the title of property, while 61 were forcefully evicted through violent means. In fact, 77 per cent of land occupation was followed by criminalisation of the leaders (Irala et al 2019), most of them through the application of terrorism legislation (García and Ávila 2019). The wave of evictions also affects Indigenous peoples. There are multiple examples of Indigenous evictions due to soy expansion. In 2012 the *Ava Guarani* people was evicted from Yva Poty community, even though they had a regular title over 600 hectares. The police burned down houses, a sacred temple, the health clinic and the school. The decision was later revoked and the land restored, but not the buildings. Furthermore, threats and violence from armed groups became frequent in the community. The Yva Poty case is exemplary, but other examples of violent-forced evictions include Y'apo (2014), Tekoha Sauce (2016), Ysati (2017), Tekoha Jetyty Mirĩ (2017), Tacuara'i (2018), Itakyry (2018), Makutinga (2018) and Ysati (2019). Some of the communities had title over their lands but this did not prevent eviction or the use of disproportionate violence (Schvartzman and Espíndola Oviedo 2019; Caceres 2018). In some cases, the state acted directly against the Indigenous communities, issuing illegal judicial decisions or using police force to perform the evictions. But the state is also liable in the cases it has omitted from taking any action, even after acknowledging violent acts, as well as not investigating or persecuting groups responsible for the violence.[51] As a backlash against the land occupations, in 2021 Law No 6830 was approved. It altered the Criminal Code in order to increase the penalties for trespassing. It established that whoever 'individually or in concert with other persons, violently or clandestinely enters another's property shall be punished with imprisonment of up to six years'. In order to tackle the issue, in 2022 the Inter-American Commission convened a hearing about forced evictions and agriculture policy in Paraguay. Participant NGOs had the opportunity to denounce forced evictions against peasants and Indigenous peoples, as well as to highlight a pattern of rights violations within the country.

A concerning consequence of agribusiness expansion is the rental of Indigenous territories. In 2012, 37 per cent of Indigenous communities said that they leased or lent the property. The situation is graver in the Eastern region of Paraguay, where the growth of soy production has been accelerated: 54 per cent of the communities rent their lands. The advance of soy production leads to deforestation and pollution by agrochemicals. Given the imperative relationship between Indigenous peoples and natural resources, several communities could no longer survive on their own means, aggravated by a lack of basic services provided by the state (Valina et al 2014: 23). Considering the low number of jobs in soy production, the renting the lands became the only way for the Indigenous people to complement their income, even though it is an illegal practice.[52] Land leasing for soy production causes deleterious effects, contaminating water sources, causing soil infertility, aggravating deforestation (Marcelo Bogado et al. 2016; Rodrigo Villagra Carron 2018) and causing an acute lack of food security, preventing Indigenous peoples from maintaining their traditional means of survival (Ramos 2014). Rent is usually valued lower than it would be in private properties and payment is most commonly performed in goods or credit, instead of money (Rodrigo Villagra Carron 2018). Considering the illegality of the

[51] Mesa de trabajo por los derechos de los Pueblos Indígenas en el Paraguay, 'Informe conjunto de organizaciones indígenas y de la sociedad civil paraguaya sobre los derechos de los Pueblos Indígenas para el segundo examen periódico universal a Paraguay' (22 June 2015).

[52] UNHRC (n 9).

practice, it is not possible to execute the contract, avoiding Indigenous peoples' access to justice in case of discordance with the terms.

A further deleterious consequence of the increased misery of Indigenous peoples and reduction of their titled lands is forced labour. This was recognised in 2005 by the ILO (Silva-Santisteban and Garland 2005) and since then multiple development projects have resulted in some decrease in forced labour.[53] In 2009, the UN Permanent Forum for Indigenous Issues affirmed that even though 84.5 per cent of the Guarani people worked in agriculture, only 27.4 per cent of them were salaried.[54] However, still in 2018, during a visit to the country, the UN Special Rapporteur on contemporary forms of slavery attested that marginalisation of Indigenous peoples was leading to their entrapment in contemporary forms of slavery, mostly in the Chaco region, relating forced labour practices to 'deep historical roots in the subjugation of Indigenous peoples' rights to land'.[55]

In this context, soy is not merely an exportation good, but becomes 'a central node in networks of social, political-economic, scientific and ecological relations literally rooted in, reshaping and reterritorialising many states in South America' (Correia 2019b), leading to what the sociologist Fogel denominated the *sojización* of Paraguay, a process that exacerbates inequality and the concentration of land, as well as contributing to the consolidation of political power by a minority of landed elites. Correia proposes three waves of *sojización* in Paraguay: from 1970 to 1995, with the introduction of conventional soy varieties; from 1995 to 2012, characterised by the introduction of genetically modified soybeans; and from 2012 onwards, characterised by 'state-led violence and new neoliberalization of nature' (Correia 2019b: 317). The soybean agribusiness influences the Paraguayan state and society by promoting simultaneously gross environmental change, dispossession and repression against peasants and Indigenous people. The increased influence of transnational business over the Paraguayan political process is explicit in the 2012 parliamentary coup (Ezquerro-Cañete and Fogel 2017; Marsteintredet et a 2013) against President Lugo, followed by massive approval of GM seeds and agrochemicals (García and Ávila 2019); as well as violent evictions of Indigenous and peasant communities with support from police forces and the justice system (Schvartzman and Espíndola Oviedo 2019).

6.6. CASES BEFORE THE COURT AS EXEMPLARY MODELS OF INEFFECTIVENESS

The land demarcation process in *Yakye Axa*, *Sawhoyamaxa* and *Xákmok Kásek* are representative of the hindrances to Indigenous territorial rights in Paraguay;

[53] UNHRC (n 7) §21.
[54] Foro Permanente de las Naciones Unidas para Cuestiones Indígenas (n 11).
[55] UNHRC (n 7) §§49–52.

therefore detailed analysis of the cases might demonstrate shortfalls for embeddedness of international decisions on the matter.

In *Yakye Axa*, an expropriation law was proposed in November 2008 (*expediente* S-08538) after attempts to negotiate the purchase of the property had failed. The draft bill is very short, detailing only the property limits and briefly mentioning the IACtHR decision. The legal reasoning presented is the Paraguayan Constitution, Article 109, regarding expropriation of private property. There is no mention to further Indigenous rights. In October 2009, the draft was discussed in the Senate. The Human Rights Commission of the Senate refused the expropriation, alleging three points: the *Yakye Axa* are a nomad people and could have accepted alternative lands; the community was manipulated by the NGO Tierraviva, which was only interested in the monetary compensation; and the Court's decision did not specifically mention that property, enabling the delivery of alternative lands. The debate was permeated by a discriminatory bias against Indigenous peoples, demonstrating a lack of comprehension of Indigenous peoples' way of life. A few examples of discriminatory sentences are: 'how can we expropriate a model estate that employs native, to give it to the native?'; 'one million hectares was transferred to Indigenous. How is the Indigenous situation so far? It is misery, poverty, neglect … [I asked the Indigenous] who pays them, what is the interest in the merely land demarcation, as they know perfectly it does not dignify the indigenous'. It was argued that the property was a productive cattle farm and could not be expropriated. The Court had tackled these arguments in the 2005 decision, saying that productivity should not prevent expropriation and that the property should be defined with the Indigenous community; alternative lands should be an exception. The draft law was recused, as the Senate followed the Human Rights Commission.[56]

Following the political failure to approve the expropriation law, the *Yakye Axa* community accepted alternative lands instead of their traditional territory – an isolated piece of land among private properties – as long as a path was constructed connecting their community to a main highway. The path would also benefit the Indigenous communities *Sawhoyamaxa, Colonia 96*, *Buena Vista* (Tierraviva a los pueblos indígenas del Chaco 2019), *Payseyamexempa'a* and *Kelyenmagategma* (Correia 2019a). Even though the construction started in 2016, it was halted considering the lack of cooperation of private estates through which the path would pass. The lack of path created a liminal situation, in which the community was the legal owner of the property, but could not benefit from the rights since it had no way to access the land (Correia 2018a). In 2019, an expropriation draft law was proposed in order to guarantee the path (*expediente* S-198570). The draft was approved by the Senate and Deputy Chamber on November 2019; during the debates the legislators affirmed the state's obligation with international organs and the historical debt with the community, deploring

[56] Camara de Senadores de Paraguay, Diario de Sesiones-11028 (15 October 2009) 58–68, silpy.congreso.gov.py.

the long delay to solve the demand (Ramírez 2019). Unfortunately, in 2020, the Ministry of Public Works realised the expropriation law wrongly identified the property and a reform in the legislation was necessary. The draft law S-201647 was proposed in August 2020 and very swiftly approved by the Senate and the Deputy Chamber in the same month.

During the several years between the Court's decision and the expropriation of the path, the *Yakye Axa* members continues to live by the side road with no change to their wretched conditions. The situation has been described by Indigenous members as 'emotionally and psychologically painful due to the harsh living conditions and uncertainty about the fate of their land and livelihoods' (Correia 2018a: 55). The state was aware of the emergency situation and yet remained inactive in resolving the land situation. In 2022, part of the community decided to occupy the acquired lands despite the absence of the path, while some members remained by the roadside.

The recognition of Indigenous rights by the legislature in 2019 is important, but meant an 11-year delay for the Indigenous community, even though the same arguments could have justified the expropriation law back in 2008. It also demonstrates how the legislature's decision whether to accept expropriation laws is more political than juridical, and that legal changes might not be enough to solve the ineffectiveness of territorial rights. Furthermore, the difficulties and the delay to construct the *Yakye Axa*'s path are representative of a common tragedy among Indigenous peoples in Paraguay, as several communities are isolated with no access path to public services, markets or sources of political power, a situation aggravated during the flood season. In fact, there are several reports of Indigenous members dying due to a lack of access to health clinics during the flood season (Correia 2018a). Ironically, the state's neglect of the access path for Indigenous peoples is simultaneous to extensive investment in roadwork infrastructure for agribusiness: in 2019 alone, the state invested one and a half billion dollars on roadwork in Paraguay (Irala 2019).

The expropriation law in *Sawhoyamaxa* case had the opposite result to *Yakye Axa*. It is important to note that before litigation in the IACtHR, the *Sawhoyamaxa* had already tried to acquire their lands through an expropriation law on two occasions: in 1997 before the Deputy Chamber; and in 2000 before the Senate (Correia 2018a). In both cases the draft bill was recused because the property was considered productive. After the IACtHR's decision and the failed attempts to negotiate purchase of the property, the state tried to offer alternative lands. Taking into consideration the *Yakye Axa* situation, which remained landless even after accepting alternative lands, the community refused it. One of the community leaders affirmed: 'we are not animals to be transferred to other place, to other estate. We are here to recover this land, this ancestral territory' (Valina 2014).[57]

[57] Original in Spanish, translated by the author.

The expropriation draft law S-131021 was proposed on October 2013 and contained details from the Court's decision (including the mandatory compliance), citing the ILO Convention 169, detailing the ancestry of the community and approaching sensitive points, such as the productivity of land. During debates in the Senate on April 2014, all manifestations were for the approval of the law and the senators mentioned the Paraguayan Constitution, the ILO Convention 169, the UNDRIP and the decision issued by the Court. The relation of Indigenous peoples with land was also explored, mentioning the long process to reobtain it and the existence of historical debt with the community. One of the parliamentarians even affirmed the concern of being penalised by an international body: 'We accept to integrate ourselves civilised to the democratic concept that we cannot do as we please here, without the international community reacting and, in this case, penalizing us; because it is the Paraguayan state that is penalized'.[58] The bill was approved and delivered to the Deputy Chamber. The discussion in the Deputy Chamber was similar to that in the Senate, as the deputies recognised historical debt with the Indigenous community, explicitly mentioned the Court's arguments and affirmed the mandatory character of the Court's decision. One councilperson argued that Paraguay should comply with the decision as it was expecting a seat in the UN Human Rights Committee. All the declarations were for the approval, except some suggesting suspension in the deliberation.[59] The draft was approved and converted into Law 5195/2014.

While the property was not guaranteed, the community had been living by the side road until, in 2014, given their hazardous situation, the community occupied the property of their ancestral territory and currently have possession of almost all property there. According to the community leaders, occupation was self-implementation of the Court's decision in the face of the state's inaction (Correia 2018b).

Four lawsuits were proposed by the owners of the estate against land demarcation of the *Sawhoyamaxa* territory. The first issue analysed by the CSJ was an unconstitutionality action against the *Sawhoyamaxa* decision issued by the IACtHR. The CSJ denied the pretension *in limine* alleging the unappealable character of the Court's decision, according to the American Convention, Article 67, and the state's duty to comply with the decision.[60] Later, with the approval of the expropriation law regarding the property of the *Sawhoyamaxa*'s traditional territory, the CSJ analysed an unconstitutionality action against the law. The CSJ decided for the compatibility between the legislation and the Paraguayan

[58] Camara de Senadores de Paraguay, Diario de Sesiones–101278 (24 April 2014), silpy.congreso.gov.py.

[59] Camara de diputados de Paraguay, Diario de Sesiones–101631 (21 March 2014), silpy.congreso.gov.py.

[60] CSJ, Inconstitucionalidad en el Juicio: Comunidad Indígena Sawhoyamaxa Vs Paraguay; Roswell Company S.A. and Kansol S.A. v. Sentencia de la Corte Sawhoyamaxa (12 May 2009) ADI 823 2008.

Constitution and the 'international treaties and conventions, approved and ratified by our country'. It recognised the binding nature of the Court's decision with the three branches of power.[61] Lastly, it approached the alleged conflict between private property and right to land demarcation by citing the Court's argumentation in the case. A second unconstitutionality lawsuit was proposed against the expropriation law, but arguing about the value of the compensation established for the property. On that occasion, the CSJ once more affirmed the binding nature of the Court's decision and the compatibility between the expropriation law and the Paraguayan Constitution.[62] A fourth lawsuit was proposed in 2015 regarding the value of the expropriation before a first instance judge and, in 2018, the first instance judge decided to raise the value of the property by 60 per cent (Ultima Hora 2018).

There is an evident lack of due process in the judicial claims regarding *Sawhoyamaxa*, as three lawsuits were proposed against the same law ignoring the *res judicata* principle. Even after the highest court of the country, the CSJ, had recognised the constitutionality of the law, a first instance procedure halted the land titling for several years. During the proceedings, the lawyer of the community, Julia Cabello Alonso, faced an administrative procedure that could have lead to her disbarment after criticising the CSJ decision, in a clear violation of her rights as a human rights defender (ABC Color 2014). Currently, the community has material enjoyment of the territorial rights, but still lacks legal recognition of the ownership.

Lastly, regarding *Xákmok Kásek*, the community followed the example of *Sawhoyamaxa* and, after the failure of purchase negotiations, occupied the property in 2015. As one community leader stated, the reoccupation was an act of resistance: 'we will no longer wait with our arms crossed for the state to act' (Correia 2020: 1). The IACtHR judgment strengthened the Indigenous movement in its struggle for their lands and members of the community recognised the importance of the Court for their decision to reoccupy their lands (Correia 2020: 7). The reoccupation was a central factor in boosting hope for Indigenous peoples, as an Indigenous member affirmed: 'now that we are back on our land our children can live in peace. We suffered a lot during the struggle but now we have a new future' (Correia 2020: 2). A few months after the occupation of the lands, the community closed the main highway of the region (*Transchaco*) for three days, in order to call attention for its demand for compliance with the

[61] CSJ, Acuerdo y Sentencia 981, Acción de Inconstitucionalidad: Kansol SA Y Roswell Company SA C/ La Ley No 5194 que Declara de Interés Social y Expropia a Favor del Instituto Paraguayo del Indigena (INDI) (30 September 2014) ADI 797 2014; CSJ, Acuerdo y Sentencia 398, Recurso de Aclaratoria Acción de Inconstitucionalidad: Kansol S.A. Y Roswell Company SA C/ La Ley No 5194 que Declara de Interés Social y Expropia a Favor del Instituto Paraguayo del Indigena (INDI) (5 June 2015) ADI 797 2015.

[62] CSJ, Acuerdo y Sentencia 384, Acción de Inconstitucionalidad Roswell Company SA y Kansol SA C/ el Art 3° de la Ley No 5194 (2 June 2015) ADI 1735 2014.

Court's decision (Correia 2020: 8). The report of the protest demonstrates the importance of the human rights discourse for the Indigenous demand:

> Xákmok Kásek leaders immediately began impassioned speeches about Indigenous rights and the IACtHR judgment on portable loudspeakers that crackled and popped under the strain of the volume. The Paraguayan national anthem blasted from a different speaker set up in the space between the protestors and police. An elder woman who had been thrown to the ground during the melee screamed that she would die on the road that day if it meant her children could live on their ancestral lands. Shamans from nearby communities began playing rattles and singing as men circled to begin a chokeo in the middle of the road that lasted for the duration of the protest. (Correia 2020: 9)

As a result of the struggle, in 2017, a considerable part of the property was acquired by the state through purchase, but the remaining part is under negotiation. Unfortunately, the final 30 per cent of the property has undergone severe deforestation and the community instead accepted alternative lands. However, in 2022, considering the state's delay in acquiring the lands, the community demanded the original territory instead of alternative lands. Information about the attempts to acquire the lands after 2022 are imprecise.[63]

The results of the detailed analysis of the three cases are emblematic of land demarcation in Paraguay and might shed light on structural discrimination that impairs the effectiveness of Indigenous rights. While the *Yakye Axa* community has legal title over the lands, they do not have physical access. On contrary, *Sawhoyamaxa* have possession over the property, but they still lack official title. Both communities are in a state of legal liminality, as the state could make their rights effective, but instead adopt a contradictory posture of only partially guaranteeing their rights, denying due process over decades and favouring the interest of agribusiness estates (Correia 2018b). It also demonstrates the influence of the landed elite within the legislative and the judicial powers and how it impairs the demarcation process. Lastly, it could show that the implementation gap is not merely a result of lack of technical means or of regulation, but instead reflect a socio-political reality.

Beyond compliance, multiple impacts of the litigation can be observed among the three communities, both positive and negative. One positive impact is the increased visibility of the communities, which received material support from civil society. The *Sawhoyamaxa* community constructed two small schools in their reoccupied land thanks to a donation from a Mennonite charitable organisation, and the *Yakye Axa* received fiberglass tanks for water storage, also donated by an NGO (Correia et al 2017: 45). Not only did the communities benefit, but also their representatives, as the decisions attracted funding to support the organisation's legal representatives (Correia et al 2017: 65). Multiple

[63] *Xákmok Kásek v Paraguay*, Monitoring Compliance (19 April 2023) §§7–10.

international NGOs (OXFAM, Survival International, Cultural Survival, Amnesty International and ESCR-Net) became involved in the post-litigation process, strengthening domestic institutions.

The litigation has also had strong symbolic impacts. It promoted empowerment and increased knowledge about territorial rights, as one *Xákmok Kásek* leader explained: 'the resolution from the court was important and it made us stronger. It spoke of a truth' (Correia et al 2017: 17). The human rights discourse changed the status of the communities, from exploited labour force, to victims of human rights abuse, to self-determinate actors of their own development (Correia 2020: 5). The process also promoted a strong cultural regeneration, including a return to speaking the traditional language, cultivating traditional goods and performing cultural rituals. Lastly, it strengthened the relationship between generations, as the elderly depended on the young members to translate their knowledge on the lands into Spanish (Beristaín 2009).

Not all impacts were positive, however. The long delay and uncertainty about the future caused considerable despair in the *Yakye Axa* community. One young member of the community stated: 'it is like I have lived my whole life in prison. We have tried everything to make them [state officials] comply [with the IACtHR], but they keep saying that it will happen soon. I … have lived my whole life on the side of the road waiting for things to change' (Correia 2018b: 77). In *Sawhoyamaxa* and *Xákmok Kásek*, the occupation of the lands exacerbated conflicts with estate owners, implying a high degree of exposure for the Indigenous leaders and their representatives (Correia et al 2017). The lawyers of the representative NGO, Tierraviva, stated that such 'backlash soon made itself felt in attempts to criminalise us, with investigations being opened into alleged offences that went as far as the courts, or the doors being shut against any possibility of working with the state, as well as a campaign to discredit us' (Miranda and Alonso 2017: 6).

6.7. FINAL OBSERVATIONS ABOUT PARAGUAY

Paraguay has adopted a position of commitment and respect towards international human rights treaties. On different occasions, it has demonstrated concrete efforts to publicise and implement international recommendations in the most diverse fields. Such international commitment has been reflected in the internalisation of several international parameters on the rights of Indigenous peoples, which was facilitated by funding from and cooperation with multiple international development programmes and agencies. It promoted an increase in the domestic level of regulation with the adoption of central legal instruments for Indigenous rights, as is the case with the Consultation and Consent Protocol, the Protocol for Isolated Indigenous Peoples and the Law on Indigenous Health. The field of access to justice saw the most commendable improvement, with the adoption of the 100 Rules of Brasilia, the Protocol for an Intercultural Justice and the Handbook Hechakuaa for an Inclusive Language, as well as wide dissemination of their content through workshops and publications. There are still some worrying shortfalls in the legislation, the most significant being the lack of an adequate remedy for land demarcation and the lack of a non-discrimination law.

Even though the country has adopted legal parameters of Indigenous rights established by the Inter-American Court (eg the right to consultation and access to justice), it is not possible to peremptorily link the increased protection with the Court's influence, as the Court has not been explicitly mentioned. However, the Court has justified the recognition of Indigenous rights by an extensive interpretation based upon the ILO 169 and the UNDRIP, and these two treaties have been cited by Paraguayan legislation on multiple occasions. It demonstrates compatibility between international, regional and domestic parameters and suggest that the Court has at least increased the domestic awareness about international Indigenous rights.

Unfortunately, the improvements in the regulation level were followed by tiny advances in the territorial situation of Indigenous peoples. In the field of access to justice, even though the conventionality control is widely accepted for several themes, in territorial rights disputes it was not mentioned and there is a consistent denial of Indigenous rights recognised both domestically and internationally. There has been an increase in the number of Indigenous properties titled, but the shortfalls in the demarcation process have not guaranteed the correspondence between ancestral territories and titled property, considering both size and borders. Furthermore, the same pattern analysed in Nicaragua is present here: property title is not enough to guarantee territorial protection, considering increased pressure from agribusiness towards Indigenous lands, which leads to deforestation, fumigation by agrochemicals, pressure to accept rentals, violence by armed groups, judicial evictions and environmental pollution.

In this context, *Yakye Axa* is emblematic of denial of rights. Fifteen years after the international victory, the community endures the same wretched conditions as before, living by the roadside without access to water, sanitation and basic public services. Despite having the title of their lands, the community waits for the construction of a path of around 30 kilometres to access their territory. This abandonment contradicts the international image of Paraguay as being deeply committed to human rights effectiveness, demonstrating what Paraguayan civil society has called a merely rhetoric commitment that disguises profound violations committed domestically (Alonso and Caceres 2018: 510; Caceres 2017). In fact, the domestic situation was described through the process of *sojización*, in which agribusiness becomes a central node in the political choices, aggravating violence and land usurpation against Indigenous peoples and favouring the concentration of political power in the hands of an economic elite.

Conclusion

THIS RESEARCH HAS conducted a reappraisal of the Inter-American jurisprudence on indigenous and ethnic peoples' territorial rights, demonstrating the different levels and dimensions of effectiveness that the Inter-American Court exerted during more than two decades of strategic litigation on the matter. The book answers specific questions regarding each dimension of effectiveness, but it also demonstrates the importance of an extended definition of effectiveness, encompassing multiple, diverse and long-lasting factors.

The central inquiry of the research was to investigate the extension of the effectiveness of the decisions issued by the IACtHR in the field of indigenous and ethnic peoples' territorial rights. As developed in the first two chapters, the Court has built an advanced framework for the protection of territorial rights. Through expansive methods of interpretation, the tribunal promoted the expansion of consolidated rights (dignified life and collective property) and the affirmation of implicit rights (self-determination and cultural identity). The decisions were reasoned upon the international *corpus iuris* of indigenous rights, the vulnerability of indigenous peoples, the non-discrimination principle and the indigenous customary law, recognising and valuing their traditional way of life. Despite clear advances, there is a lack of coherence among some decisions and insufficient reasoning in others. The central problem highlighted was the insufficient protection of ancestral territory, caused by an undue emphasis on the property right and the insufficiency of the procedural safeguards for the exploration of natural resources, jeopardising the physical and cultural survival of indigenous peoples.

Considering that the reparation system was adopted for the redress of territorial rights violations, the Court has built a multidimensional approach, issuing forward-looking reparation measures that are focused on non-monetary remedies and which are sensitive to cultural peculiarities. The reparation system adopted by the Court was a laudable effort to guarantee the enjoyment of territorial rights based upon the following principles: the victims' centrality; respect for cultural identity; and the integrality of the reparations. However, the book has detailed some shortcomings in the reparation system, mostly in terms of compensation (the paternalistic method of payment and the insufficient method for the evaluation of damages) and restitution measures (the possibility of delivering alternative lands).

In order to increase the Court's norm-development effectiveness, the book has proposed an interpretation model connecting self-determination, cultural identity and territory. It is crucial to recognise the rights to property, cultural identity and self-determination as being a complex and inseparable ensemble of rights, strengthening the judicial protection of indigenous peoples and guaranteeing their physical and cultural survival. The contributions of the interconnected approach were presented, indicating paths for future decisions, including the reinforced protection of traditional territory; the recognition of the right to free, prior and informed consent; the increase in the protection of human rights defenders; the strengthening of the protection of a healthy environment; and the adequacy of reparation measures for the indigenous and ethnic peoples' self-determination.

Regarding case-specific effectiveness, the book analysed both the implementation and the compliance rates with the measures. The compliance rate with territorial cases is considerably low. In addition, when complied with, the reparation measures are only delivered after considerable delay. Compliance rates are greater among satisfaction and compensation measures. Accountability and rehabilitation measures have never been complied with. Low compliance is observed in restitution and non-repetition measures. The research concluded that compliance is a domestic matter and that the Court can increase the effectiveness of its decisions since it facilitates domestic processes of implementation. The influential factors were classified as enabling, constricting and blocking. The enabling elements include: the active role of the Court during supervision; the low political cost of the measure; the creation and strengthening of an active network of NGOs; the pre-existence of a domestic indigenist framework; and the consolidation of a framework for the implementation of international decisions. The constricting factors included: the vagueness of the measure; the involvement of multiple state organs; and the lack of accountability of private companies. The only blocking factor identified was the incomplete transition from dictatorship. Despite the identification of general patterns for compliance with territorial cases, the study also indicated that compliance is closely linked to the domestic context and influenced by a myriad of socio-economic elements. Therefore, implementation can vary over time, in response to domestic changes. The book also demonstrated how norm-development impacts the implementation, considering both the design of the reparation measures and the consistency and coherence of the decision.

Lastly, in order to comprehend the embeddedness of the decisions, the research detailed how the Court strengthened domestic human rights institutions and organised civil society, while simultaneously promoting the embeddedness of international parameters for the protection of territorial rights in the domestic legal system. However, it also demonstrated that the Court alone could not transform de facto situations of exclusion and marginalisation of indigenous and ethnic peoples, which are deeply ingrained in historical and socio-economic contexts. Focusing on three countries (Nicaragua, Paraguay and Brazil), which are representative of the Latin America and the Caribbean context, the research considered the level of protection of territorial rights, the level of openness to international law and the factual situation of traditional peoples. Therefore, the results can be expanded, despite possible singularities, to other countries condemned by the Court in territorial cases.

In the three countries analysed in this study, the IACtHR's decisions impacted the domestic legal system beyond compliance with reparation measures, even though it was not enough to guarantee the full enjoyment of territorial rights. In Nicaragua, in the years that followed *Awas Tingni*, there was a consistent expansion of the protective legislation of territorial rights and in the land demarcation process. However, land encroachments, the persecution of land defenders and violence against indigenous and ethnic people have only increased over the years, especially following the 2018 socio-political crisis. Paraguay has gone to great effort to build an international image of commitment to indigenous rights, approving multiple laws which adopt international parameters. This image is contradictory to a neoliberal economic project of development that favours agribusiness over indigenous peoples' rights, with an increasing number of cases dealing with land encroachment, lack of access to basic services and goods and water, air and soil pollution. Lastly, despite the short period of time since *Xucuru v Brazil*, some effects are already observable in Brazil, most of which include the strengthening of the indigenous movement both within civil society and the state, enhancing their legal arguments in the struggle against legal and judicial setbacks.

There are similarities between the Nicaraguan and the Brazilian situations. Both countries are facing, with contrasting levels of intensity, a human rights crisis that has impacted territorial rights and aggravated violence against HRD. In both cases, the Inter-American System has become an instrument in the struggle for the effectiveness of territorial rights, but while Nicaraguan human rights organisations continue to directly claim protection in the Inter-American System as a main strategy, the Brazilian organisations primarily use case law to domestically claim changes in the protection of territorial rights.

Analysing the state of affairs of territorial rights in Nicaragua, Paraguay and Brazil after the international litigation in the IAS, different levels and categories of impacts in the domestic legal system were detailed, thus indicating how the IACtHR's parameters were embedded in the domestic sphere. The study concludes that effectiveness cannot be dually assessed (effective/ineffective) due to the risk of oversimplification. Furthermore, the study detailed the variation of effectiveness in time, demonstrating that its level is neither a constant element nor does it steadily evolve; on the contrary, effectiveness might contract depending on the domestic context. The Nicaraguan case exemplifies this variation in clear detail. Until 2010, an effectiveness assessment would be optimistic in terms of the impacts of the IACtHR, considering the full compliance with *Awas Tingni* and the comprehensive process of land demarcation. However, the current assessment indicates a concerning weakening in the indigenist framework, with worsening land insecurity and increased violence against HRD.

Beyond the effectiveness assessment presented, three important lessons from the territorial cases for future strategic litigation can also be learned, suggesting paths for the enhancement of the effectiveness of territorial rights. First of all, full compliance with territorial rights does not represent a complete enjoyment of rights on behalf of the litigants and compliance analysis for the assessment of rights effectiveness is insufficient. On one hand, demarcation had unforeseen negative impacts both in the Nicaraguan and in the Paraguayan cases, namely the increase in conflicts with neighbouring communities, the increase of violence by third-party occupants and the persecution of land defenders and their representatives. On the other hand, formal title was not enough to guarantee full use and enjoyment of the territory. This last element is indicative of the fact that the right to collective property might be ineffective unless it encompasses the duty to perform title clearance and the protection of natural resources.[1] In the first territorial cases before the Court, the central concern was to guarantee formal title of the property to indigenous and ethnic peoples' ancestral territories. This changed in 2015 with *Garífuna Triunfo de la Cruz* and *Garífuna de Punta Piedra*, both against Honduras, when for the first time the Court affirmed the obligation to perform *saneamiento* under Article 21 of the Convention. The duty was later clarified in the most recent case, *Xucuru v Brazil*. This development shows that the Court later recognised that mere formal title is not a guarantee for full use and enjoyment, affirming the state's duty to eliminate any obstacle that hinders the exercising of the property right. Unfortunately, in the precursor case *Awas Tingni*, *saneamiento* had not been stipulated and the duty to demarcate was declared complied with despite increased land encroachment. During supervision of the Paraguayan cases, it is essential that, before declaring full compliance, the Court is aware of the limitations of the mere property title and verifies the performance of *saneamiento*, considering its own thresholds for property rights as recognised in *Xucuru v Brazil*.

Furthermore, the lack of full enjoyment of the property right in *Awas Tingni* despite compliance is related to a failed design of the reparation measures, as is the concerning matter of deforestation in the lands of the *Xákmok Kásek* community in Paraguay. With regards to the restitution of territorial protection, the Court ordered the delimitation, demarcation and titling of the traditional territory, as well as the abstention from any act, caused by both state or third party, that could affect the full use and enjoyment of the property until final titling. However, the measure not to harm was only temporarily issued and thus limited to the moment of obtainment of the property title. In *Awas Tingni*, despite the existence of third-party occupation in the territory after titling, the measure not to harm was declared complied with, considering its temporal nexus to the demarcation measure. A possibility for improvement could be to

[1] Some scholars are sceptical about the configuration of indigenous rights based upon property rights, indicating that title clearance would not be enough to guarantee territorial rights, but a focus on self-determination would instead be necessary. The hindrance would be the use of a liberal right (property) to protect indigenous peoples, since they are incompatible. See Offen (2003); Wainwright and Bryan (2009); and Wetterslev (2020).

consider the measure not to harm as being a separate reparation measure and to include monetary penalties in case any harm is caused to the territory, as well as the duty to rehabilitate environmental damages caused directly by the state or by third parties with its acquiescence. This suggests a correlation between the three layers of effectiveness (norm-development, case-specific and embeddedness), demonstrating that effective law-making when building reparation measures has a central role not only in compliance with the cases, but also in future impacts the decision might have.

The second lesson of the study to be learned for future litigation is that compliance is also not sufficient for an effectiveness assessment since the positive impacts of the Court's case law go beyond the reparation measures. Following a detailed analysis of the domestic levels of protection of territorial rights, the book presented two positive central impacts: the strengthening of a network of key actors, which includes domestic and international NGOs and NHRI; and the changing of domestic political disputes through the unblocking of debates on indigenist policies and the empowering of the indigenist institutional framework. Regarding the latter, the adoption of legal standards on indigenous and ethnic territorial protection in Nicaragua and Paraguay enhanced the protection of the rights following international litigation. In that sense, the Court's parameters were adopted in the domestic legal system, thus demonstrating embeddedness. Embeddedness reaches subjects that have not been reviewed by the Court in the cases against the country, ie the right to consultation in Paraguay and positive measures against discrimination in Nicaragua. It demonstrates the wide reach of the Court's impact beyond compliance. One caveat is necessary, however, regarding the application of the conventionality control. The research revealed timid outcomes, since the IACtHR was only recently directly cited by the Brazilian Supreme Court and only laterally.

Regarding the former impact, the Court has strengthened domestic institutions acting in the defence of territorial rights, both within civil society and in the state. The study of the three countries reveals that the tribunal has strengthened indigenous movements in their claims for land regularisation, unlocking discussions that could not be tackled domestically and strengthening legal arguments in the struggle for territorial self-determination. In order to improve the effectiveness of its decisions, the active role of the Court during supervision facilitated the dialogue among these actors and promoted operational frameworks that enhanced the effectiveness of territorial rights. Regional litigation has constituted discourses and practices, since it offers domestic organisations a legal lexicon for the identification of violations of rights, responsible actors and adequate remedies. It also promotes the legitimacy of domestic organisations, influencing their identities and promoting the legitimacy and publicity of their actions. In the current situation of indigenous and ethnic peoples, this is a crucial effect, considering the increase in campaigns that aim to discredit NGOs and the NHRI, some of which are promoted directly by states themselves. Furthermore, the Court's proceedings during supervision can serve as conduits for the flow of material and human resources, enabling NGOs and the NHRI to build networks, establish alliances, exchange valuable information and gain international funding. In this sense, hearings and visits are valuable opportunities in which the Court promotes this flow of resources, thus strengthening domestic institutions. From another perspective, the depth of the impact on the domestic legal system is directly related to the formation of influential pro-compliance coalitions, composed of the NHRI, NGOs, international agencies and programmes and domestic political structures.

Finally, the third lesson is that a full understanding of systemic legal transformation entails extensive systemic analysis and cannot be exclusively linked to international strategic litigation. The case analysis revealed a multitude of evidence pointing to the fact that the Court influenced the enhancement of territorial rights in Nicaragua, Paraguay and Brazil, but there are also elements indicating the concurrence of other variables. As Offen (2003) stated, since the 1990s there has been a 'territorial turn' in domestic and international orders, increasingly recognising indigenous and ethnic rights over the territory. Very diverse groups have included territorial demarcation in their claims, ie multilateral and bilateral lending groups, conservation organisations and human rights mechanisms, simultaneously promoting extensive land demarcation processes all throughout Latin America and the Caribbean. Similarly, the impacts of the growth and strengthening of indigenous movements in LAC over the last decades have been the subjects of research. The Inter-American Court's case law is only a piece of the jigsaw puzzle and its impacts can only be understood as one element in a more complex scenario. Former research on the effectiveness of international courts has restricted the analysis to the behaviour of the courts or of their domestic compliance partners. The present research moves one step further by detailing the influence of various international organisations in the impact that the international court had domestically. Considering the influence exerted by UN human rights mechanisms, international financial institutions and conservationist funds on the effectiveness of the regional tribunal, the research suggests that these international and regional organisations should hold dialogues in order to promote a common agenda, which would thus support the indigenous and ethnic peoples' struggle for self-determination.

In Nicaragua, it is clear that the Court influenced the approval of Law 445, followed by the extensive land demarcation programme that was promoted in the country. However, tending to social movements' claims was benefited simultaneously by a (temporarily) favourable political arrangement and by consistent funding from international financial organisations and international development programmes. These two elements were so central that, when they were absent, no effort to implement the rights was observed, seen in the lack of *saneamiento*. Similarly, in Paraguay, the adoption of protocols for access to justice, consultation and consent, and the protection of indigenous peoples in voluntary isolation, were the results of recommendations from multiple UN human rights mechanisms and funding from international development programmes, so the influence of the Court can only be understood in the wider context of the international monitoring of human rights in the country. Lastly, the increased use of the IACtHR's parameters for territorial rights in Brazil is related to the increase in legal setbacks in indigenous and ethnic peoples' rights and the need to reinforce the constitutional arguments in the struggle against the threats.

Regarding the analysis of the transformative potential of the Court's decisions, the study underlined limitations for the transformation of factual circumstances of marginalisation. Despite the contributions of the Court towards the embeddedness of territorial rights, the book identified a common implementation gap in the three countries, considering the factual situation of indigenous and ethnic people. The term 'implementation gap' was first conceived by Stavenhagen in 2006, analysing the simultaneity in the rising recognition of territorial rights and the continuous violation of indigenous and ethnic people's rights. According to the former UN Special Rapporteur on the situation of human rights and fundamental freedoms of indigenous peoples, the causes of the gap were related to a lack of political participation, a lack of consultation mechanisms, a lack of systematic policies and a 'malfeasant bureaucracy'.[2] A similar evaluation is still present in the UN, as the 2019 report on the State of the World's Indigenous Peoples demonstrates. The report identifies four of the most pressing areas for domestic implementation of the UNDRIP: the recognition of and respect for indigenous rights; an assessment of the progress in the field; awareness, information and coordinated action; and the practical constraints, including, among others, a lack of funding, weak domestic partnership and lack of political will.[3]

The book demonstrated the maintenance (and worsening) of the implementation gap in three different countries years after the territorial turn. It also revealed that the implementation gap might be more closely related to historical and socio-economic grounds rather than to the institutional framework, since increasing and improving the regulation of territorial rights, even with the introduction of consultation and participation mechanisms, has not been enough to tackle the lack of effectiveness of territorial rights. In that sense, the case study reveals that the lack of implementation of rights is neither merely an unexpected outcome nor the result of the lack of institutional mechanisms, but instead a consequence of years of marginalisation rooted in colonisation and slavery regimes.

In Nicaragua, the existence and consolidation of systematic policies were not enough to guarantee the overcoming of the gap, revealing that the implementation gap is derived from the history of abandonment of the Caribbean Coast. The history of Nicaragua could be described through an analysis of the conflict

[2] Economic and Social Council, Human rights and indigenous issues, Report of the Special Rapporteur on the situation of human rights and fundamental freedoms of indigenous peoples (16 February 2006) UN Doc E/CN.4/2006/78.

[3] United Nations, 'State of the World's Indigenous Peoples: Implementing the United Nations Declaration on the Rights of Indigenous Peoples' (2019).

between the Pacific and the Caribbean coasts, which actually represents a racial conflict between indigenous and non-indigenous peoples (Larson et al 2016; Baracco and Gonzales 2016; Baracco 2016). The conflict manifested differently over the years, passing through colonisation (Spanish in the Pacific, British in the Caribbean), the *contra* war and the opposition of the political party YATAMA against the Sandinista movement (Sierra Cadena 2016). The current abandonment of the indigenous population and the lack of effectiveness of territorial rights are a voluntary condition and a consequence of a long history of conflict. Just like Nicaragua, there is a clear implementation gap in Paraguay, as even though the country boasts a robust legal framework, including active mechanisms for participation, the implementation politics are characterised by a lack of will to guarantee those rights in a timely and effective manner. It is clear that the Paraguayan implementation gap cannot be considered merely a technical issue or suggested as simply a lack of political will. On the contrary, it is a product of a socio-economic model that prioritises agribusiness production over the life and well-being of indigenous peoples (CORREIA 2018b). Lastly, in 2006, Stavenhagen identified the Brazilian situation as an example of the implementation gap, describing a context very similar to the current situation presented in this work. It reveals that little has changed in 15 years in regard to the implementation of territorial rights, and the legal and institutional gains were not enough to avert the current setbacks.

The non-repetition measures issued by the Court in the territorial cases are based upon the 2006 implementation gap analysis, since they propose coordination among organs, courses on human rights or the implementation of legislative frameworks. There is no question that these measures are essential and that they might promote, at some level, the effectiveness of territorial rights. But what the present case analysis shows is that they are not enough to guarantee the physical and cultural survival of traditional peoples, and that only the comprehension of systemic historical and socio-economic conditions can provide the answer as to why rights are not effective. As already mentioned, it suggests a correlation between norm-development and embeddedness effectiveness.

This book has detailed how the Court can – it has repeatedly done so – polarise and strengthen human rights institutions and organised civil society, both domestically and internationally, as well as promote the internalisation of international parameters for the protection of territorial rights. However, it alone will not transform de facto situations of exclusion, which are deeply ingrained in historical and socio-economic contexts. Different levels of effectiveness were identified in each of the three dimensions analysed. Therefore, to answer the research question from two angles – effective or non-effective – would be an oversimplification of the results. The IACtHR demonstrated great effectiveness in the following aspects: the development of international parameters for the protection of territorial rights; the development of a reparation system for the violation of territorial rights, while simultaneously restoring the enjoyment of the rights and fostering social transformation; the strengthening of domestic indigenist institutions and NGOs; and the promotion of the domestic adoption of international parameters on territorial rights. However, the Court has demonstrated a low level of ability to compel states to comply with its decisions. It does not represent a lack of effectiveness, considering the wide range of reparation measures issued. The effectiveness has varied considerably over time and according to each domestic context. Lastly, however, the improvement on the legal parameters on territorial rights did not guarantee full enjoyment of the rights, since the implementation gap is a consequence of deep social and historical elements. Indigenous peoples' struggle for self-determination continues to remain decades after the strategic litigation and even after full compliance with international decisions, demonstrating the persistence of discrimination and the inability to overcome the impacts of colonisation.

Bibliography

ABC Color, 'Critican a ministra por sumario a abogada' (14 April 2014), www.abc.com.py/edicion-impresa/politica/critican-a-ministra-por-sumario-a-abogada-1356266.html.

—— 'Tribunal ratifica condena a Quesnel' (17 April 2018), www.abc.com.py/nacionales/tribunal-ratifica-condena-a-quesnel-1805559.html.

Abramovich V, 'From Massive Violations to Structural Patterns: New Approaches and Classic Tensions in the Inter-American Human Rights System' (2009) 6 *SUR – International Journal on Human Rights* 6.

Academia de Ciencias de Nicaragua (ed), *El Canal Interoceánico por Nicaragua: Aportes el debate*, 2nd edn (Managua, Academia de Ciencias de Nicaragua, 2015).

Acosta, ML, 'Awas Tingni Versus Nicaragua, y el Proceso de Demarcación de Tierras Indígenas en la Costa Caribe Nicaragüense' (2006) 47 *Wani Revista del Caribe Nicaragüense* 6.

—— 'Los Retos del Proceso de Titulación y Saneamiento Como Protección a la Propiedad Indígena' (2011) 60 *Wani Revista del Caribe Nicaragüense* 5.

—— 'La Autodeterminación de los Pueblos Indígenas del Pacifico, Centro y Norte de Nicaragua' (2012) 62 *Wani Revista del Caribe Nicaragüense* 62.

—— 'El Impacto de la Ley del Gran Canal Interoceánico de Nicaragua sobre los Pueblos Indígenas y Afrodescendientes de Nicaragua' (2016) 1 *Cuaderno Jurídico y Político* 21.

—— 'El Título del Territorio de los Creoles de Bluefields y el Gran Canal Interoceánico por Nicaragua' (2017) 2 *Cuaderno Jurídico y Político* 5.

—— 'Nicaragua' in IWGIA (ed), *Indigenous World 2019* (Copenhagen, IWGIA, 2019) 111–19.

Alessandri PS, 'Algunas Reflecciones Encuanto el Impacto Estructural de las Decisiones de la Corte Interamericana de Derechos Humanos' in Juan I Ugartemendia Eceizabarrena, Alejandro Saiz Arnaiz and Mariela Morales Antoniazzi (eds), *La garantía jurisdiccional de los Derechos Humanos: Un estudio Comparado de los Sistema Regionales de Tutela: Europeo, Interamericano y Africano* (Bilbao, Bilbao Instituto Vasco de Administración Pública 2015).

Alfred-Cunningham, AB, 'Derechos Territoriales de los Pueblos Indígenas y Comunidades Afrodescendientes en Nicarágua' in M Aparicio Wilhelmi (ed), *Los Derechos de los Pueblos Indígenas a los Recursos Naturales y al Territorio. Conflictos y Desafíos en América Latina* (Barcelona, Icària, 2011) 203–21.

Alianza de Pueblos Indígenas y Afrodescendientes de Nicaragua, 'Informe sobre la Situación de los Derechos Territoriales de los Pueblos Indígenas y Afrodescendientes de Nicaragua' (2017).

Alonso, JC, and Caceres, MB, 'Doble Discurso en la Política Internacional de Protección de Derechos Humanos. Sistema Internacional de Derechos Humanos' in CODEHUPY (ed), *Derechos Humanos Paraguay. 2018* (Asunción, Paraguay, Arandurã, 2018) 509–22.

Alvarado, L, 'Prospects and Challenges in the Implementation of Indigenous Peoples' Human Rights in International Law. Lessons From the Case of Awas Tingni V Nicaragua' (2007) 24/3 *Arizona Journal of International and Comparative Law* 609.

Amnesty International, *Danger, Rights For Sale: The Interoceanic Grand Canal Project in Nicaragua and The Erosion Of Human Rights* (Amnesty International, 2017).

Anaya, S, *Indigenous Peoples in International Law* (New York, OUP, 2000), gbv.eblib.com/patron/FullRecord.aspx?p=279562.

Angelo, M, 'Movimento Indígena Impede Retrocessos no Atendimento à Saúde', INESC (29 March 2019a), www.inesc.org.br/movimento-indigena-impede-retrocessos-no-atendimento-a-saude.

—— 'Por Decreto, Bolsonaro Força a Municipalização da Saúde Indígena', INESC (27 May 2019b), www.inesc.org.br/por-decreto-bolsonaro-forca-a-municipalizacao-da-saude-indigena.

Antkowiak, T, 'Remedial Approaches to Human Rights Violations. The Inter-American Court of Human Rights and Beyond' (2008) 46 *Columbia Journal of Transnational Law* 351.

—— 'Rights, Resources and Rhetoric. Indigenous Peoples and the Inter-American Court' (2014) 33 *University of Pennsylvania Journal of International Law* 113.

Anzola, S, Eugenia Sánchez, B and Urueña, R, 'Después del Fallo. El Cumprimento de las Decisiones del Sistema Interamericano de Derechos Humanos. Una Propuesta de Metodología' in L Burgorgue-Larsen (ed), *Derechos Humanos y Políticas Públicas.* Manual (Barcelona, UPF, 2014) 447–517.

APIB, 'Campanha Sangue Indígena, Nenhuma Gota Mais!' (2019) en.nenhumagotamais.org/objetivos.

Apipé, G, 'Aumentan Limitaciones de los Mercados a los Residuos de Plaguicidas' in M Palau (ed), *Con la Soja al Cuello.* 2019 (Asunción, Paraguay, BASE, 2019) 24–27.

Astigarraga, G (ed), *La Protección de la Persona Humana, el Caso Indígena, su Relevancia Histórica, Derechos Fundamentales y su Vinculación con la Justicia* (Asunción, Paraguay, CSJ, 2019).

Ayala, C, Alvarez, I, Baluarte, D et al, 'Conference: Reparations in the Inter-American System. A Comparative Approach Conference' (2007) 56 *American University Law Review* 1375.

Baltodano, ML (ed), *La Entrega de un País: Expediente Jurídico de la Concesión Canalera en Nicarágua* (Popol na; Eco Abogados, 2017).

Baluarte, DC, and Vos, CM de, *From Judgment to Justice: Implementing International and Regional Human Rights Decisions* (New York, NY, Open Society Foundations, 2010).

Baracco L, 'The Historical Roots of Autonomy in Nicaragua's Caribbean Coast: From British Colonialism to Indigenous Autonomy' (2016) 35 *Bulletin of Latin American Research* 291.

Baracco L and Gonzalez M, 'Introduction to Special Issue: 25 Years of Autonomy on Nicaragua's Caribbean Coast: Cultural Diversity and Governance in Indigenous Regions of Latin America' (2016) 35 *Bulletin of Latin American Research* 289.

Barreto, V (2017), 'Sintomatología de la Agudización Neoliberal en Agravio a los Pueblos Indígenas en el Paraguay. Derecho de los Pueblos Indígenas' in CODEHUPY, *Derechos Humanos Paraguay 2017* (Asunción, Paraguay, CODEHUPY, 2017) 59–74.

Barros, C, 'Os Indígenas e Quilombolas Ameaçados pela Soja, Veneno, Portos e o Preconceito' Agência Pública (1 October 2019), apublica.org/2019/10/os-indigenas-e-quilombolas-ameacados-pela-soja-veneno-portos-e-o-preconceito.

Basch, FF, 'The Doctrine of the Inter-American Court of Human Rights regarding States' Duty to Punish Human Rights Violations and Its Dangers' (2017) 23 *American University International Law Review* 195.

Basch, F, Filippini, L, Laya, A et al, 'The Effectiveness of the Inter-American System of Human Rights Protection. a Quantitative Approach to its Functioning and Compliance with its Decisions' (2010) 7 *SUR – International Journal on Human Rights* 9.

Bassi, SB (2018), 'Fumigações Ilegais de Agrotóxicos São Arma na Guerra Contra Camponeses e Indígenas', deolhonosruralistas.com.br/deolhonoparaguai/2018/08/29/chuva-de-veneno-fumigacoes-ilegais-sao-arma-na-guerra-contra-camponeses-e-indigenas-paraguaios.

BBC News, 'Amazon fires. Brazil threatened over EU trade deal' (23 August 2019), www.bbc.com/news/world-latin-america-49450495.

Beristaín, CM, *El derecho a la reparación en los conflictos socioambientales: Experiencias, aprendizajes y desafíos prácticos* (Bilbao, Universidad del País Vasco; Hegoa, 2010).

—— (ed), *Diálogos sobre la Reparación: qué Reparar en los Casos de Violaciones de Derechos Humanos* (Quito, IIDH, 2009).

Bernardes, MN, 'Sistema Interamericano de Direitos Humanos como Esfera Pública Transnacional. Aspectos Jurídicos e Políticos da Implementação de Decisões Internacionais' (2011) 8 *SUR – International Journal on Human Rights* 135.

Bernardi, BB, 'O Sistema Interamericano de Direitos Humanos e o Caso da Guerrilha do Araguaia. Impactos no Brasil' (2017) 22 *Revista Brasileira de Ciência Política* 49.

Boadle, A, 'Amazon fires could burn Brazil's bid to join OECD rich nations club' Reuters Media (23 August 2019), www.reuters.com/article/us-brazil-environment-wildfires-oecd/amazon-fires-could-burn-brazils-bid-to-join-oecd-rich-nations-club-idUSKCN1VD2A9.

Bogado, M, Portillo, R and Villagra, R, 'Alquiller de Tierras y Territorios Indígenas en el Paraguay' (2016) 1 *Cadernos do LEPAARQ (UFPEL)* 106.

Bonilla Toruño, WA (ed), 'Factibilidad de la Etapa de Saneamiento de los Territórios Indígenas de Bosawás y de la RAAN' (2010).

—— 'Diagnóstico sobre el Saneamiento de los Territorios Indígenas y étnicos de la RAAN' (2019).

Bowman, M and Boyle, A, *Environmental Damage in International and Comparative Law: Problems of Definition and Valuation* (Oxford, OUP, 2002).

Brito, B, Barreto, P, Brandão Jr, A et al, 'Stimulus for Land Grabbing and Deforestation in the Brazilian Amazon' (2019) 14 *Environmental Research Letters* 1.

Brook, MF, 'Territorial 'Fix'? Tenure Insecurity in Titled Indigenous Territories' (2016) 35/3 *Bulletin of Latin American Research* 338.

Brook, MF and Offen, K, 'Bounding the Commons. Land Demarcation in Northeastern Nicaragua' (2009) 28 *Bulletin of Latin American Research* 343.

Burgorgue-Larsen, L, 'El Contexto, las Técnicas y las Consecuencias de la Interpretación de la Convención Americana de Derechos Humanos' (2014) 12 *Estudios constitucionales* 105.

—— 'Inter-American Added Value' in AV Bogdandy et al (eds), *Transformative Constitutionalism in Latin America: The Emergence of a New Ius Commune* (Oxford, OUP, 2017).

Caceres, MB, 'La Instrumentalización Política de la Justicia, una Amenaza para la Realización Integral de los Derechos Humanos' in CODEHUPY (ed), *Derechos Humanos Paraguay* (Asunción, Paraguay, CODEHUPY, 2017) 575–90.

—— 'Resulta Imperativo Revertir el Patrón de Muerte y Amedrentamiento como Respuesta a las Reinvindicaciones Territoriales. Derecho de los Pueblos Indigenas' in CODEHUPY (ed), *Derechos Humanos Paraguay* (Asunción, Paraguay, Arandurã, 2018) 53–66.

—— 'Yemtelhek Nengeleyvaam. Haave Saat Nengaayóo-Ngkatnahamkok, Haave Saat Nahan Nentemesseeykam' na'sa Nengelaankeklhoo Nengnaykam' in CODEHUPY (ed), *Derechos Humanos Paraguay* (Asunción, Paraguay, 2020) 71–88.

CADPI and Mairena, DA (eds), *Demarcación y Titulación de Territorios Indígenas, la Reinvindicación de Derechos Ancestrales: Estudios de Caso en la Región Autónoma Atlántico Norte (RAAN)* (Bilwi, Nicaragua, 2014).

Canova, P, 'Reflexiones Sobre el Proceso de Consulta Previa y la Participación Indígena en Proyectos Gubernamentales en el Chaco Paraguayo' (2018) 53 *Suplemento Antropológico* 19.

Canuto, A, Luz, CRS and Santos, PCM (eds), *Conflitos no Campo*: Brasil 2019 (2020).

CAPECO, 'Área de Siembra, Producción y Rendimiento', capeco.org.py/area-de-siembra-produccion-y-rendimiento.

Cavallaro, J, 'Toward Fair Play. A Decade of Transformation and Resistance in International Human Rights Advocay in Brazil' (2020) 3 *Chicago Journal of International Law* 481.

Cavallaro, JL and Brewer, SE, 'Reevaluating Regional Human Rights Litigation in the Twenty-First Century: The Case of the Inter-American Court' (2008) 102 *American Journal of International Law* 768.

Cavallaro, JL and Schaffer, EJ (2004), 'Less as More. Rethinking Supranational Litigation of Economic and Social Rights in the Americas' (2004) 56 *Hastings Law Journal* 217.

—— 'Rejoinder: Justice Before Justiciability. Inter-American Litigation and Social Change' (2006) 39 *NYU Journal of International Law* 345.

Cavalli, G (ed), 'Congresso Anti-indígena: os Parlamentares que Mais Atuaram Contra os Direitos dos Povos Indígenas (CIMI)' (2018).

CEJIL, 'Resistencia Miskitu: una Lucha por el Territorio y la Vida' (2019).

Charters, C (ed), *Making the Declaration Work: The United Nations Declaration of the Rights of Indigenous Peoples* (Copenhagen, IWGIA, 2009).

Chiriboga, OR, 'O Direito à Identidade Cultural dos Povos Indígenas e das Minorias Nacionais. um Olhar a Partir do Sistema Interamericano' (2006) 3 *SUR – International Journal on Human Rights* 42.

Chiriboga, OR and Donoso, G, 'Jurisprudencia de la Corte IDH sobre los Pueblos Indígenas y Tribales' in C Steiner and M-C Fuchs (eds), *Convención Americana sobre Derechos Humanos. Comentario*, 2nd edn (Bogotá, KAS, 2019) 1131–202.

Citroni, G and Osuna, KQ (2008), 'Reparations for Indigenous Peoples in the Case Law of the Inter-American Court of Human Rights' in F Lenzerini (ed), *Reparations for Indigenous Peoples. International and Comparative Perspectives* (Oxford, OUP, 2008) 317–44.

CODEHUPY, 'Situación de los Derechos a la Tierra y al Territorio de los Pueblos Indígenas en el Paraguay' (2013).

—— 'Derechos Humanos Paraguay 2019' (2020).

Colombia, *Decreto 4633*. Por medio del cual se dictan medidas de asistencia, atención, reparación integral y de restitución de derechos territoriales a las víctimas pertenecientes a los pueblos y comuni-dades indígenas (2011a).

—— *Decreto 4635*. por el cual se dictan medidas de atención, asistencia, reparación integral y de restitución de tierras a las víctimas pertenecientes a comunidades negras, afrocolombianas, raizales y palenqueras (2011b).

—— 'Ley 1448. Ley de Victímas y Restituición de Tierras' in *Diário Oficial* (2011c), wsp.presidencia.gov.co/Normativa/Leyes/Documents/ley144810062011.pdf.

Comunidad Mayagna de Awas Tingni, and Gobierno Territorial Amasau, Caracterización 'Jurídica de Terceros en el Território Ancestral de la Comunidad Mayangna de Awastingni – Awastingni Mayangnina Sauni Umani(AMASAU): Fortalecimiento de las Experiencias de Ordenamiento Territorial de dos Pueblos Indígenas en Colombia y Nicaragua (Waspá)' 2012).

CONAQ and Terra de direitos, *Racism e Violencia contra Quilombolas no Brasil* (2018).

Correa, C, 'Artículo 63. Reparaciones y Medidas Provisionales' in C Steiner and P Uribe (eds), *Convención Americana sobre Derechos Humanos*. Comentada (México, DF, Suprema Corte de Justicia de la Nación; Fundación Konrad Adenauer, 2014) 817–86.

Correia, JE, 'Adjudication and Its Aftereffects in Three Inter-American Court Cases Brought against Paraguay: Indigenous Land Rights' (2018a) 11 *Erasmus Law Review* 43.

—— 'Indigenous Rights at a Crossroads. Territorial Struggles, the Inter-American Court of Human Rights, and Legal Geographies of Liminality' (2018b) 97 *Geoforum* 73.

—— 'Arrested Infrastructure. Roadwork, Rights, Racialized Geographies' (2019a) 2 *Roadsides* 14.

—— 'Soy States. Resource Politics, Violent Environments and Soybean Territorialization in Paraguay' (2019b) 46 *The Journal of Peasant Studies* 316.

—— 'Unsettling Territory. Indigenous Mobilizations, the Territorial Turn, and the Limits of Land Rights in the Paraguay-Brazil Borderlands' (2019c) 18 *Journal of Latin American Geography* 11.

—— 'Reworking Recognition. Indigeneity, Land Rights, and the Dialectics of Disruption in Paraguay's Chaco' (Geoforum, 2020).

Correia, JE, Gilbert, J, and Subramaniam, Y, 'Strategic Litigation Impacts: Indigenous Peoples Land Rights' (Open Society Injustice Initiative, 2017).

Corte Suprema de Justicia, *Digesto Normativo sobre Pueblos Indígenas en el Paraguay: 1811–2003* (Asunción, Paraguay, 2003).

—— *Beneficiarios de las 100 Reglas de Brasilia: Índice Rormativo Referencial* (Asunción, Paraguay, 2012).

—— *Derechos Humanos y Pueblos Indígenas: por una Justicia Intercultural* (Asunción, Paraguay, 2010).

—— 'Transfieren Tierras a Favor de Pueblo Ayoreo Totobiegosode' (2019) www.pj.gov.py/notas/16440-transfieren-tierras-a-favor-de-pueblo-ayoreo-totobiegosode.

Daly, TG, 'Brazilian "Supremocracy" and the Inter-American Court of Human Rights. Unpicking an Unclear Relationship' in P Fortes, V Boratti, A. Palacios Lleras et al (eds), *Law and Policy in Latin America. Transforming Courts, Institutions, and Rights* (London, Palgrave Macmillan, 2017) 3–20.

del Cid, V (2019) (ed), *Pueblos Originarios y Afrodescendientes de Nicaragua: Etnografía, Ecosistemas Naturales y áreas Protegidas* (URACCAN, 2019).

Del Popolo, F (ed), *Los Pueblos Indígenas en América (Abya Yala): Desafíos para la Igualdad en la Diversidad* (Santiago, CEPAL, 2017).

Della Barba, M, 'Agrotóxico foi Usado Como Arma Química Contra os Indígenas, Diz Procurador' *Repórter Brasil*, 27 August 2019, reporterbrasil.org.br/2019/08/agrotoxico-foi-usado-como-arma-quimica-contra-os-indigenas-diz-procurador.

Della Barba, M and Junqueira, D, 'Omissão do Estado e Impunidade. o que Está por Trás do Massacre dos Guajajara no Maranhão' *Repórter Brasil*, 4 April 2020, reporterbrasil.org.br/2020/04/omissao-do-estado-e-impunidade-o-que-esta-por-tras-do-massacre-dos-guajajara-no-maranhao.

Desierto, D (2018), 'Environmental Damages, Environmental Reparations, and the Right to a Healthy Environment. The ICJ Compensation Judgment in Costa Rica V Nicaragua and the IACtHR Advisory Opinion on Marine Protection for the Greater Caribbean', www.ejiltalk.org/environmental-damages-environmental-reparations-and-the-right-to-a-healthy-environment-the-icj-compensation-judgment-in-costa-rica-v-nicaragua-and-the-iacthr-advisory-opinion-on-marine-protection (14 February 2018).

Dolce, J, 'Marco Temporal. Datar Terras Ancestrais Viola Direitos Indígenas, diz Relatora da ONU' *Brasil de fato* (26 June 2020), www.brasildefato.com.br/2017/08/16/marco-temporal-datar-terras-ancestrais-viola-direitos-indigenas-diz-relatora-da-onu.

Donoso, G, 'Inter-American Court of Human Rights' Reparation Judgments. Strengths and Challenges for a Comprehensive Approach' (2009) 49 *Revista Instituto Interamericano de Derechos* Humanos 29.

Dulitzky, A, 'When Afro-descendants Became "Tribal People". The Inter-American Human Rights System and Black Rural Communities' (2010) 15 *UCLA Journal of International Law and Foreign Affairs* 29.

Engstrom, P, and Low, P, 'Mobilizing the Inter-American Human Rights System. Regional Litigation and Domestic Human Rights Impact in Latin America' in P Engstrom (ed), *The Inter-American Human Rights System. Impact Beyond Compliance* (Cham, Palgrave Macmillan, 2019) 23–58.

Engstrom, P, Hillebrecht, C, Huneeus, A et al, 'Strengthening the Impact of the Inter-American Human Rights System Through Scholarly Research' Inter-American Human Rights Network Reflective Report (2016).

Estupiñan-Silva, R, 'La Vulnerabilitad en la Jurisprudencia de la Corte Interamericana de Derechos Humanos. Esbozo de una Tipología' in L Burgorgue-Larsen (ed), *Derechos Humanos y Políticas Públicas*. Manual (UPF, 2014) 193–231.

European Commission, 'EU and Mercosur Reach Agreement on Trade', trade.ec.europa.eu/doclib/press/index.cfm?id=2039 (2019, updated 7 July 2020).

Ezquerro-Cañete, A and Fogel, R, 'A Coup Foretold. Fernando Lugo and the Lost Promise of Agrarian Reform in Paraguay', (2017) 17 *Journal of Agrarian Change* 279.

FAO, 'El programa ONU-REDD', www.fao.org/redd/initiatives/un-redd/es.

FAPI and FPP, 'Estudio del Marco Legal de Paraguay sobre los Derechos Humanos de los Pueblos Indígenas Relacionados con los Posibles Proyectos de REDD+' (2015a).

—— 'Situación Territorial de los Pueblos Indígenas en Paraguay' (2015b).

FIDA, 'Project to Improve Indigenous and Family Farming in Value Chains in the Eastern Region' (12 August 2017) No del proyecto 2000002377 www.ifad.org/es/web/operations/project/id/2000002377.

—— 'Proyecto Mejoramiento de Ingresos de la Agricultura Familiar Campesina e Indígena en Departamentos de la Región Oriental del Paraguay (PROMAFI)' (28 November 2015) No del proyecto 1100001750, www.ifad.org/es/web/operations/project/id/1100001750.

Finer M and Mamani N, 'Amazon Gold Mining, part 2: Brazil' (6 April 2020).

Fonseca, B and Oliveira, R, 'Com Bolsonaro, Fazendas Foram Certificadas de Maneira Irregular em Terras Indígenas na Amazônia' *Agência Pública* (19 May 2020), apublica.org/2020/05/com-bolsonaro-fazendas-foram-certificadas-de-maneira-irregular-em-terras-indigenas-na-amazonia.

Forero-Nino, L, 'Colombia's Historic Victims and Land Restriction Law' (2017) 18 *Law and Business Review of the Americas* 97.

FUNAI, 'Índios no Brasil, quem são?', www.funai.gov.br/index.php/indios-no-brasil/quem-sao?limitstart=0#.

G1 RR, 'Mais de mil indígenas Yanomami em estado grave foram resgatados nos últimos dias, diz secretário', G1 Roraima (24 January 2023), g1.globo.com/rr/roraima/noticia/2023/01/24/mais-de-mil-indigenas-yanomami-em-estado-grave-foram-resgatados-nos-ultimos-dias-diz-secretario.ghtml.

García, L and Ávila, C (eds), *Atlas del Agronegocio en Paraguay* (Asunción, Paraguay: BASE, 2019).

GAT, 'Petición 850-15 CIDH: inició proceso de negociación entre el Estado Paraguayo y los Ayoreo Totobiegosode' (22 February 2017), gat.org.py/noticias-del-gat/peticion-850-15-cidh-inicio-proceso-de-negociacion-entre-el-estado-paraguayo-y-los-ayoreo-totobiegosode-1558.

Gilbert, J, *Indigenous Peoples' Land Rights under International Law: from Victims to Actors* (Leiden, Brill, 2007).

GIZ, *Stärkung indigener Organisationen in Lateinamerika* (PROINDIGENA), www.giz.de/de/weltweit/12304.html.

Global Witness, 'Enemies of the State?: How Governments and Business Silence Land and Environmental Defenders' (2019).

Gómez Bote, JM, 'La Política Indigenista en el Paraguay Desde 1992 Hasta Nuestros Días. Integración y Desafíos de las Comunidades Nativas Actuales' Masters thesis (Bergen, Bergen University, 2019).

Gómez, N, 'Indigenous Peoples and Psychosocial Reparation. the Experience with Latin American Indigenous Communities' in F Lenzerini (ed), *Reparations for Indigenous Peoples. International and Comparative Perspectives* (Oxford, OUP, 2018) 143–59.

Góngora Mera, ME, 'La Difusión del Bloque de Constitucionalidad en la Jurisprudencia Latinoamericana y su Potencial en la Construcción el Ius Constitutionale Commune Lationo-americano' in AV Bogdandy, H Fix Fierro and M Morales Antoniazzi (eds), *Ius Constitutionale Commune en América Latina. Rasgos, Potencialidades y Desafíos* (México, DF, Universidad Nacional Autónoma de México, Instituto de Investigaciones Jurídicas; Instituto Max Planck de Derecho Público Comparado y Derecho Internacional, 201) 301–30.

Gonzalez, M, 'The Unmaking of Self-Determination. Twenty-Five Years of Regional Autonomy in Nicaragua' (2016) 35 *Bulletin of Latin American Research* 306.

Gonzalez-Salzberg, DA (2017), 'Complying (Partially) with the Compulsorty Judgments of the Inter-American Court of Human Rights' in P Fortes, LV Boratti, A Palacios Lleras et al (eds), *Law and Policy in Latin America. Transforming Courts, Institutions, and Rights* (London, Palgrave Macmillan, 2017) 39–56.

Gori, E de, 'Una Crisis Insospechada y la Convulsión de un Orden. Entrevista al Dr. Salvador Martí i Puig' in Z Villacorta (ed), *Nicaragua en Crisis. Entre la Revolución y la Sublevación* ([S.l.]: CLACSO, 2017) 260–63.

Grigori, P, 'Em Decisão Inédita, Indígenas Vítimas de "Chuva de Agrotóxico" Recebem R$ 150 mil de Indenização' Agência Pública (22 January 2020), apublica.org/2020/01/em-decisao-inedita-indigenas-vitimas-de-chuva-de-agrotoxico-recebem-r-150-mil-de-indenizacao/#Link2.

Grossman C, 'The Inter-American System and Its Evolution' (2009) 2 *Revista interamericana y europea de derechos humanos* 49.

Guajajara, S, 'Governo Bolsonaro. o Retrato da Barbárie Contra os Povos Indígenas e a Vida' in A Canuto, Luz, Cassia Regina da Silva, and PCM Santos (eds), *Conflitos no Campo* Brasil 2019 (2020) 182–89.

Guerena, A (ed), *Desterrados: Tierra, Poder y Desiguladad en América latina* (2016).

Hale, CR, '*Resistencia Para Que?* Territory, Autonomy and Neoliberal Entanglements in the 'Empty Spaces' of Central America' (2011) 40 *Economy and Society* 184.

Hawkins, D and Jacoby, W, 'Partial Compliance. A Comparison of the European and Inter-American American Courts for Human Rights' (2010) 6 *Journal of International Law and International Relations* 35.

Helfer, LR, Madsen, MR, and Alter, KJ, 'How Context Shapes the Authority of International Courts' in KJ Alter, LR Helfer, and MR Madsen (eds), *International Court Authority* (Oxford, OUP, 2018).

Hillebrecht, C, 'Rethinking Compliance. the Challenges and Prospects of Measuring Compliance with International Human Rights Tribunals' (2009) 1 *Journal of Human Rights Practice* 362.

—— *Domestic Politics and International Human Rights Tribunals: the Problem of Compliance* (Cambridge, CUP, 2014).

Hitters JC, 'Control de Constitucionalidad y Control de Convencionalidad: Comparación (Criterios fijados por la Corte Interamericana de Derechos Humanos)' (2009) 7 *Estudios constitucionales* 109.

Huete-Perez, JA, Meyer, A and Alvarez, PJ, 'Rethink the Nicaragua Canal' (2015) 347 *Science* 355.

Huneeus, A, 'Compliance with Judgments and Decisions' in C Romano, KJ Alter and Y Shani (eds), *The Oxford Handbook of International Adjudication* (Oxford, OUP, 2014) 438–60.

—— 'Courts Resisting Courts. Lessons From the Inter-American Court's Struggle to Enforce Human Rights' (2011) 44 *Cornell International Law Journal* 493.

Huneeus, AV, 'Reforming the State from Afar. Structural Reform Litigation at the Human Rights Courts' (2015) 40 *Yale Journal of International Law* 1.

Hutukara Associação Yanomami and Associação Wanasseduume Ye'kwana, 'Yanomami sob ataque: Garimpo ilegal na terra indígena Yanomami e propostas para combatê-lo' (2022).

IACHR, 'IACHR Concludes Working Visit to Paraguay. Press Release 89/2011' (2011, updated 23 May 2020), www.oas.org/en/iachr/media_center/PReleases/2011/089.asp.

—— 'CIDH saluda los avances de Paraguay en el cumplimiento del acuerdo de solución amistosa suscrito en el Caso 12.629 Comunidad Indígena Kelyenmagategma. Comunicado de prensa 233/19' (2019, updated 23 May 2020), www.oas.org/es/cidh/prensa/comunicados/2019/233.asp.

IBGE, 'O Brasil indígena, Censo demográfico 2010', indigenas.ibge.gov.br/estudos-especiais-3/o-brasil-indigena.

ILO and CEACR, 'Observation, Indigenous and tribal peoples Convention, 1989 (n. 169) – Brazil', adopted 2019, published 109th ILC session (2020).

INCRA, 'Quilombolas' (28 January 2020), www.incra.gov.br/pt/quilombolas.

INPE, 'A taxa consolidada de desmatamento por corte raso para os nove estados da Amazônia Legal (AC, AM, AP, MA, MT, PA, RO, RR e TO) em 2019 é de 10.129 km2' (updated 28 June 2020), www.inpe.br/noticias/noticia.php?Cod_Noticia=5465.

—— DETER, online system Terrabrasilis, terrabrasilis.dpi.inpe.br/app/dashboard/alerts/legal/amazon/aggregated.

—— PRODES, online system Terrabrasilis, terrabrasilis.dpi.inpe.br/app/dashboard/alerts/legal/amazon/aggregatedcf.

Irala, A, 'Obras viales, el tributo de los estados a la integración de capitales' in M Palau (ed), *Con la Soja al Cuello*. 2019 (Asunción, Paraguay, BASE, 2019) 48–52.

Irala, A, Kretschmer, R and Palau, M (2019), *Ocupaciones de Tierra: Marcas del Conflicto Rural (1990–2019)* (Asunción, Paraguay, BASE, 2019).

ISA, 'O que Muda (ou Sobra) Para os Índios com a Reforma de Bolsonaro?' (2019a), www.socioambiental.org/pt-br/noticias-socioambientais/o-que-muda-ou-sobra-para-os-indios-com-a-reforma-de-bolsonaro.

—— 'Ministério age para acabar com controle social da Saúde Indígena' (2019b), www.socioambiental.org/pt-br/noticias-socioambientais/ministerio-age-para-acabar-com-controle-social-da-saude-indigena.

—— 'Placares', widgets.socioambiental.org/pt-br/placares.

—— 'Situação jurídica das TIs no Brasil hoje' (28 June 2020), pib.socioambiental.org/pt/Situa%C3%A7%C3%A3o_jur%C3%ADdica_das_TIs_no_Brasil_hoje.

—— 'Terras indígenas no Brasil', terrasindigenas.org.br.

Isa, FG, 'The Decision by the Inter-American Court of Human Rights on the Awas Tingni vs. Nicaragua Case (2001). the Implementation Gap' (2017) 8 *The Age of Human Rights Journal* 67.

IWGIA, 'Indigenous World 2019' (2020).
Jarquín, L, 'El Nuevo Marco Jurídico de la Propiedad Comunal de la Costa Atlántica y de los Ríos Bocay, Coco, Indio y Maíz' (2003) 32 *Wani Revista del Caribe Nicaragüense*, 6.
Joaquín Delgado Martín, 'Guía comentada de las Reglas de Brasilia: Comentarios a las Reglas de Brasilia sobre acceso a la Justicia de las personas en condición de vulnerabilidad' (Eurosocial, 2019).
Jucá, B, 'Decreto de Bolsonaro com Mudanças na Saúde Indígena Dispara Alerta no Movimento Indigenista' *El Pais* (1 June 2019) brasil.elpais.com/brasil/2019/05/30/politica/1559238132_162541.html.
Kapiszewski, D and Taylor, MM, 'Compliance. Conceptualizing, Measuring, and Explaining Adherence to Judicial Rulings' (2013) 38 *Law & Social Inquiry* 803.
KAS and IDEHPUCP, *Avances y retos en materia de derechos de los pueblos indígenas y tribales. Reflexiones del primer conversatorio en jurisprudencia interamericana* (Lima, IDEHPUCP; KAS, 2017).
Koorndijk, JL, 'Judgements of the Inter-American Court of Human Rights Concerning Indigenous and Tribal Land Rights in Suriname. New Approaches to Stimulating Full Compliance' (2019) 23 *The International Journal of Human Rights* 1.
Krsticevic, V, 'Reflexiones Sobre la Ejecución de las Decisiones del Sistema Interamericano de Protección de Derechos Humanos' in V Krsticevic and L Tojo (eds), *Implementación de las Decisiones del Sistema Interamericano de Derechos Humanos. Jurisprudencia, Normativa y Experiencias Nacionales* (Buenos Aires, CEJIL, 2007).
Kumari Rigaud, K, Sherbinin, AD, Jones, B et al, *Groundswell: Preparing for internal climate migration* (Washington, WBG, 201).
Kunz, R, 'Judging International Judgments Anew? The Human Rights Courts before Domestic Courts' (2019) 30 *European Journal of International Law* 1129.
Kuokkanen, R, 'Self-Determination and Indigenous Women's Rights at the Intersection of International Human Rights' (2012) 34 *Human Rights Quarterly* 225.
Larson, A, Soto, F, Mairena, DA et al (2016), '"*The Challenge of 'Territory*. Weaving the Social Fabric of Indigenous Communities in Nicaragua's Northern Caribbean Autonomous Region' (2016) 35 *Bulletin of Latin American Research* 322.
Le Monde avec AFP, 'Emmanuel Macron Assure le Chef Amazonien Raoni du Soutien de la France' *Le Monde* (16 May 2019), www.lemonde.fr/planete/article/2019/05/16/emmanuel-macron-assure-le-chef-indigene-raoni-du-soutien-de-la-france_5463077_3244.html.
Londoño-Lázaro, MC, Thoene, U and Pereira-Villa, C, 'The Inter-American Court of Human Rights and Multinational Enterprises: Towards Business and Human Rights in the Americas?' (2017) 16 *The Law & Practice of International Courts and Tribunal* 437.
Lunelli, I, and Silva, FB, 'Etnografia do assédio institucional na FUNAI' in JC Cardoso Jr (ed), *Assédio institucional no Brasil. avanço do autoritarismo e descontrução do Estado* (Brasília, Associação dos Funcionários do Ipea, 2022) 726–63.
Macdonald, T, and Wetterslev, J, 'Accompanying a Search for Self-Determination. Mayagna Awas Tingni and Indigenous Land Rights in Nicaragua' (2019) *ReVista Harvard Review of Latin America*.
Mac-Gregor E, Antoniazzi M and Pantoja R (eds), Inclusión, Ius Commune y Justiciabilidad de los DESCA en la Jurisprudencia Interamericana: El Caso Lagos del Campo y los Nuevos Desafíos (Instituto de Estudios Constitucionales de Estado de Querétaro, 2018).
Mac-Gregor E, 'The Conventionality Control as a Core Mechanism of the Ius Constitutionale Commune' in Armin v Bogdandy and others (eds), *Transformative Constitutionalism in Latin America: The Emergence of a New Ius Commune* (Oxford OUP 2017).
Machado, AM, Bedinelli, T and Brum, E (2023), 'Não estamos conseguindo contar os corpos' Sumauma (20 January 2023), sumauma.com/nao-estamos-conseguindo-contar-os-corpos.
MacKay, F, 'Addressing Past Wrongs Indigenous Peoples and Protected Areas. The Right to Restitution of Lands and Resources' FPP Occasional Paper (2002).

—— 'The Case of the Kalina and Lokono Peoples V Suriname and the UN Declaration on the Rights of Indigenous Peoples: Convergence, Divergence, and Mutual Reinforcement' (2018) 11 *Erasmus Law Review* 31.

Magalhães, BB, Uchoa, BF and Bemerguy, RC, 'A Recepção da Convenção Americana sobre Direitos Humanos pelo Supremo Tribunal Federal (2009-2015) e a Supralegalidade. o Discurso Engajado e a Prática Resistente' in AM Maues and BB Magalhães (ed), *O Cumprimento das Sentenças da Corte Interamericana de Direitos Humanos. Brasil, Argentina, Colômbia e México* (Rio de Janeiro:, Lumen Juris, 2017) 17–60.

Manzoni, M, 'Os brasileiros Mataram meu Papai?' *Agência Pública* (12 February 2020), apublica.org/2019/12/os-brasileiros-mataram-meu-papai.

Márquez Domínguez, JA, and Díaz-Diego, J, 'The Nicaragua Interoceanic Grand Canal in the Central American Regional Development Context. Considerations for the Debate' (2016) 66 *Investigaciones Geográficas* 27.

Marsteintredet, L, Llanos, M and Nolte, D, 'Paraguay and the Politics of Impeachment', (2013) 24 *Journal of democracy* 110.

Martí i Puig, S, 'Nicaragua. Desdemocratization and Caudillism' (2016) 36 *Revista Ciencia Politica* 239.

—— 'Nicaragua. the Roots of the Current Crisis' (2019a) *ReVista Harvard Review of Latin America.*

—— 'Nicaragua: Análisis de una Crisis Inesperada' (2019b) 10 *Documentos de Trabajo.*

Maues, AM, 'Supra-Legality of International Human Rights Treaties and Constitutional Interpretation' (2013) 10 *SUR – International Journal on Human Rights* 205.

—— 'Brasil. As Promessas não Cumpridas da Supralegalidade' in AM Maues and BB Magalhães (eds), *O Controle de Convencionalidade na América Latina.* Experiências Comparadas (Rio de Janeiro, Lumen Juris, 2018) 157–70.

McCall, S, and Taylor, MJ, 'Nicaragua's 'Grand' Canal: Cuento Chino? Rhetoric and Field-Based Evidence on the Chinese Presence in Nicaragua' (2018) 17 *Journal of Latin American Geography* 191.

Médici Colombo, G, 'El Acuerdo Escazú: La implementación del Principio 10 de Río en América Latina y el Caribe' (2018) 9 *Revista Catalana de Dret Ambienta.*

Melo, PPC, 'Constitucionalismo, Transformação e Resiliência Democrática no Brasil. o Ius Constitucionale Commune na América Latina Tem uma Contribuição a oferecer ?' (2019) 9 *Revista Brasileira de Políticas Públicas* 253.

Meyer, A, and Huete-Pérez, JA, 'Conservation: Nicaragua Canal Could Wreak Environmental Ruin' (2014) 506 *Nature* 287.

Ministerio de Justicia, 'Histórico: establecen protocolo de actuación con el pueblo Ayoreo Totobiegosode' (30 April 2018), www.ministeriodejusticia.gov.py/noticias/historico-establecen-protocolo-de-actuacion-con-el-pueblo-ayoreo-totobiegosode.

—— 'Prosigue mesa de trabajo entre el Estado paraguayo el pueblo Ayoreo Totobiegosode' (27 September 2018), www.ministeriodejusticia.gov.py/noticias/prosigue-mesa-de-trabajo-entre-el-estado-paraguayo-el-pueblo-ayoreo-totobiegosode.

Miranda, MM, 'La Luta ante la Estigmatización, el Amedrentamiento y la Criminalización del Estado paraguayo. Defensoras y Defensores de Derechos Humanos y Liberdades Fundamentales' in CODEHUPY, *Derechos Humanos Paraguay 2017* (Asunción, Paraguay CODEHUPY, 2017) 601–90.

—— 'El Riesgo que Implica ser Defensora y Defensor de Derechos Humanos y Libertades fundamentales en Paraguay, y la Necesidad de un Mecanismo Nacional de Protección' in CODEHUPY (ed), *Derechos Humanos Paraguay 2018* (Asunción, Paraguay Arandurã, 2018) 541–54.

Miranda, MM, and Alonso, JC (2017), *Advancing Indigenous Peoples' Rights Through Regional Human Rights Systems: The Case of Paraguay* (London, IIED, 201).

MPF, *Reconhecimento de Direitos Territoriais de Comunidades Quilombolas* (2018), www.mpf.mp.br/atuacao-tematica/ccr6/documentos-e-publicacoes/manual-de-atuacao.

—— *Manual de Jurisprudência dos Direitos Indígenas* (2019), www.mpf.mp.br/atuacao-tematica/ccr6/documentos-epublicacoes/manual-de-atuacao.

MRE Paraguay, 'Cancillería monitorea solución amistosa con comunidad indígena Kelyenmagategma' (updated 23 May 2020), www.mre.gov.py/index.php/noticias-de-embajadas-y-consulados/cancilleria-monitorea-solucion-amistosa-con-comunidad-indigena-kelyenmagategma.

Muller, T, 'Nicaragua's Chinese-Financed Canal Project Still in Limbo' (20 August 2019) *The Diplomat*.

Muñoz Machado, S, *Diccionario del Español Jurídico* (Referencia, Barcelona, Madrid: Espasa Libros; *Real Academia Española*; Consejo General del Poder Judicial, 2020), www.rae.es/sites/default/files/Diccionario_juridico_de_espanol._Indice_prologo_y_presentacion.pdf.

Nash Rojas, C (2009), *Las Reparaciones ante la Corte Interamericana de Derechos Humanos* (1988–2007), 2nd edn (Santiago, Andros, 2009).

Navarro, GCB, and Calabria, C (eds), *Direito dos povos indígenas* (Brasília, CNJ; STF; MPIL, 2023).

Offen, KH, 'The Territorial Turn: Making Black Territories in Pacific Colombia' (2003) 2 *Journal of Latin American Geography* 43.

OHCHR, 'Indigenous and Environmental Rights under Attack in Brazil, UN and Inter-American Experts Warn' (2017; updated 26 June 2020), www.ohchr.org/EN/NewsEvents/Pages/DisplayNews.aspx?NewsID=21704&LangID=E.

Oliveira, R, 'Centro de Cultura Indígena Huni Kuin é Destruído pelo Fogo no Acre', *Agência Pública* (29 August 2019), apublica.org/2019/08/centro-de-cultura-indigena-huni-kuin-e-destruido-pelo-fogo-no-acre.

Oltermann, P, 'Austria Rejects EU-Mercosur Trade Deal Over Amazon Fires' *The Guardian* (19 September 2019), www.theguardian.com/world/2019/sep/19/austria-rejects-eu-mercosur-trade-deal-over-amazon-fires.

Paiva Godoy, R (ed), *Cuadernillo de Jurisprudencia N° 1*, Fallo de la Corte IDH, Fallos de la CSJ: Caso Yakye Axa (Asunción, Paraguay, 2016).

Parra-Vera, O, 'Institutional Empowerment and Progressive Policy Reforms. the Impact of the Inter-American Human Rights System on Intra-State Conflicts' in P Engstrom (ed), *The Inter-American Human Rights System. Impact Beyond Compliance* (Cham, Palgrave Macmillan, 2019) 143–66.

Pasqualucci, JM, 'The Right to a Dignified Life (Vida Digna). The Integration of Economic and Social Rights with Civil and Political Rights in the Inter-American Human Rights System' (2008) 31 *Hastings International and Comparative Law Review* 1.

—— 'International Indigenous Land Rights. A Critique of the Jurisprudence of the Inter-American Court of Human Rights in Light of The United Nations Declaration on the Rights of Indigenous Peoples' (2009) 27 *Wisconsin International Law Journal* 51.

Pérez Liñán, A, Schenoni, L and Morrison, K, 'Time and Compliance with International Rulings. The Case of the Inter-American Court of Human Rights', Max Planck Institute for Comparative Public Law & International Law (MPIL) Research Paper No 2019-17 (2019), papers.ssrn.com/sol3/papers.cfm?abstract_id=3463105.

PNUD, 'Programa nacional conjunto de reducción de emisiones de la deforestación y la degradación de los bosques' (1 June 2011), www.py.undp.org/content/paraguay/es/home/operations/projects/poverty_reduction/reduccion-de-emisiones-de-la-deforestacion-y-la-degradacion-de-l.html.

Posner E and Yoo J, 'Judicial Independence in International Tribunals' (2005) 93 *California Law Review* 1.

Prado Jr, MB and Scotti, G, 'Normas Cosmopolitas e Efetivação dos Direitos Humanos. uma Análise do Caso do Povo Xukuru vs. Brasil perante a Corte Interamericana de Direitos Humanos'(2022) 13 *Revista Direito e Práxis* 552.

Prieto, E, *Protocolo de Actuación para una Justicia Intercultural: los Pueblos Indígenas* (Asunción, Paraguay, Corte Suprema de Justicia, 2016).

Puente, SG, 'Legislative Measures as Guarantees of Non-Repetition. a Reality in the Inter-American Court, and a Possible Solution for the European Court' (2009) 49 *Revista Instituto Interamericano de Derechos Humanos* 69.

Ramírez, LN, 'Aprueban Expropiar Tierras en Beneficio de la Comunidad Yakye Axa' (updated 30 May 2020), www.senado.gov.py/index.php/noticias/noticias-generales/4785-aprueban-expropiar-tierras-en-beneficio-de-la-comunidad-yakye-axa-2019-11-14-19-07-15.

Ramos, NR (ed), *Informe Nacional: Diagnóstico y Propuestas Para el Desarrollo de una Política Pública de Seguridad Alimentaria y nutricional de los Pueblos Indigenas en Paraguay* (Asunción, Paraguay, 2014).

Ramsoeh, H, 'Democracy and Political Culture in Suriname' in ML Bishop, P Clegg and R Hoefte (eds), *Post-colonial Trajectories in the Caribbean. The Three Guianas* (London, New York, Routledge Taylor & Francis Group, 2017) 30–45.

—— 'Desi Bouterse. de lange mars van een putchist naar het presidentschap' (2016; updated 12 August 2019), spectator.clingendael.org/nl/publicatie/desi-bouterse-de-lange-mars-van-een-putchist-naar-het-presidentschap.

Ribbota, S, 'Reglas de brasilia sobre acceso a la justicia de las personas en condición de vulnerabilidad. Vulnerabilidad, pobreza y acceso a la justicia' *Revista Electrónica Iberoamericana,* V 1988, P 0618 (2012).

Robles GMY, 'La Compensación Colectiva en la Corte IDH. a Propósito de la Sentencia Triunfo de la Cruz y sus Miembros vs. Honduras' in J Mejia Rivera (ed), *Obligaciones Internacionales del Estado de Honduras en Materia de Derechos Humanos y Bienes Naturales* (Yoro, ERIC-S, 2018) 315–45.

Rocha Reis, R, 'Transnational Activism and Coalitions of Domestic Interest Groups. Reflections on the Case of Brazil' in P Engstrom (ed), *The Inter-American Human Rights System. Impact Beyond Compliance* (Cham, Palgrave Macmillan, 2019) 199–219.

Rodriguez, E and Peralta, V, 'Escuelas Rurales Fumigadas. el Paradigmático Caso de la Escuela San Jorge de Itapuá Poty' in M Palau (ed), *Con la Soja al Cuello* (Asunción, Paraguay: BASE, 2019).

Rodríguez-Garavito, CA and Kauffman, C, 'De las Órdenes a la Práctica. Análisis y Estrategias para el Cumplimiento de las Decisiones del Sistema Interamericano de Derechos Humanos', in Dejusticia, *Desafíos del Sistema Interamericano de Derechos Humanos.* Nuevos Tiempos, Viejos Retos (Bogotá, DC, Dejusticia, 2015).

Rojas, M, *La Restitución de Tierras y Territorios: Justificaciones, Dilemas y Estrategias* (Bogota, Dejusticia, 016).

Rombouts, B, Meijknecht, A and Asarfi, J, 'The Implementation of IACtHR Judgments Concerning Land Rights in Suriname – Saramaka people V Suriname and Subsequent Cases: International Law Association (ILA) Committee on the implementation of the rights of indigenous peoples, case study' (2016).

Rufino, MP, 'The equality trap. notes on indigenist policies in the Bolsonaro government' (2022) 19 *Vibrant, Virtual Brazilian Anthropology.*

Ruggie, J, 'Report of the Special Representative of the Secretary-General on the Issue of Human Rights and Transnational Corporations and other Business Enterprises' (2011) 29 *Netherlands Quarterly of Human Rights* 224.

Ruggie, JG, 'Business and Human Rights: the Evolving International Agenda' (2007) 101 *American Journal of International Law* 819.

Ruiz, O and Donoso, G, 'Pueblos Indigenas y la Corte Interamericana. Fondo y Reparaciones' in C Steiner and P Uribe (eds), *Convención Americana sobre Derechos Humanos. Comentada* (México, DF, Suprema Corte de Justicia de la Nación; Fundación Konrad Adenauer, 2014) 947–1026.

Russo, AM, and Wences, I, 'De los Derechos de los Miembros de las Comunidades a los Derechos de la Comunidad y sus Miembros. la Diversidad Cultural y el Reconocimiento de la Propriedad Colectiva de los Pueblos Indigenas en la Corte Interamericana de Derechos Humanos' in P Santolaya Machetti and I Wences (eds), *La América de los Derechos* (Madrid: Centro de Estudios Políticos y Constitucionales, 2016) 281–325.

Sandholtz, W, 'Human rights courts and global constitutionalism. Coordination through judicial dialogue' (2020) 10 *Global Constitutionalism* 1.

Sandholtz, W, Bei, Y and Caldwell, K, 'Backlash and International Human Rights Courts' in A Brysk and M Stohl (eds), *Contracting Human Rights. Crisis, Accountability and Opportunity* (Cheltenham, UK, Northampton, MA, Edward Elgar Publishing, 2018) 159–73.

Sandoval, C, 'Two Steps Forward, One Step Back. Reflections on the Jurisprudential Turn of the Inter-American Court of Human Rights on Domestic Reparation Programmes' (2018) 2 *The International Journal of Human Rights* 1192.

Sarfaty, GA, 'The World Bank and the Internalization of Indigenous Rights Norms' (2005) 114 *The Yale Law Journal* 1792.

Säuberli, G, 'The Case of Kichwa peoples of the Sarayaku V Ecuador. Constructing a Right to Consultation and Cultural Identity?' in Y Haeck, O Ruiz-Chiriboga and C Burbano Herrera (eds), *The Inter-American Court of Human Rights. Theory and Practice, Present and Future* (Cambridge, UK, Antwerp, Belgium, Portland, Oregon Intersential, 2015) 573–92.

Sauer, S, Tubino, N and Leite, A, 'Governo Bolsonaro Amplia A Grilagem De Terras Com Mais Uma Medida Provisória', Dataluta 144 (December 2019) 2–11.

Schettini, A, 'Por um Novo Paradigma de Proteção dos Direitos dos Povos Indígenas. uma Análise Crítica dos Parâmetros Estabelecidos pela Corte Interamericana de Direitos Humanos' (2012) 9 *SUR – International Journal on Human Rights* 63.

Schneider, J, 'Reparation and Enforcement of Judgments. A Comparative Analysis of the European and Inter-American Human Rights Systems' Dissertation (Mainz, Johannes Gutenberg-Universität, 2015).

Schneider, N, 'Impunity in Post-Authoritarian Brazil: The Supreme Court's recent Verdict on the Amnesty Law' (2011) 90 *European Review of Latin American and Caribbean* Studies/*Revista Europea de Estudios Latinoamericanos y del Caribe*, 39.

Schonsteiner, J, 'Dissuasive Measures and the "Society as a Whole". A Working Theory of Reparations in the Inter-American Court of Human Rights' (2007) 23 *American University International Law Review* 127.

Schramm, FP (2019), 'No Atual Ritmo, Brasil Levará Mil Anos Para Titular Todas as Comunidades Quilombolas' (updated 28 June 2020), terradedireitos.org.br/noticias/noticias/no-atual-ritmo-brasil-levara-mil-anos-para-titular-todas-as-comunidades-quilombolas/23023.

Schvartzman, L and Espíndola Oviedo, S, 'Nueva Ola del Agronegócio Avanza sob Tierras Indigenas. Desalojos Irregulas de Comunidades Ava Guarani' in M Palau (ed), *Con la Soja al Cuello* (Asunción, Paraguay: BASE, 2019) 84–85.

Shalders, A, 'Funai Suspende Atendimento e Famílias Indígenas Passam Fome no Mato Grosso do Sul' BBC News Brasil (2 April 2020) www.bbc.com/portuguese/brasil-51272231.

Shelton, D, 'Reparations for Indigenous Peoples. Present Value of Past Wrongs' in F Lenzerini (ed), *Reparations for Indigenous Peoples. International and Comparative Perspectives* (Oxford, OUP, 2008) 47–72.

—— 'The Inter-American Human Rights Law of Indigenous Peoples' (2013) 35 *Harvard Law Review* 937.

Sierra Cadena, G, 'República de Nicaragua' in L Burgorgue-Larsen, R Estupiñan Silva, LM Gutiérrez Ramírez et al (eds), *Derechos Humanos en Contexto en América Latina.* El Impacto del Sistema Interamericano de Derechos Humanos en los Estados Partes (Colombia, Ecuador, Haití, México, Nicaragua, Perú, República Dominicana, Uruguay, Venezuela) (Ciudad de Mexico, Tirant lo Blanch, 2016) 537–619.

Silva, CTD, 'A Homologação da Terra Indígena Raposa Serra do Sol e seus Efeitos. uma Análise Performativa das 19 Condicionandes do STF' (2018) 33 *Revista Brasileira de Ciências Sociais* 2.

Silva, LAL da, 'Consulta Prévia e Livre Determinação dos Povos Indígenas e Tribais na América Latina. Re-existir para Co-existir' Thesis (Curitiba, Pontifícia Universidade Católica do Paraná, 2017).

Silva, LAL da and Souza Filho, CFMD, 'Marco Temporal Como Retrocessso dos Direitos Territoriais Originários Indígenas e Quilombolas' in AC Wolkmer, CFM Souza Filho and MCVB Tarrega (eds), *Os Direitos Territoriais Quilombolas. Além do Marco Temporal* (Goiânia, GO: Editora da PUC-Goiás, 2016) 55–75.

Silva-Santisteban, AB and Garland, EB, *Servidumbre por deudas y marginación en el Chaco de Paraguay*. Declaracioń relativa a los principios y derechos fundamentales en el trabajo documento de trabajo 45/2005 (Geneva, ILO, 2005).

Skaar, E, 'Wavering Courts. From Impunity to Accountability in Uruguay' (2013) 45 *Journal of Latin American Studies* 483.

Soley, X, 'The Transformative Dimension of Inter-American Jurisprudence' in AV Bogdandy, E Ferrer Mac-Gregor, M Morales Antoniazzi et al (eds), *Transformative Constitutionalism in Latin America. The Emergence of a New Ius Commune* (Oxford, OUP, 2017) 337–55.

—— 'The Crucial Role of Human Rights NGOs in the Inter-American System' (2019) 113 *AJIL Unbound* 355.

Soley, X and Steininger, S, 'Parting ways or lashing back? Withdrawals, backlash and the Inter-American Court of Human Rights' (2018) 14 *International Journal of Law in Context* 237.

Souza, IF, Leme, LR and Scherf, EDL, 'Creating Bridges Between International Relations Theory and International Human Rights Law. Constructivism and the Role of Brazil in the Inter-American System of Human Rights' (2019) 15 *Revista de Direito Internacional* 179.

Starck, G and Bragato, FF, 'O Impacto da Tese do Marco Temporal nos Processos Judiciais que Discutem Direitos Possessórios Indígenas' (2020) 8 *Revista Direitos Sociais e Políticas Públicas* (UNIFAFIBE) 245.

Staton, JK and Romero, A, 'Rational Remedies. The Role of Opinion Clarity in the Inter-American Human Rights System' (2019) 63 *International Studies Quarterly*.

Stec, S and Jendrośka, J, 'The Escazú Agreement and the Regional Approach to Rio Principle 10: Process, Innovation, and Shortcomings' (2019) 31 *Journal of Environmental Law* 533.

Stiansen, Ø, 'The Politics of Compliance with International Human Rights Court Judgments' Dissertation (Oslo, University of Oslo, 2019).

STP (2019), 'Comunidad indígena de Kelyenmagategma avanza en acuerdo amistoso sobre tierras' (updated 10/18/2019), www.stp.gov.py/v1/comunidad-indigena-de-kelyenmagategma-avanza-en-acuerdo-amistoso-sobre-tierras.

Sylvander, N, 'Saneamiento Territorial in Nicaragua, and the Prospects for Resolving Indigenous-Mestizo Land Conflicts' (2018) 17 *Journal of Latin American Geography* 166.

Terra de Direitos (2020), 'Nota Técnica' (12 May 2020), terradedireitos.org.br/noticias/noticias/7-razoes-para-nao-aprovar-a-mp-da-grilagem/23306.

Thornberry, P, *Indigenous Peoples and Human Rights* (Manchester, Manchester University Press, 2005), www.jstor.org/stable/10.2307/j.ctt155jg1p.

Tierraviva, 'Camino a Yakye Axa' (2019), www.tierraviva.org.py/camino-a-yakye-axa.

Tierraviva a los pueblos indígenas del Chaco, *Violencia e Impunidad Hacia el Pueblo Paĩ Tavyterã-Kaiowa: Aproximación a la Situación de Violaciones de Derechos Humanos en la Frontera Paraguayo-brasileña* (Asunción, Paraguay, 2014).

Tigroudja, H, 'La Satisfaction et les Garanties de Non-repetition de l'illicitedans le Contentieux Interamericain des Droits de l'Homme' in E Lambert-Abdelgawad and K Martin-Chenut (eds), *Réparer les violations graves et massives des droits de l'homme. La cour interaméricaine, pionnière et modèle?* (Paris, Société de Législation Comparée, 2010) 69–90.

Tomaselli, A, *Indigenous Peoples and Their Right to Political Participation: International law standards and their application in Latin America* (Baden-Baden, Nomos, 2016).

Torelly, M, 'Transnational Legal Process and Fundamental Rights in Latin America' in P Fortes et al (eds), *Law and Policy in Latin America: Transforming Courts, Institutions, and Rights* (London, Palgrave Macmillan, 2017).

—— 'Domestic Rule of Law Gaps and the Uses of International Human Rights Law in Post-Atrocity Prosecutions: Argentina, Brazil, and Chile Transitional Justice Experiences' in M Bovero (ed), *Teoria Politica* (Madrid, Marcial Pons, 2017) 345–61.

Torres Kirmser, JR, 'Diálogo Jurisprudencial entre la Justicia Nacional y las Cortes Internacionales' (2014) 1 *Revista Facultad de Derecho y Ciencias Sociales* 1.

Ultima Hora, 'Totobigosode y el Estado se reúnen en Montevideo' (24 October 2017), www.ultima-hora.com/totobigosode-y-el-estado-se-reunen-montevideo-n1114777.html.

—— 'Por Desidia, el Estado Pagaría más de G 24.000 Millones por Tierras' (31 January 2018), www.ultimahora.com/por-desidia-el-estado-pagaria-mas-g-24000-millones-tierras-n1131376.html.

—— 'Ayoreos Celebran Titulación de sus Tierras Ancestrales' (30 March 2019), www.ultimahora.com/ayoreos-celebran-titulacion-sus-tierras-ancestrales-n2810642.html?fbclid=IwAR348WF1gfZ4PlxG-Ko9I2lpvjEliGBblm9Z6dFrKxmwyM1jzXlRy3Bzx3M?fbclid=IwAR348WF1gfZ4PlxG-Ko9I2lpvjEliGBblm9Z6dFrKxmwyM1jzXlRy3Bzx3M.

UNICEF and MEC, 'Fortaleciendo la Educacion Inicial en Escuelas Indígenas Urbanas' (Asunción, Paraguay, 2012).

United Nations Development Program, 'Human Development Reports. Paraguay', hdr.undp.org/en/countries/profiles/PRY.

Universidad de Arizona, Programa de derechos y políticas indígenas, Diagnóstico de Tenencia y Uso de la Tierra de la Comunidad Mayangna de Awas Tingni: Resumen Ejecutivo (2004).

Valente, R (2020), 'Moro Usa Parecer de Temer e Trava Demarcação de 17 Terras Indígenas no País' *Folha de São Paulo* (20 January 2020), www1.folha.uol.com.br/poder/2020/01/moro-usa-parecer-de-temer-e-trava-demarcacao-de-17-terras-indigenas-no-pais.shtml.

Valina, L (ed), *Paraguay, Diálogo con los Pueblos Indígenas: Participación y Consulta* (Asunción, Paraguay, 201).

Valina, L, Rojas, I and Prieto, E (eds), *Diálogos con Representantes de Organizaciones Indígenas 2013–2014: Fortalecimiento de los Derechos de los Pueblos Indígenas sobre sus Tierras Ancestrales* (Asunción, Paraguay, ONU Derechos Humanos Paraguay, 2014).

van Boen, T, 'Reparations. a Requirement of Justice' in AAC Trindade (ed), *El Sistema Interamericano de Protección de los Derechos Humanos en el Umbral del Siglo XXI*, 2nd edn (San José, Costa Rica, Corte Interamericana de Derechos Humanos, 2003).

Vannuccini, S, 'Member States' Compliance with the Inter-American Court of Human Rights: Judgments and Orders Requiring Non-Pecuniary Reparations Section V: Procedural Aspects' (2014) 7 *Inter-American and European Human Rights Journal* 225.

Veenendaal, W, 'Does Smallness Enhance Power-Sharing? Explaining Suriname's Multiethnic Democracy' (2019) 25 *Ethnopolitics* 1.

Villagra Carron, R, 'Diagnóstico Socio-jurídico de Tierras y Territorios Indígenas en Paraguay' (2018) 53 *Suplemento Antropológico* 129.

Vos, CM de, *From Rights to Remedies: Structures and Strategies for Implementing International Human Rights Decisions* (New York, Open Society Foundations, 2013).

Wainwright, J and Bryan, J, 'Cartography, Territory, Property: Postcolonial Reflections on Indigenous Counter-mapping in Nicaragua and Belize (2009) 16 *Cultural Geographies* 153.

Wetterslev, J, 'Surrounded by Settlers: The Creation and Fragmentation of Indigenous Territories in Nicaragua' Annual Conference of the Latin American Studies Association (2020).

Wiggins, A, 'El caso Awas Tingni o el Futuro de los Derechos Territoriales de los Pueblos Indígenas del Caribe Nicaragüense' (2002) 30 *Wani Revista del Caribe Nicaragüense* 6.

Xanthaki, A, *Indigenous Rights and United Nations Standards: Self-determination*, Culture and Land (Cambridge, CUP, 2007), doi.org/10.1017/CBO9780511494468.

Yamada, EM, and Villares, LF, 'Julgamento da Terra Indígena Raposa Serra do Sol: Todo Dia era Dia de Índio' (2010) 6 *Revista Direito GV* 145.

Index

www.ingramcontent.com/pod-product-compliance
Ingram Content Group UK Ltd.
Pitfield, Milton Keynes, MK11 3LW, UK
UKHW020805290926
15470UKWH00003B/959

9 781509 979066